Imperialism and Chinese Nationalism

Germany in Shantung

Harvard East Asian Series 58

The East Asian Research Center at Harvard University administers research projects designed to further scholarly understanding of China, Japan, Korea, Vietnam, and adjacent areas.

Imperialism and Chinese Nationalism

Germany in Shantung

John E. Schrecker

Harvard University Press
Cambridge, Massachusetts
1971

Distributed in Great Britain by Oxford University Press, London

Preparation of this volume has been aided by a grant from the Ford Foundation.

Library of Congress Catalog Card Number 73–129119

SBN 674-44520-1

Printed in the United States of America

For my mother,
Marianne Schrecker-Strauss

Contents

Contents

Preface

In the late 1890s, fifty years of imperialism in China reached a climax with the scramble for spheres of influence and broad economic concessions. This period is one of the critical turning points in modern Chinese history. Not only did the Middle Kingdom face the prospect of foreign economic domination, and perhaps even of disintegration into separate colonial areas, but the period also witnessed crucial changes in Chinese attitudes toward the West.

However, apart from the diplomatic maneuverings of the foreign powers while they acquired the new privileges, very little is actually known about the spheres of influence or about how China survived the threat which they represented. Thus there is little or no information about what occurred within a sphere, the amount of political and economic power the imperialist nation attained, or how its activities affected the development of the area. At the same time, little is known about the Chinese approach to the spheres or, indeed, about Chinese foreign policy in general during the last decades of the Ch'ing. Yet such knowledge is vital for an overall understanding of the era from 1895 to the Revolution of 1911, a period that is attracting increasing historical attention and in which concern with imperialism was perhaps the most significant driving force.

The purpose of this study is to investigate such questions by examining one important sphere of influence and the Chinese response to it: the German sphere of influence in Shantung and the German leasehold at Chiao-chou Bay. Although this investigation was originally envisaged as concentrating almost exclusively on Chinese history, once work had begun it quickly became clear that considerable attention must also be devoted to the German side of the story. First, there was no other way to understand and describe what occurred in Shantung. Second, an examination of the German presence in the province proved to have intrinsic significance as an important but as yet unstudied example of German colonialism. In particular, it constituted a case study of the colonial policies of the German navy, which was one of the important sponsors of German imperialism but had direct control over only one colony, the leasehold at Chiao-chou Bay.

I must begin my acknowledgments by joining the very long line of authors who owe their primary and deepest thanks to Professor John K. Fairbank of Harvard University. This work began as a dissertation under Professor Fairbank's direction, and at every stage of its development (and even before in his superb seminars) he has served subtly, but with inestimable effect, as teacher, critic, goad, and support. Actually, I find myself at a loss to describe, or even to understand, the exact nature of much of his assistance, yet I am peculiarly certain that without it this book would not have appeared. Others who have helped and who deserve thanks are Professors Samuel Bowles, Lamar Cecil, Marius Jansen, Stanley Kelley, Jr., George Lensen, K. C. Liu, Arno Mayer, Benjamin Schwartz, Edward Tufte, and Robert Tignor; as well as Mr. Robert Irick, Dr. Li Kuo-ch'i, Dr. Jonathan Rubinstein, Mr. Raymond Sokolov, and Dr. Leo Strauss. The late Professor Mary C. Wright, who did more than any other historian to arouse interest in and to elucidate the last years of the Ch'ing, deserves a special acknowledgment. I was particularly stimulated by attending the conference which she organized on the Revolution of 1911; and her work and her great integrity made her an inspiration to me and to all others who had the good fortune of knowing her. She will be greatly missed.

I am indebted to the librarians of Harvard, Princeton, Columbia, and Florida State University who helped me in my research. The Deutsches Zentralarchiv in Potsdam, and in particular Dr. Enders of Historical Section I, was extremely helpful and generous in establishing a film exchange which enabled me to use vital German materials. On the American side this exchange was efficiently handled and also financed by the Princeton University Library, a service for which I am extremely grateful. While working on this book I received financial assistance from the Princeton University Council on International and Regional Studies, the Princeton University Council on the Humanities, and the Shelby Cullom Davis Fund of the Princeton Department of History. Portions of the book originally appeared in somewhat different form in my article "The Reform Movement, Nationalism, and China's Foreign Policy," *The Journal of*

Asian Studies, vol. 29, no. 1, pp. 43–53. I would like to thank the Association for Asian Studies, Inc., which holds the copyright, for permission to use this material.

I would also like to take this opportunity to acknowledge my debt to my teachers of East Asian studies at the University of Pennsylvania who, while I was an undergraduate, first aroused and fed my interest in Chinese history: Professors Derk Bodde, Schuyler Cammann, and Hilary Conroy.

My mother, to whom this book is dedicated, aided my endeavors directly by helping to decipher some particularly horrifying examples of German gothic handwriting. The dedication is for much more than that, of course. Finally, I must admit that it is especially useful if one's wife is not only able to assist in all the expected ways but can also contribute the talents of a trained historian. I have had this double good fortune. My wife, Ellen, from the earliest stages of this work, has not only given me all the domestic support for which any author could hope but has also read all the material carefully, made comments and criticisms, provided stylistic and even orthographic help, and, in innumerable other ways, been of immense assistance. For this I give her my admiration and my sincerest thanks.

John E. Schrecker

Tokyo, July 1970

Imperialism and
Chinese Nationalism

Germany in Shantung

Notes on Romanization and Maps

Romanization. The romanization system used in this book is the Wade-Giles, modified in the usual way by dropping unnecessary umlauts and circumflexes. Some place names, well known in their Post Office form, have been romanized by that system. One special convention has been employed for clarity. Except in a few quotations translated from the German, the word "Kiaochow" is used only to refer to the German leasehold in Shantung. The nearby Chinese prefecture from which the leasehold took its name is called Chiao-chou, and the bay within the leasehold, which was also named for the prefecture, is called Chiao-chou Bay. Similarly, "Tsingtao" refers only to the German city established in the leasehold, while the bay, island, and village from which the German name came are called Ch'ing-tao.

Maps. The appendix contains three maps of the areas covered in the book, as well as a list of place names keyed to these maps. When a place name occurs in the text, it can best be located by looking first at the list and then at the appropriate map or maps.

I. The Acquisition of the German Sphere of Influence

Germany and China through 1895

In 1898 Germany established a colony at Chiao-chou Bay in the Chinese province of Shantung and obtained privileges which made the entire province into a German sphere of influence. The German drive for the status of a world power in the 1890's precipitated these acts of imperialism. Fundamentally, however, they grew out of the rapid expansion of German activity in China in the latter half of the nineteenth century. As the German stake in China grew, the German government began to play an increasingly active role there, both to support existing German endeavors and to stimulate new ones. The acquisition of Chiao-chou Bay was the culmination of Berlin's involvement and also fulfilled the longstanding desire of many Germans, particularly commercial groups, for a foothold on the coast which would serve German interests as Hong Kong served British.[1] A sense of rivalry with England permeated every step toward the creation of the leasehold.

The German navy was the government department which most consistently advocated the establishment of a colony in China and which ultimately was most instrumental in obtaining the sphere of influence in Shantung. The navy shared the goals of the German commercial groups because it believed in these goals and also valued the political support which groups of this type could give to general naval interests.[2] The ideological and political ties between the navy and commercial circles rested partially on the fact that the liberals who dominated commerce traditionally supported the fleet because its origins lay in the German movement for unification and because they believed a powerful navy was a prerequisite for the commercial strength of a nation, as was the case with Britain. The ties also derived from the related circumstance that the

1

navy, lacking the aristocratic background of most Prussian institutions, came to be dominated by men from the middle class and, hence, frequently reflected commercial attitudes. This sympathetic relationship between the navy and the German commercial interests proved to be of great significance not only in the acquisition of Chiao-chou Bay but also in the actual development of the German colony there, which the navy administered.

The roots of German imperialism in China can be traced back to the second half of the eighteenth century, when significant commercial relations first developed between Germans and Chinese.[3] In that period a fairly substantial overland trade grew up between North China and Prussia by way of Siberia and the Russian trading posts on the Chinese border. At the same time Prussians and other Germans began to enter into the sea trade at Canton. The land trade came to an end in the early nineteenth century largely as a result of Russian tax policy; however, the Canton trade continued on a small scale and formed the basis of German involvement in nineteenth-century China.

When the Opium War began in 1839, the German share of the trade at Canton was still rather insignificant and was far smaller than that of other important powers. Nevertheless, in their attitude toward the war German commercial circles already displayed concerns similar to those which would preoccupy them in later decades.[4] They looked forward to the possibility that the British pressure on China might bring about increased commercial opportunities. At the same time they feared that the war might conceivably result in a British monopoly over the trade. Therefore they urged the Prussian government to intervene in the fight against China in order to defend German interests. The government declined, and its refusal shows how the concerns of commercial groups involved in China became linked with the navy. For the government said that, even if German interests in China warranted intervention, and it did not believe they did, such intervention was impossible because Prussia had no fleet.

At the end of the Opium War the Prussian government continued to maintain a cautious posture toward involvement in China and, unlike England, the United States, and France, did not sign a commercial treaty with the Middle Kingdom. As a result, in the years between the war and the second treaty settlements of the late 1850s, German activities in China were particularly dependent upon the auspices and protection of England, a position which probably served to reinforce among German merchants a sense of unwilling subordination to English power along the coast.[5]

The most important German commercial venture in this period was in the coasting trade. This trade was still dominated largely by the Chinese themselves, but one estimate places under the German flag three quarters of the part in foreign hands. German Protestant missionary groups also began to operate in China during these years, concentrating their endeavors in Kwangtung. As German activities in China increased, interested groups continued to press the various German states for active manifestations of official support. This pressure was generally unsuccessful. Until the late 1850s only Prussia, Saxony, and Hamburg responded, and they limited themselves to appointing a few merchants as consuls in some of the more important of the open ports.

A crucial turning point in Sino-German relations came in 1859 when Prussia finally decided to accede to the requests for more positive governmental action in China by sending a fleet to the Middle Kingdom to negotiate a commercial treaty for the German states.[6] This was to be the first expedition of its type undertaken by the new Prussian fleet, which from its beginning, thus, had links with Germany's involvement in China. One reason for the government's decision to act was the fact that in 1858 at Tientsin and then in 1860 at Peking, England and France imposed a new set of treaties on China which expanded and consolidated the system of foreign privileges that had grown out of the Opium War. An additional factor which influenced Berlin's decision was that the new round of commercial negotiations in China coincided with the so-called "New Course" in Prussian politics. The New Course was partly designed to convince the liberal middle class interested in German unification that Prussia was a modern progressive state worthy of their support. Using the new Prussian fleet to intervene in China for commercial purposes was a move well calculated to have great appeal to such liberals. Indeed, the expedition was something of a milestone not only in the history of Sino-German relations and in the growth of the navy but also in the unification of Germany. For it marked the first time that Prussia represented a united Germany in international negotiations, having been authorized by all the other German states to bargain with China on their behalf.

The four ships that composed the expedition left for China early in 1860. Friedrich von Eulenburg headed the diplomatic mission, which included, among others, Max von Brandt, a future minister to Peking, and Freiherr Ferdinand von Richthofen, the geologist whose economic studies of China were to play a vital role in the selection of Chiao-chou Bay as the location for a German colony. Because of the importance of the mission to the navy, the ships' companies had a particularly strong complement of promising young officers and naval cadets. Several later rose high in the service, which may have contributed somewhat to the navy's interest in China.

Eulenburg's orders showed that the German government was very self-conscious about Germany's inferiority to Britain on the China coast. The orders stressed that Eulenburg was to demand the same commercial privileges and protection for Germans as the British had obtained in their treaty. He was also instructed to examine the possibilities for obtaining a German naval and commercial base in China similar to Hong Kong; Formosa was suggested as the likeliest prospect.

When the fleet arrived in East Asian waters, the English and the French were still negotiating the final settlements at Peking, and Eulenburg, aware of Germany's weak position, realized that he could not intervene there while they were still at work. Therefore, he directed the fleet toward Japan, where he was also supposed to sign a commercial treaty. Japan had recently made treaties with the other important powers, and Eulenburg obtained one with little difficulty. In March 1861 the expedition finally arrived at Tientsin.

Eulenburg hoped to expand on the privileges which the English and the French had just obtained in their treaties. The Chinese negotiators, however, were not impressed with the Prussians and not only refused to grant them any new privileges but were unwilling to deal with them at all. This was essentially because, in 1861, the Chinese knew little and cared less about Germans.[7] Before the Opium War a handful of scholars and officials had become aware of the existence of a place called Prussia. However, their knowledge, weak even on those nations which had more contact with China, reflected only the most confused ideas about Prussia's location and characteristics. After the war, the works of such pioneer experts on the West as Wei Yuan and Hsü Chi-yü finally provided some accurate information about Germany, but this information failed to make any noticeable impact on Chinese officialdom.

Eulenburg attributed his difficulties in opening negotiations to the jealous machinations of the English and French. In this he was, of course, incorrect. In fact, the Chinese officials only agreed to open talks with the newcomers after the other two powers urged them to do so. The Germans eventually signed a treaty in September 1861, modeled almost exactly on those obtained by the other powers. Significantly, the agreement specified that Prussia would continue to represent the other German states on the ministerial level, although the Hansa towns were allowed to establish consuls in the ports.

After the conclusion of the negotiations Richthofen and another specialist visted Formosa. Their report about the island was not unfavorable. Nevertheless, Eulenburg was evidently unimpressed and reported home that Formosa had a poor climate and was devoid of good harbors. He added, however, that in the "not too distant future" Germany would require a base in China if the privileges obtained in the treaty were to be fully realized.[8]

In the decade following the treaty, both the navy and the commercial circles interested in China continually pressed the Prussian government to consolidate its position as a growing East Asian power. One demand of these groups was that the government display a commitment similar to that of Britain and the other powers by sending a permanent squadron of ships to China in order to enforce the treaty and protect Germans.[9] At first the government rejected the idea in favor of dispatching ships to Asia on temporary missions. However, the pressures continued, and in 1867 the navy established a depot and hospital in Yokohama. The next year the government agreed to send some corvettes to East Asia on a permanent mission and began building two shallow-draft, heavily armed gunboats of the type favored for facilitating diplomatic relations with China. When the first corvettes arrived in 1869, the government announced the formation of the East Asian fleet command. Once again development of the navy was related to China, for this was the first command of the Prussian fleet in foreign waters.

A further demand of the commercial and naval circles in the years after the treaty was for a German territorial foothold in China.[10] One of the most articulate proponents of this idea was Richthofen. Between 1868 and 1872 he made seven trips to different parts of China and visited thirteen provinces. His trips, paid for by the Shanghai Chamber of Commerce, were for the overall purpose of surveying the mining potential of the Middle Kingdom. However, as he traveled, Richthofen kept an eye open for the best location for a German colony.

Richthofen stressed that he was searching for a spot which not only could serve as a naval base but which could also become an important trading center. The potentialities for turning Chusan Island into a "German Hong Kong" impressed him the most, and he sent the government several memoranda about the advantages of obtaining it for Germany.[11] He claimed that the island provided limitless commercial opportunities because it was located directly off the Yangtze River, China's chief avenue for commerce. He predicted that a new port there would "quickly attract a large part of the trade from Shanghai" which currently dominated the Yangtze trade despite its comparatively unfavorable location at the river's mouth. Indeed, since a German Chusan would be a "free port under foreign protection" in a better location than Hong Kong, it could even "take over the combined role of Hong Kong and Shanghai for the greater part of Chinese commerce." It is significant that Richthofen, in his eagerness to acquire Chusan in order to compete with the English, was apparently unimpressed by the fact that in 1846 Britain had extracted a promise from China never to give the island to any other power.[12]

Despite Richthofen's extremely optimistic reports and the urgings of others, the government made no serious move toward obtaining a foothold in China. However, it occasionally toyed with the idea. Bismarck himself even considered taking a base.[13] In 1870 he ordered Rehfues, the Prussian minister in Peking, to open negotiations in the name of the North German Confederation for the purpose of obtaining a centrally located naval base on the China coast. Richtofen's memoranda about Chusan may have had some influence on Bismarck's request. As things turned out, Rehfues did not carry out the order, reporting home that China would not agree to the German demand and that Berlin could expect no support from the other European powers. Bismarck then apparently dropped the project. Nevertheless, the incident is of interest, for Bismarck generally supported colonial ventures only when they were warranted by genuine commercial interests or by the exigencies of internal politics. Thus his brief but early concern with a base in China suggests that the belief was becoming widespread in Germany that the nation had an economic stake in the Middle Kingdom.

After the signing of the commercial treaty, Chinese interest in Germany gradually increased, rising sharply in the decades after the Franco-Prussian War and the unification of the Reich. At the same time the attitude of many members of the Chinese elite became one of admiration and respect for what they considered to be Germany's success as a nation in the second half of the century. These years also witnessed the enormous growth of Germany's involvement in China, a development which the new Chinese attitudes naturally assisted.

In China the 1860s and '70s witnessed the rise of the self-strengthening movement, the first comparatively widespread effort to respond to the West with a major program of change and reform. During these early years the self-strengtheners were primarily interested in developing China's military capabilities. Germany was a natural source of inspiration in this field, and respect for German military power and efficiency became the first, and remained the most persistent, aspect of the Chinese admiration for the Reich. An outstanding example of this attitude is to be found in the book *Record of the Franco-Prussian War* (*P'u-fa chan-chi*), written by the well-known journalist and advocate of reform, Wang T'ao.[14] In this work, published in 1871, Wang described and lauded the German army and urged that China reform its own military along German lines in order to provide national security and domestic order. Because its point of view perfectly complemented the ideals of the early self-strengthening movement, the book achieved great success and influence. It was also popular in Japan, where interest in Germany was widespread and developed along much the same lines as in China.

As time passed, the self-strengthening movement began to turn away from its preoccupation with narrow military reforms and became interested in discovering how the broader economic and political aspects of Western society could contribute to enriching and strengthening China. With its later perspective, the movement's admiration for Germany continued unabated;[15] for the new German Reich, just entered upon its own great era of economic development, provided an outstanding model of how a weak nation could, through planning and effort, increase its power rapidly and efficiently. By the late 1890s some Chinese reformers had even become interested in the German governmental system and were advocating the idea, which became popular in later years, that it was more appropriate to Chinese traditions than the English system because it had an independent and powerful executive. For example, Hsü Chien-yin, the well-known Western specialist of the Kiangnan Arsenal translation department, argued in his book *Statutes of the German Reichstag* (*Te-kuo i-yuan chang-ch'eng*) that the most serious drawback in a democracy was that it had no way of resolving differences of opinion, a problem which only the German system had been able to overcome. On the whole, until the Sino-Japanese War, Chinese leaders had a positive attitude toward Germany. It was a country with much to recommend it and one which, at the same time, did not appear to pose a major threat to China.

The expansion of Germany's role in China was especially aided by the fact that Li Hung-chang, the most powerful political figure in China in the decades before 1895, shared this favorable assessment of the Reich.[16] Li, the leading advocate of self-strengthening, also influenced the Chinese government to adopt a foreign policy which aimed at fending off the Western powers by balancing them against one another. As a result, during the 1870s and particularly in the early '80s, Li carried out policies which reflected his belief that Germany was the best military model for China as well as a particularly good counterweight against the incursions of other nations. For example, Li tried to maximize the use of German personnel in order to undercut the monopoly which the British had obtained as foreign advisers through their domination of the Imperial Maritime Customs. It was partially for this reason that he selected a German commissioner of customs, Gustav Detring, to be his chief adviser on foreign affairs.

The Germans understood Li's attitude and, in order to further their own interests, cultivated him assiduously.[17] They actively encouraged his inclination to look toward Germany for help in military matters and other aspects of self-strengthening. Moreover, the German minister, von Brandt, intervened energetically on Li's behalf in a number of diplomatic crises beginning with the negotiations over the Chefoo Convention of 1876. As a result of von Brandt's efforts, in 1880 Germany became the first power to agree on a supplementary commercial treaty with China, a treaty whose terms struck most Old China Hands as overly acquiescent toward the Chinese.

After 1885, Li began to alter his pro-German policies because of Germany's behavior during the Sino-French War.[18] The Reich, for reasons of international politics, had adopted a position of pro-French neutrality during most of the fighting. This seriously disappointed Li, who had counted on more German assistance in limiting the conflict. In addition, Li's futile attempt to woo Germany had become a target for militant conservatives who were opposed to the viceroy's moderate approach to foreign affairs. Therefore, Li abandoned his efforts to seek Germany as an ally. Nevertheless, the Reich still continued to enjoy much favor in China, and this contributed to the striking growth of German activities.

By 1895 the volume of German business in China was second only to that of Great Britain. Germany still stood far behind; nevertheless, the German rise had been so spectacular that a strong competition had developed between the citizens of the two nations. In the economic sphere, as in other fields, the German government actively cooperated with private interests in the enhancement of Germany's position. In many cases the government not only supported its citizens but actually encouraged them to undertake specific activities.[19]

One area of business in which the Germans were extremely successful was the development of shipping under the German flag. In the 1860s the Germans lost much of their share in China's coastal trade when the traffic changed over to steam. This happened partly because Germany as a nation was comparatively slow in adapting to steam navigation and also because the Germans could not compete with large British firms when the latter finally decided to enter the coasting trade. Although the first direct steamer service between Germany and China began in 1871, the German role in the carrying trade between Europe and China was extremely small through the 1870s. Even German goods went on English ships and were frequently transshipped in England.

The turning point for German shipping in China came in the early 1880s when the German government began to encourage it, striving in particular to reduce the role of English middlemen. Bismarck fought hard against considerable opposition at home in order to obtain for a German steamship line the type of subsidy which carriers of other nations enjoyed for their runs to China. The bill granting the subsidy was finally passed in 1885. The Norddeutscher Lloyd received the concession and in 1886 began service to China. The line, as had been expected, made a tremendous difference to German shipping. By 1895 tonnage under the German flag moving at Chinese ports stood second only to England; and the direct shipment of German goods going to China was greater than the amount transshipped in England. Nevertheless, Germany, though gaining on Britain, still remained far behind her. In 1895 the total British tonnage cleared inwards and outwards at Chinese ports was about 20,500,000 tons. The Germans had 2,400,000 tons; but their closest rivals, the Swedes, carried only 400,000 tons.[20]

By 1895 Germany was also probably the second most important source of China's imports. It is extremely difficult to obtain figures relating to this aspect of Chinese trade, for the customs never kept such records but only concerned itself with the immediate port of origin of foreign goods. Nevertheless, estimates generally agree that Germany ranked next to England and that about 9 per cent of the goods brought in were of German origin. A large portion of the German products consisted of inexpensive consumer goods such as matches, needles, and cloth.

Military equipment accounted for another important segment of German exports to China. For a while, in the early 1880s during the period of Li Hung-chang's greatest interest in Germany, the Reich had close to a monopoly over Chinese imports of weapons and munitions.[21] During these years Li made Germany the major supplier for his Peiyang fleet, the most powerful in China. He also appointed a German, Constantin von Hannecken, to supervise the development and fortification of Port Arthur, later China's greatest naval base but then only a "windbound junk harbor." [22] The impressive fortifications and installations of Port Arthur used a great deal of German equipment and weaponry, especially from Krupp. After 1885, Li no longer had ships constructed in Germany, although that nation remained China's primary supplier of military equipment. The rivalry between Germany and England was particularly fierce in this profitable area of trade, partially because Germany was doing so well and also because of the apparent strategic importance of dominating the supply of arms and influencing China's military development.

By the 1890s the Germans had also prospered in the field of finance and, indeed, had become the first group to challenge the long-standing British monopoly over foreign banking in China. This development came comparatively late, primarily because, of all German business interests, financial circles were among the most hesitant to participate in Chinese enterprises.[23] In part this was because the return on investments in China was frequently not high enough to rival the pull of capital to Europe or the United States. Other business groups, however, felt that the establishment of German credit facilities in China would aid them, and so the government tried strenuously to induce German financial concerns to begin operations in the Middle Kingdom.

In the early 1870s one of the so-called great German banks, the Deutsche Bank, opened a branch in Shanghai, which, however, did not prosper and was quickly closed. In the following years the German government sought the establishment of a new German bank. Minister Brandt was particularly concerned with the problem, and he frequently spoke of the contribution which a German bank would make to German commerce. For example, he cited the advantage which British merchants and British goods received from the fact that loans from British banks were often granted on the condition that the money be spent with British firms. Bismarck also supported the establishment of a bank in China. For many years, however, the idea was received with little enthusiasm by the German financial groups.

In 1885 a combine of great German banks and industrial concerns sent a study commission to China in order to investigate the prospects for banking and investment. The group returned with a rather pessimistic assessment, though it did report that a bank was a prerequisite for any major expansion of the German commercial position in China. During the next few years there were protracted negotiations between the government and the reluctant financial interests over the opening of a bank in China. The financiers demanded, and finally received, very favorable guarantees of support from the government before they were willing to act.

Finally, in 1889 and 1890, a combine of great banks, representing almost all German finance capital with overseas interests, organized the Deutsch-Asiatische Bank and the Konsortium für asiatische Geschäfte. The bank was capitalized at 5,000,000 taels and opened its doors in Shanghai in 1890, becoming the first financial institution in China operated by foreigners other than the British. By 1896 the bank had become so strong that the British banks were willing to make an agreement with it for an equitable distribution of loans to the Chinese government.

One sign of the growing importance of German business in China was the establishment of a German language newspaper in Shanghai in 1886. The paper, the *Ostasiatischer Lloyd*, was meant to serve as a spokesman for German interests on the coast, just as the British papers did for British interests. A number of German companies in China supported the paper. In 1890 it temporarily met financial difficulties, and the German Foreign Office succeeded in getting the Deutsch-Asiatische Bank to grant the paper a subsidy.

The number of German firms in the Middle Kingdom provides a final indication of the extent of the German involvement in economic affairs and of the reasons for the sense of rivalry with England. By 1895 Germany stood second to England in this regard and, in view of Britain's general dominance in China, a rather good second. There were 361 British firms and 92 German; Japan was next with 34. Evidently Germans also comprised the second largest group of individuals engaged in business in China, though the precise figure is difficult to determine.[24]

China's use of German military instructors and specialists further enhanced Germany's position in the latter part of the century. The Germans were eager to be selected because this increased their general influence and, in particular, permitted them to encourage the purchase of German military equipment. As a result the German government and Krupp, the prime supplier of arms, made considerable efforts, through the use of such means as subsidies to prospective instructors, to ease the way for Germans to serve the Chinese. These measures met a warm response from Chinese military reformers, who frequently found it both difficult and expensive to hire foreign military specialists. Even after 1885, therefore, German military advisers played an exceptionally prominent role in China. Because of the advantages of supplying military specialists, the competition between Germany and England for the privilege was extremely sharp.

Finally, a significant part of Germany's growing stake in China in the late nineteenth century was in the field of missionary work.[25] Two developments in particular played a vital role in setting the stage for future German imperialism in Shantung: Germans established a new Catholic mission in that province, and the German government assumed the role of protector of all German Catholics in China.

In the 1870s the French government was still the official protector of all Catholic missionaries in China, whatever their nationality. French consuls acted for the missionaries in dealing with the Chinese government and also granted them the passports required for residence and travel in the interior. The French government used its relation to the missionaries as an important method of increasing French influence in China and of extracting concessions from the Chinese government. As early as 1877 Minister Brandt suggested that the German government should replace the French as the protector of German Catholic missionaries. Brandt wanted the change not only to increase German power directly but also, apparently, to further his efforts to win favor from the Chinese government, which had long resented the French protectorate. Berlin, however, in the midst of the Kulturkampf with the Church, showed no interest in Brandt's suggestion.

The government's eventual decision to become the official protector of German Catholic missionaries was brought about primarily through the efforts of the Steyl Missionary Society. The Steyl Society was founded in 1875 by a group of nationalist Germans partly to break the dominance which the French held over Catholic missionary work around the world. Ironically, the group had to organize itself in Holland because of the Kulturkampf. In 1879 the society dispatched its first two missionaries to China. One of these was Johann Anzer, who was to become the most important German clerical figure in China. In addition to his religious concerns, Anzer was an ardent advocate of expanding German power abroad. When he arrived in Shanghai, Anzer told the German consul general that he planned to open a major mission in China and that he wanted to obtain German passports for travel in the interior and to place the mission under German protection. The consul refused, and Anzer had to accept French passports and travel under French auspices.

In 1880 Anzer went to Shantung, and the next year the Italian Franciscans, who had been active there since 1838, agreed to give the Steyl mission jurisdiction over the southern half of the province. Anzer then became head of the new Bishopric of South Shantung. The new bishopric comprised an area famous for its hostility to missionaries; indeed, the French Treaty of 1860 had even banned missionaries from one section around Yen-chou because it was the birthplace of Confucius. There is no solid evidence why Anzer decided to work in southern Shantung. However, it may have been because he was directed there by hostile superiors or even because the area presented such a challenge. Anzer continued to seek German protection as he began his evangelical activities.

It was not until 1886 that the German government became interested in replacing the French as the protector of the German Catholics. Domestic politics helped to bring about this reversal of policy, for this was the period when the government gradually realized that the Catholic Center might become a useful prop for the Reich rather than a permanent opposition. The new policy was also calculated to recoup some of the good will which Germany had lost in China as a result of its attitude during the French War, for after the conflict Peking made a particularly strong effort to end the French protectorate. The Tsungli Yamen urged the Vatican to send a minister to China to take over the role of protector, for the Chinese believed that the pope would be less interested than the French in utilizing Christian missions to obtain political and economic concessions.

In 1888, after considerable diplomatic interplay, the Germans and their Italian allies finally announced that they no longer recognized passports issued to their nationals by other governments. Since French pressure on the Vatican had blocked the appointment of a papal emissary, the Chinese government welcomed the decision of the two powers. Brandt immediately informed Anzer that the Steyl mission was, henceforth, under German protection. The change, however, did not become official until 1890 because of the necessity for further negotiations in Peking and Rome.

Anzer and the Steyl missionaries were, of course, delighted by the German protectorate. Shortly after it was declared, the first official German government representative visited the seat of the bishopric in Shantung. The description of his arrival, written by one of the missionaries, bears testimony to the overtly nationalistic commitment of Anzer's mission.[26] The missionary proudly noted that "the apostolic residence was richly decorated and there were innumerable banners, including a huge German flag, hanging from the church steeple and the buildings. The bells rang their salvo. Over the door of the house richly ornamented lettering read, 'A Hearty Welcome,' and over the veranda, 'Vivat, crescat, floreat Germania [May Germany live, flourish and grow].' The 'Kaiser-Hymne' and other German songs were sung enthusiastically." The government representative was deeply moved by his reception and reported home that "it made an almost overpowering impression when a fifteen year old blind youth . . . with a clear and bright soprano voice flawlessly sang 'Hail to Thee with the Victor's Wreath, Ruler of the Fatherland' to the accompaniment of a harmonium."

Almost as soon as the German government became the protector of the missionaries it began to intervene on their behalf as the French had done. One of the first fruits of such intervention was Chinese permission to move the seat of the bishopric from the small town where it had been located to the more important Chi-ning. When the famous opponent of Christianity, Li Ping-heng, became governor of Shantung in 1894, there was a notable increase in violence against the mission.[27] The Germans used the outbreaks to obtain further concessions from China, including, by 1896, the right to live and work in formerly closed Yen-chou. Such concessions, of course, did nothing to improve the relations between the Germans and the officials and people of Shantung.

Clearly, the German government played a decisive role in stimulating and assisting the growth of German interests in China. Nevertheless, prior to 1895 Bismarck's attitude toward imperialism placed some limits on what he and his immediate successors would consider doing. Thus Berlin was willing, indeed eager, to aid private activities in China if it felt that such activities were important for German economic interests or if it believed that its actions gained support for the government at home. However, the government was careful not to undertake action in China which conflicted with broader considerations of German international policy.[28] Among other things this meant that, despite the growth of the nation's stake in the Middle Kingdom, the German government continued to resist pressure to take territory there. The reason Berlin did not seize a base was probably because it felt that any such aggressive action in China would create unnecessary friction with England, whose friendship constituted one of the fundamental pillars of Bismarck's foreign policy. In addition, during the late '80s and early '90s the navy because of a change in command may have been temporarily less concerned with East Asia and may have relaxed its pressure on the government to obtain a colony in China.[29]

Chiao-chou Bay

Chiao-chou Bay is a large inlet of the Yellow Sea located about half way up the southern side of the Shantung peninsula. It is about fifteen miles long and fifteen miles wide, with a two-mile-wide opening into the sea.[30] In the late nineteenth century the bay and the land around it lay within Lai-chou-fu (Lai-chou Prefecture).[31] The northeastern part and the peninsula formed by the bay and the Yellow Sea were in Chi-mo-hsien (the district of Chi-mo), and the area to the northwest and west were in Chiao-chou (Chiao-chou Department), from which the bay took its name.

Prior to the 1890s the bay and its environs were remarkably isolated from the impact which the West had made elsewhere on the China coast.[32] No Western trading vessels called there, and there were no Western goods. Indeed, even the Mexican dollar and the missionaries, those two harbingers of the Occident, had never made an appearance in the area.

14

Nevertheless, from a nautical point of view, the bay had considerable potential for Western shipping. It was from ten to thirty fathoms deep where it joined the sea, and there were a number of spots along its southeastern shore near the tip of the peninsula where the water was deep enough for the largest vessels.

In the 1880s Chiao-chou Bay was a moderately important terminus for a junk-borne commerce with South China.[33] This trade had begun almost a thousand years earlier during the Sung dynasty. In the thirteenth century, under the Yuan, the government had connected several rivers across Shantung to form a canal which joined the bay to the Gulf of Pechihli. This waterway, whose primary purpose was to avoid sending tribute rice around the dangerous Shantung peninsula, had contributed to the growth of commerce at the bay. Although silting made the ambitious canal difficult to maintain and caused it to fall out of use by the end of the next century, the bay remained a junk port. In the eighteenth century a customs barrier was established at its mouth to tax all incoming and outgoing vessels. By the late nineteenth century the total value of the junk trade had reached something over 3,000,000 taels annually.[34]

Because of the poor facilities for inland transport, however, the market area for the trade remained limited to the districts immediately adjacent to the bay.[35] The major junk ports were all located, therefore, in the shallow sections of the bay, on its north and northeast side, which were closest to the important towns in the interior. The most important of these ports was T'a-pu-t'ou in the north, the outlet for the largest town in the vicinity, Chiao-chou, which was about five miles inland. T'a-pu-t'ou, which handled about half of the junk trade at the bay, was the headquarters of the important Fukien and Chekiang firms which dominated the commerce. There were two other significant junk ports, Nü-ku-k'ou and Ts'ang-k'ou; they served the town of Chi-mo located about ten miles from the coast.

The future site of the German leasehold on the southeastern peninsula between the Yellow Sea and the bay did not even participate in the traditional commerce to the north.[36] This isolation was partially caused by the area's distance from the important towns in the interior and partially by the Lao-shan Mountains, which stretched from the sea nearly to the bay and which separated the peninsula from the rest of Chi-mo-hsien. The only connection between the peninsula and the areas to the north was a strip of flat land which ran around the edge of the bay. At the tip of the peninsula this strip of land broadened out, and it was there that the Germans eventually established a port. On the future site of the port were a few small villages which lived from a combination of farming and fishing. On the ocean side there was an inlet with a small island called Ch'ing-tao (Green Island). The inlet was known as Ch'ing-tao Bay, and one of the small villages was also called Ch'ing-tao. The Germans, therefore, called the city which they erected Tsingtao (Tsingtau), although the anchorage for the future port was actually on the inside of Chiao-chou Bay rather than on Ch'ing-tao Bay.

Chiao-chou Bay became well known to Westerners in the 1880s. This was partly because of the reports of naval personnel along the coast but more importantly because of the publication in 1882 of the second volume of *Trips through China*, Richthofen's massive report on his travels in the Middle Kingdom.[37] Richthofen had searched for coal because he felt that the exploitation of Chinese mines by Westerners would provide the basis for the overall foreign development of China's communications, commerce, and industry. In volume two, which dealt with North China, he devoted considerable attention to Shantung.

This was because the province was an outstanding example of the sort of area Richthofen had in mind for Western activity. It had a dense population, estimated at 30,000,000. In addition, it was reputed to be extremely rich in untapped mineral wealth, particularly coal. It also produced a wide variety of inherently valuable agricultural products, such as silk. However, the province remained comparatively poor and underdeveloped, even for China. The most striking reason for Shantung's failure to exploit its economic potential was, as one observer wrote, because "in no province has trade and commerce had to contend with such difficulties of transport and shipment as in this." [38] Transportation by land in Shantung, as in much of China, was of the most rudimentary and mediocre sort; however, unlike other more favorably endowed provinces on the coast, it had few navigable rivers or inland waterways to make up the deficiency. Shantung also had only one port of any significance, Chefoo, which had been opened as a treaty port in 1858. Chefoo, however, had a poor harbor and, even more serious, was located at the northeastern tip of the peninsula, cut off from the rest of the potentially rich province by a broad band of mountains.

In his description of Shantung, Richthofen delineated coal fields at Po-shan, Chang-ch'iu, Wei-hsien, and I-chou-fu which were later to be included in the German mining concession.[39] He also pointed out that Chefoo was still the only outlet for the coal which might be produced in these areas. However, the mountains which surrounded that port would make it very difficult to build a railroad between it and the fields; and Richthofen stressed that a railroad into the mineral-rich areas was absolutely essential if the mines were to be developed. According to him,

16

it was Chiao-chou Bay which was the logical outlet for Shantung's minerals since it was "the largest and best harbor in the whole northern half of China." [40]

Not only was the bay excellent for shipping, Richthofen said, but in addition a railroad could easily be constructed across the Shantung plain between it and the provincial capital, Tsinan. He pointed out that such a rail line would traverse the important coal beds and would also provide a very convenient outlet for the other products of the province, which were mostly produced in its central areas and had to be carted over the mountains to Chefoo to reach any wider markets. As Richthofen saw it, a port at Chiao-chou Bay and a railroad from there into the interior would become the basis for the economic development of the entire province. Indeed, "only Chiao-chou Bay" was a "suitable" location north of the Yangtze for the terminus of a "far wider railroad net" which would cover all of North China and for which the "connection to Tsinan would only be the beginning." [41]

In the 1880s a few important Chinese officials also became interested in Chiao-chou Bay.[42] The Sino-French War ushered in a new wave of interest in naval development in China, and during the period immediately after the conflict there were a number of attempts at reform, including the establishment in 1885 of China's first national Bureau of the Navy. It was this concern with naval matters which focused attention on the bay and, in particular, on its potential as a base.

In 1886, Hsü Ching-ch'eng, the minister to Germany and one of the leading advocates of naval reform, memorialized on the importance of the bay. Significantly, he had become aware of its value primarily from the works of Richthofen.[43] Hsü's basic point was that the unopened bay was an ideal spot for China to build a secure naval base in the north. "Western military ships have surveyed every point on the China coast," Hsü said, "and all report that Chiao-chou Bay is the best spot for a harbor." The minister pointed out that the bay not only provided excellent anchorage but was also easy to defend. He stressed that, since it had no commercial importance, it was preferable as a naval base to an important trading center, which would be more vulnerable to a blockade in time of war. Finally, Hsü said, the bay was ideally located for both the northern and the southern fleet commands, since it was within one or two days' sail from each. He, therefore, urged the government to begin developing it immediately and insisted that if this were done "within ten years" Chiao-chou Bay "would become a great harbor."

Shortly after Peking received Hsü's memorial, a censor, Chu I-hsin, presented another memorial on naval matters which once again reiterated that Chiao-chou Bay was the most suitable place for a naval base in the north.[44] Thereupon, the question of developing the bay was turned over for comment to Li Hung-chang in his capacity as head of the Peiyang fleet and vice-president of the new Bureau of the Navy. Li responded that he, too, had heard that Chiao-chou Bay was the best harbor in China; during the French War he had even heard rumors that the French were planning to occupy it and use it as a base for attacking North China.[45] Therefore he had already had the place thoroughly investigated. The results of these investigations, while not quite so glowing as the reports of Hsü or Chu, did tend to support their conclusions. Nevertheless, Li said, Chiao-chou Bay was not properly situated for the main northern base. "Port Arthur and Taku are exactly opposite each other; thus, they are so well placed strategically that we must work on them first," he wrote of the two spots he already was developing into bases. Only when they were ready, he continued, could "discussions begin about starting work on Chiao-chou Bay," which was "more than 300 li" from the vital Gulf of Pechihli. Still, acknowledging the potential importance of the place, Li did suggest that the governor of Shantung should be ordered to send some troops to the bay to build fortifications there. (If such orders were issued, they were not carried out.)

By 1891, however, Li decided that it was necessary to begin fortifying Chiao-chou Bay. In that year he made a tour of inspection of the northern coast, visiting the bay among other places. After his return the viceroy memorialized that Chiao-chou Bay and Chefoo should be armed as soon as possible.[46] Li said that since Port Arthur and Weihaiwei (the latter having been substituted for Taku) were already becoming naval bases, an enemy fleet, seeking a base from which to launch an attack, would choose a suitable, undefended anchorage such as Chiao-chou Bay. Hence, he wrote, the fortification of the place could "not be delayed any longer," and he suggested that the normal contribution of Shantung to the navy should be diverted to fortifying the bay and Chefoo.

As a result of Li's memorial, four battalions of Huai Army troops under the command of General Chang Kao-yuan, which had been based elsewhere in Shantung, were transferred to Chiao-chou Bay.[47] Chang and his forces remained there, except for a short stint in Manchuria during the Japanese War, until the Germans came in 1897. Chang stationed his forces at the tip of the southeastern peninsula, just to the north of Ch'ing-tao Bay. He constructed barracks and a telegraph line to the interior and began to build three gun batteries. The last work went extremely slowly and, by 1897, Chang had only completed one battery and part of another, leaving the bay still essentially undefended.[48]

Despite the comparative lack of activity at the bay during the early '90s, its potential was not forgotten. For example, in 1893 a correspondent from Shantung wrote to the *North China Daily News* that the bay should be opened as a treaty port because it was the most "strategic point of Shantung commerce." [49] China's defeat in the Sino-Japanese War virtually obliterated her naval strength, and in July 1895 the leading reformer, Chang Chih-tung, wrote a memorial containing a set of proposals for once again developing the nation's capabilities.[50] Among other things, he suggested that China build two naval bases, one at the Hu-men in Kwangtung and the other at Chiao-chou Bay. Since the war had destroyed China's dreams of developing a modern navy, Chang's suggestions were ignored, at least with regard to the bases. The general lack of interest in naval matters after 1895 may also have been the reason why Chang Kao-yuan's activities at Chiao-chou Bay made so little headway.

Just after the Japanese War, an event occurred which should have dramatized the value of the bay to the Chinese government. The conflict convinced the Russians that they could no longer freely rely on Japanese ports for wintering their fleet as they had done in the past.[51] Some anchorage to the south of Russian territory was still vital, however, because Vladivostok froze over in the winter. The commander of the Russian fleet had apparently heard the favorable reports about Chiao-chou Bay and suggested that it might be a good place to use. In the fall of 1895, therefore, the Russian government obtained permission to anchor ships at the bay during the coming winter. Peking acceded to the Russian request because of the increasingly good relations between the two nations, but the decision was a reluctant one. The Tsungli Yamen explicitly told the Russians that they could only use the bay as a "temporary anchorage" and that when spring came they would have to "depart immediately." [52] A few Russian ships actually did spend the winter of 1895–1896 at Chiao-chou Bay.

The Immediate Background, 1894–1897

Germany's campaign to obtain a foothold in China began during the Sino-Japanese War, which coincided with the heightened demand of influential sections of German society for a more ambitious foreign policy. Many of the key factors which contributed to the drive for the status of a *Weltmacht* in the '90s had long been characteristic of the German involvement in China. Thus the Middle Kingdom was a fitting stage for the Reich's most important colonial venture of the period, the acquisition of the sphere of influence in Shantung.

The German navy provided the vital connection between the nation's quest for world power and its imperialism in China. This was because the navy, which had long been interested in the Middle Kingdom, also played a crucial part in developing Germany's new foreign policies.[53] The impetus for the navy's role was provided by a new group of naval leaders, typified by Alfred Tirpitz. The rise of this group to power began about 1895, and in 1897 Tirpitz became the Secretary of State of the Naval Ministry (*Reichsmarineamt*). Although Germany was probably the second most powerful nation in the world, her navy, partially through neglect in the late '80s and early '90s, ranked fifth, even behind that of Italy. Alfred Tirpitz and his supporters engineered the movement to remedy the situation and, in so doing, became not only the leaders of the German naval revival of the '90s but also the creators of the German colony in China.

Tirpitz' theories about naval power and the problem of obtaining support for increasing it clearly indicate why the desire to become a *Weltmacht* ultimately found a focus in China through the activities of the navy. Tirpitz fought to strengthen the German navy because he considered a great fleet the primary basis of national power. This was because for Tirpitz, as for many other thinkers of the late nineteenth century, national power consisted of a worldwide system of military strength, political influence, and, above all, economic involvement. A strong fleet not only protected the homeland against possible rivals but also directly supported the activities around the world which were so crucial in establishing a nation's international position.

Such a conception of national power, of course, contributed directly to Tirpitz' interest in imperialism in the non-Western world, particularly in regions where Germans played an important economic role. China was such an area, and an especially striking one, because the navy's traditional concern with the German position in the Middle Kingdom had always been, if only implicitly, based on the same sorts of considerations as those which dominated the new ideology of navalism in the 1890s.

The feeling of rivalry with Great Britain, which permeated the whole German drive for a place in the sun, was a particularly important component of Tirpitz' own credo and further served to direct both his and the nation's attention to China. The competition existed, of course, because England was the greatest power in the world and, indeed, provided the model for the definition of power in the 1890s. England's fleet was the world's largest, she was the acknowledged leader in international trade, her colonies circled the globe, and her economic influence predominated in many other places outside the Empire. Tirpitz, like many other naval leaders, was particularly prone to the sense of rivalry with England, not only because of his direct concern with naval power but also because of his middle-class background. This segment of German society had what has been described as an "undeniable England-complex" and, in its attitudes and policies, displayed a combination of admiration for and jealousy of Britain totally alien to the "self-contained old Prussian mentality of the generation of Bismarck." [54]

No place provided a more appropriate locale for competing with England than China, where the Anglo-German rivalry was of long standing. Indeed, in the Middle Kingdom the Germans faced a small-scale version of the relationship with Britain which they believed existed in the world at large; they felt that they were beginning to challenge England's preponderant position while still being forced to compete in an environment dominated by Britain and her power. Not only did the rivalry with England push Tirpitz and the navy toward activism in China in the late '90s; it also encouraged them to make the future German possession a model colony in order to equal the vaunted English competence in the colonial sphere.

For the government to build a powerful navy required enormous budgetary expenditures which in turn necessitated widespread political support.[55] Fortunately for his goals, Tirpitz was a brilliant politician and one of the great parliamentary tacticians of the German Empire. He realized clearly that the relationship between a strong navy and the expansion of German colonial power provided one of the most persuasive arguments for enlarging the fleet. Therefore, he also espoused imperialism, especially in a place like China, because it gained support for him from important swing groups in the Reichstag.

What success the navy had in winning the backing of liberals was frequently due to Tirpitz' emphasis on the connection between a fleet and world trade and economic power. Action in China, where Germany had a strong Catholic missionary interest, was also an effective way of obtaining crucial support for the fleet from the Center Party, the most important pivotal group in the Reichstag. The Center eventually supported the navy primarily for domestic reasons. However, Tirpitz hoped to convince the party that the fleet could benefit its specific interests as well, and one of the ways he planned to do this was by showing how German power abroad could provide assistance and protection to German missionaries. It should be noted that Tirpitz' interest in missionary work was essentially Machiavellian; for, unlike his fervent belief in the economic necessity of a fleet, he seems to have had no particular concern for religion. This was to become obvious in later years when commercial and missionary interests in Shantung appeared to clash and the navy opted for the former.

Tirpitz' political perspicacity thus strengthened his own commitment to the need for world power. However, this sensitivity also conditioned the methods by which he was willing to pursue that goal. In particular, the admiral was reluctant to indulge in activities which would lead to open military hostilities, since many of the pro-imperialist groups whose support he needed disliked actual warfare. World power might have an appeal in the Reichstag, but conflict itself was unpopular. Many politicians who gave qualified support to the fleet felt that the major drawback of Germany's quest for the status of a world power was its expense. As a result, any action which brought about hostilities might be roundly condemned as unnecessarily wasteful. Similarly, some of the liberal groups interested in trade and commerce felt that fighting within a colony or trading area not only hurt business but demonstrated a policy of militaristic atavism rather than sound commercial planning.

Hence, when an action might result in military conflict, Tirpitz frequently backed away from it. Some of his contemporaries, like Holstein, attributed this tendency to a personality trait, a "lack of nerve" on the admiral's part.[56] Although such a psychological factor may have been operative, Tirpitz' avoidance of conflict was definitely also a conscious policy. As one student of the admiral has written, Tirpitz "disliked direct confrontation and, contrary to the common impression, shied away from open pitched battles . . . He was *par excellence* the politician and the manipulator of men." [57] In later years, Tirpitz' particularly keen political sense was to differentiate him from some of his own allies in the search for increased national power and to work in the interest of Chinese autonomy in Shantung.

The kaiser agreed with the views of Tirpitz and his circle, though he tended to embrace the position with even greater fervor due to his racialist view of world politics and rather atavistic concern for national glory, neither of which was particularly characteristic of Tirpitz and the navy. Thus, it was the kaiser who initially responded to the Sino-Japanese War with the suggestion that the time might have come for Germany to contemplate a territorial acquisition in China.[58] Ever since his accession to the throne, Wilhelm had felt that Germany's power in China was not commensurate with the Reich's growing interest there. In November 1894 he warned the Foreign Office that Germany's rival, Britain, might use China's defeat in the war to initiate the dismemberment of the Middle Kingdom and that, if this occurred, Germany "must not under any circumstances be put on the wrong end of the stick" but should be ready to grab its share of the spolis.[59] For, he pointed out, "we also need a secure place in China, where our trade turnover comes to four hundred millions a year." This figure is an interesting indication of the impact which the growth of German commerce in China was making at home, for, no matter what monetary system the kaiser may have had in mind, it was a tremendous exaggeration.[60]

The Foreign Office itself was not very interested in obtaining a base in China. At least until 1897, when Bülow replaced Marschall as foreign minister, the Wilhelmstrasse was rather skeptical of the whole drive for world power. Its attitude toward imperialism remained closer to the moderate one inherited from the Bismarck era. Nevertheless, when it received the kaiser's letter, the Foreign Office agreed that Germany ought to be prepared to capitalize on the break-up of China if the war should happen to lead in that direction.

In early 1895, therefore, it asked the navy to outline the requirements for a naval base in China and at the same time entered into negotiations which were to lead eventually to the triple intervention against Japan.[61] By the beginning of April, it became evident that Japan planned to follow up her crushing defeat of China by exacting a harsh peace which would include the cession of the Liaotung peninsula and Port Arthur. Russia decided that the cessions would constitute a threat to her interests in Manchuria and Korea and, encouraged by Li Hung-chang, the chief Chinese negotiator, worked to thwart Tokyo by organizing a concerted international attack on the proposed terms. The Treaty of Shimonoseki which contained Japan's demands was signed on April 17, and a few days later Russia, Germany, and France handed notes to the Japanese government ordering it to retrocede Liaotung to China. Tokyo, in a militarily weak position, reluctantly agreed despite widespread and bitter domestic desentment against the move, which, it should be noted, left a deep residue of hostility against the three powers involved. The Germans participated in the intervention because of their desire to neutralize the Franco-Russian alliance. There was also the feeling in German diplomatic circles that such a move would put the Reich in a good position from which to profit from any impending division of Chinese territory, something which still seemed a possibility.

As events unfolded in the spring and summer of 1895, however, it became clear that China was not going to split up, and the Foreign Office lost interest in trying to obtain a foothold there.[62] But by then a broad range of German press and public opinion, with commercial and colonial groups in the lead, had begun to campaign seriously for the German colony in China which they had coveted for so long.[63] Japan's military triumph aroused racial fears in the kaiser, and he too began to press harder than ever for a base. As Holstein later described the war's effect on Wilhelm, the "kaiser had formerly spoken sympathetically of the 'plucky little Japs,' but now the picture of a future 'Yellow Peril' took root in his mind and gave rise to a definite program" for greater activism in the Far East.[64]

It was the navy, however, which became the most powerful advocate of a German move in China. It embraced the idea that the war might permit the Reich to obtain a foothold in the Middle Kingdom and quickly developed extremely grandiose plans for the future German possession. Thus, in accord with the thinking of Tirpitz and the new group which was coming to dominate naval policy, the navy abandoned the idea of simply establishing a naval base in China and insisted that what Germany needed was a sphere of influence which included a major commercial depot like Hong Kong and a hinterland which could be developed by Germans.

The evolution of these goals was already evident in early 1895 in the navy's initial response to the Foreign Office's request for a list of the requirements for a suitable naval base in China. Admiral Hollmann, then Secretary of State of the Naval Ministry, wrote the reply.[65] He had been secretary since 1890 and was Tirpitz' chief rival in the navy until the latter replaced him in 1897. Hollmann answered the Foreign Office essentially in terms of a naval base. He paid considerable attention to the value of such a station in time of war and stressed the importance of bases for other purely naval purposes. Hollmann even suggested that two bases would probably be desirable in view of the East Asian fleet command, which stretched from Singapore to Hakodate.

Nevertheless, in line with the navy's traditional orientation toward commerce, Hollmann was also highly interested in the role which a base could play in furthering German trade in China. "When there is peace and order abroad, the advantage of a base is basically in the economic sphere," he wrote. "Its position raises the political power and prestige of the owner . . . and creates an ability to influence far beyond its borders which can, indeed, be obtained in no other way." Significantly, Hollmann insisted that the spot to be selected should be economically important in itself and not simply serve German interests indirectly by acting as a naval base. "The stations," he wrote, "must be located on the principal trade routes and must have already attained some commercial importance; dead places which have no capability for development have no value."

By early 1896, perhaps because the new group surrounding Tirpitz had become increasingly influential, the navy had already decided not to seek a mere naval base in China but, rather, a complete territorial sphere which would be suitable for economic exploitation. For example, Captain Jaeschke, head of the Naval General Staff and a future governor of the German colony, wrote a long report giving the navy's desiderata for the foothold in the Far East.[66] Jaeschke laid the greatest emphasis on economic criteria, stipulating that "the place must be in or near a zone which we contemplate taking, it must already economically dominate this zone, or it must, after suitable measures have been taken, be able to dominate the zone economically. The more developed the place is already, the better . . . If underdeveloped, it needs to have its capabilities for development taken into account through the quality of the area around it and behind it and the ease of transportation to it."

In addition to sketching out the ideal qualifications of a base, Jaeschke also provided detailed descriptions of many possible sites on the East Asian coast. His discussion of Shantung, a province which he considered "very desirable for Germany," indicated how unsympathetic the navy was to the idea of taking a base solely for military purposes and how dedicated it had become to the notion of seizing an entire sphere of influence with a port which, although militarily useful, would serve also as the outlet for the sphere. Basing his report largely on the writings of Richthofen, Jaeschke listed all the products of the province and described its trading patterns. With reference to Chiao-chou Bay, Chefoo, and other places on the coast, the memorandum concluded, "As one can see . . . Shantung has no good harbor as yet which in nautical or military terms is acceptable. Nevertheless, it might be useful to take one of the spots while paying attention to the goal of later taking possession of the whole province . . . only the expectation of the whole province would make the cost of developing the harbor worthwhile."

From an economic point of view, of course, there was something fundamentally irrational in the plans which the navy was developing for China. For, like Britain, Germany was a major trading power and, hence, not a nation which would profit from breaking up the Middle Kingdom into spheres of influence. However, the navy did not see this situation clearly until after the acquisition of Chiao-chou Bay, testimony to the strength of its sense of rivalry with Britain and its adherence to the ideology of navalism.

Significantly, although the naval leaders advocated that Germany's foothold in China should be more than simply a naval base, they did not suggest that the new possession be removed from naval control and placed, like the other German overseas territories, under the Colonial Section of the Foreign Office. This was primarily because of the dissatisfaction which German colonial circles felt with the Colonial Section. The bureau had originally been established in lieu of an independent colonial ministry, partly in order to de-emphasize the significance of overseas expansion. As a result, German colonialists considered the Colonial Section to be something of a symbol of the nation's supposed diffidence toward imperialism. They complained that the section received little attention from either the Foreign Office or the government as a whole and that it was chronically short of funds. More important, the commercially oriented colonial groups felt that the men who administered the colonies were conservative bureaucrats who, if they appreciated the importance of overseas possessions at all, understood only their military and political value and not their economic significance. As a result, it was claimed, such officials overlooked the need for administering the colonies rationally and efficiently and had no interest in making plans for economic development.[67] While this assessment of the Colonial Section is open to dispute, the navy apparently agreed with it.[68] Therefore, because it hoped for political gains among colonialist groups, as well as because it genuinely wanted to improve and stimulate German colonialism, the navy was eager to try its own hand at colonial administration.

The Foreign Office, which from the first had been lukewarm about obtaining a naval base in China, became the main source of opposition to the navy's broadened colonial desires. The Wilhelmstrasse fought the navy's scheme because it feared that activity on the scale envisioned by the naval leaders would exacerbate Germany's increasingly poor relations with Great Britain. In addition, a calmer assessment of the rivalry with England may have enabled a few persons in the Foreign Office to recognize the economically irrational element in the navy's plans for a sphere in China.[69] In later years the Foreign Office became the chief advocate of limiting German activity in Shantung lest it hurt Germany's overall diplomatic position and her economic activities elsewhere in China.

Because of the clash between the broad desires of the navy and the hesitations of the Foreign Office, it took the German government until 1897 to decide where to move in China. As a member of the Foreign Office complained in the beginning of that year,[70] "The whole thing started two years ago when the Foreign Office wrote the Naval Ministry and suggested that the Sino-Japanese War, which was then still in progress, *might* lead to the seizure of territory in China by the European powers; and so, perhaps, we might get an opportunity to obtain a *coaling station* there for our navy. Under the hands of the navy, the coaling station gradually turned into a fleet base and then into a point of support for our trade. The navy pushed the concept of a *commercial* base ever more into the foreground . . . Finally we were asked to get a place which would be suitable for *the jumping-off point for the establishment of a German colonial sphere.* There is no doubt the thing has become harder and slower because all these new points of view were dragged in. Many good chances to get a place have been lost because of this delay . . . If the original and moderate point of view of the Foreign Office had been followed, i.e., the goal of obtaining a coaling station for the navy, we might have had it long ago" [emphasis in original].[71]

After the kaiser reopened the discussion about a foothold in China, a number of places quickly suggested themselves as the best location for the colony.[72] Among those most frequently mentioned were Chusan Island, Chiao-chou Bay, Mirs Bay (north of Hong Kong), the Pescadores, or one of the islands off Amoy. During 1895 and most of 1896, Chusan was apparently the navy's first choice. Richthofen had predicted that Chusan could not only become the economic fulcrum of the Yangtze Valley, the most important economic region in China, but could also take the trade of South China away from Hong Kong. The acquisition of Chusan would, of course, have led to the gravest difficulties with Great Britain. Not only had China promised England not to alienate the island, but Britain also dominated the foreign trade of China through her commercial control of the Yangtze Valley, and she had always considered the region as her special sphere of action. However, Admiral Knorr, the new Chief of the Naval High Command and the navy's main spokesman in the deliberations over a site, was not particularly concerned about the possibility of tension with Britain.[73]

Naturally, the Foreign Office strongly opposed the acquisition of Chusan because of the international complications involved. Foreign Minister Marschall thought that a more acceptable, and less dangerous, choice might be a spot like Quemoy or Amoy, or "some other place of minor importance, suitable for narrow naval purposes."[74] But Knorr, for example, had doubts about Amoy: it was a treaty port which had never developed because it had "no suitable hinterland for trade."[75]

Chiao-chou Bay received little consideration after early 1895 because Admiral Hollmann reported that it was not ice-free in winter. If it had not been for this false information, the German government would probably have reached its decision to take Chiao-chou Bay much more quickly, for the bay was otherwise the sort of place which was acceptable to both the navy and the Foreign Office. It was fairly satisfactory from a diplomatic point of view because it was located in an area in which no other power appeared to have a strong interest. Even Russia's right to anchor there was not an overwhelming obstacle because Russia's major interests lay farther north. The navy could also agree to Chiao-chou Bay because of the area's importance for the economic and commercial development of Shantung Province.

In addition, the presence of the Steyl mission in Shantung made the bay a particularly appropriate location for Germany's foothold in China. Throughout this period Bishop Anzer called vociferously for a more powerful German presence in China. Thus, in late 1895, a Foreign Office spokesman noted that, according to "the repeated complaints of Bishop Anzer," Germany had "no respect now among the people and officials of Shantung . . . Anzer stormily demands an energetic act which will get some respect," the official continued; "he says otherwise the mission may force him to return to the protection of the French, which was more effective." [76] Anzer probably had a hand in the suggestions of the minister in Peking that Germany might obtain a base in China as a reparation for the repeated missionary cases at Yen-chou and that the best location for such a base would be Chiao-chou Bay.[77]

As the discussions over what spot Germany should acquire continued, Berlin made its first overtures to the Chinese government about obtaining a foothold in China.[78] The Germans hoped to get the territory peacefully, perhaps as a form of compensation for the German role in the triple intervention. This approach, however, was doomed to certain failure because Chinese foreign policy had just undergone a radical change. The Sino-Japanese War had called into question the earlier policy of balancing off the powers against one another. As a result, Li Hung-chang and most other important officials became convinced that the best method of maintaining Chinese security would be to rely on Russian protection alone. One result of the new approach was the Chinese decision to let the Russian fleet anchor at Chiao-chou Bay. Another (and the most important) was the secret treaty of alliance with Russia of 1896. A third was that in late 1895 and early 1896, when the Germans first broached the subject of a base, Peking was willing to give some concessions to keep German friendship, but certainly not a piece of Chinese territory.

In October 1895 the Foreign Office asked the Tsungli Yamen and the Chinese minister to Germany, Hsü Ching-ch'eng, if it would be possible for Germany to obtain a base. The Wilhelmstrasse, however, did not mention a specific location. The Chinese answer was a flat refusal which stressed that, while China valued German friendship, it could not satisfy Germany's request without having all the other powers ask for territory too. In the same month the Germans received something which they had long desired, separate German concessions in Tientsin and Hankow. In March 1896, Peking granted the second loan for the Japanese indemnity to the consortium of the Hong Kong Banking Corporation and the Deutsch-Asiatische Bank but continued to ignore Germany's territorial desires. In June, when Li Hung-chang arrived in Berlin on his world tour, the Germans made another unsuccessful attempt to obtain Chinese permission for a base.

Though the Germans met no response from Chinese authorities, the debate in Berlin over what place to obtain dragged on. In the spring of 1896, therefore, Tirpitz himself went to the Far East as commander of the German East Asian squadron in order to discover the best location for the German foothold in China.[79] Tirpitz claimed in later years that, from the beginning of the debate, he had realized clearly on the basis of Richthofen's and others' reports that "there was only one place" which was suitable for a base, "the unset pearl Tsingtau." [80] This view from hindsight was an oversimplification of his actual position at that time. Tirpitz, like the other new naval leaders, was envious of Great Britain's position in China, and his respect for the English increased when he observed their activities at first hand after his arrival in East Asia.[81] Therefore, like Knorr, he apparently felt at first that the best location for a German base in China would be at the mouth of the Yangtze River.[82] Nevertheless, perhaps because of his political sensitivity and desire to avoid conflict, he was willing to compromise with diplomatic reality and pick another site as long as it was capable of economic growth. In any case, Tirpitz developed a favorable opinion of Chiao-chou Bay, and his reports on it ultimately proved decisive.

After he arrived in China, Tirpitz learned, probably from Russians who had wintered there, that Chiao-chou Bay was free of ice. This information cleared up the vexing doubt which had precluded the bay from serious consideration as the German base. By July, Tirpitz thought highly enough of the bay to send a ship to have a look at it. He also requested the minister to Peking, Edmund Heyking, to ask the Russian minister if the latter's country had any claims on the area because of the ships which had wintered there.[83] In August the admiral sailed to the bay to study its potentialities for himself. He was pleased with what he found, and his subsequent reports extolled the virtues of the place.

His most crucial and comprehensive report,[84] written in September, emphasized the economic advantages of the bay. It was based as usual on the writings of Richthofen but carried added weight because of Tirpitz' personal observations. Tirpitz again stressed that Chiao-chou Bay was the "only natural, good harbor in the whole of China northwards from Shanghai to Newchang" and explained how it could be made into the chief outlet not only for the wealth of Shantung but also for the whole of North China. In addition, the admiral made the significant observation that developing the bay would ease communications with the western part of Shantung "where German missionaries are active."

The report also included a lengthy discussion of the maritime and military capabilities of the bay. In it Tirpitz reiterated that the area was free from ice at all times of the year. He emphasized the feasibility of developing the bay into a harbor, though he pointed out that a more expert opinion would be required to make a final assessment about the patterns of tides and silting. In addition, the admiral described the bay's advantages from the point of view of defense. Finally, he discussed the weak Chinese military preparations there and actually appended a tactical plan for occupying the area. After Tirpitz' reports reached Berlin, a consensus about the desirability of Chiao-chou Bay rapidly developed.

Nevertheless, the final selection of the bay was complicated by the sudden possibility, in the fall of 1896, that the Russians might have too great a claim on the area.[85] This situation developed as a result of the so-called Cassini Convention. The convention is a mysterious document, or set of documents, whose exact status and even existence have been matters of dispute; however, there does appear to have been some sort of understanding, referred to in the Chinese text as the "New Russian Treaty." [86] Article 9 of the convention stated, "Russia has no ice-free port in Asia; therefore, if there were military complications in the area . . . the Russian fleet would be very inconvenienced. The Chinese government is, therefore, willing temporarily to lease Chiao-chou Bay to the Russians for a period of fifteen years." However, "if there is no military danger, the Russians may not immediately send troops to occupy the bay, lest the suspicions of other powers be raised." This concession may have been part of a conscious Chinese plan to block German designs on Chiao-chou Bay by placing it under Russian protection. Even though the German government had not yet asked China for the bay, Peking and Saint Petersburg were aware that the Germans were becoming increasingly interested in taking it.

The news of the new Russian privileges predictably made its greatest impact on the Foreign Office. In a last-minute attempt to stave off what seemed like an imminent decision for Chiao-chou Bay, the Foreign

Office suggested that Germany should take Samsah Bay instead.[87] Samsah Bay was a place which was considered good for a naval base but which the navy had rejected long ago because it had no economic potential. Although the Foreign Office admitted that "one can't tell if Samsah Bay has a commercial future," it pointed out that at least the area was politically feasible. For the present, Germany "must be satisfied with the military significance" of the place, insisted the Wilhelmstrasse, adding that "when we have a secure place there, we will later still be able to put our hand on another spot with some economic value, if the chance should appear."

By late 1896 this rather vague suggestion had no chance of blocking the drive to occupy an area which, like Chiao-chou Bay, had broad economic significance. In November a crown council consisting of the top diplomatic and naval officials met and tentatively decided to acquire Chiao-chou Bay.[88] The final decision was delayed only in order to let a professional engineer complete a topographical survey of the area. The day after the meeting the kaiser ordered Knorr to prepare plans for the military occupation of the bay. It was decided, over the objections of Foreign Minister Marschall, who remained displeased, that the Russian claims to the area could be settled by negotiations.

After the decision the Germans began to take the final steps necessary to acquire Chiao-chou Bay. In December, Heyking approached the Tsungli Yamen to ask, for the first time, if China would cede the area to the Germans.[89] He was rebuffed. He continued, however, to press the Chinese, and as it became clear that they would not yield willingly, the minister began to search for some incident which could serve as a pretext for seizing the bay by force. Some of the incidents which Heyking tried to exploit were oddly petty. In February 1897, for example, the minister caused a tremendous fuss by claiming that he had been seriously insulted by Ching-hsin, the president of the Board of Finance. Ching-hsin had evidently done nothing more than pull Heyking's sleeve when the minister made a ceremonial mistake upon leaving the presence of the emperor at a New Year's presentation. Nevertheless, Heyking threatened that if the Chinese official did not come immediately to the German embassy and apologize, Germany would break diplomatic relations with China. The Tsungli Yamen agreed to the demeaning request, for it realized that Heyking was looking for an excuse for action.

While Heyking was concocting incidents in Peking, Georg Franzius, who was famous in Germany as the director of the harbor works at Kiel, went to China to study the topography of Chiao-chou Bay to ascertain if it was suitable for a German base. By early summer he reported back favorably, maintaining that from a technical point of view it was the finest location for a harbor on the coast.[90] The German government then began to negotiate with the Russians for their acquiescence in Germany's occupation of the area.[91] By August 1897, after discussions with the czar at Peterhof, the kaiser felt that he had received Russia's consent, although some members of his government still harbored doubts on the matter. In September, Heyking received orders to tell Peking that if the need arose, the Germans planned to anchor warships at the bay during the coming winter.

As Berlin's desire for Chiao-chou Bay became increasingly clear to China, the Chinese government's main hope for warding off the German threat was the Russian alliance. However, Peking also undertook what proved to be last-minute efforts to strengthen the bay's military defenses. In February the Tsungli Yamen memorialized that Heyking had recently come to the Yamen seeking a base in China, but that he had not designated a place until the previous month "when he finally named Chiao-chou Bay." The Yamen said that since the bay was "strategically vital" it should immediately be built up "to defend itself and to block the desire of those who would seize it." The Yamen, therefore, had orders sent to Wang Wen-shao, the Commissioner of Northern Ports (Pei-yang ta-ch'en), and to Governor Li Ping-heng asking them to draw up plans for converting Chiao-chou Bay into a naval base. At the same time, the Grand Council ordered the naval and land forces to bolster all coastal defenses.[92] In July, Wang reported back that plans were complete for developing the defenses of the bay and that work was about to begin.[93] Time had run out for China, however.

By the fall of 1897 only the modalities of the actual seizure of Chiao-chou Bay were still being debated in Berlin. The basic decision to take the area had been made, and the government, strongly prodded by the kaiser, was ready to move when a proper opportunity presented itself. On October 30, when Heyking was in Wuchang visiting Chang Chih-tung and inspecting the new German concession, townspeople threw stones at some German sailors from the ship *Cormoran,* which had brought the minister up the Yangtze.[94] Heyking immediately sent Chang Chih-tung an insulting demand for restitution, and the kaiser ordered the Foreign Office and the navy to confer on how to use the incident as a pretext for seizing Chiao-chou Bay. Chang Chih-tung was certainly aware of Heyking's intentions, and he immediately agreed to the minister's demands. Unfortunately for China, however, two days after the stoning at Wuchang another and more serious act of violence gave the Germans the chance they had been waiting for.

The Acquisition of the Sphere of Influence

On the night of November 1, 1897, in a small village in Chü-yeh-hsien in southwestern Shantung a band of local people killed two of Anzer's missionaries. The circumstances surrounding the murder of the two German priests, Henle and Nies, have been in dispute ever since. However, the best evidence would indicate that the attack was motivated by typical antimissionary sentiments and that it was organized, led, and largely perpetrated by members of the famous secret society, the Ta-tao-hui.[95] The attack, because it was a direct and serious offense against Germans and because it took place in Shantung itself, provided Berlin with the perfect excuse for seizing Chiao-chou Bay.

The kaiser, who had grown increasingly impatient while waiting for his government to act in China, apparently made the initial decision to move promptly on the basis of the Chü-yeh case.[96] When he first heard of the murders, on November 6, Wilhelm was almost euphoric about what he considered a "splendid opportunity" for taking action.[97] He immediately drafted a telegram ordering the East Asian squadron to occupy Chiao-chou Bay. The Foreign Office and the chancellor, however, urged the kaiser not to send the order until he had made absolutely certain that the Russians had definitely relinquished their interest in the area and would not oppose the German action. The kaiser thereupon cabled his intentions to the czar, and Nicholas' reply, "Cannot approve nor disapprove your sending German squadron to Kiaochow," [98] became the signal for action. On November 7 the kaiser's telegram went out to Admiral Diedrichs, Tirpitz' successor as commander of the East Asian squadron.

Bishop Anzer, who was in Berlin when the missionaries were killed, also recognized the opportunity offered by the incident and began to agitate for the seizure of Chiao-chou Bay, seemingly as unconcerned about the two dead priests as was the kaiser.[99] On the seventh, Anzer told a representative of the Foreign Office that he hoped Germany "would now use the opportunity to occupy Kiaochow, by far the best and from every vantage point the base with the finest capabilities for development for us." A few days later he warned the kaiser, "It is the last chance for Germany to get a possession anywhere in Asia and to firm up our prestige which has dropped . . . no matter what it costs, we must not under any circumstances give up Kiaochow. It has a future for economic development as well as industry, a future which will be greater and more meaningful than Shanghai is today."

On November 10, Admiral Diedrichs left Wusung with the cruisers *Kaiser, Prinzess Wilhelm,* and *Cormoran* and headed north for Chiao-chou Bay.[100] The ships arrived at the bay early on November 14, and Diedrichs landed 700 men near the Chinese garrison. Although Chang Kao-yuan had between 1600 and 2000 troops, he made no attempt to stop the German ships from sailing into the bay or the landing parties from coming ashore. At noon of the same day, Diedrichs issued an ultimatum to Chang ordering him to evacuate his troops within three hours and to withdraw to Ts'ang-k'ou, about seven miles to the north, leaving behind all weapons but rifles. Chang wanted to remain where he was until he heard from Li Ping-heng or Wang Wen-shao. Diedrichs, however, pressed him and threatened to eject the Chinese by force; and, at two-thirty in the afternoon, Chang withdrew to the north.

Diedrichs immediately raised the German flag over the Chinese installations and issued a proclamation announcing the German occupation of Chiao-chou Bay. Diedrichs had been a fervent supporter of the navy's plans to acquire the bay for Germany,[101] and he did not doubt that his landing was to be the beginning of the permanent occupation of the area. Therefore, before he concluded his activities on the fourteenth, the admiral issued a supplementary edict in which he referred to himself as "governor" and, in order to ward off speculation, forbade the sale or purchase of land.[102]

Meanwhile, in Berlin, the German government was experiencing second thoughts about the possible dangers involved in seizing the bay.[103] Even after Czar Nicholas' telegram had arrived, the Foreign Office remained apprehensive about the threat of Russian intervention. These fears became profound when the Germans learned, on November 9, that the czar had spoken without the advice of his government, which was hostile to the German plans. Significantly, Tirpitz, now returned to Germany as naval secretary, shared the anxieties of the Foreign Office and argued that the time was not ripe for the occupation of the bay.[104] By expressing these reservations, Tirpitz put himself in disagreement with his allies in the navy, Admiral Knorr and Admiral Senden-Bibran, Chief of the Naval Cabinet. Tirpitz feared that if any conflict arose out of the occupation it would hurt the passage of the great naval bill which he was about to submit to the Reichstag. As soon as he heard of the Russian protests, the admiral telegraphed Chancellor Hohenlohe that he regarded "the action against China as unfavorable for the Navy Bill and in the proposed form very dangerous. The consequences of this sort of action must lead to serious threat of hostilities." [105] Holstein, who was handling the matter for the Foreign Office, appreciated Tirpitz' position and, in a letter otherwise critical of the navy's attitude, wrote, "By 'navy' I mean Senden and Knorr . . . Tirpitz is superb — and deeply disturbed." [106]

What disturbed Tirpitz most, of course, was the possibility of hostilities with Russia. However, he was also afraid that China might resist the landing and force Germany to engage in military action. Hohenlohe shared Tirpitz' concern about Chinese opposition and feared that "an actual war with China would have . . . the result that German trade with China would be ruined for a decade to the advantage of England." [107]

The fear of Russian intervention began to abate fairly quickly, and Diedrichs' fait accompli at Chiao-chou Bay militated against the possibility of surrendering the area. On November 15, a crown council decided rather definitively that the time had in fact come to obtain Chiao-chou Bay from China.[108] In addition to sending military reinforcements to the area, the council made plans to initiate a diplomatic campaign to obtain the bay. However, in deference to views like those held by Tirpitz and Hohenlohe, the council suggested that "in order to hinder China from making war on us (either openly or latently), her sovereign rights are to be protected wherever possible in the occupation, perhaps by only leasing the territory for a long period of time." [109] This suggestion is significant because, of course, the Germans did lease Chiao-chou Bay rather than annex it. It is also interesting because it was a harbinger of future compromises the Germans were to make in Shantung out of their desire to avoid conflict with China.

After the decision to keep Chiao-chou Bay, the German government began negotiating with Russia and England to make certain that the two powers would not interfere with German actions or come to the aid of China. These negotiations, which have been discussed thoroughly elsewhere,[110] concerned general international questions far broader than the issue of Chiao-chou Bay. Within a month Germany had succeeded in obtaining Russia's acquiescence to the German seizure of the bay and, indeed, had encouraged the Russians to participate in the division of Chinese territory by taking Port Arthur. Saint Petersburg's decision, of course, robbed China of its chief prop, the Russian alliance. The English also quickly decided not to interfere with Germany, as they did not wish to drive Germany and Russia together. Moreover, Great Britain rather welcomed the idea of a German buffer between the Russian zone in Manchuria and the center of England's activities in the Yangtze Valley.

At the same time the Germans began negotiations with the Chinese government. After Heyking heard of the murders of the missionaries, he hurried back to Peking. En route to the capital he stopped at Wusung to speak with Admiral Diedrichs, who was about to sail north, for he was anxious to coordinate his position with that of the navy, whose views he continued to consult throughout the coming months. Together Heyking and Diedrichs settled on terms which the minister would present to the Chinese if talks were begun.[111] Before he reached Peking, Heyking learned that Diedrichs had taken Chiao-chou Bay and that Berlin wished to keep the area.

On November 20, he presented to the Tsungli Yamen the demands which he and Diedrichs had decided upon.[112] Some of these demands, and others submitted soon afterward, were concerned with the missionary case. They called for punishment of the officials involved, reparations to the missionaries in the form of buildings, and a guarantee from the Chinese government that it would strive to prevent future violence. The most significant part of the ultimatum, however, dealt with Germany's imperialist desires in Shantung. First of all, Heyking asked China to give Germany a major compensation for the incident, by which he meant the leasing of Chiao-chou Bay. Secondly, the minister demanded that Germans receive the right to operate railroads in Shantung and open mines along the roadbeds.

The Germans achieved their goals in Shantung quickly and easily. The leading Chinese officials felt that China was too weak to resist Germany alone, and no other power proffered any assistance. The cornerstone of Chinese foreign policy since 1895 had been Li Hung-chang's Russian alliance. When it proved useless in the face of German and, indeed, Russian aggression, Peking quickly decided it would be impossible to resist the German pressure. There was important opposition to the government's attitude, but although this proved to be of great significance later, it had little effect during the period when Germany was seizing its sphere of influence in Shantung.

The Tsungli Yamen had not known of the murders at Chü-yeh until it received a telegram from Heyking in the south.[113] The Yamen reprimanded Governor Li Ping-heng for not reporting the incident more promptly and ordered him to investigate and settle it at once in order to prevent the Germans from obtaining a pretext for aggrandizement.[114] Li reported back immediately that he was sending the provincial judge, Yü-hsien, to Chü-yeh to look into the case.[115] By the fourteenth, when the Germans took Chiao-chou Bay, Yü had already rounded up about ten men who he said had been involved in the murders.[116]

When the Germans landed in spite of his efforts to settle the case, Li Ping-heng began to call for armed resistance against them.[117] The

Tsungli Yamen, highly conscious of China's military weakness, rejected this appeal. Instead, Peking sought to appease the Reich on the slim chance that the Germans might be interested only in the missionary case.[118] Through Minister Hsü the Chinese government urged Berlin to withdraw, stressing that Governor Li would be punished and that vigorous steps were being taken in Shantung to settle the missionary case. The Yamen informed Li that he was to be replaced and ordered his successor, Chang Ju-mei, to hurry to Shantung. The latter did so and took over the seals of office at Tsinan before the end of the month. At the same time, the Yamen turned its attention to seeking aid from the Russians. This diplomatic effort was begun after Diedrichs landed and was handled, appropriately enough, by Li Hung-chang himself.[119]

It was obvious virtually from the start that both the Chinese government's attempt to appease the Germans and its effort to solicit Russian assistance were going to fail. The demands Heyking presented to the Yamen on November 20 revealed the extent of Germany's ambitions. At the same time, the Germans continued to consolidate their position at Chiao-chou Bay. Diedrichs demanded that General Chang move his troops even farther to the north and withdraw from the area of the bay altogether.[120] After checking with Peking, Chang complied. As a result, by early December the Germans occupied not only the tip of the southeastern peninsula but also all the territory which surrounded the bay, including the administrative centers, Chi-mo and Chiao-chou.

Meanwhile, Russian ships which had been heading for Chiao-chou Bay, leading the Tsungli Yamen to believe that Russia was going to intervene, turned back. By the beginning of December many important Chinese officials had even begun to argue that the German demands ought to be accepted as quickly as possible in order to settle the Shantung crisis before other powers, particularly the Russians, thought of emulating Germany.[121] Their worst fears were realized when, in the middle of December, Russia announced its intention of occupying Port Arthur.

Under such conditions, the Chinese government found itself forced to yield with almost pathetic haste to the German ultimatum.[122] On November 27 the emperor appointed Weng T'ung-ho and Chang Yin-huan to negotiate with Heyking. By December 3 the two officials had agreed to almost all the demands which the minister had presented, though they still hesitated to surrender Chiao-chou Bay. Instead, Weng tried to get Heyking to accept the opening of the bay as a treaty port. Naturally, in view of the German goals, such efforts were bound to be unsuccessful. The minister rejected Weng's suggestion along with every other alternative plan the Chinese side presented. On December 15 the Chinese agreed informally to the leasing of Chiao-chou Bay; from then on only details remained to be settled.

During the negotiations which followed, Heyking and the Foreign Office worked closely with Diedrichs and Tirpitz.[123] As a result the minister tried to obtain the sort of sphere of influence in Shantung which the navy had been advocating since 1896. He sought to make the leased territory at Chiao-chou Bay into a German Hong Kong and, hence, as independent of China as possible. In addition, he strove to secure a German monopoly over the development of the interior of the province and to maximize German political influence there.

The navy wanted to lease somewhat more land than did the Foreign Office, and this was the main disagreement which arose between them during the negotiations.[124] The naval leaders felt that the northern border of the leased territory should run along the ridge of the Lao-shan Mountains and then follow the course of the Po-sha River across the plain to Chiao-chou Bay. The navy wanted this border because the 2400-foot-high ridge constituted a natural defensive barrier, and the thickly populated area just to the south of the riverbed was the "richest section" of the peninsula, where both agriculture and livestock raising flourished.[125] The Foreign Office, arguing that Germany should rule as little territory and as few Chinese as possible, wanted the boundary line placed somewhat farther down the peninsula. The result of this difference of opinion was evidently a compromise, for the eventual treaty with China left the precise delineation of the northern border for later discussions between the two nations.

During the negotiations the Germans continued to strengthen their military position. On December 17, Prince Heinrich left Germany with several troop ships bound for Chiao-chou Bay. The evening before, the kaiser celebrated his brother's departure with one of the most famous of his bombastic speeches, telling the prince, among other things: "Make it clear to every European there, to the German merchant and, above all things, to the foreigner in whose country we are . . . that the German Michael has set his shield, decorated with the imperial eagle, firmly on the ground. Whoever asks him for protection will always receive it . . . But if anyone should undertake to insult us in our rights or wish to harm us, then drive in with the mailed fist." [126] The prince's armada arrived at the bay on January 26 and landed a contingent of 1155 marines and 303 members of the naval artillery, under the command of Captain Oskar Truppel.[127] These forces were to become the basis of the permanent garrison of the German colony.

A continuing series of violent incidents involving Germans supplied Heyking with further ammunition for his negotiations. In late December there were attacks against the Steyl missionaries in Ts'ao-chou Prefecture, the location of Chü-yeh where the original two murders had taken place.[128] In addition, a German missionary was murdered in January in Kwangtung Province, and a German soldier died in a clash with some local people at Chi-mo.[129]

By the middle of January, agreement was reached in the Peking negotiations on the final terms for settling the Chü-yeh case.[130] The settlement complied with Germany's demands and provided ample compensation to the Steyl mission. The Chinese government agreed to pay the missionaries monetary damages as well as build three cathedrals and seven residences for the bishopric. It also promised that Li Ping-heng would never again receive high office. At the same time the Tsungli Yamen accepted a draft treaty which spelled out Germany's new privileges at Chiao-chou Bay and in the interior of Shantung. This treaty, with some further concessions to the Germans, was formally signed on March 6, 1898.

The Treaty of March 6 [131] opened with a humiliating reference to China's gratitude for German assistance in 1895: "The incidents connected with the mission in the prefecture of Ts'ao-chou-fu in Shantung being now closed, the Imperial Chinese Government consider it advisable to give a special proof of their grateful appreciation of the friendship shown them by Germany." Section I of the treaty dealt with the lease of Chiao-chou Bay. The Germans were given the area for ninety-nine years. The leasehold included the entire surface of the bay up to the high-water mark, and land on the southeastern peninsula up to a line drawn from the top of Potato Island to Lao-shan Harbor. It also included the entire peninsula which formed the southwestern side of the entrance to the bay, as well as "all islands lying seaward from Chiao-chou Bay which may be of importance for its defense."

The exact boundaries were to be negotiated later "in accordance with local traditions . . . by means of commissioners to be appointed on both sides." A boundary commission, headed by two Shantung taotai and some naval topographical specialists, did meet a few months later; and though it is difficult to know precisely how the Germans accomplished it, the decisions of the group were uniformly favorable to the Reich.[132] The crucial northern border of the leasehold encompassed more territory than the treaty had envisioned. In accordance with the navy's original desires, the final boundary line ran along the ridge of the Lao-shan Mountains and along the Po-shan River. In addition, the high-water mark was defined so as to include the junk port of T'a-pu-t'ou, and the Germans obtained all the islands which lay southwest of 121° east longitude and between 35°40' and 36°10' latitude.

The March 6 treaty granted the Germans the sole right to exercise sovereignty within the leased territory for a period of ninety-nine years. This made their position during the term of the lease analogous to that of the British at Hong Kong; and there is no indication that the Germans, either when the treaty was signed or later, ever desired or considered the leased territory to be anything but a German colony. They were permitted to establish their own tariff system in the leasehold, though they did promise "to come to an agreement with the Chinese government for the definitive regulation of the customs frontier" between the leased territory and the interior, and to do so "in a manner which will safeguard all the interests of China." Although the Germans were not allowed to sublet the leasehold, they could return it to China before the ninety-nine years, receive payment for the costs they had incurred, and obtain "a more suitable" place in return.

The treaty further permitted the free passage of German troops at any time within a fifty-kilometer zone around the leased territory. Although China retained sovereignty within the zone, it agreed to "abstain from taking any measures, or issuing any ordinances therein, without the previous consent of the German government." For the sake of military security, the Germans wanted a buffer between themselves and the Chinese, and this neutral zone provided the territorial protection they sought without increasing the amount of territory Germany had to administer.

Section II of the treaty delineated Germany's economic privileges inside the province. The Germans were given a concession to build three railway lines and to operate mines within thirty li (ten miles) of the roadbeds on either side. The projected routes of the railways not only assured that the leasehold could become Shantung's chief commercial outlet but also traversed almost every coal field Richthofen had mentioned. One line ran from Chiao-chou Bay to Tsinan, via Wei-hsien and Po-shan; another went from Chiao-chou Bay to I-chou-fu; and the third from Tsinan to I-chou-fu, via Lai-wu-hsien. In addition, the Germans received the right to extend the first line to the border of Shantung, once service had reached Tsinan.

Both the railways and the mining concessions were to be exploited by "Sino-German" companies in which "both German and Chinese merchants" would be "at liberty to invest" and to "share in the appointment of directors for the management of the undertaking." The firms involved were to receive "all the advantages and benefits extended to other Sino-foreign companies operating in China." In addition, the two governments agreed that in the near future they would "draw up a further agreement relative to the management" of the undertakings. Apparently the Germans did not consider the provisions for joint control of the enterprises particularly important. The spirit and rhetoric of the rest of the treaty, which spoke of giving the concessions to "Germany" or "German subjects," diminished the impact of such stipulations. Nevertheless, in the future the two clauses proved to be a useful wedge for Chinese officials trying to gain control over the German railways and mines.

Section III of the treaty granted the Germans further privileges in the interior which, in essence, reduced the province to a German sphere of influence. The section said that the Chinese government "binds itself in all cases where foreign assistance, in persons, capital, or material, may be needed for any purpose whatever within the province of Shantung, to offer the said work or supplying of materials in the first instance" to Germans.

Even before the negotiations were over, the Germans had already tried to capitalize on their new position in Shantung, and, within a day or so after March 6, they had actually succeeded in enforcing their monopoly privileges. In November 1897, Yung Wing, the American-educated entrepreneur and advocate of reform, had sought the right to construct a railway from Tientsin via Shantung to Chinkiang on the Yangtze River. The plan had aroused the immediate and fervent hostility of Chang Chih-tung, the leading patron of railway expansion, and Sheng Hsuan-huai, the official supervisor of railways. They feared that the new line would compete with the proposed Peking-Hankow railway, to which they were both heavily committed and which they hoped would become China's chief north-south trunk. The two officials had, therefore, launched a major campaign against Yung's project.[133] Nevertheless, on February 11 he obtained the concession for his railway, which by then held the added attraction for Peking of preventing a German railroad monopoly in Shantung.[134] The Germans immediately complained that the project infringed on their rights, especially since Yung planned to use foreign capital. The Chinese government, already under pressure from Chang and Sheng, capitulated shortly after the treaty had been signed, rescinded Yung's concession, and promised to negotiate the matter with Germany.[135]

By the beginning of 1898 the Germans had achieved their goal in China. They had acquired a colony on the coast which could be developed into a great port and, at the same time, had extracted concessions which opened the way to economic and political domination over the important Chinese province which formed the colony's hinterland. Other powers were obtaining similar privileges elsewhere in China, and it appeared to many observers that the Middle Kingdom, having finally succumbed to half a century of heightening imperialist pressure, would find itself bereft of all political and economic autonomy and, perhaps, carved up into separate colonial areas. As the scramble for concessions occurred, however, crucial political developments were taking place within China which were eventually to play a large part in saving the nation from this fate.

II. The Chinese Response

Tradition and Change in Chinese Foreign Policy

The German seizure of Chiao-chou Bay, the Treaty of March 6, and the scramble for concessions all conjured up the specter of the disintegration of the Middle Kingdom and revealed the utter inability of the Chinese government to fend off the Western powers. In response, important segments of the Chinese political elite began to put forward new formulas for dealing with the foreign threat and for saving China. As a result, the crisis of 1897–98 was to become one of the key turning points in the history of Chinese foreign relations and, indeed, in the whole history of her difficult adaptation to the new conditions of the modern era.

In order to understand the nature and significance of the Chinese response to the imperialist onslaught of the late '90s, it is necessary to re-examine the traditional Chinese attitudes toward foreign policy, for the usual conceptualizations of these earlier approaches must be somewhat altered in order to explain the changes which were to occur. Prior to the 1890s, Ch'ing officials were probably confronted with a wide range of alternative approaches to foreign policy. Two schools of thought, however, predominated and are particularly essential for understanding the significance of the crisis of 1898. One of these represented what may be called the mainstream approach. It reflected a basically pragmatic and, in some respects, rather passive attitude toward international affairs. The fundamental goal of the mainstream approach was to minimize the impact which foreign pressures could have on the Middle Kingdom. In concrete terms, this meant that the proponents of this approach sought to maintain enough control over the activities of the foreigners who were residing in China or were in close contact with her so that they would not constitute a danger. Most of the leading national and provincial officials, including Li Hung-chang, who were directly concerned with foreign affairs subscribed primarily to this position, making it the predominant element in Chinese policy throughout most of the nineteenth century.

The practitioners of the mainstream approach were quite flexible with regard to the means they adopted in pursuit of their goal, the control of foreigners. These measures included such things as the efforts at self-strengthening, attempts to balance the Western powers against each other, and the granting of a role to foreigners in China's administrative and legal affairs. This last method, exemplified in practice by the treaty system with its extraterritoriality, foreign control of customs, and other features of inequality, underscored the flexibility of the mainstream approach, as well as its incompatibility with the modern Western conception of international relations. No Western government would have tolerated the unequal treaties; yet the mainstream officials could accept them as a useful method for managing the foreigners in a manner which did not threaten the existing Chinese polity in any concrete way. One tactic which the adherents of the mainstream approach generally shunned was the use of force. They preferred to employ administrative and political techniques in order to attain their goals and considered violence to be a sign of failure.

The mainstream approach, when viewed in terms of its own criteria, had considerable success, at least up to 1895, since the West, despite its obviously superior military power, was not threatening to conquer the Middle Kingdom. The new barbarians were strong, but, unlike so many of their predecessors, they apparently did not have insatiable appetites for domination in China and seemed to be successfully pacified by comparatively moderate changes in administrative and commercial practices. It can be argued, therefore, that the limited nature of China's response to the West in the 1870s and '80s was largely due to the nature of the mainstream's goal and was not simply the effect of general conservatism or ignorance.

It should be stressed that this description of the mainstream foreign policy is not meant to imply that the officials involved did not subscribe to the Chinese universalistic world-view which held that there was only one truly civilized culture, Chinese culture, and that the center of cultural and political authority in the world ought to be China, nor that they did not view foreigners as inferior and probably as barbarians. Rather, what is being suggested is that their foreign policy was not based on a simple one-to-one relationship with this world-view and can be fruitfully analyzed separately from it.

The second major approach to foreign affairs was, in comparison with the mainstream, ideologically rather than pragmatically oriented. In this sense, it had a more direct relationship to the Chinese world-view, although it, too, can be analyzed in other terms. Its primary goal was not the control of foreigners but rather the maintenance in the purest possible form of China's Confucian way of life, as manifested in the existing intellectual orthodoxy, social organization, and political system.[1] In addition, the adherents of this position adopted an extremely militant attitude toward foreigners who threatened the Middle Kingdom. This view of foreign relations, with its combination of orthodoxy and fervor, represents what can be called the militant conservative approach to foreign affairs.

Unlike the mainstream officials, militant conservatives tended to oppose all innovations from the West, except perhaps for weaponry, which could be used against the foreigners themselves. This was because products of the barbarian culture could corrupt Confucian purity and hence work against the very goal of the militant conservative foreign policy. Missionaries aroused some of the bitterest hostility on the part of the militants, perhaps because Christianity, of all the elements of the Western onslaught, represented the most direct ideological threat.

Militant conservatism was closely associated with the various *ch'ing-i* groups which gained prominence in the 1870s and '80s as a result of their opposition to the government's policy of accommodation with the West; and the general methods by which the proponents of this position hoped to implement their foreign policy goals were heavily influenced by the so-called *ch'ing-i* approach to statecraft. Thus militant conservatives stressed above all the need to arouse and unite the Chinese people against the foreign danger. Similarly, they emphasized the importance of unity between ruler and subject and made much of the need to keep the lines of communication to the throne open. They urged, in addition, that their own fervor and sense of commitment be disseminated as widely as possible through the society and be particularly implanted in the military. For war and violence against foreigners were considered indispensable modes of action by the militant conservatives, who displayed a constant readiness and, indeed, eagerness to take up arms against the West whenever it threatened China.

By the late 1890s, in addition to the mainstream and militant conservative positions, a third, and new, approach to foreign policy had emerged, one which was to play a key role in the Chinese response to the crisis of 1898. This was the attitude toward international relations espoused by the radical reform movement under the leadership of K'ang

Yu-wei. K'ang had begun to develop his political views and to call for reform in the late 1880s. However, it was the Sino-Japanese War which thrust him and his followers into national prominence and revealed that a new and major political movement calling for radical reform had appeared. K'ang showed considerable respect for Chinese tradition and Confucianism and even attempted to defend his position in Confucian terms. The main significance of his group, however, was that they advocated extremely broad and far-reaching institutional changes in order to solve China's problems. At the same time the modes of political action which they espoused were also highly radical, for they hoped to mobilize the scholar-elite class, both inside and outside the government, to struggle for reform. This was a sharp departure from the traditions of the Ch'ing dynasty, which had succeeded in its careful effort to prevent any political action by persons not in the government, particularly by organized groups.

In 1895 K'ang Yu-wei was in Peking for the triennial examination for the *chin-shih* degree, and he used the crisis engendered by the defeat by Japan to mobilize support for his cause. Among other things he organized a protest meeting of examinees out of which came a mass memorial to the throne denouncing the peace treaty and demanding radical reform. This was the famous "Petition from the Degree Candidates" ("Kung-ch'e shang-shu"), which has been characterized as "the beginning of mass political action in China." [2] K'ang and his supporters also founded a study club, the Society for Self-strengthening (Ch'iang-hsüeh Hui), whose purpose was to mobilize scholars for the tasks of reform.

In the immediate crisis of the war, K'ang received considerable support from important officials in Peking. However, once the worst had passed, opposition to the unorthodox goals and methods of the reformers began to develop, and K'ang and his followers were forced to suspend their activities in Peking. Nevertheless, they continued their efforts in the provinces, and in 1896 and 1897 they founded dozens of study associations and newspapers in order to encourage the scholar elite to undertake political action for radical reform.

The approach to foreign affairs which K'ang's reform movement espoused was completely new to China. For the reformers, the basic goal of foreign policy was the preservation and strengthening of China's national sovereignty. This conception of international relations was, in a crucial respect, qualitatively different from that of either the mainstream officials or of the militant conservatives, for their objectives, the control of foreigners and the preservation of the Confucian system, represented legitimate, though differing, traditional attitudes toward foreign relations. The goal of the reformers, though related to these earlier approaches, was essentially a product of the impact of Western ideas and, in particular, of Western theories of international law. Although an understanding of the Western notion of sovereignty and a grasp of its importance in foreign relations may have appeared earlier among a few Chinese intellectuals,[3] prior to the reform movement these concepts were not adopted by any important group of officials or by any political movement. From the 1860s onward, international law had, of course, been known to the Chinese officials concerned with foreign affairs. Significantly, however, the mainstream only considered it to be another efficacious technique for controlling a particular set of barbarians in particular circumstances and did not adhere to the basically different outlook on foreign affairs which its acceptance would seem to imply.[4] The reformers, however, adopted international law as the fundamental perspective from which to formulate and judge Chinese policy.

Hence, for the reform movement, sovereignty had essentially its modern connotation. It stressed the absolute national autonomy of China. In addition, it embraced the idea that China's status should in no way be inferior to that of any other nation in the international community. When the reformers spoke of the need to *pao-kuo* (protect the state), they gave the term "protect" an altogether new interpretation. No longer did it mean simply to defend the existing government or territory of China; rather it suggested a defense of all those rights which accrued to China as a fully sovereign nation in the Western sense. This Western conception of sovereignty, it should be noted, is not defined in a narrowly pragmatic way, since it also includes assumptions and practices not specifically associated with national defense which serve to manifest the absolute autonomy of the state involved. As a result, the new approach to international relations involved the reformers in an entirely new range of attitudes and policies, among which was the desire to eradicate those institutions which had been established by the mainstream in order to control the West but which violated and insulted China's sovereignty.

Indeed, since so many of China's problems manifested themselves in her inability to resist the West, an understanding of the reformers' desire to secure full sovereignty for their country can provide a framework for analyzing their overall approach to reform. It also suggests that what set K'ang and his followers apart from earlier reform movements was not simply the scope of what they recommended but also the fact that they took Western models or a Western frame of reference as their basis. This is not surprising because the radical reformers represented a new generation which had grown to maturity when the presence of the West was already an integral part of the Chinese scene. K'ang Yu-wei was born in 1858, twenty to thirty years after the great leaders of the self-strengthening movement, and most of his followers were even younger.

In any case, the reformers' attitude toward foreign affairs, involving a fervent desire to be equal to the West in terms of the West's own categories and a sense of shame at the inferiority implied by inequality, was soon to become enormously significant in China, just as it had in Japan. For this viewpoint comprised what can be considered to be the essential ingredient of a nationalistic foreign policy. Indeed, if Chinese nationalism is analyzed as a phenomenon composed of positive elements rather than as a negation of older values, then it can be argued that one of its most crucial elements was a genuine understanding of and commitment to a modern conception of sovereignty.

The Response to the Scramble for Concessions

The adherents of the different schools of foreign policy each responded differently to the German seizure of Chiao-chou Bay and the ensuing scramble for concessions. As might be expected, the important officials who handled foreign affairs, both in Peking and the provinces, responded to the German occupation in the manner characteristic of the mainstream. It was they who stressed the need to avoid violence and advocated the policy of nonresistance which dominated the government's actions. At the same time, however, their response was not entirely static, though it only concentrated on developing a fresh diplomatic strategy for dealing with the crisis. Specifically, the mainstream officials decided to end China's exclusive reliance on Russia and to return to the policy of balancing the powers against one another.

Early in December 1897 the Tsungli Yamen began to turn away from Russia and sought unsuccessfully to obtain assistance against the Germans not only from Saint Petersburg but also from Russia's chief rival, Great Britain.[5] After the Russian occupation of Port Arthur, of course, the campaign to seek new international connections gained considerable momentum. It received particular support from the great Yangtze viceroys, Chang Chih-tung and Liu K'un-i, who had direct contact with low-ranking British and Japanese military officers.[6] These viceroys did not want to bind China as exclusively to England and Japan as she had been tied to Russia. Rather, they hoped to develop some relationship with them which would make use of their opposition to Russia while at the same time controlling the two nations themselves, which the viceroys did not trust. As Liu K'un-i wrote, "now England and Japan are anti-

Russian, so besides allying ourselves with the Russians we should also join England and Japan so that there can be no suspicion of favoritism." [7] Apparently, however, both Liu and Chang wanted a formal agreement or treaty which would codify the new relationships.

The central government agreed that the time had come to return to the policy of balancing off one power against another. However, the Tsungli Yamen rejected the idea of obtaining a formal agreement with Britain and Japan.[8] This was partly because of internal politics. Li Hung-chang still exerted great influence, and he opposed an outright alliance with England because it would have been a delayed triumph for those of his political opponents, like Weng T'ung-ho, who had long advocated relying on Britain rather than Russia. Another reason the Yamen decided against an alliance was that, unlike the viceroys, it was aware there had been no high-level offers from either England or Japan. Finally, and most important, Russia's aggressive actions convinced the Yamen that, in view of China's weakness, no new alliance could really be in the nation's interest but could only be at her expense. This, it believed, would be particularly true if a treaty with Britain or Japan were to touch off an even more intense competition among the powers in East Asia.[9] The situation as the Yamen saw it was that "Russia grows daily more avid, all nations are fearful and envious of it, England and Japan especially. The reason they may want an alliance is only to use us as a cover, not to help us . . . If an alliance became public, our relations with Russia would be destroyed, and Germany and France would have a pretext for action. The disaster would be too terrible to contemplate." [10]

Therefore, the Yamen decided that the only proper course of action was to work with all the powers. "This would be an alliance without an alliance," it observed, and would be the best way to assure peace in East Asia and security for China.[11] In practice, the adoption of this policy meant that in the following months China made no new formal arrangements, although England received considerably more concessions and favors than she had obtained in the past three years.[12] China's decision to return to the policy of balancing the powers was essentially a negative approach to the problems of 1897 and 1898. However, after the Boxer Rebellion and the Anglo-Japanese Alliance, when the Chinese government adopted the nationalist framework for foreign policy, the manipulation of international rivalries proved to be an effective diplomatic strategy for reasserting China's independence.

While the leading members of the bureaucracy sought a diplomatic solution to the crisis of 1897–98, another group of officials, exemplified by such men as Li Ping-heng, the governor of Shantung, offered a different approach. When the attitudes and suggestions of this group, which came to dominate government policy from late 1898 through 1900, are examined, it becomes evident that they represent a continuation of the militant conservative and *ch'ing-i* tradition of the 1870s and '80s.

After he became governor of Shantung in 1894, Li strenuously opposed innovations from the West and succeeded, against the wishes of the central government, in curtailing modern industrial activities in the province.[13] In a famous memorial which he wrote in 1895, Li attacked railroads, mines, telegraph lines, paper currency, factories, a modern army, a modern navy, Western schools, and even a postal system.[14] He was particularly hostile to Western missionary activity and criticized the missionaries sharply after cases of violence in which they were involved, repeating the usual anti-Christian arguments and stressing how much missionary activity tended to disrupt an area.[15] As soon as he became governor, missionary cases in Shantung proliferated.

Li's views on foreign policy were archetypical of militant conservatism. He rejected the idea that China should defend itself through the use of diplomacy, alliances, or any other type of accommodation. Rather, he urged that resistance to the West, military resistance if necessary, be based on a revival of orthodox values and a mobilized and dedicated population. His ideas on the eve of German aggression in Shantung are clearly presented in a long memorial he composed in 1897 attacking the Russian alliance and, in particular, the Cassini Convention.[16] "I beseech my holy emperor," the governor wrote, "to increase his awesomeness daily and to enforce the established rules of his ancestors and to keep strict control over the evil of debating about these rules and confusing government. The proper way to defend against foreigners is still to use the concept of 'Hsia converting the barbarians.'" Specifically, Li suggested, the emperor "should clearly raise and demote in order to spur the officials, use rewards and punishments to spur on the troops, pare away all unneeded expenses in order to replenish the treasury, and seek commanders for the borders who are willing to die." Then, he continued, "when ruler and minister are united and aroused and those above and below are of one heart, the feeling of complacency and fear will be destroyed, and the method of retrieving the situation from the brink will have been achieved." For the foreigners "will then become very fearful, and they will not dare to spread their evil."

Such an approach was the only way to resist the West, Li concluded, and if it were used, the false idea of self-strengthening could be abandoned and there would "really be no reason to wrangle and quarrel about railroads and mines as the way to become strong." Such views are clearly in striking accord with the position of the militants of the '80s who, deprecating the self-strengtheners' belief that China's best hope was to adopt some European innovations while maintaining a cautious diplomatic approach to the West, argued instead, as one scholar has written, that "the barbarian could be expelled not by the use of cunning Western gadgets but by the militant and aroused spirit of the Chinese people." [17]

When the Germans landed at Chiao-chou Bay, Li's reaction was, naturally, to urge that China use force against them, and he sharply attacked the government's pacifistic response. In accord with his militant perspective on foreign policy, Li insisted that armed resistance was the only way to retain the respect of the West and, perhaps more important, to maintain the army's morale. "I cannot express the depth of my sorrow and anger," he wrote of the plans to appease Germany.[18] Peking, of course, restrained Li from acting and quickly replaced him as governor. For a short time after the landing, however, he remained officially in control at Tsinan and devoted himself to expressing his bitterness and disillusionment with the government's policy.

In one of his memorials from Tsinan, Li summed up his feelings in a direct attack on orders he had received from Peking which had insisted that nonresistance was the best way for China to "avoid later disaster" and to "defend the overall situation." [19] Li stressed that nonresistance would promote a set of "disasters" that threatened to destroy China. The first "disaster," he warned, was that "because they fear Germany, all the other countries will begin to wrangle together; then our treaties will no longer be reliable . . . and no harbor will remain ours. Who can imagine what will happen to the 'overall situation' then." Normally, it was the mainstream Tsungli Yamen which defended the importance for China of diplomacy and treaties; therefore, it was a particularly pointed argument for Li to claim that military resistance was the only way to ensure the effectiveness of such agreements. The second "disaster" was that Chinese troops would lose their spirit because they had been forced to sit on their hands while the Germans occupied the area they were defending, "as if it were a place without any people at all . . . I fear," he wrote, "commanders of all places will consider nonresistance to be the proper way to care for the 'overall situation.' If there is need for battle, who will then be willing to risk his life to fight?" In his conclusion Li pointed out that "the court basically feels that not fighting is the 'way to block later disaster.' I believe that if one fights no one can tell who will win or lose. But the real 'later disaster' is only if a country does not fight, for then every country will think of attacking her. This 'disaster' is the one which cannot be exceeded."

51

Li's advocacy of resistance probably found some support in all sections of government, including the Tsungli Yamen.[20] Significantly, however, the branch of the bureaucracy which was most in accord with his position was the censorate, long a center of militant *ch'ing-i* attacks on the West and on change.[21] In December a large group of censors drew up a secret memorial which pointed out that all the foreign powers were clearly hostile to China and were threatening her with force.[22] Because military power had become so important, the censors argued, if China were to lose Chiao-chou Bay it would be better to do so fighting. They suggested specifically that the relatively modern Chihli armies of Nieh Shih-ch'eng and Yuan Shih-k'ai should start marching toward the bay. The government could then inform Germany that China had agreed to the points at issue in the missionary case and that the Germans should therefore leave Chiao-chou Bay or else they would be driven out by force. Needless to say, this memorial made no impact on policy.

Like the militant conservatives, K'ang Yu-wei and the radical reformers also proposed an activist policy for countering the foreign aggression. The German landing and the subsequent crisis marked a critical turning point in the history of the reform movement. Not only did it enable the reformers to shift their base of operations from the provinces back to Peking, but by the summer of 1898 it had played a major role in catapulting K'ang and his followers into power.

After K'ang had heard of the German landing, he hastened back to the capital to renew his work there; similarly, Liang Ch'i-ch'ao, his chief lieutenant, also hurried to Peking despite a serious illness. They both arrived in December 1897 and immediately plunged into political activity, sending memorials to the throne and organizing officials, particularly the licentiates who had once more gathered for the triennial examination.

The reformers' prescription for countering the new wave of imperialism was the initiation of a thoroughgoing national renovation and a massive commitment to reform. In terms of foreign policy this effort would mobilize and unite society in order to achieve the institutional and economic changes required to preserve national sovereignty. In his first memorial to the throne after the German landing, K'ang Yu-wei outlined what China's immediate response should be to the new Western incursions.[23] "In view of the sudden warning of the Chiao-chou incident," the reformer wrote, "I want my illustrious sovereign to issue a decree which will bring forth a great effort, a decree in which he heightens the people's spirit by blaming himself above all for our difficulties." Then the ruler should "encourage memorials from all over the empire in order to learn the feelings of those below" and, when this was accomplished, should issue a comprehensive decree which would reorient the nation's policy.

K'ang stressed that it was necessary to follow the procedure he had outlined as quickly as possible in order to block the Germans by threatening them with the possibility of opposition from a united and powerful China. If decrees on civil and military reform appeared, K'ang claimed, "even if" these edicts "were not carried out, the Germans would hear of them and withdraw." It is interesting to note that when the reform movement eventually came to power, decree after decree was issued with comparatively little concern about whether or not any were implemented. The reformers have been criticized for this. However, in view of what K'ang wrote in 1897, it would appear that he considered the promulgation of decrees to be an act which in itself could be a powerful step toward uniting the nation and eradicating the foreign menace.

In his memorial, K'ang showed some interest in the idea of combating the heightened international threat by seeking new foreign alliances, particularly with England and Japan; but he seemed to feel that diplomatic maneuvering was basically ineffectual in comparison with a radical program of internal change.[24] For example, the memorial contained a sophisticated description of what has since been called the "Diplomacy of Imperialism"; and K'ang used the idea to explain why all the powers were aggressive in East Asia and could not, therefore, be trusted. He pointed out that "because the partition of Africa has been completed, during the past three years the West has begun to speak about dividing up China." Furthermore, "if one were to say that when the West speaks this way it is just empty talk and were to ask for concrete acts, then I would ask: For what other purpose have Russia, Germany, and France signed a secret alliance? For what other purpose have England and Japan decided upon close relations? In the war between Greece and Turkey why did all the countries guard their military power and not use it [in Europe]? Why are they all competing to strengthen their warships and wrangling among themselves while they do it? . . . It is obvious," K'ang emphasized, "that while telling their multitudes, 'we are protecting the peace of Europe,' they are spreading their poison to Asia." The point was clear: "Today, in the great competition among the powers, if we want to preserve our independent existence, there is only one plan, and that is to establish reform."

In his second memorial about the new Western incursions, K'ang explained the rationale behind some of the institutional changes which were required to save China.[25] In doing this he laid considerable emphasis on economic matters, and particularly on the need for China to assert control over the use and development of her own resources. He felt that it was especially important for Chinese foreign policy to concentrate on this objective because economic progress was indispensable if China was ever to become strong enough to resist the West. In addition, and of even more immediate concern, he recognized that the most dangerous imminent threat to Chinese sovereignty came from the increasing likelihood that the Western powers would take over China's economic resources.

The memorial began by citing numerous examples of countries which had "lost control of their wealth" and so had "perished" with varying degrees of speed. China was in the same position, it continued: "though we are called a country, we are losing control of our land, railroads, steamships, commerce, and banks . . . Though we may not have perished on the surface, in reality we have perished." The memorial contained K'ang's specific plans for reorganizing the government, and these showed the premium which he placed on economic matters. Of the twelve ministries which he recommended to replace the old boards, five — the Ministries of Agriculture, Industry, Commerce, Railroads, and Mines — dealt directly with economic development, and a number of others had important economic functions.

K'ang also explained that the implementation of his reforms would enable Peking to begin the assault against the worst blemish on Chinese sovereignty, the unequal treaties and their attendant institutions. The way to do this would be to establish legal and administrative systems which would be compatible with Western ideas and which would, therefore, convince the powers to surrender their rights. Thus, at the head of his list of suggested ministries K'ang placed a Ministry of Law, whose main task would be to make the necessary reforms and, in particular, to combat extraterritoriality, the "extreme national disgrace."

Despite his concern with economic and political reforms, K'ang did not ignore the role of military power as a means of deterring the West. In his first memorial of 1897, for example, he said that one crucial reason it was necessary to arouse the nation was that "the determination of the determined has grown dull and should be stimulated to establish brave men and strengthen their valor. Afterwards, the militia can be reformed so that there will be 30,000 men in each province who have received better training, and there must be considerable purchasing of warships . . . which will be prepared for naval war." Two of the ministries which he proposed were those of the army and navy. K'ang also urged that

China's military forces be under the command of Chinese officers rather than foreign advisers, as had frequently been the case.

By the end of March 1898 it was clear that the government had failed to prevent the establishment of spheres of influence. K'ang was very depressed. He wrote later that he had realized then that his "memorials would not be put into practice" and that he had actually thought about leaving the capital again.[26] Instead, however, his organizational activities there reached a peak in April with the founding of the Pao-kuo Hui (Society to Preserve the Nation). Like K'ang's earlier organizations, the Pao-kuo Hui was intended to inspire the literati to spread the doctrine of national renovation and pressure the government to initiate reform. In their writings for the group the reformers bitterly attacked the government for not preventing the recent Western encroachments. They also criticized the bulk of officials who seemed to be passively awaiting "butchering" and who did not "read books or tend to affairs" but preferred to "smell flowers and drink wine." In addition, the society's propaganda stressed the need to "preserve the sovereignty of the nation" and established the connection between doing this and maintaining economic independence. For example, in an introduction which he prepared for the organization, K'ang pointed out, "If we are weak and have land cut off, then with our vast territory . . . we are still a great nation; but if the power to build railroads and use men are both lost, the national territory is like a colony and our sovereign is equivalent to a slave." [27] The Germans, of course, had just robbed China of both powers.

During the early years of the German presence in Shantung, the Chinese government was dominated consecutively by the two groups with a comparatively activist approach toward the Western incursions, the nationalistic reformers and the militant conservatives. K'ang Yu-wei and his followers tasted power during the crucial Hundred Days of reform in the summer of 1898; and then, for the next two years, the conservatives gained increasing influence until their disastrous involvement with the Boxer Rebellion. These two groups and their differing attitudes were extremely important to the Germans in Shantung because they determined the initial development of Chinese policy toward the sphere of influence. Naturally the reformers, with their sensitivity to any act which violated Chinese sovereignty and their emphasis on economic autonomy, developed a policy very different from that of the warlike conservatives, who stressed cultural purity and were more alarmed by missionary activities than by Western economic encroachments.

The differences between the reformers and the conservatives are, therefore, crucial. However, the fact that they both presented positive alternatives to the mainstream and that in 1897 they both demanded an extreme and massive response to the German aggression suggests that there may have been some connection between the two factions. There is evidence that this was the case, and the link shows up most clearly when one notes that *ch'ing-i* ideas had an important influence on the outlook, rhetoric, and modes of political action of both groups. They both rejected moderate, sometimes manipulative, approaches to foreign affairs in favor of an extensive and essentially internal response based on a united and mobilized nation. Furthermore, the language of each group was, often in strikingly similar ways, extremely passionate and militant, permeated by a sense of crisis and urgency which bristled with hostility toward the passive complacency of the majority of officials. Finally, like the conservatives the reformers apparently drew on those elements of the *ch'ing-i* tradition which emphasized the role of dedicated and sincere scholars working outside the centers of power for a change in policy. In this connection, the reformers stressed the need to keep the lines of communication open between the emperor and his officials and the importance of uniting the ruler and his subjects in a common endeavor.

K'ang and his followers were conscious of the ties between themselves and the *ch'ing-i* tradition. When they began political agitation in the period before their rise to power, for example, they frequently called attention to similar activities by earlier groups which had been associated with the *ch'ing-i* approach.[28] After the failure of the Hundred Days, when the reform leaders resumed political action from the sidelines, they named one of their first newspapers the *Ch'ing-i pao* (Ch'ing-i newspaper).

Thus, there seems to be little doubt about the existence of significant ideological affinities between the reformers and the militant conservatives. Nevertheless, it is perhaps more interesting to speculate upon whether the reform movement drew upon the generally conservative *ch'ing-i* movement of the nineteenth century for support and personnel. The answer to this question must await further studies of the actual make-up of the two groups. However, among several provocative indications that such a tie may have existed is the case of Chang Chih-tung. Chang, among all the great officials in 1898, seemed closest in spirit to the reformers, and after 1900 he led the movement which made their nationalistic approach the basis of China's foreign policy. Chang was also the most famous official connected with the *ch'ing-i* party of the 1880s to remain in public life.

Another interesting indication of such a connection is the fact that K'ang Yu-wei's first attempt to mobilize broad political support, the

"Petition from the Degree Candidates," was not only the type of act associated with the *ch'ing-i* approach but was also a call for militancy which exhorted the government to continue the war against Japan at all costs. In the petition K'ang listed some military and civilian officials who he felt could be relied upon to unite and defend China; significantly, the two civilians he mentioned were Chang Chih-tung and Li Ping-heng.[29]

Whether the connection between nationalism and militant conservatism was one involving personnel or was simply an ideological tie, it would still indicate that, once Chinese nationalism is viewed as a complex of positive features, strong elements of support for it within Chinese tradition begin to emerge. Indeed, the spirit and even the content of nationalism may have owed as much to extreme and militant culturalism as to the more widespread, moderate objective of simply keeping foreigners under control. Such a derivation is understandable in the sense that a militant commitment to Chinese culture, existing in perfection solely within China, needs only a subtle substitution of goals to become a fervent devotion to Chinese sovereignty. Both are nonpragmatic, essentially ideological approaches to foreign relations. A similar shift was a common and important characteristic of Bakumatsu Japan, and the results of the change there were analogous to what later occurred in China.

In conclusion, it becomes evident that the broad significance of the Chinese response to the Western onslaught of 1897–1898 is that it precipitated a crisis for the mainstream position which had been brewing since the Sino-Japanese War and, thus, ended the dominance of this approach over Chinese foreign policy. In part, this occurred because the mainstream approach seemed to be failing in terms of its own criteria of success; the foreigners were no longer under control but were actually threatening to occupy and dismember China. An equally important aspect of the crisis, however, was the fact that, when judged in terms of the alternative conceptions of foreign affairs, particularly that of the reformers, the situation was a disaster. Thus it is important to stress that the sense of crisis which developed so rapidly in China in the last years of the nineteenth century was not simply the result of increased foreign pressures but was also attributable to the sudden prominence of different perspectives on international relations and the concomitant extension of the objectives of foreign policy. Militant conservatives had, after all, always felt a greater sense of urgency than mainstream officials, and the reformers were equally hostile, in retrospect, to the quiescence of the Chinese government in the '70s and '80s in the face of what K'ang and his followers felt should have been recognized as an intolerable situation.

It was the decline of the mainstream, of course, which opened the way for the application of the two alternative approaches to foreign policy at the end of the century. It was also this decline which, after the Boxer Rebellion had discredited militant conservatism, allowed the reformers' nationalistic conception of foreign affairs to become almost universally accepted and, among other things, to play a crucial role in destroying the German sphere of influence and saving China as a whole from subjugation.

III. The Establishment of the Leasehold, 1898–1900

The Naval Administration of Kiaochow

Shortly after Germany acquired the leasehold at Chiao-chou Bay, the kaiser officially declared the area to be a German colony.[1] The new colony was named Kiaochow (Kiautschou) and was placed under the jurisdiction of Tirpitz' Naval Ministry. The goals which the ministry established for the new territory developed out of the same considerations as those which had originally impelled it to work for the acquisition of a sphere of influence in China rather than a mere naval base. Thus the ministry was not exclusively concerned with the military development of the leasehold. Rather it sought a larger goal, to make Kiaochow into a model colony. This meant that the navy hoped to develop the new German acquisition into a place which would reflect the navy's competence in all areas of colonial administration, from taxation to education. Most importantly, it meant turning the leasehold into a great commercial entrepôt which would enhance German trade as well as become the focal point for economic development in Shantung.

The navy hoped that success in Kiaochow would not only promote German interests in China but would also popularize the cause of German colonialism in the homeland. In addition, the successful development of the leasehold would vividly indicate the ability of the Reich, and particularly the navy, to match the supposed prowess of Germany's rival, Great Britain, in the field of colonialism. Finally, a triumph at Kiaochow would garner political support for the navy at home among the liberal commercial groups it had traditionally cultivated.

Between 1898 and 1900 the navy concentrated on setting up an administrative system at Kiaochow and on developing methods for handling a variety of problems which were involved in establishing a new colony, such as the allotment of land and the implementation of public health measures. The navy carefully excluded both the Chinese central government and the provincial authorities in Tsinan from the administration of Kiaochow. Even though the new territory was technically a leasehold, the Germans never considered its status to be different from that of the other German colonies.[2] Indeed, the navy, looking upon the territory as Germany's Hong Kong, was especially concerned with making certain that there was not the slightest trace of Chinese authority at Kiaochow which might dilute Germany's complete sovereignty there.

The chief administrative official of the colony was the governor of Kiaochow, a naval officer who had, essentially, total authority. He administered both the military and civilian affairs of the leasehold for a population which consisted of German troops and civilians of several nationalities. The civilians, both Chinese and foreign, were entirely under Germany's administrative and legal jurisdiction.

The military authority of the governor rested on his rank and on his position as the commander of a German naval base.[3] His civilian power was based primarily on his authority to issue local ordinances. In addition to granting the governor wide responsibility within the colony, the navy also sought to allow his administration "as great a degree of autonomy as possible in relation to the homeland authorities." [4] According to a naval spokesman, this was done in order to give him flexibility in making decisions which needed "to take local conditions into consideration," as well as to permit him to act "vigorously and without loss of time" to meet the needs of a "fast-growing and quickly changing community." [5] The local ordinances which the governor issued took effect immediately. Theoretically, they could be revoked by the German chancellor, but none ever was. Tirpitz, as the naval secretary, was both the military and administrative superior of the governor and so was, of course, ultimately responsible for the colony.

The governor's authority was not supposed to extend beyond the borders of the leasehold, nor was he to be responsible for dealings with the Chinese officials of Shantung. This limitation was formally recognized in an understanding between the navy and the Foreign Office which was agreed upon in early 1898.[6] The understanding was that "political and commercial matters which concern German undertakings outside of Kiaochow, such as railroads and mines, will remain in the competence of the Foreign Office." However, during the first two years of the German presence in Shantung, this agreement remained in abeyance and the governor of Kiaochow was also the main German official concerned with German activities in the interior.

The governor's immediate subordinates in the Kiaochow administrative hierarchy were a chief of staff who commanded the garrison and a civilian commissioner who administered the civilian population.[7] The commissioner, even though he took orders from the governor, a military officer, and supervised a considerable number of naval men, was to be a civilian. The governor also had direct jurisdiction over three semi-administrative bodies which exercised both civilian and military functions, the Bureaus of Health, Public Works, and Finance. The chief of staff, the civilian commissioner, and the three bureau heads formed the governor's council, which was the highest policy organ in the colony. The Post Office constituted a fourth bureau, but it was managed by the Imperial German Postal Administration in Berlin and was the only part of the administrative structure at Kiaochow completely independent of the authority of the navy and the governor.

There were about 1500 German troops in the leasehold during the early years.[8] The largest unit in the Kiaochow garrison was a newly created marine battalion, the III Marine Battalion, which had a complement of 1132 men and 22 officers. The forces also included a new naval artillery detachment, the Kiaochow Naval Artillery Detachment, with 272 men and seven officers. In addition, there were 50 or so high officials of the colony who were naval officers but were not either in the marine battalion or the artillery detachment. In order to assist the German troops, particularly in keeping order, the navy also organized a Chinese unit of about 100 cavalry and infantry.[9] The military headquarters of the leasehold were at Tsingtao, where most of the troops were stationed. Detachments were also placed along the borders and at other locations in the colony.

The civilian administration of Kiaochow was organized into two separate structures, for Westerners and Chinese.[10] It was also divided geographically into an urban and a rural zone. The urban zone included the town of Tsingtao and its surroundings, and the rural zone constituted the rest of the leasehold. Since virtually every foreigner resided in the urban zone, this territorial division essentially affected only the administration of the Chinese population.

The civilian commissioner himself was directly responsible for governing the Western civilians, a legal category which also included Japanese. He worked with the semi-administrative bureaus directly under the governor, as well as with his own subordinate agencies, the most important of which were the Police Department and the Cadastral Office.

Since German colonial groups sometimes complained that the German inhabitants of a colony did not participate sufficiently in its administration, the navy made a point of stressing that it was establishing "organs of self-government" at Kiaochow which would bring the "skills of the civilian population, and especially of the economically important members . . . into the service of the colonial administration." [11] A decree of 1899 organized a committee of Westerners to advise the governor and his council. The committee consisted of three members, one picked by the governor with the advice of the council, one elected by the foreign business community, and one elected from among those landowners who paid at least fifty dollars in land tax. Like the governor's council, this committee was purely advisory and so, despite the navy's claims, had no official authority.

The judicial system for Westerners consisted of a judge and an Imperial German court, whose members included the judge and a varying number of *Beisitzer* (lay assessors) selected from among the merchants and other European civilians.[12] Appeals from the court went to the German consul general's court in Shanghai. There was no extraterritoriality at Kiaochow as there was in the treaty ports, and the leasehold's legal system applied German law to all Western residents, no matter what their nationality. The fact that Westerners living in China were not under the jurisdiction of their own consuls underlined the status of Kiaochow as a piece of German territory under full German sovereignty.

The non-Chinese community remained fairly small during the first two years of the occupation. It consisted largely of representatives of the old German firms from the China coast which had established branches at Tsingtao, personnel of the companies which had been organized specifically to exploit the German sphere in Shantung, and missionaries. Although the navy did not publish figures on the size of the European community until 1902, there is evidence that by 1900 there were about two hundred Western civilians at Tsingtao.[13]

The system of administration for the Chinese community was headed by a commissioner for Chinese affairs who was a subordinate of the civilian commissioner.[14] The Chinese commissioner's primary lieutenants were two German officials who headed district offices known as *Bezirksämter*. One of these officials administered the urban zone and the other the rural. Although there were *Bezirksämter* in other German colonies, the Chinese term meaning district magistrate is an appropriate designation for the two officials who administered the zones at Kiaochow. For the functions of these two men were patterned to a considerable degree upon those of a Chinese *chih-hsien* (district magistrate). The two German magistrates exercised both administrative and judicial functions and, in fact, like their Chinese counterparts, were meant to have complete governmental responsibility for the inhabitants of their district.[15] In addition, the legal system which they enforced was designed "to come as close as possible" to Chinese practices;[16] and its basic ordinance included the stipulation that the magistrate should "learn Chinese law by listening to village elders and other suitable persons." [17]

Like a Chinese *chih-hsien,* the rural magistrate had comparatively few basic responsibilities other than maintaining local order. Indeed, prior to 1900, the Germans had essentially no other goals in the rural zone. The magistrate kept order much as a *chih-hsien* would have. He worked with the local Chinese elite and, when necessary, used troops and police. In the urban zone the Germans administered the Chinese community with far more care. Like the civilian commissioner, the urban magistrate worked with the semi-administrative bureaus, the police, and the Cadastral Office. Although there was initially no formal procedure for bringing members of the Chinese community into the urban administration, the navy claimed that, whenever possible, it sought the advice and cooperation of the "most distinguished" members of the local population.[18]

The Chinese population at Tsingtao rose sharply during the first two years. However, it is difficult to arrive at an exact figure for the "thousands and thousands" of persons who reportedly flocked to the new town.[19] The most precise information available indicates that in 1899 the Chinese population of the urban zone had already increased by about 4,000, while the population of the rural zone had remained steady at approximately 80,000.[20]

On the whole, the Chinese population of the leasehold adjusted rather smoothly to German rule. Although difficulties were to be expected during the early years, there is no evidence of serious opposition by the local people to the new German administration. The Germans' attempt to accommodate themselves to traditional Chinese methods of government, especially in the rural zone, contributed to this tranquillity. In addition, the naval administration did not hesitate to use military force swiftly and draconically whenever the governor felt it was required. For example, in February 1899 some of the markers set up by an official survey team were stolen.[21] Twelve villages were suspected of complicity and were ordered to deliver up the guilty parties or suffer a fine. The threat brought no result, so the governor sent a naval detachment to the scene, where it took payment for the markers by seizing cattle. Some of the villagers protested, and a confrontation took place in which two Chinese were killed.

From the start, the navy based its criteria for assessing the effectiveness of the administration which it had established at Kiaochow upon how well the system furthered the navy's hopes for the colony, particularly with regard to economic development.[22] The importance of these criteria becomes clear in the attitude of Tirpitz and the Naval Ministry toward those officers at Kiaochow who had substantial military responsibilities. The first governor, Captain Rosendahl, was transferred six months after he arrived at Tsingtao because, despite his military competence, he did not pay enough attention to his civilian functions. Tirpitz explained to the kaiser that he was replacing the governor because Rosendahl was "not able to set his sights . . . on the great goal of the economic development of Kiaochow or to contribute to the furtherance and achievement of this goal." This was the case despite the fact that Tirpitz had repeatedly told the governor that development was his "primary task" there and that he had been given "as free a hand as possible" to carry it out. Rosendahl had done well with the garrison, but his very military orientation and effectiveness, Tirpitz said, had "turned him all the more from his higher task" of developing the colony.[23] Appropriately, Rosendahl's replacement was Captain Jaeschke, who had written one of the crucial naval reports in 1895 which urged the acquisition of a sphere of influence in China. Jaeschke generally agreed with Tirpitz' plans for Kiaochow, and he successfully directed the navy's initial efforts to develop the colony.

Even the rank and file of the German troops were judged to a surprising degree in terms of their effectiveness in contributing to the development of the colony. The garrison's primary function was, of course, to provide security for Kiaochow and, to a lesser extent, for German interests in the interior of Shantung and the rest of China. However, the troops also carried out many nonmilitary tasks, such as construction work, health work, road building, and surveying. For example, in 1900 Jaeschke commented on the importance of the contribution which they had made during the first two years by noting that at Kiaochow "until now all colonial activity, even including labor, has rested on the troops." Indeed, while the governor recognized the importance of this work, he seemed to feel that too much of the troops' time was being devoted to it, and he wrote to Tirpitz that, among other things, the nonmilitary activities were acting as "sources of difficulty" which "obstructed the training" of the troops.[24] In commenting on Jaeschke's report, the secretary emphatically told the kaiser that the garrison's extracurricular activities were no cause for concern because the development of the leasehold depended upon them. Tirpitz pointed out that "it is the recurrent experience of all nations that at the start of colonial activity one falls back on troops to do the labor required," and he insisted that it was "the common work of officials, colonists, and troops" which "leads to a bond between them that is vital in order for the colony to thrive." [25]

Tirpitz' concern with the successful economic development of Kiaochow was deep and genuine, and his private utterances about the colony did not differ from his public ones. Nevertheless, political considerations also influenced the direction of the navy's colonial activity, and Tirpitz, a master propagandist, made certain that the Reichstag was kept fully informed about the navy's plans for Kiaochow and their successful implementation. Tirpitz did this not only to garner general support for the navy as the manager of Germany's best-run colony but also to convince the legislature to appropriate the funds needed to develop Kiaochow. From 1898 through 1900 the leasehold received 23,280,000 marks, a very substantial sum compared to what the Foreign Office got for the other colonies.[26]

Every year at budget time the Naval Ministry prepared a lavish publication for the Reichstag entitled "Memorandum concerning the Development of the Colony of Kiaochow." These annual memoranda contained tables, maps, and photographs in addition to the text and have remained an important source of information about the colony. They were quite accurate, because the ministry knew the Reichstag deputies had other ways of finding out about Kiaochow and also because the reports were designed to embody the image of accuracy and competence in administration which the navy was trying to cultivate.[27]

The Land System

The navy believed that the successful growth of Kiaochow would depend upon a carefully elaborated system for the utilization and taxation of land. Such a system, it believed, was needed in order to provide a continuous supply of inexpensive building lots for the growing needs of Tsingtao, to retain extensive administrative control over urban development, and to provide revenue for the colony. To fulfill such diverse goals, as well as to establish Kiaochow's image as a model colony, the navy developed an extremely elaborate, almost utopian, program to control every aspect of the disposition of land from its original acquisition from the Chinese landowners to its eventual use.

An important source of information on the development of the land system, as well as on the early years of the colony in general, is the writings of a scholarly German official, Wilhelm Schrameier.[28] He was an interpreter in the consulate in Shanghai who was sent to Kiaochow after the German occupation. He became active in the organization of the German administration, especially the land system, and eventually remained at Kiaochow as Chinese commissioner.

An essential feature of the system was a government monopoly over the purchase of land from its original owners. This policy was designed to head off any attempt by the local people to raise their prices and was also intended to stop outside speculators from buying up the best land.[29] The first measure aimed at establishing the monopoly was a decree issued by Admiral Diedrichs on the day he occupied Kiaochow, which declared that no land could henceforth be bought or sold without his express consent.[30] This and subsequent decrees quickly froze the ownership of land at the tip of the peninsula, the area in which the Germans were interested and which was to become the urban zone. The procedures for purchasing Chinese land were not codified formally until general land regulations were issued on September 2, 1898.[31] However, most of the preparation for and the actual initiation of land buying started during the first five months of the occupation, while Chinese officials were theoretically responsible for the area. The German sources stress the cooperation which the navy received during this period from local officials and especially from the magistrates of Chi-mo and Chiao-chou.[32] In view of the Chinese decision not to resist the occupation and of the German military presence in the area, the navy probably did receive substantial Chinese aid in dealing with the local population.

Because of the complicated Chinese land tenure system, the first and, according to the navy, most difficult task in purchasing local land was to ascertain who actually owned each plot.[33] By early 1898 the Germans had "demanded and obtained" the tax books of the areas involved from the two magistrates.[34] However, these books were in poor condition. Because the government extracted a variety of payments in order to register a sale of land, those concerned frequently did not notify the local officials of their transaction. It was Schrameier's impression that the books for the Kiaochow area were several generations out of date.[35]

As a result, an accurate picture of land holdings could only be obtained by consulting the village heads and local officials.[36] The most useful official involved in this process was the tax collector, who kept his own lists in addition to the regular ones; these lists were used, though they also proved to be inaccurate. Proceeding thus, collecting records and supplementing the contents with the knowledge of local notables, the Germans managed to find out who owned the land at the tip of the peninsula. By the time the March 6 treaty was signed, the Germans had ascertained the ownership of more land than they actually purchased from the Chinese during the first two years.[37]

While the cadastral survey was going on, Admiral Diedrichs persuaded "thousands of villagers" to sign *Vorkaufsrecht* (right of pre-emption) agreements.[38] These gave the Germans the sole right to buy the land of the people involved at the price which had been current before the occupation. The villagers received an amount of money equal to twice the yearly tax in exchange for signing — something which Schrameier said they did "with understandable eagerness." The money was to be deducted from the sale price when the navy actually bought the land. By the time the treaty was signed, the government had spent 3,000 marks to sign such agreements covering a square mile of territory. This system of preliminary agreements did not continue after March 6, although, of course, no one but the government could buy land from the local property owners.

Admiral Diedrichs also initiated the actual purchase of land by buying the property occupied by the Chinese barracks and military installations.[39] It was bought from General Chang to be used for similar military purposes by the Germans. The task of buying land from private individuals proved more difficult, however, for the navy could not reach an agreement with the owners on the going price for the area, as had been stipulated in the pre-emption agreements. According to the government, this was because a group of villagers banded together to charge for their land considerably more than the navy thought it was worth.[40]

The administration solved the impasse by issuing a decree on February 10, 1898, which authorized the government to expropriate land through purchase.[41] The decree said that "since the landowners of Ta-pao-tao and Tsingtao have made unreasonable demands" with regard to price, "we have learned that General Chang paid the following when land was bought for official purposes: for first-class land $37.50, for land of the second class $25.00, and for land of the third class $12.50 per *mou*. Henceforth this is the price which will be paid by the German government when it buys land." This scale of prices remained in effect throughout the first two years of the German occupation.

Chinese dissatisfaction with the navy's land purchases continued, although there is no evidence that this opposition was ever very effective. In April 1898, Governor Rosendahl issued a decree aimed at placating the landowners in the village of Ta-pao-tao, who had complained that the Germans were destroying their livelihood by expropriating their land.[42] Rosendahl said that he hoped the people would be able to continue earning their living and added that "although I must buy the land, as long as we do not need it for our purposes we will lease it to you for a low price." Moreover, he claimed, when the land was finally bought "there will be houses, warehouses, and other establishments in which you can find employment . . . and earn more money than you have as farmers."

In addition to the normal attachment of peasants to their land, another reason for the villagers' reluctance to accept the Germans' terms may have been that the prices Chang had originally paid for land were not necessarily equitable. Schrameier admitted that "investigation into the interior of the province showed that these prices were rather low, although considering the poor quality of the land on the coast . . . they were fitting." [43] Furthermore, land prices had been rising gradually in Shantung, which, coupled with a slight monetary inflation, probably meant that even if Chang had been scrupulously fair, the amount he had paid five years earlier was no longer high enough. Altogether the Germans purchased about two and a half square miles of land during the first two years.[44]

The administration established a careful procedure for selling land to civilians at Tsingtao, one which was intimately related to the tax structure of the colony. Schrameier drew up the outlines of the system during the summer of 1898,[45] and his suggestions were codified in the regulations of September 2.[46] Their essential stipulations were these:

1. "The government will hold public land auctions from time to time as needed . . . The announcement for these sales . . . will give a description of the plots based on the building plan for Tsingtao and the minimum price which will be charged for each piece of land. The sale shall . . . be made to the highest bidder."

2. "People, in order to bid, must tell the government . . . their general plan for the use of the plot . . . there will be a three-year time limit for carrying out this plan . . . which in extraordinary circumstances can be extended to five years."

3. "Important changes in the plan without the consent of the government, as well as the failure to carry it out within the designated time limit, will result in confiscation of the plot. In such instances the person involved will be paid one half of the original sale price."

4. "Persons who have bought land shall pay a yearly land tax of 6 per cent of the value . . . until January 1, 1902, this shall be based on the original sale price." (The navy said that 6 per cent was not too high; the going interest rate in China was high, and a lower rate would not have discouraged speculation.)

5. "If the buyer wishes to sell his land, he obligates himself to pay the government a fee of 33 1/3 per cent of his net profit on the sale . . . after the deduction of the cost of all improvements on the land . . . The government reserves the right to buy all land at the price reported by the seller."

6. "If a piece of land is not sold for a period of twenty-five years . . . the government shall levy an extraordinary fee" which shall not exceed 33 1/3 per cent of the estimated value at that time.

According to the administration, the system was partially intended to preclude the sort of speculation from which other places on the China coast had suffered.[47] Equally important, the plan guaranteed that the government would share in all rises in land value. The navy justified such a share on the ground that appreciation in the value of real estate would come "not through circumstances created by the owner, but rather through the activity of the government or of the whole society" at Tsingtao.[48]

This rationale gives an insight into the theoretical considerations about land reform which played some role in the genesis of the system. Schrameier, the plan's originator, became associated with the land reform movement in Germany and was a fervent admirer of Henry George.[49] He wrote that soon after the regulations appeared at Tsingtao people began "to associate them with the teachings of land reformers and especially their gifted representative Henry George." [50] In addition, Schrameier boasted, it was worthy of note that "shortly after this restless pioneer of rational land reform passed away in America, work was begun in the new German position on the China coast, which, for the first time, sought a large-scale, practical solution to the questions which his life work opened up, and that the birthday of this towering man . . . September 2, was also the birthday of the land regulations of Kiaochow." Henry George was an important influence on Sun Yat-sen, and it is interesting to note that a leading specialist on Sun's ideas about land reform has stated that it was the land system at Kiaochow, as well as personal contacts with Schrameier, which were most important in showing the Chinese leader how George's ideas could actually be implemented.[51]

Before the government could sell any land, it had to formulate guidelines for the physical development of the future town. The elaborate plans which the administration drew up not only reveal the navy's interest in land control but are also symptomatic of its desire to exert careful supervision over every aspect of Tsingtao's development.[52] The broad outlines of the building plan for the harbor and town were completed in time for the first land auction, in October 1898, and were actually adhered to as the town developed.

Technical criteria determined the selection of the site for the chief commercial and military harbor. It was to be located off the villages of Yang-chia-ts'un and Hsiao-chu-t'an within Chiao-chou Bay near Woman's Island. A second smaller harbor was to be located farther south within the bay near the village of Ta-pao-tao. Near the main harbor would be a "harbor town." Because this area was north of the ring of hills on the peninsula and therefore lacked "any protection against the north to northwest wind in winter and received no refreshing breeze from the south to southwest during the hot summer," it was not considered "a comfortable place for Europeans" and, thus, was not slated to become the center of the future city.

"For the actual residence and business areas the only possible place" was "the southern slopes of the hills which ran down to Ch'ing-tao Bay." These slopes ringed the bay and ran east and west of the existing village of Ch'ing-tao. The most detailed parts of the urban plan concerned this section, the heart of the new town of Tsingtao. The heights east of the site of the old village were to be used exclusively for a European "villa and bathing area" and for the barracks of the III Marine Battalion. West of the old village was an area reserved for administrative buildings, commercial establishments, and European residences. North of this area, centering on the village of Ta-pao-tao, would be the Chinese residential section. Although it was still south of the hills, the Chinese quarter was not quite so well protected as the European sections. West of the city and nearer the tip of the peninsula was an area set aside for warehouses and industry. The railroad station was planned for the western end of the European commercial area; from there the tracks would go underground into the warehouse area, then surface, and follow the shore of Chiao-chou Bay to both of the harbors.[53]

The necessary concomitant of erecting a planned town was that the Germans had to raze the Chinese homes and villages which occupied areas intended for other purposes. The navy did not feel that it was necessary to justify this procedure or to supply any lengthy explanation for another essential feature of the plan, the separation of the Chinese and the German residential areas and the prohibition against Chinese settlement in the German section. This policy of racial segregation was generally listed among the various "sanitary measures." [54] Schrameier claimed that "it was in the interest of the convenience of the Chinese as well as the non-Chinese." [55]

Besides drawing up a master plan for the town, the navy had to make a topographic survey, divide the land into parcels, and set a minimum price for them. These tasks were performed by a naval surveying detachment which ultimately became the permanent Cadastral Office.[56] At the end of the first two years this office had prepared maps of the entire urban zone of 7500 acres which were detailed enough for administrative purposes; it had also made even finer maps, with a scale of 1:1000, of the center of Tsingtao in order to show the area to prospective buyers. By 1900, about 200 acres of land had been completely prepared for sale.

The first auctions took place during a five-day period beginning on October 3, 1898. The minimum prices for plots ranged from 12 1/2 cents per square meter for land in the area set aside for villas to 27 cents per square meter for the choicest lots in the European business section.[57] The best land at Ta-pao-tao was priced at 19 cents per square meter. According to observers, few of the plots went for the minimum price, which turned out to be quite low.[58] Altogether, a total of 105,390 square meters (26 acres) were sold at an average price of $1.00. The minimum price at succeeding auctions was based on the average price paid for similar real estate in the first auction. The navy reported that during the first two years building plots rarely fetched more than the minimum price because there was no competition for land and everyone could get as much as he pleased.[59] By the end of 1899, the navy had sold a total of 51 acres and had received $161,921.

In addition to auctions there were other methods of distributing land. Thus, regulations allowed the government to give land free and without tax obligations to groups which were adjudged to serve the public interest.[60] The chief beneficiaries of this policy were the missionaries and the Chinese Imperial Maritime Customs, which obtained their property for nothing, and the railroad, which got it at a reduced price. The government also leased land to private individuals. This was especially common during the early years with land along Ch'ing-tao Bay, where temporary installations were built to serve until the permanent harbor on Chiao-chou Bay was completed.

At first the entire land system, and particularly the tax on increments in land value, came under heavy attack from German private interests.[61] The administration responded in 1899 by issuing a special memorandum which reiterated the practical and philosophical bases of the land regulations, and within a short time the navy claimed that criticism of the system had begun to abate. In 1899, for the first time, the navy levied the 6 per cent tax on real estate purchased from the government. This was the only land tax collected in 1899 in the urban zone, and it yielded a total of $11,355 during the year.[62] The imposition on private real estate profits did not yield any revenue because no land was resold before 1900.

Most of the land in the leasehold lay within the rural zone and remained in the hands of the original Chinese owners. In accordance with its general policy of administration, the German government made no attempt to alter traditional real estate activities there or to impose a monopoly on the purchase of land. The September 2 regulations had declared that the permission of the governor was required before any land could be sold or used for a new purpose in the rural zone. However, according to Schrameier this stipulation was purely nominal.[63] Its purpose was to ensure that there were no major changes in the zone which would make it more difficult for the German government to buy land eventually or which would circumvent the land system as a whole.

During the first two years of the occupation the Germans not only allowed the Chinese tax collectors in the rural zone to continue assessing the normal Chinese land tax but probably even let them continue giving the receipts to the local Chinese magistrates.[64] At the same time, however, the Germans also began a cadastral survey in the area similar to the one they had undertaken in the urban zone.[65] This was done with the long-term goal of reforming and rationalizing the system of taxation in the rural zone. As usual, the Germans received considerable cooperation from the Chinese magistrates, who turned over the tax lists for the areas involved. Perhaps one reason the Chinese officials were so helpful was that temporarily the Germans let them continue to keep the tax receipts.

When the Germans tried to obtain the more up-to-date tax lists used by the tax collectors, however, they ran into some of the strongest opposition they were to encounter within the leasehold. In April 1899, Jaeschke reported to Tirpitz that "the people find themselves in a definite excitement. This is because the administration has called for the tax lists from the village elders." [66] He added that the Germans' request for the lists had touched off a rash of rumors, including one which claimed that the new government wanted to collect a tax of 300 cash per *mou* per month. As a result, the governor continued, "several villages did not send in their lists. Punishments were threatened, and finally there was no alternative but to arrest the village tax collectors." An expedition went out and brought the collectors back to Li-ts'un, the administrative center of the rural zone; immediately about a thousand people gathered in front of the town to protest the arrests. The commanding officer at Li-ts'un called for reinforcements. Jaeschke responded by sending Schrameier out from Tsingtao under the protection of a patrol. According to the governor, Schrameier spoke to the people and "told them that their taxes to us would be no higher than had hitherto been paid to the Chinese government . . . The mob dispersed and the tax collectors were freed." Trouble continued, for Jaeschke complained later in April to the district magistrate of Chiao-chou, who still had "considerable influence" in the zone, about the appearance of posters along the border which said, among other things, that "foreigners have come to Tsingtao . . . Now they want to collect taxes, later they will take more land. We must plan resistance." [67] The naval administration countered by posting its own signs in the villages of the leasehold explaining its tax plans. By 1900 the cadastral survey of the rural zone had made some progress, but, because of the local opposition and the inherent difficulty of the task, it was far from completed.

The Tariff System

Adopting an appropriate tariff policy was one of the most important problems which faced the new administration at Kiaochow. In later years the tariff system established during 1898–99 was fundamentally altered because of opposition from the Imperial Maritime Customs and because it contained too many practical disadvantages. Nevertheless, the original system represented a careful attempt on the navy's part to make certain that Kiaochow achieved the goal of becoming a major port, as well as a base for economic activity in the interior.

The navy was deeply committed to the idea that if Kiaochow was to develop into an important commercial center the colony would have to be a free port.[68] This was an article of faith among the administrators of the leasehold, primarily because of the navy's liberal orientation but also because of Hong Kong's success as a free entrepôt on the China coast. At the same time, the naval officials felt that a tariff barrier between the leasehold and the interior would hamper the colony's trade with Shantung and thus reduce Kiaochow's effectiveness in the development of the German sphere of influence.[69] The problem as the administration envisioned it was, therefore, to establish a customs system in the leasehold which would not only provide ready and free access to Tsingtao for sea-borne trade but also permit the free movement of goods between the port and the "tightly tariffed" interior.[70]

The most significant step which the navy took to implement these goals was its decision to let the Chinese Imperial Maritime Customs (IMC) open a branch at Tsingtao. The customs house had extremely circumscribed powers. Nevertheless, its presence represented a compromise with the navy's desire to keep Tsingtao free of any hint of Chinese sovereignty, a compromise indicative of the navy's overriding interest in the commercial development of the port and the sphere of influence.

The administration's projected tariff system was based on a memorandum drawn up by Zimmermann, the civilian commissioner of Kiaochow.[71] In July 1898 negotiations over the scheme began in Peking between Heyking and Robert Hart of the IMC. The negotiators quickly reached a general agreement. This was probably because Hart was pleased simply to be allowed to establish a station at Kiaochow, a concession which gave the Chinese customs a much larger role in the colony than was to have been expected. The first customs commissioner, E. Ohlmer, arrived at Tsingtao in August, and on September 2, 1898, the Germans officially proclaimed the port to be open "to the trade of all nations." [72] A formal customs treaty was not signed until April 17, 1899, however, and it did not take effect until July 1, a year after the initial negotiations had begun.[73] The tariff system which was embodied in the treaty provided the free access to both sea and interior which the navy had desired. Thus, it was a truly ideal situation from the administration's point of view, one in which Kiaochow was "assured the advantages of a Chinese treaty port without losing its character as a free port." [74]

The entire leased area functioned as a free port primarily in the sense that goods which came by sea and which had Kiaochow as their final destination paid no duty upon entering. This was the case for both foreign and Chinese goods, coming either from abroad or from a treaty port. For foreign goods which arrived at Tsingtao from a treaty port where customs had already been paid, the duty was refunded. The treaty further stipulated that all Chinese merchandise or products shipped from another Chinese port to Tsingtao and reshipped from there to places outside China should pay no export duty. At a treaty port Chinese goods had to be re-exported within one year in order to be exempt from customs; thus, while the freer procedure at Kiaochow did not differ radically from the normal one, it could, nevertheless, help Kiaochow to become a depot and distributing point for coastal goods. Finally, the treaty said that produce raised in and merchandise manufactured from produce raised in or imported by sea into the German territory paid no export duty, a stipulation which opened up the possibility of developing an industrial system at the depot. Thus, Kiaochow enjoyed all the advantages which Hong Kong legally had as a free port.

The colony acted like a treaty port in relation to goods entering or leaving the Chinese hinterland. The Chinese government established a regular customs house of the Imperial Maritime Customs at Tsingtao, which, when appropriate, exercised its normal collecting functions at the usual treaty rates. As in a treaty port, it collected no export duty on Chinese goods whose final destination was the leasehold. It did collect import duties on all foreign goods which crossed the border of the German colony and entered Chinese territory, as well as export duties on Chinese goods which left Tsingtao for abroad. Coastal rates were collected on Chinese goods from another treaty port when they entered the interior, and the customs house could issue receipts on Chinese goods which had paid the export duty so that they could enter another port at coastal rates. The customs house was also empowered to sell transit passes for goods heading into the interior. While the duties involved in each case were theoretically due when the goods crossed the border, they were actually collected at the customs house in Tsingtao. According to the treaty, the German authorities agreed to "take suitable measures to assist . . . in the prevention of merchandise passing the German frontier when not provided with a permit or pass by the Maritime Customs Office." Special arrangements were made for the control and taxation of opium, but these never became significant because virtually none ever reached Tsingtao.

The customs house and Tsingtao's similarity to a treaty port gave the leasehold several advantages which were not enjoyed by Hong Kong.[75] First of all, goods which came from the interior and which were consumed in the colony or were used for any purpose there were tax-free. Secondly, goods could go into the interior without unpacking or reloading; this was particularly significant because the major form of transportation inland would be the railroad. Finally, Kiaochow could serve as a free depot for provincial products, which could be sorted, sampled, and finished there before shipment.

The navy managed to obtain these commercial advantages while at the same time keeping to a minimum the Chinese encroachment on Kiaochow's autonomy, which the customs house represented. This was done by embodying in the agreement what the Germans considered "a sharp limitation of the powers" of the office and its personnel. First of all, in contrast to the Imperial Maritime Customs stations elsewhere, the one at Tsingtao was "limited to the raising of customs" and lacked control over the harbor administration and the Post Office;[76] and the treaty specifically stated that the IMC "shall take no part in the collection or administration of tonnage dues, lighthouse dues, or port dues." In addition, the agreement gave the Germans influence over the choice of personnel for the station. The first three articles stipulated that "the Chief of the Maritime Customs office at Tsingtao is to be of German nationality. The Inspector General of Customs will come to an understanding with the German legation at Peking in case of appointing a new Commissioner." Moreover, "the members of the European staff . . . shall, as a rule, be of German nationality . . . the Inspector General . . . will inform the Governor of Kiaochow beforehand about all changes in the staff." Article 4 even specified that "all correspondence between the customs office . . . and the German authorities and German merchants shall be conducted in the German language." Finally, in order to reduce Chinese authority within the leasehold as much as possible, the IMC was also made responsible for the functions of a Chinese customs taotai at a treaty port and thus collected the native customs as well as the foreign.[77]

Although the navy was very pleased with the tariff arrangements for Kiaochow, the German merchant community on the China coast was rather hostile to the new system. Indeed, Schrameier noted, during the early years "hardly any institution of the leasehold met with as much opposition as the customs arrangements." [78] Reports and letters in the *North China Herald* during the summer of 1899 bear out the existence of such hostility, which was aimed chiefly at the Chinese customs house. For example, on July 10 the paper reported that "the German merchants at Tsingtao" were "strongly opposed" to the plan, adding that they "complain that the establishment there of a Chinese Custom-house will soon prove to be an intolerable obstacle to the full development both of the import and export trades." [79] A dispatch by a merchant at Tsingtao said that the customs was "a disadvantage for our place, its location should be on the frontier, not here." [80]

The attacks have the flavor of writings by Old China Hands opposed in principle to any concessions to the Chinese government, for they neither present any rational argument against the considerations which lay behind the settlement nor describe the advantages of rival schemes. The prevalent attitude of the opposition is revealed in a report on the situation written by the German consul at Shanghai.[81] It shows that the merchants combined traditional fears which were not confined to Tsingtao — "the German colony will be surrounded by customs houses . . . not only of the Imperial Maritime Customs but also likin" — with a generally tough attitude toward China — "China has got all the advantages of an open port complete with customs house without having to contribute the slightest to the cost." The basic complaint was always that "the Chinese flag waves again at Tsingtao, raised up with great fanfare by the highest officials of the colony."

Ironically, the IMC was also unenthusiastic about the newly established customs system. It soon became obvious that smuggling would be a serious problem because of the difficulty of adequately patrolling the border between the leasehold and the interior.[82] Furthermore, the German government did not cooperate fully with the customs house; the naval administration was frequently more concerned with making certain that the station did not, in fact, become a symbol of Chinese sovereignty than it was with helping the IMC enforce the Chinese customs regulations efficiently.[83]

The navy's insistence on the selection of a German as commissioner did not, however, result in any particular favoritism toward Germany on the part of the station. Ohlmer, who had been born in Hanover, had joined the customs service in 1868 when he was twenty-one.[84] He had risen steadily in the service until he received the post at Tsingtao and, after thirty years in the IMC, had come to view himself essentially as an official of the Chinese government. As Stanley Wright wrote later, "During his sixteen years' tenure of office at Kiaochow" Ohlmer "watched over China's Customs interests at the port . . . zealously and efficiently."[85] The Germans also treated Ohlmer as a representative of China and from the start always judged his behavior as if it were that of a Chinese official who was in the leased territory at the sufferance of the German government.[86]

The customs agreement had specified that the IMC should also collect the native customs, and therefore branch offices for this purpose were established at the important junk ports around the bay.[87] By 1900 there were facilities for handling the native customs at T'a-pu-t'ou, Nü-ku-k'ou, Ts'ang-k'ou, Tsingtao, Sha-tzu-k'ou, and Ling-shan-wei (which was actually just over the border to the south). The original plan had stipulated that the duties and other charges collected from Chinese-built vessels at the junk ports should not be changed. However, Ohlmer found that it was virtually impossible to operate the traditional system.[88] Each of the eight different landing places on the bay had its own extremely complicated tariff schedule as well as its own system of weights and measures. By 1900 the customs house had decided to set an arbitrary levy of $2\frac{1}{2}$ per cent on the junk trade, an amount which Ohlmer believed was a low but fair figure. Goods which came in junks were not affected by the German free zone. This was not significant, however, because the junk ports were not important places themselves but served almost completely for the transshipment of goods to Chiao-chou and Chi-mo in the interior.

After the customs house opened, the most crucial issue facing it was the demand of the railroad company that the material for the construction of the Tsingtao-Tsinan Railroad enter the interior duty-free. In July 1899, when the company asked Ohlmer for a ruling on this question, he replied that according "to instructions of the Tsungli Yamen . . . all railroad materials without exception must pay the treaty tariff."[89] Gaedertz, the director of the firm, then wrote to the chancellor urging that the German minister be ordered to press for a separate ruling on the question from the Tsungli Yamen and the Maritime Customs.[90] He pointed out that the estimated cost of the materials destined for the interior was 27,000,000 marks, which would result in a tariff of 1,350,000 marks. He added that no tariff had been paid on the materials for the construction of the Manchurian railroad; therefore, the most powerful argument in favor of a new ruling was that the Kiaochow treaty had stipulated that the Shantung railroad would receive most-favored-nation treatment. Soon afterward the minister presented the issue using this argument, and in October 1899 the Yamen agreed that the railroad materials were entitled to enter the interior free of duty.[91]

There was little commercial development at Tsingtao during the early years of the leasehold for the obvious reason that neither the harbor facilities nor the railroad into the interior had been built. In 1899, 205 foreign vessels came to Tsingtao, about half from a small subsidized steamship line, Diederichson, Jebson and Company.[92] However, almost all the goods carried on these ships were intended either for consumption by the foreigners at Tsingtao or for the construction of the railroad.[93] Since such goods were not subject to customs, there are no statistics concerning them. Some foreign merchandise, notably cotton goods and kerosene, did apparently enter the surrounding areas for the first time as a result of the German presence.[94] All these goods were transshipped at either Chefoo or Shanghai, and none came directly from abroad. The value of such imports for the last six months of 1899 was only about 200,000 Haikwan taels.[95] The establishment of the leasehold had little effect on the junk trade during the early years. Not only was there no significant change in the size of the traffic, but it also did not shift from the older ports on the bay to Tsingtao, which handled only 2½ per cent of the total.[96] The navy reassured the Reichstag that the growth of commerce would accelerate as soon as the leasehold's communications facilities developed.[97]

Social Services

Because of the navy's desire to turn Kiaochow into a model colony, the administration was anxious to improve the living conditions in the leasehold. Before 1900, however, the actual results in the chief areas of activity involved, health and education, frequently did not go beyond the recognition of problems and the formulation of goals.

The activities of the missionaries at Kiaochow were an indispensable element in the government's efforts to provide adequate social services. By 1900, the four missionary societies which were to establish themselves in the colony had already arrived.[98] These included one Catholic and three Protestant groups. The Catholics were represented by the Steyl Society. After the Germans took Kiaochow, the society had obtained jurisdiction over the leasehold and the surrounding districts of Chiao-chou, Chi-mo, Kao-mi, and Chu-ch'eng, which had formerly been under the French Franciscans based at Chefoo. Two of the Protestant groups were German and one was American. The German societies were the Allgemeine evangelischprotestantische Missionsverein (General Evangelical Protestant Missionary Society, the so-called Weimar Mission) and the Berliner Gesellschaft zur Beförderung der evangelischen Mission unter den Heiden (The Berlin Society for the Promotion of Evangelical Missions among the Heathen, the so-called Berlin Missionary Society). Neither had ever worked in Shantung before. The American group was the Presbyterian mission, which had long been active in the province but had not previously worked in the Tsingtao area.

Neither the German Protestants nor the Catholics concentrated solely on evangelical work at Tsingtao but instead devoted many of their resources to welfare activities. For the Protestants, the emphasis on non-evangelical activities partially reflected the general transformation of the Protestant missionary movement in China in the early twentieth century. The movement was growing progressively less concerned with simply amassing converts and was becoming more interested in tackling China's social ills and, thus, making Christianity seem more important and relevant to the nation. The Protestant societies at Tsingtao were among those most committed to the new approach. The Berlin Mission, from its earliest years in China, had been primarily interested in educational work.[99] Similarly, the Weimar Mission specialized in "literature education and medicine" while, indeed, "gathering no Christian communities of its own."[100]

This drift away from simple evangelization received a special boost at Kiaochow as a result of particular circumstances there which stimulated even the Steyl Mission to concentrate more on secular activities than was perhaps usual for Catholic groups. The navy openly encouraged the missionaries to become service organizations which would assist both the government and private interests in developing Kiaochow and realizing Germany's goals in Shantung. For example, the reason the navy gave the missionaries free land was to reward them for undertaking activities which were useful to the colony.[101]

Health conditions at Kiaochow were extremely poor during the early years. In 1898 there was widespread colitis, dysentery, venereal disease, and malaria.[102] In 1899 the situation grew worse when a major epidemic of typhus and relapsing fever struck the Chinese community, and typhoid fever spread among the troops and the foreign population. During the eighteen months from October 1, 1898, to April 1, 1900, 38 members of the garrison died of illness, mainly typhoid fever and dysentery.[103] The daily rate of hospitalization among the troops was also extremely high; in October 1899, for example, it averaged 161.2 per 1000 in the III Marine Battalion. There are, unfortunately, no statistics available concerning the health of the Chinese community; however, all sources would indicate that it was far worse than that of the troops.[104]

The navy doctors attributed the bad situation to the generally poor health conditions in China made acute by Tsingtao's particular problems: a rapid increase in population, unsatisfactory housing conditions, and the lack of good drinking water.[105] The troops, who comprised the vast bulk of Europeans, lived in the old Chinese barracks. The navy doctors complained that these quarters, damp, dark, overcrowded, and lacking modern sanitary facilities, were natural breeders of disease.[106] The Chinese who came to the colony were even worse off. They settled primarily in a large ring around Tsingtao which formed the improvised "mat-village of Ta-pao-tao." [107] There, the navy said, "among the dirty, thickly settled, and poverty-stricken" residents, relapsing fever and typhus from the interior easily developed into epidemics. The navy was partly responsible for this overcrowding. For by 1899, in accord with its urban plan, the administration had destroyed the village of Upper Ch'ing-tao and a good part of Lower Ch'ing-tao, forcing the former residents to seek new housing. The original Chinese homes which continued to stand at Tsingtao were also a major cause of illness, for almost all of them were built directly on the ground on "contaminated soil." [108] The contamination of the soil was the cause of the bad water, since germs easily seeped into the wells, which were the sole source of drinking water for the colony.

The navy considered the dismal health of the colony to be one of Kiaochow's most serious problems and quickly developed plans to improve the situation. The administration felt that it was vital to raise health standards not merely for the sake of the present inhabitants of the leasehold but also because good health conditions would make Tsingtao attractive for settlement and would thus aid development. In addition, the navy believed that the public health of Kiaochow provided a significant criterion for assessing the merits of the location chosen for the colony as well as the skill with which it was being run. The notion of judging the leasehold's administration according to its success in public health was to some extent forced on the navy because the Reichstag showed particular interest in the health conditions at Kiaochow.[109]

Therefore, in addition to taking steps to improve the health situation, the navy strove to refute publicly any suggestion that Kiaochow was situated in a poor location or that the hygienic conditions would remain bad.[110] The administration stressed that the health problems were temporary, the "usual phenomenon at the beginning of any colony." It "asserted unconditionally" that the "climatic and other fundamental conditions" of the area were extremely favorable. Not only was Kiaochow located on the sea, but, unlike Shanghai, it was not at the mouth of a great river which would bear disease. Moreover, because it was in the north, its climate was more suitable for Europeans than that of most of the other treaty ports. The navy, insisting that Kiaochow's conditions would improve markedly as soon as the proper measures were instituted, promised that the administration would turn the leasehold into one of the "healthiest places in East Asia" with hygienic standards which "essentially would not lag behind those of the mother country."

To meet the immediate needs of sick Europeans the government established a temporary hospital in tents and sent patients requiring greater care to the German naval hospital in Yokohama.[111] Meanwhile, construction began on a large permanent hospital to serve the European community, both military and civilian. The navy doctors set up a free clinic for the Chinese residents, and the Weimar Mission started work on a hospital. In addition, the administration began to promulgate a variety of health regulations.[112] Ordinances were issued, for example, governing the inspection of food sold in the town, and these were enforced with the aid of a bacteriological laboratory and testing station which the navy established. To guard against the spread of illness from outside the colony, German consuls elsewhere in China supplied the Kiaochow authorities with information on the health conditions along the coast so that incoming ships and merchandise could be met with the necessary precautions.

Since the poor housing was a major cause of the health problem, the administration also became active in this area. A government building department erected residences for the governor and other officials.[113] It also began to build new barracks for the troops; by the end of 1899, however, only a small portion of the III Marine Battalion was actually provided with new quarters. In the meantime, the administration refurbished the old Chinese barracks and attempted to provide them with modern hygienic facilities.

It was soon evident that government intervention was also required to solve the long-term housing problems of the Chinese population. Although many of the local business firms began to build homes for their staffs, it was not feasible for private initiative to undertake the provision of "mass dwellings" for the Chinese workers.[114] Among other things, the government tried to encourage such construction by setting aside a section of the city especially for the residences of workers. This area, which became known as T'ai-tung-chen, was located near the village of Yang-chia-ts'un, on land which the government had purchased for the urban zone. There, private firms were allocated large tracts for the erection of "cheap coolie houses." [115] The builders received the land free. However, the occupants were responsible for a yearly tax of 70 pfennigs per square meter, which accorded with the general 6 per cent tax on the value of land. In order to maintain control over the construction at T'ai-tung-chen, the administration stipulated, among other things, that "if there should be an epidemic there at any time or if the health needs of the colony should make the destruction of the houses desirable, the property and all that stands on it would return to the government." [116] The navy reported that by the end of 1899 both Chinese and German companies had begun to build blocks of houses at T'ai-tung-chen for their employees. It is difficult to learn how many people the new area actually housed in its initial stages. However, the navy reported that "after the destruction of Upper Ch'ing-tao" the former residents "found homes" in the new development, and another contemporary source indicates that it began to absorb the homeless Chinese ringing Tsingtao.[117]

The administration drafted building codes for the urban zone, largely in order to enforce sanitation measures. The stringency of these regulations differed according to the area, with the strongest restrictions in the European sections of Tsingtao and the mildest in T'ai-tung-chen; however, no area was exempted altogether.[118] The first of these building codes appeared together with the original land laws in September 1898. Among other things, it prohibited any building that was over two or three stories and stipulated that only 55 per cent of the land could be built on in the European part of town and 75 per cent in the Chinese sector. Later codes gave detailed specifications for such things as the amount of space required in buildings constructed for Chinese use, and numerous regulations required all homes and work areas to contain sufficient toilet facilities.[119]

The government also tried to alleviate the water problem.[120] In order to prevent the contamination of the soil, construction began on a sewage system for Tsingtao and Ta-pao-tao. The navy hoped that this system, coupled with the destruction of the old villages and a plethora of regulations prohibiting the disposal of waste in the streets of the urban zone, would assure Tsingtao safe wells. However, the administration knew that in the long run the growing town could not continue to depend on wells for its water supply. Therefore, in 1898 the government began preliminary surveys for a projected central system which would bring in water from the north.

Primarily in order to improve the situation with regard to water the government also developed a program for halting soil erosion on the hills surrounding Tsingtao and for repairing its ravages there and in the town itself.[121] The project was also intended to prevent silting of the harbor, to improve the scenic character of the area, and to hide gun emplacements. The administration planned to construct earthworks to reduce run-off and fill in gullies and ravines and also to initiate a foresta-tion program. The government claimed that these efforts would consti-tute a major undertaking involving the greatest difficulty, and it pains-takingly described the engineering techniques to be employed, the types of trees to be imported, and the methods to be used in planting and nurturing them. In 1899 the German government sent forestry officials to Tsingtao to supervise the undertaking. By the end of that year, however, only a small area of about twenty-five acres had actually been planted and a few preparatory steps had been taken to repair the effects of erosion.

The navy's desiderata for Kiaochow also included the establishment of a comprehensive educational system.[122] The administration believed that good facilities for Europeans were desirable not only to meet the needs of the colony but also to fulfill the educational requirements of Germans all over East Asia. The navy pointed out that the level of Ger-man education in the Far East was considerably below what it should have been, given the number of Germans in the area and the nation's role there. Naturally, the provision of good educational facilities for the German commercial community in Kiaochow and the rest of East Asia could not fail to have considerable appeal in the homeland.

The administration stressed that a good system of schools for Chinese was vital too, both in order to further the development of the colony and to help control it politically. Moreover, such a Chinese educational sys-tem would directly contribute to the attainment of one of the navy's sub-ordinate but frequently mentioned goals for the colony, to make Kiao-chow a showplace of German culture which would have an appeal for all China and especially for Shantung.[123] By doing this, the Germans hoped to use Kiaochow to stimulate the modernization of the province and at the same time increase German influence over the process.

Nevertheless, despite the interest of both the naval administration and the missionaries in educational work, little was actually accomplished before 1900. This was probably because educational development, though crucial, was a less pressing problem than health. The Berlin Mission took advantage of government aid to open one Chinese school. It had three grades and fifty pupils in 1899. European children were taught by missionaries at a school established by the navy and the foreign residents. In 1900 it had only about a dozen pupils.

In addition to the provision of community services, both the navy and the missionaries undertook a number of "scientific investigations" of the leasehold. These studied the "natural condition of the area as well as . . . its culture and its political system." [124] Not only was such research intrinsically valuable, but the navy also considered it important for the rational administration and development of the colony. The completed surveys are particularly interesting, for, in addition to illustrating the systematic approach to colonization which characterized the navy, they also provide significant and detailed information about the leased area in a period when German influence was still negligible.

For example, an interesting study was prepared in 1898 and early 1899 by several navy officers and published as a separate volume entitled *The German Colony of Kiaochow and Its Population*.[125] According to the navy the authors "personally examined the whole colony, village by village, and hut by hut." [126] The bulk of the study consists of information which the survey team compiled in answer to the following questions about each of the 301 villages examined: "How many huts are there and among them how many large ones? What is the approximate number of residents in each hut and in the village as a whole? Is there a temple — how many side buildings does it have? What does the population do — farming, grazing, fishing, etc.? Does the village give the impression of being poor or wealthy? Are there vegetable gardens or commercial farms? How many wells are there, how are they supplied? . . . Is there straw and firewood available? Of what is the village constructed? . . . How do the villagers react to Europeans?" [127]

The navy also conducted extensive hydrographic surveys for the purpose of preparing charts of the bay and its approaches.[128] Further, it established an astronomical station, which was assigned the tasks of determining the exact location of Tsingtao and of maintaining a tide indicator. Finally, the government set up a modern meteorological station which kept records and provided daily forecasts based on its own observations and on the telegraphic exchange of information with stations in other parts of China.

IV. The Germans in the Interior, 1898–1900

The Reform Movement and the Initial German Activities

Between 1898 and 1900 the Germans began to exploit the privileges which they had obtained in Shantung. They started work on one of the railroad lines stipulated in the March treaty, that from Tsingtao to Tsinan. They also carried out preliminary mining operations in a few spots along the proposed route of this and the other lines. All these activities had political significance because they contributed to the extension of German power in the province. The German entrepreneurs consciously strove to remain free of any interference by the provincial government at Tsinan and sought to keep their enterprises under the administrative control of the authorities at Kiaochow. Furthermore, the naval administration provided military protection for the railroad and mining operations and, for a time, for the German missionaries of the Steyl Mission. In these years also, the Germans used their general claim to a sphere of influence in Shantung to seek additional concessions for investment in the province.

The Chinese reaction to these German activities varied, depending on whether it was informed by a nationalistic or militantly conservative point of view. These were years of flux in Chinese politics and, both in Peking and Tsinan, proponents of the two approaches alternated in power. The conservatives showed comparatively little interest in developing policies, short of a military confrontation, which would thwart the expansion of German economic and political power. In addition, their permissive attitude toward violence against foreigners, especially missionaries, provided Germany with opportunities to intervene militarily and to strengthen its influence in the interior. The nationalistically oriented officials, on the other hand, worked consistently to develop policies which, by asserting and upholding the privileges of Chinese sovereignty, would neutralize the impact of the German undertakings.

The influence of the radical reformers, with their nationalistic approach to foreign affairs, was at its height when the Chinese central and provincial authorities developed their initial policies toward the German activities in Shantung. On June 11, 1898, three months after the Kiao-chow Treaty, the young Kuang-hsü Emperor issued a decree, heavily influenced by the thought of K'ang Yu-wei, which called for the beginning of the great national renovation K'ang and the other reformers had advocated. This decree marked the beginning of the famous Hundred Days of reform of 1898. A few days after the edict, K'ang had an audience with the emperor. Thereafter the ruler, with the close and continuous advice of K'ang and his followers, issued a stream of edicts aimed at implementing the reformers' program and renovating virtually every facet of Chinese government. By the middle of September over forty significant edicts had been promulgated, and the reformers had begun to consolidate themselves in power. Although few of the decrees had been implemented and there was considerable hostility to the reform from within the ruling family and the bureaucracy, the direction of change was clear. As a result, on September 21 the empress dowager, who did not share the emperor's attachment to the reformers and who was fearful for her own power and that of the dynasty, engineered a coup which brought the Hundred Days to a sudden halt. The emperor was stripped of power, and six of the leading reformers were summarily executed. K'ang and Liang Ch'i-ch'ao barely escaped and sought refuge in Japan.

During the Hundred Days, the reformers formulated many programs which were designed to attain their goal of restoring full sovereignty to China. The most important of these from the point of view of the early German activities in Shantung were those that dealt with the economic privileges which the Germans and other Westerners had recently obtained in China. What the reformers sought to do was to regulate and control the actual operation of the new concessions in order to limit their political impact, circumscribe the role of foreigners in the future economic development of China, and insure Chinese entrepreneurs a real opportunity to control this development.[1] Perhaps the most significant new institution which was actually established during the summer of 1898 and which was aimed at implementing these goals was China's first national Bureau of Railways and Mines (K'uang-wu t'ieh-lu tsung-chü, or K'uang-lu-chü). Once established, the bureau attempted to regulate the new concessions and to prevent future economic encroachments. Among other things, it drew up, for the first time, nationwide railway and mining regulations whose basic purpose was to limit the use of foreign capital and to protect and encourage the growth of Chinese investment.

The Germans' objectives in Shantung were, of course, completely antithetical to such efforts. From the beginning the Germans hoped to organize the railway and mining enterprises in the province as purely German enterprises under German control and to use them to increase German influence in the province. Shortly after the Kiaochow Treaty was signed, the German government, without consulting any Chinese officials, initiated discussions in Berlin with the main German banks and commercial firms interested in China.[2] The purpose of these discussions was to establish a German syndicate which could take up the economic concessions in Shantung. At the same time, representatives of the firms involved in the talks began investigating the interior of the province in order to determine its suitability for such economic development.[3] These surveys were also undertaken unilaterally, without involving Chinese merchants or officials.

The first German mining engineer to enter the province was Karl Schmidt of Carlowitz and Company, who in the spring of 1898 arrived at Wei-hsien on the route of the proposed Tsingtao-Tsinan line.[4] By July he had already purchased several plots of land in the coal field at Fang-tzu, which lay south of the district capital, and had begun preparations for test borings. Soon after, other German engineers began to explore the coal fields at I-chou-fu on the Tsingtao-I-chou line.[5]

The governor of Shantung at this time was Chang Ju-mei,[6] a man about whom little information is available but whose response to these early German activities was in keeping with the outlook of the reform movement. When the first German mining engineers appeared, Chang started a drive to encourage local Chinese merchants to open mines along the routes of the proposed railway lines before the German monopoly within the thirty-li zone could become operative. He issued proclamations to this effect, which were posted at Wei-hsien and I-chou-fu and probably elsewhere in the province.[7] They pointed out the threat posed by the foreigners and warned that, if the people did not "accommodate" themselves to the situation, they would "lose the profit" to be obtained from mining. The proclamations also promised that the provincial government would subsidize merchants who were willing to open mines. In this early period, however, there does not seem to have been any response to the governor's efforts.

While Chang worked in Tsinan, in Peking the Tsungli Yamen was developing another aspect of Chinese policy. This was the attempt to enforce the provisions of the Kiaochow Treaty in such a way as to permit Chinese merchants to participate in the German economic activities, as well as to bring these enterprises under Chinese administrative control. The Yamen enunciated this policy in July when Schmidt asked the magistrate of Wei-hsien to register the land which he had purchased.[8] The magistrate doubted whether he had the authority to do this, explaining to Schmidt that "although the treaty permits mining along the railroad, this must be done within thirty li of the line. Now, since the railroad has not yet been surveyed, how can you start buying land and digging shafts?" Schmidt answered that since the railroad would definitely pass through the field at Fang-tzu, there was no possibility that his work would violate the treaty. The magistrate, unconvinced, asked Chang Ju-mei for instructions, and the governor in turn reported the matter to the Tsungli Yamen.[9]

The Yamen responded by citing Section II, Articles 3 and 4 of the Kiaochow Treaty.[10] These showed, it said, that the magistrate was correct in thinking that mining operations could not begin until the location of the thirty-li zone had been ascertained. Furthermore, the articles also specified that the mines along the railroad were to be undertaken by a joint Sino-German company and that before it could legitimately begin its work, this company was required to negotiate "regulations" with the Chinese government for the operation of the mines. The Yamen pointed out that Schmidt had complied with none of these requirements and, therefore, he was in "extreme violation of the treaty" and was acting without any authority. The Yamen ordered the magistrate not to register the land and to have Schmidt stop work.

Chang Ju-mei continued to apply the policies of the reformers toward the Germans in Shantung even after the reform movement itself came to an end in September. Significantly, however, the Tsungli Yamen's support for his efforts gradually declined as it came to reflect the resurgence of conservatism in the central government. In November the magistrate of Wei-hsien complained to Chang that Schmidt had stubbornly refused the orders to halt work.[11] The governor reported this to the Tsungli Yamen and added that Schmidt's activities should be stopped immediately because no regulations had yet been written and no Chinese were participating in the enterprise.[12] The Yamen agreed and wrote to Heyking asking him to order Carlowitz and Company to cease operations.[13] The minister evaded the request by replying that Schmidt was still only collecting samples and was not really mining.[14] He added,

"I know the treaty says we must discuss regulations soon, but to do this carefully will take considerable time . . . If we wait until then . . . to collect samples, there will be delay in reaping profits from the mines. Carlowitz and Company plans to sell stock to Chinese merchants, but before it can do so it must have the results of the tests . . . so that it can tell potential buyers what profit can be expected."

After it received the minister's reply, the Yamen agreed to order the local officials "not to interfere" with the engineers so long as they confined their activities to testing.[15] The Tsungli Yamen's willingness to compromise with the Germans proved to be the first indication of a divergence between the policies of Tsinan and Peking. This split widened as the central government became increasingly less interested in protecting China's sovereignty and economic interests in Shantung. At the end of December, when the German engineers were beginning to survey the route of the railway between Tsingtao and Wei-hsien, Heyking succeeded in having the Tsungli Yamen order the governor to "tell the local officials that the engineers must be protected . . . when they come." [16] Chang responded that he would, of course, comply. At the same time, however, he took the unusual step of writing a private letter to the Yamen, pleading for more attention to the burgeoning German activities.[17]

"The railroads and mines which are to be built," Chang wrote, "require the negotiation of separate regulations and are supposed to be joint Sino-foreign companies. But there are still no regulations, and no stock has been sold to Chinese. Yet the Germans, having established a company independently, are already . . . surveying the railroad and buying land for mines." This not only constituted a case of "clamoring guests grabbing the authority of the host" but also violated the accepted procedures of "friendly intercourse among nations" and was "at variance with the original treaty" of Kiaochow. Therefore, the governor recommended, "since Heyking constantly speaks of acting according to the treaty, you should negotiate detailed regulations with him for opening the railroad and mining operations in Shantung."

Chang further pointed out that the negotiation of regulations and the transformation of the company into a joint enterprise would not only defend Chinese rights generally but might also bring in additional revenue. "When foreigners open a railroad or a mine . . . whether in their own country or abroad . . . they give 25 or 40 per cent of their extra profit to repay the nation . . . we can incorporate this into the regulations for the Sino-German company in Shantung." He added that regulation and joint control might also "secretly" be a way to minimize the military threat posed by the line.

On the other hand, he warned, if the Germans were not controlled by regulations which forced them to obey the treaty, they would "imitate the methods used by the Sino-Russian company to manage the railroads in Manchuria . . . They will begin by coercing us for whatever they like, and end by trying to steal everything. If we want to limit them then, it will be too late." Specifically, he added, by letting the Germans achieve the autonomous position of the Russians, China would be "permitting them to station troops along the line to defend it, allowing them to pay a reduced tariff . . . on goods, allowing them to be oppressive in the purchase of land, and permitting them to open mines with no restrictions whatever."

Greater concern for Chinese prerogatives was essential, he concluded, or the results would be grave indeed. "The officials, the gentry, the merchants, and the people will have nowhere to turn. The German slyness for seizing power and profit will be a disaster not only for Shantung but for the situation of the whole country." Despite this plea, the Yamen was apparently content to have the governor merely avoid trouble with the Germans in Shantung by protecting the engineers along the railway, and it ignored Chang's request to pursue the question of regulations with Heyking.

Chang, however, persisted. In March 1899, shortly before he was removed from office, the governor reported that Schmidt had come to Po-shan on the proposed Tsingtao-Tsinan line to buy land and begin tests.[18] He said that this case was, therefore, probably analogous to that at Wei-hsien, when he had faithfully carried out the orders of the Yamen and told the local magistrate "to obey the treaty" and permit the test borings to proceed. But, the governor added with a touch of sarcasm, "I think if there is talk of 'obeying the treaty' one should wait until regulations have been written before acting" to allow the work to begin. This would not only be "in accord with a specific Sino-German treaty," he reminded the Yamen, but also "with what you told me earlier." The governor then proceeded to quote the original dispatch which the Tsungli Yamen had issued during the reform movement, ordering Schmidt to halt work until the regulations were written. Chang said that this policy was still correct and that Schmidt should be told to stop all his activities. There are some indications that, just before Chang left the province, he proceeded to raise the matter directly with Governor Jaeschke,[19] though there are no indications that the Yamen did so with Heyking in Peking.

The Rise of Militancy: Anti-Missionary
Violence and German Intervention

The end of the reform movement marked a decline in Peking's efforts to control the nascent German economic activities in Shantung. At the same time, the change in government inaugurated a new wave of violence against the Steyl Mission. These disturbances are significant because they provided the opportunity for a major German military expedition into the interior and, for the first time, forced the navy to consider its future role outside the leasehold. The unrest is also of interest because it coincided with the early activities of the Boxer movement then beginning in Shantung. The Boxers were a secret society, strongly antiforeign and anti-Christian, which became prominent in 1899 because of its attacks on missionaries and Chinese Christians. Boxer activities were centered in the western parts of Shantung rather than the areas where the Germans were active. Nevertheless, the events in the German areas can give some insight into the causes and nature of antiforeign violence in Shantung at this time and into the relationship of government officials and government policy to that violence.

The attacks on the German missionaries, which began in the fall of 1898, occurred for the most part in the eastern half of the Bishopric of South Shantung, primarily in I-chou Prefecture. In November a Steyl missionary, Peter Stenz, was kidnapped, beaten, and held prisoner in a small village in Jih-chao-hsien in the eastern part of the prefecture.[20] Soon afterwards, nearby mission stations were also attacked by mobs, and as the unrest spread, both the American Presbyterians and the German miners began to feel threatened.[21] By March the foreigners claimed that the situation "could not be described" and that it was the "worst in twenty years."[22]

The attacks on the missionaries grew out of earlier disturbances at I-chou which were not, originally, directed against foreigners.[23] The area had been plagued by bad weather for a year, and the resulting crop failures had caused widespread suffering. In addition, because of the high food prices the government had reduced the size of its military forces and discharged some of the troops it was supporting. According to Chang Ju-mei, by April 1898 such "dispersed troops joined together with bandit leaders, laborers, and refugees . . . collected weapons and wandered about nearby villages on the pretext of getting food but actually to rob the people."[24] The provincial forces partially succeeded in putting down this unrest, but some of the leaders escaped and the threat of renewed outbreaks remained. Later, when Bishop Anzer claimed that the attacks at I-chou were led by a secret society called the Hei-hui (Black Band), which had connections with former military men, he may have been referring to these ex-soldiers.[25]

To some extent, the actions of the missionaries contributed to the renewal of the unrest and to the fact that it was directed against them. All observers, except the members of the Steyl Mission itself, leveled against the missionaries the usual charge of seeking improper protection for themselves and their converts.[26] The actively interventionist policy which Bishop Anzer pursued would seem to support this accusation. For example, Stenz reached an amicable agreement with the magistrate of Jih-chao, which settled the case of his own kidnapping.[27] However, Bishop Anzer considered Stenz' agreement a "light peace" which only egged on the antimissionary elements. He "overthrew" it and renegotiated a far more stringent settlement which, among other points, called for an indemnity of 25,000 taels for Stenz and a humiliating mass apology by the local gentry to the Steyl Mission. Nevertheless, the missionaries did not act in any unusual or particularly aggressive manner in the fall of 1898, and their behavior was not the main reason that attacks on them began at this time.

Rather, the new violence against the missionaries was apparently a manifestation of the reformers' fall from power and the increasing influence of militant conservatives in Peking. The reformers, because they opposed the West primarily for nationalistic rather than cultural reasons, and perhaps because there was nothing in modern international practice which required the exclusion of foreigners from one's land, had not been hostile to missionaries unless they were used to undermine Chinese sovereignty. Indeed, the reformers valued missionaries and had been profoundly influenced by several Protestant authors. The militant conservatives, on the other hand, were particularly hostile to missionaries and Christianity. The result of these differing attitudes was that during the Hundred Days antimissionary attacks came to a halt all over China but after the coup of September started again, not only in Shantung but in many other provinces.[28]

The impact which the attitude of higher government authorities had on the incidence of local antimissionary violence is frequently overlooked. However, the existence of this influence is not surprising in view of the well-documented role which the local elites, the gentry and the officials, played in missionary cases. Whereas the persons who actually attacked the missionaries were not necessarily aware of the feelings of Peking or of their provincial governor, the politically oriented local

elites certainly were. In addition, specific local appointments of magistrates who were either friendly or hostile to missionaries could not only
change policy directly but could also serve to indicate the views of higher
authorities. The important influence which the central and provincial
governments' attitudes had on the number of missionary cases was a
fact well known to foreigners in the nineteenth century. The reformers
were also cognizant of the implications which the differences between
their attitude toward missionaries and that of the militants had in this
regard. For example, in commenting on a decree against antimissionary
violence issued during the Hundred Days, Liang Ch'i-ch'ao wrote that
missionary cases rested on local grievances: "however, they also grow out
of the fact that the court and senior officials hate foreigners, so that evil
people follow their lead and use it. If one examines the three months
when the emperor was pursuing reform, one notes that there was not a
single missionary case, but that on the fourth day after the coup the
violence in Peking began, and within two months there were already
five or six cases involving the murder of missionaries. One can see that
the thing which directs the behavior of the people in this regard is the
attitude of the court." [29]

The foreigners at I-chou all claimed that the unrest there reached
major proportions because the local officials showed no desire to protect
Christians; and they stressed that a crucial reason for this diffidence was
the widespread knowledge that Peking, while not openly advocating antimissionary violence, had become rather sympathetic to it. To back their
contention, they cited numerous examples of laxity on the part of district
authorities and described how incumbent subprefects and district magistrates were being replaced by men who were more hostile to missionaries.[30]

The most important personnel shift of this type, and one which clearly
revealed the political pressures which must have affected the provincial
and local authorities during this period, occurred in March 1899, when
Yü-hsien was named to replace Chang Ju-mei as governor. Yü had been
the provincial judge under Li Ping-heng and was a close political ally
of the former governor. He shared Li's militant hostility to the West and,
indeed, has been described as being even more antiforeign than his
former chief. Yü was to become one of the leading patrons of the Boxers,
first in Shantung and then in Shansi, and he was eventually to be executed on the demand of the Western powers as part of the Boxer settlement.[31]

When the violence at I-chou began, the German missionaries first tried
to restore order there by following the normal procedure of complaining

to the Tsungli Yamen through their minister in Peking, while at the same time negotiating directly with the Chinese officials on the scene. They quickly realized, however, that the existence of the new German sphere of influence in Shantung held out the possibility of direct military intervention from Tsingtao; and they began to work for such intervention.[32] The missionaries called for a military expedition, which they claimed was absolutely essential in order to protect their own lives and those of their converts. Not only did they appeal directly to German officials, but they also used the Catholic press in Germany to generate political pressure for their demands.[33]

One argument employed by the missionaries in soliciting intervention was the claim that the navy owed them military assistance because the unrest at I-chou was caused by anti-German feelings which had been aroused by the seizure of Kiaochow. Bishop Anzer, for example, wrote that "the disturbances come not from religious fanaticism but from patriotism," [34] and he noted that the Hei-hui, which carried banners inscribed "Destroy the Europeans and support the Ch'ing," [35] had been organized to drive out the Germans and thus to avenge the loss of Kiaochow.[36]

It is clear that the local population of I-chou received stimulation and even support from higher authorities and members of the local elite, whose hostility to the Germans had increased because of the loss of Kiaochow; and in this sense Bishop Anzer's claim was correct. However, it should be remembered that there is no evidence to suggest that on the popular level the unrest was directly related to the German occupation. In fact, the causes of anti-German violence, even on or within the borders of the leasehold itself, indicate that popular opposition to the Germans had its roots in local anti-German grievances and not in anger over the occupation of Tsingtao. In addition, if Yü-hsien was typical of the militant officials who condoned the violence at I-chou, it would suggest that even the higher authorities with this perspective were as concerned with the missionaries as with the seizure of Kiaochow. Yü, for example, did not attack the leasehold in his writings but concentrated instead on criticizing the missionaries in the interior.[37]

Bishop Anzer made his first request for armed intervention to Jaeschke and Heyking in December, and throughout the winter the bishop continued to demand "strongly that German troops be marched to I-chou in order to make an impression on the mandarins." [38] In March, Anzer sent Stenz and another missionary to Jaeschke, and the two priests finally succeeded in convincing the governor to launch the expedition.[39] The Stenz case was still the most important in the eyes of the German government because it involved a German citizen; and apparently, in their eagerness for action, the missionaries did not tell Jaeschke that it had already been settled. Later the governor was to regret this omission bitterly and to note that when he made his final decision for intervention he "was not in a position to judge the facts correctly." [40]

Although the main pressure on Jaeschke came from the missionaries, considerations of German power in Shantung also influenced him. In the first place, the unrest at I-chou had also disrupted the initial mining surveys in the prefecture, and both Jaeschke and Heyking felt that a passive response to these disturbances would set a bad precedent and endanger the future of German economic activities in the interior.[41] Jaeschke even wrote Tirpitz that he favored an expedition "less because of the missionaries than because of our economic interests." [42] Similarly, Heyking defended the propriety of protecting Chinese Christians, who were, after all, not German citizens, by pointing out that "with development of our economic undertakings in Shantung, we will have to create a 'clientele' from within the native population . . . for this the Christian congregations are our first good source . . . so the violence against them and the efforts to drive them out can't be viewed calmly." [43] These arguments frequently sound like rationalizations, intended to appeal to Tirpitz' concern about the economic development of the sphere; yet they certainly played some role in Jaeschke's decision.

In the second place, the Germans felt that they had to undertake military action in order to assert their recently acquired preeminence in Shantung and to discourage the claims of rival powers. In particular, they feared possible American competition in the province, and Heyking warned that "if the unrest continues," the United States could "use the danger to its missionaries as a basis for interfering in Shantung." [44] The American missionaries contributed to these fears. They complained to their consul in Chefoo about the disturbances and, at the same time, asked the Germans for protection both directly and through the articles they wrote for the *North China Herald*.[45] In January, for example, the Jih-chao correspondent noted that the German authorities "must do something of a very striking and decisive character if their prestige in their chosen sphere of influence is to be maintained," [46] and a month later he declared himself "amazed that the German Government has not made itself felt as yet." [47]

The Germans may have worried also about the possibility of renewed French involvement in Shantung. France was in the middle of negotiations for an improvement in the status of Catholic clergy in China. As a result, Bülow suspected that the French were again "seeking a protectorate over all Catholic missions in China." Therefore he stressed that it was in the government's interest to be "particularly careful in dealing with the missionary matters" in Shantung.[48]

By the middle of March, Jaeschke had definitely decided to send a military expedition to the troubled areas. Its immediate purpose was to obtain an indemnity for the Stenz case, but its broader mission was to "put pressure on the officials in southern Shantung so that they will act vigorously against anti-Catholic activities." [49] Through consultations with Anzer, Jaeschke decided that the basic objective of the expedition was to be the occupation of Jih-chao city.[50] Heyking, who was also in close touch with the bishop, acquiesced quickly. Bülow and Tirpitz likewise gave their assent, although with hesitation. Tirpitz, for example, was bothered by the fact that "the reports of the minister and the governor are based on the news given out by Bishop Anzer," and he urged the men on the scene to search for a political settlement if possible.[51]

While Jaeschke was awaiting Berlin's approval of the expedition, he sent reconnaissance patrols to I-chou-fu in order to study its potentialities for sustaining troops.[52] One such party, consisting of two officers and a mining engineer, landed on the southern coast of the prefecture and marched inland toward its capital, I-chou-fu city. On the morning of March 22, near the villages of Han-chia-ts'un and Pai-lien-ts'un, the three men clashed with a band of Chinese who, they claimed, were armed with cannon, guns, and lances and were in "good marching order." [53] In the fight two of the Chinese were killed and four severely wounded. In its protest over the incident Peking maintained that the band was probably a part of the local militia then being organized in the area. As such, the Chinese minister told Bülow, the group's purpose was to stop "local bandits" from "persecuting missionaries and Chinese Christians," and therefore there could have been "nothing further from its intentions than to attack the three Germans." [54]

From the available information it is impossible to ascertain what actually happened in this incident, which became famous as an example of European fighting ability.[55] In any case, its main result was that Jaeschke, angered by what he considered an unprovoked attack on his men, decided to give the forthcoming expedition the added task of burning down the two villages involved.

After final approval arrived from Berlin, the expedition left Tsingtao aboard the cruiser *Gefion* on the evening of March 29.[56] It consisted of two sections. The first, made up of 120 marines, a naval artillery detachment of ten men, and two machine gun units, was landed on the morning of the thirtieth at Shih-chiu-so near Jih-chao. The second section, consisting of 40 marines, was put ashore farther down the coast opposite the villages of Han-chia-ts'un and Pai-lien-ts'un. Simultaneously, Heyking notified the Tsungli Yamen of the landings and stressed in his note that the troops were not hostile to China but, rather, were sent "to support the local officials in protecting German engineers and missionaries and in quieting the population." [57] Berlin also sent dispatches to the major world capitals in order to assure the other powers that the expedition had "no territorial goals" and was merely a "police measure." [58]

The unit in the south marched inland toward the two villages. It reached them on the morning of April 2 and proceeded to burn them down. The unit's commanding officer reported that the villagers "were given an hour to clean up" and then a horn sounded indicating that the fires would be lighted. He was pleased to note that "the people felt the punishment was completely justified and no attempt was made to stop us; yes, not a single one asked us to spare his house . . . in almost every one there were rifles, swords, and lances, and four of them . . . blew up because of the powder inside." Besides what was burned, of course, "nothing was taken from the people but a few weapons . . . They were completely quiet and showed not the slightest trace of agitation or bitterness." [59] After this reprisal raid, which became the most notorious act committed by the Germans in Shantung, the detachment marched directly back to the coast and boarded the *Gefion* for Tsingtao.

The other company arrived at Jih-chao city on March 30 and immediately secured the town gates and occupied the hsien yamen. The commanding officer presented the magistrate with a letter which said that the troops had come because no action had been taken against the attackers of Stenz.[60] The letter also contained an ultimatum, a threat to take the magistrate back to Tsingtao as a prisoner unless the guilty parties were arrested within three days and punished within ten. The next day the magistrate began hearings at the yamen under the supervision of German officers and interpreters. When the deadline passed without any arrests, Jaeschke toyed with the idea of carrying out the ultimatum by taking hostages away and so creating a "lasting impression" in the area.[61] Instead, he decided to prolong the occupation of Jih-chao. He did so primarily because of the requests of the Westerners in the prefecture, who insisted that if the expedition were "withdrawn too early it could lose whatever progress has been made to date." [62] The American missionaries had welcomed the German landing and were among the most anxious to have troops remain.[63] They even asked the Germans to increase the scope of the expedition and occupy the prefectural capital at I-chou-fu; however, this request was denied.

Another reason Jaeschke did not withdraw immediately was that Hey-king felt the presence of German troops at Jih-chao gave him leverage in his negotiations with the Tsungli Yamen over the Tientsin-Chinkiang Railway.[64] These negotiations were then in their final phase. Similarly, Anzer wanted the expedition to remain until he had obtained compensation for the missionaries and converts who had suffered damages in the original riots.[65] Thus, on April 17, despite the fact that peace had been restored, Jaeschke strengthened the German force with fifty-two more men and awaited a "satisfactory situation" for its withdrawal.[66]

The troops did not finally leave Jih-chao until May 25, after the railway negotiations had been successfully concluded. However, as it departed, the detachment forcibly seized five "literati" and took them back to Tsingtao as hostages.[67] This was done ostensibly in order to have a guarantee for the punishment of the ringleaders of the Stenz attack who had not yet been captured; but, in reality, it was to provide Bishop Anzer with leverage in his forthcoming negotiations at Tsinan for a financial settlement.[68] Anzer reached an agreement on June 25, when the provincial authorities promised the mission an additional indemnity of nearly 80,000 taels. Thereupon, the bishop finally closed the Jih-chao incident by telegraphing Jaeschke to free the hostages.[69]

Understandably, both Yü-hsien and the Peking government were enraged by the expedition. Their reaction was based not only on the fact that foreigners had once again used military force against China but, perhaps even more, on their hatred of the missionaries, who, it was believed, had caused the intervention. The Chinese officials were also upset by the violence of the German troops and worried about the military threat which the expedition posed to Shantung and Peking. However, neither Yü nor the Grand Council appears to have opposed the intervention because it was an affront to Chinese sovereignty in the interior, or because it violated the treaties; they did not discuss it in such terms but rather denounced it as a "wanton" attempt on the part of the Germans "to create strife" in Shantung.[70] As a result, in dealing with the expedition, these authorities limited their objectives to obtaining the withdrawal of the German troops and preventing them from advancing farther into the interior.

The concrete steps taken by the central government to achieve these goals clearly indicate the strength which militancy had gained since 1897. Not only did Peking employ the normal mainstream procedure of protesting to the foreigners while attempting to quiet the unrest, but it also began to develop plans for dealing with the Germans militarily.

This latter approach paralleled a decision taken a few weeks earlier to resist by force the Italian demands for a leasehold in China.

On the day Peking learned of the landings, an imperial decree was issued denouncing as a "pretext" the German claim that the troops had been sent to help Chinese officials. The decree also ordered General Hsia Hsin-yu, commander of the brigade at Teng-chou, to bring his troops to I-chou-fu "in order to repress the rising firmly and protect the missionaries . . . If there are people who spread rumors to drive out the missionaries," the decree continued, "they are to be arrested and punished in order to show the Germans we are just and protect both the people and the converts." [71] On the same day the Chinese minister in Berlin, Lu Hai-huan, was ordered by telegraph to go to the Foreign Office and inform it of the decree in order to let the Germans know that the Chinese government was intent on keeping the peace alone, and that "German troops need not bother to assist." [72] Lu carried out the order and requested the Foreign Office to telegraph Tsingtao to have the troops withdrawn immediately.[73]

Thereafter, Peking issued a series of decrees ordering local officials to treat the Christians fairly despite the injustices which the converts might have caused in the past. At the same time, the central government continued its protests to the Germans. These became particularly bitter after the burning of the two villages, which was denounced as an "atrocity." [74] The Chinese government warned the Germans that a gunboat policy would only engender widespread hatred and violence against them by the "poor but proud" people of Shantung,[75] and it pointed out that such a policy was particularly dangerous "in view of the intended mine and railway developments" and could "hurt the future of Germany in East Asia." [76]

There is some evidence that, in order to make the German troops withdraw, Yü-hsien actually tried to prevent the German engineers from continuing their activities in Shantung.[77] When the Germans complained, however, the Tsungli Yamen quickly told the governor to stop so that the foreigners would find no further "pretense to cause trouble." [78] The threat to German economic interests implied by the Chinese diplomatic notes, coupled with Yü-hsien's actions, may, to some extent, have contributed to Tirpitz' growing awareness that the attainment of Germany's goals in Shantung required peace with the local population and officials.[79]

The Chinese decision to use force, which was intended to block any further penetration by the Germans, was evidently taken after the destruction of the two villages. On April 6 the Grand Council responded to

Tsinan's report of the burnings by ordering General Hsia to proceed by forced marches to Lan-shan-hsien, where the two villages were located.[80] The council explained its order by saying that "if the armies of the two nations are too far apart, how can one hope to make a defense." On April 10, Hsia arrived in Lan-shan with about 1500 men. Since the Germans had already left, he was given new orders to hurry to Jih-chao, "publicly, in order to repress" the unrest, but "secretly, to defend ourselves." [81] He arrived there on April 16 and stationed his forces about three miles outside the town. He reported that, in order "to dispel their worries," he had told the Germans that he had come to keep the peace, but that he had actually deployed his troops so as to guard against the foreigners.[82]

The Peking government also began to prepare for the possibility of a broader military confrontation. On May 1, the Grand Council warned Yü-hsien that since "the Germans are unfathomable," Shantung, "the gateway to the capital," would have to be "strictly defended" against their encroachments. Yü was told to draw up a plan for the defense of the province which would pay particular attention to the placement of troops so that they could guard the coast.[83] At the same time, Yuan Shih-k'ai was ordered to move some of his modern troops from the Tientsin area to Te-chou.[84] Though ostensibly for drill and training, this move was really intended to contain the German threat. On May 13, Yuan arrived at Te-chou with two battalions totaling about 5000 men. There is also evidence to suggest that two other divisions of the Peiyang Defense Corps, those under Nieh Shih-ch'eng and Tung Fu-hsiang, received similar orders and also moved in the direction of Shantung.[85]

None of these Chinese armies ever went into action against the German expedition. Therefore the Germans, who had not planned to move beyond Jih-chao, did not realize that, had they done so, they might have clashed with the Chinese forces. The Germans, for example, considered the arrival of General Hsia solely as a sign that the expedition was "showing good effects" and that the Chinese authorities were now really interested in maintaining order.[86] The *North China Herald* reported from Lan-shan that as the troops passed through, "there was much talk of exterminating the foreigners," but this and later British reports were discounted by the Germans as "pure fiction." [87] Nevertheless, the Chinese defensive measures made some impression on the Germans, again particularly on Tirpitz, who during this period became increasingly concerned about the danger of having to fight China.

The impact of the Jih-chao expedition on the Chinese attitude toward the Germans in Shantung was to heighten suspicion of every German activity in the province. In addition, the intervention left Peking and Tsinan more ready to employ force against future German incursions.[88] However, neither the conservative court nor Yü-hsien viewed the crisis from a perspective which encouraged it to develop a policy to protect Chinese interests in the sphere of influence. The task of continuing the work of the reformers in formulating such a program was to be left to Yü's successor, Yuan Shih-k'ai, who first concerned himself with the German activities in Shantung as a result of the Jih-chao episode.[89]

The expedition also influenced the overall development of Chinese foreign policy by bolstering the government's increasing militancy, a development which was to culminate in official support of the Boxers. This is clear, for example, in the case of Yü-hsien, who, while castigating the missionaries for their role in the incident, was formulating his plans for dealing with the anti-Christian activities of the Boxers, then gaining strength in the western part of the province. "The people's hatred of the missionaries has been accumulating," the governor wrote in his comments on the final Tsinan settlement with Bishop Anzer. "Those among the people who are weak fear them; those who are strong are roused to precipitous action. The people have not yet finished causing trouble for the missionaries." He added, as usual, that he would keep order, but the increasing emphasis on the retribution which the missionaries deserved is clear.[90]

On the German side the most significant result of the expedition was Tirpitz' decision that the interior of Shantung was not, with regard to military intervention, to be automatically treated as an extension of Kiaochow. Tirpitz' position was a natural outgrowth of his characteristic disinclination for warfare. Specifically, he was convinced that the indiscriminate use of German troops in Shantung would have adverse repercussions on the sound economic development of the sphere of influence and might even be militarily dangerous. Tirpitz had never been enthusiastic about the expedition and, from the first, had stressed the importance of withdrawing the troops as soon as possible.[91] After the intervention was over, Jaeschke requested permission to launch similar actions on his own authority in the future, arguing that such measures were only local in character and were needed to defend German economic development in the interior. Tirpitz' response summarized his recently developed objections to a policy of military activism.[92]

The admiral began by rejecting Jaeschke's request because of the "formal" exigencies of international politics. "I cannot share your feeling that the expedition was of only local importance . . . Though we have by treaty economic privileges in Shantung, we must remember that outside the leasehold and the fifty-kilometer zone the province is an area under foreign sovereignty, even if Chinese sovereignty only. If we were simply to ignore this fact and let the governor begin war activities there on his own (and this is what such expeditions are despite all claims of peaceful intentions), this would be justifiably exploited by our enemies . . . So we must base ourselves on the standpoint of international law until some other can be decided upon in line with overall German policy."

In addition, he continued, there were also "material" reasons why the request could not be granted. "I believe the idea that such an expedition presents no danger and that a state of war is impossible is a dangerous underestimation of the power of the Chinese population to resist . . . the Chinese government has influenced the people's actions in the past and will continue to do so," and therefore "the expedition cannot possibly be considered a local undertaking. For one must consider the fact that the opposition to us could become much more serious and we could find ourselves in a sort of latent war. Though the results of this war would not be unclear, it would necessitate a great sacrifice in time, money, personnel, and material and would ultimately have an effect contrary to your goal, the 'peaceful development of our colony.' "

Tirpitz' endemic suspicion of Britain appeared in the unlikely suggestion that China might choose to fight because she was "supported or encouraged by a third power, which would have an interest in keeping us busy in Shantung and turned away from the Yangtze . . . We do not yet have sufficient forces directly available for war with China, and there is no need to mention that our troops at Kiaochow are not sufficient."

The admiral continued by launching into a sharp attack on the missionaries, claiming that they presented an especially "serious danger to the development" of the German sphere of influence. "There is no doubt that the uproar in Shantung was caused by the Catholic missionaries in general, and the provocative behaviour of the Chinese Christians in particular . . . The miners were hampered in their work," Tirpitz admitted, "but this was only a backlash." He warned Jaeschke that "although it is in our interests both internal and external to treat the missionaries well, as you yourself said, this must not reach the point where the governor becomes their blind tool."

In regard to the Jih-chao incident, he commented rhetorically, "So what has been accomplished? In my opinion only what you did not want, and nothing different from what would have happened had Anzer told you of his agreement in the Stenz case. I can only partly guess why you were not told when I note that compensation took the form of money and 'land to build churches' . . . You can see how extremely careful you must be toward the missionaries, and what weight you should give to their complaints and demands."

He added that he and the Foreign Office had decided in May that, in the future, Germany would stand on "the only possible position of international law, that is, one country can only demand guarantees for the rights and interests of its own citizens in another country. This does not include the Chinese Christians." The legation no longer planned, "even as a matter of form," to present "the demands of injured Chinese" to the Chinese government. Therefore, said Tirpitz, "How much less can one speak of armed intervention. I think henceforth when the missionaries request something . . . you should refer to international law and thus direct them to the legation; this will indirectly indicate to them that, as you expressed it, the governor and his troops are not supernumeraries for the missionaries." With his usual sensitivity to political nuances, Tirpitz assured the governor that "the Catholic German circles here agree completely" and "strongly wish not to have us dragged into war by the missionaries. This view will get high level and influential expression in the *Koelnische Volkszeitung* and will also be conveyed to Anzer."

The letter concluded with a general outline of the proper way for Germany to get control of Shantung. "I believe much can be achieved in China by small and essentially personal means. But this needs time and leisure . . . In view of the attitude of the Chinese government, which is passive at best, the same goals could only be achieved quickly with the greatest sacrifices; for the more sharply we act, the greater the opposition will grow. Therefore, I believe that the best policy to expand our influence in Shantung is to proceed from Tsingtao and to base ourselves on it. Our most essential interest is furthering the railroad construction from Tsingtao to Tsinan . . . As the railroad grows we will be able to expand our influence outwards from it more and more widely and to gradually establish ourselves ever more firmly in the province. This may be slower, but its result will, therefore, be all the surer."

Tirpitz' primary concern in writing to Jaeschke was to caution him against further military adventures in the interior on behalf of the missionaries, with whom the naval secretary had little sympathy. Tirpitz did not discuss the possibility that German economic activities might also need German military support; however, he seemed to imply that, even for such a purpose, intervention should not be undertaken lightly.

103

The Railroad and the Variations in Chinese Policy

The Governorship of Yü-hsien

On June 1, 1899, Chancellor Hohenlohe issued a charter which gave the concession for the construction and operation of the railroad line from Tsingtao to Tsinan to a German syndicate.[93] This syndicate was dominated by the same prominent financial houses which had organized the Deutsch-Asiatische Bank. It also included some of the firms, such as Carlowitz and Company, which were involved in Chinese enterprises. On June 14 the syndicate formed the Schantung Eisenbahn Gesellschaft (Shantung Railroad Company, or SEG), a joint stock company with a base capital of 54,000,000 marks.

According to the terms of the concession[94] the company was to have the railroad in operation as far as Wei-hsien within three years, and the whole line, including the branch to Po-shan, within five. The government promised that the company would be granted the right to build the other lines mentioned in the Treaty of Kiaochow if it asked for them before 1908. The concession obligated the company to route the railroad through the chief towns and cities along the way and also to make the "best possible connection with the most important coal fields." Although the line was to be standard gauge and single track, the company was required to buy enough land for an eventual second track. German materials were to be used throughout, in so far as possible.

During the discussions in Berlin, the syndicate told the German government that it did not want to hold any negotiations with China about the railroad.[95] Therefore, the concession placed the firm under the jurisdiction of the German authorities at Kiaochow and did not acknowledge any relationship to either Peking or Tsinan. Among other things, German officials were given considerable influence over the railroad's rates and schedules as well as over the selection of its main executives. Furthermore, the company was not permitted to begin work within the leasehold without the permission of the governor of Kiaochow, nor within the province without the permission of the German minister. In addition, it had to pay a yearly tax on its profits, which was "to be applied to the expenditures of the government" of Tsingtao "for the harbor works . . . and also to the general running expenses of the protectorate." The company was responsible solely to the German government for violations of the concession agreement. Finally, the government reserved the right to purchase the line after sixty years.

The only references to China in the concession were the provision that the Schantung Eisenbahn Gesellschaft was to be a joint Sino-German company, and the stipulation that "care is to be taken that Germans as well as Chinese may participate in the public subscription to the stock of the company. More especially, subscriptions shall be opened in the suitable commercial centers of East Asia." However, the syndicate initially planned to use its own vast resources to build the line. Therefore, during the early years, the provisions for Chinese participation in the concession, as well as the sections in the Kiaochow Treaty upon which they were based, remained a dead letter.

In the summer of 1899 the newly established company made arrangements with German firms to supply it with building materials and rolling stock, and by the beginning of 1900 it had already ordered 85,000 tons of goods worth 20,000,000 marks.[96] The company also reached an agreement with the two great German steamship lines, the Hamburg-Amerika and the Norddeutscher Lloyd, to transport these materials to Tsingtao. In December 1899 the first shipment left Germany for China. It consisted of 4,200 tons of rails, iron ties, and fishplates to be used in constructing the first 15 miles of line.

The company established a field office in Tsingtao in order to supervise the construction and operation of the line. Heinrich Hildebrandt was named manager. He was an official of the Prussian railway administration, who had been in China since the early 1890s as a representative of German interests and as an adviser on Chinese railway projects.[97]

The actual work on the line, which had begun before the concession was granted, proceeded rapidly. By the summer of 1899 the areas nearest Kiaochow were being surveyed in order to establish the precise location of the roadbed. Earthwork began at Tsingtao on September 23 with a formal ground-breaking ceremony presided over by Prince Heinrich. Construction got under way at a number of places along the sixty-mile section extending to Kao-mi, and by early 1900 most of the embankment to that point had been completed.[98] Because the docking facilities at Tsingtao were still undeveloped, the biggest technical problem during the early years involved the unloading of the heavy building materials from ships anchored out in the harbor. The construction of some of the bridges on the route to Kao-mi also presented significant engineering problems.

The actual work on the line was handled mainly by Chinese contractors. Sometimes they received payment for completing a given task or for moving a fixed amount of earth. At other times they supplied the Germans with a certain number of men for those jobs, such as the construction of bridges, which were supervised directly either by German contractors or by the railroad officials themselves. The workers were predominantly peasants who lived along the route, and there is evidence that the local population quickly grew to appreciate the possibilities for employment afforded by the railroad.[99] The contractors also brought in workers from the north who had had experience working on the railroads there. The construction involved great numbers of men; one source says that at times there were from 20,000 to 25,000 working on the railroad.[100] Because foreigners commanded extremely high wages in China, the SEG founded a small school for Chinese in 1899 in order "to create . . . the necessary personnel for stationmasters, conductors, firemen, and watchmen, etc." [101]

From the start, the SEG realized that the greatest problems which it would face during the construction of the line would involve the related tasks of buying land and of maintaining security as the work progressed into the interior.[102] In purchasing land, the company encountered problems similar to those which had confronted the navy when it bought property at Tsingtao. The peasants were frequently unwilling to sell their land, and every transaction was complicated by the difficulty of determining the exact ownership of the property involved. Security was vital to the railroad because it was extremely vulnerable to disturbances caused by its acquisition of land and other activities. If there was unrest, not only would the company face losses from damage to its property, but the ensuing delays in construction would be extremely costly in themselves.

Therefore, the SEG wanted the Chinese authorities to guarantee that the railroad work would be protected and that the local officials would help the company purchase land. The Germans, of course, hoped to obtain these benefits without having to negotiate regulations with the Chinese government which might limit the independence of the firm or open the way to Chinese participation in it. Eventually, it was this urgent need on the part of the SEG for the untroubled and rapid construction of the railway which enabled Tsinan to gain increased administrative control over the line.

However, in 1899, while Yü-hsien was governor, the company succeeded in obtaining these assurances without having to make concessions in return. This was primarily because Yü was not interested in the structure or operations of the railway enterprise. Nor did the Tsungli Yamen threaten the independence of the SEG in 1899, for its main concern was the maintenance of stability along the roadbed. There are some indications that the Tsungli Yamen may have been somewhat more interested in having the Germans live up to the Kiaochow Treaty than was the governor,[103] though this was not one of its primary objectives. The Yamen's greater interest in the status of the railroad probably resulted from the fact that in 1899 it still contained some members who had been fairly sympathetic to the reform movement or in any case, were not militants.[104]

For a brief period after its organization, the SEG actually considered negotiating directly with the Chinese government in order to obtain the cooperation which it desired. In June the company made plans to send Franz Urbig, the director of the Deutsch-Asiatische Bank in Shanghai, to the Tsungli Yamen to carry out this mission.[105] The orders prepared for Urbig cautioned him not to allow himself to be drawn into a broad discussion involving the railroad. If the Yamen wanted to begin such discussions, Urbig was "to convince it that it was too late now to discuss the general foundations, legal principles, character, and scope of the concession" and was to stress that all that remained to be dealt with were a few "details" which could and should be cleared up quickly.[106] Ultimately, the company decided not to send Urbig. This was partially because the SEG feared that he might compromise the railroad's independence. It was also because the company decided that it could achieve its goals with less risk by negotiating a limited agreement with local officials.

The opportunity to do this came in June when the first disturbances struck the railroad. In Kao-mi-hsien the peasants ripped out the surveyors' rods which were used to mark the route.[107] On the eighteenth they clashed directly with some German engineers south of the district capital. The underlying cause of the trouble was that the inhabitants did not understand what the rods were being used for and were upset by the prospect of losing the property on which they were placed.[108] The Germans also said that the people were "encouraged" in their actions by the district magistrate and by the creation of a local militia.[109] These charges would seem to indicate that the unrest, like that at I-chou-fu, grew out of local grievances but gained momentum because the local authorities reflected the antiforeign sentiments then in ascendancy among their superiors.

On June 21, Hildebrandt requested military assistance from Jaeschke on the ground that the work at Kao-mi could not continue. He insisted that occupation of the district capital was "absolutely necessary" if the construction was to progress.[110] It is possible that the unrest at Kao-mi was not the only reason why Hildebrandt requested help. He may also have wanted troops in order to put pressure on the local authorities to get the agreement which the railway company desired concerning the purchase of land and the security of the line. For there are indications that, at the same time it had been considering Urbig's mission, the SEG had also tried to get Yü-hsien to accept an agreement similar to that which Urbig was to seek, but that Yü had ignored the request.[111]

Tirpitz' letter counseling against precipitous military intervention had not yet arrived at Kiaochow, and Jaeschke responded to Hildebrandt's request promptly by dispatching a force of marines and mounted artillery to Kao-mi. He maintained that he did so because the railroad construction schedule was very crucial for both the company and the leasehold, and therefore "diplomatic treatment of the situation would take too long." [112] Another reason Jaeschke authorized the expedition was that he felt it was strategically necessary to Kiaochow for German military power to be strengthened in the fifty-kilometer zone. Diplomacy, the governor said, might even provide Chinese authorities with "a pretext for sending large numbers of troops into the zone, which would be inconvenient for us." [113]

The expedition remained at Kao-mi for only two weeks. In this time, however, the troops put down the unrest harshly and quickly and succeeded in preventing it from spreading to other points along the route.[114] In order to do this, the Germans occupied the district capital. They also fought two battles against what were apparently local militia; and, in one of these, they took by force the walled village of Ti-tung, near the site of the original riot. While the expedition was at Kao-mi, the SEG submitted its draft agreement to the local officials. On July 5, after peace had been definitely restored and the agreement signed, the troops were withdrawn.[115]

Yü-hsien and the Chinese government treated the expedition to Kao-mi much as they had the intervention at I-chou earlier in the year. Their policy still consisted of acquiescing to German demands at the scene of the unrest in order to encourage the withdrawal of the foreign troops, while at the same time preparing for the possible use of force, should this become necessary to prevent further German advances. During the entire period of the crisis, however, neither Yü nor the central government seemed concerned that the company was still operating in flagrant violation of the treaty or that its activities represented a serious threat to Chinese economic independence and sovereignty. Nor did they think of using the pressure created by the crisis to force the Germans to negotiate formal regulations which would define the railroad's relationship to the Chinese government and guarantee Chinese participation in the enterprise. The agreement which was signed at Kao-mi was written by the Germans and was, of course, designed to avoid these issues.

In practice, Yü and the local officials tried to calm the population and to stop the disturbances directly.[116] They also launched repeated appeals to the German naval commanders to stop their advance. The Tsungli Yamen promised the German chargé that the government would take "energetic measures to put down the movement," [117] and the Grand Council ordered Yü to send troops to restore order.[118] In order to block further German penetration, the council also told Yü to have the troops "plan for defense" against the foreigners. Throughout the crisis, Peking continued to order the governor to strengthen his forces for the same purpose.[119] On June 29, 200 Chinese infantry approached Kao-mi.[120] The Germans did not doubt that they were sent solely to help them put down the populace, but they nevertheless asked the Chinese troops to return at least to the border of the neutral zone.[121] The Chinese complied by withdrawing to Chang-ling, about 18 miles from the town of Kao-mi.

From the SEG's point of view the most important thing Yü-hsien did to bring about the German withdrawal was to allow the local officials, the magistrate of Kao-mi, the subprefect of Chiao-chou, and the prefect of Lai-chou-fu, to accede to the company's request and sign the agreement which it had prepared.[122] The agreement, which was officially signed on July 2, allowed the SEG to circumvent the difficulties of buying land by making the local officials act as intermediaries for all transactions with the peasants.[123] The magistrates agreed to the principle that "all land shall be sold to the railroad company which it requires, at a fair market price and without the slightest hindrance." In return the company promised only to pay this price, as well as to recompense residents for moving graves and for any other damage to property or crops. According to the detailed procedure agreed upon for buying land, the SEG would simply survey and select the land which it wanted and then have the magistrate purchase it and transfer payment to the owner. Similarly, all claims for damages against the company were to be taken to the officials who were responsible for dealing with the Germans. In the company's opinion, this system solved the problem of procuring land "as simply as possible" and was particularly desirable because it used Chinese officials without having to give them any control over the railroad.[124]

The agreement settled the question of security in an analogous manner. The three officials pledged to "protect the railroad work along the length of the roadbed" and to insure that there would be "no more damage or disturbances" in their areas. They were to carry out this pledge by themselves, enforcing it in any way they desired. The company's role in keeping order was limited to establishing a scale of fines for different types of damage, which the magistrates were responsible for collecting if trouble did occur.

The techniques which the local officials planned to use to keep order are interesting and may be seen in a proclamation which the magistrate of Kao-mi issued at the time.[125] He resorted both to exhortation — "The railroad construction in this district is being undertaken with the permission of the emperors of China and Germany . . . henceforth, you must act in a peaceful and friendly way, not just outwardly but also in your heart" — and to threats based on the principle of mutual responsibility — "If someone should, nevertheless, transgress . . . then for every surveyor's rod which he destroys he will have to pay an indemnity of five taels, and if he cannot be found, then the village heads will be responsible for raising the money. If a Chinese or European worker on the railroad is killed or injured, and if the evildoer cannot be found, then the whole village will be severely punished." The Germans were especially pleased when the subprefect of Chiao-chou had twenty villages along the route sign bonds acknowledging their responsibility for defending the work in their area.[126]

The SEG hoped to extend the system which it had established at Kao-mi to the entire length of the Tsingtao-Tsinan Railroad, and to do so without any further negotiations. The company wanted Yü-hsien to obtain bonds of mutual liability from all the villages on the route to Wei-hsien and even asked him to enforce the agreement of July 2 throughout the province.[127] Both these requests were ignored, perhaps because the expedition had already withdrawn. Thus, when disturbances began again at the end of 1899, the SEG was forced to reopen negotiations.

While the SEG was beginning operations in Shantung, the Germans also reached a preliminary agreement with China for the loan to construct the Tientsin-Chinkiang Railway, which the Germans had successfully claimed on the basis of their sphere of influence in Shantung. In September 1898 the Deutsch-Asiatische Bank and a British syndicate reached an understanding over the loan for the line.[128] The Germans were to lend the money for the section from Tientsin to the southern border of Shantung, while the British would handle the section from the southern border to Chinkiang.

In December, negotiations for the concession began with the Chinese government.[129] The preliminary agreement on the loan, signed in May 1899, was not a good one from China's point of view.[130] The financial terms were not favorable, and, even more important, the foreigners received the right not only to lend the money for the line but also to equip and operate it. On the other hand, the Germans did not succeed in making the section of the railroad from Tsinan to the southern border a private German line that would replace the Tsinan-I-chou railway, which was now rendered rather superfluous. However, they did reach an understanding with the Chinese negotiators that the mining privileges associated with the proposed German line would be transferred to the Tientsin-Chinkiang route if the German road was not built. It is possible that the increasing power of the conservatives in Peking, who were less touchy about giving up economic concessions, may have played some role in enabling the Germans to win these terms. In addition, the troops at Jih-chao were used as a lever in the last stages of the negotiations.

Yuan Shih-k'ai as Governor

The SEG experienced peace from July until December; then attacks on the work began again at Kao-mi, this time on a wider scale than before.[131] Local residents stole surveyors' rods, ripped out rails, and even attacked a number of the railroad's construction headquarters, forcing the German engineers to flee. By the beginning of February 1900, most work had come to a halt over a long section of the line on both sides of Kao-mi city.

Much of this unrest was not the result of isolated and unrelated attacks. Rather it was the work of a local villager, Sun Wen, and a military licentiate, Li Chin-pang, who had succeeded in organizing a large number of villagers north and west of Kao-mi into an armed band whose aim was to stop the intrusion of the railroad.[132] Contemporary Chinese historians consider Sun Wen's activities to be the most important instance of popular resistance to the Germans in Shantung.[133]

The main reason for the "spirit of opposition" at Kao-mi continued to be the hostility aroused by the foreigners and their continued quest for land.[134] These feelings were intensified by the end of 1899 because the railroad had begun large-scale construction activities in this isolated rural area. The uprising led by Sun stemmed specifically from the fear on the part of the peasants that the railroad dam would block the drainage of water in the reclaimed lowlands where they lived and would thus cause recurrent flooding or dryness. There are also indications that the villagers objected to the importation of labor from other areas, partly because this practice supplanted their own opportunities for employment and partly because the outside coolies tended to be less chary of damaging local property and crops.[135]

The Germans maintained that the new magistrate at Kao-mi, upon whom they depended for their dealings with the villagers, was hostile to the railroad and therefore contributed to the unrest.[136] They claimed, for example, that he purposely misrepresented the proposed route of the line so as to arouse the peasants' fears of improper drainage. They also said that he ignored the agreement with the railway company by refusing to send someone to Tsingtao to pick up the money which was to reimburse the landowners for their property, graves, and crop damage.

Just as the unrest in Kao-mi began again, Yü-hsien was removed as governor because of Western protests over his laxity toward the Boxers in western Shantung. On December 26 the new governor, Yuan Shih-k'ai, arrived in Tsinan.[137] Under Yuan a striking reversal took place in the provincial government's treatment of the Germans. For, in contrast to Yü's militant conservative approach, the new governor again pursued a nationalistic foreign policy. Yuan, who ultimately became one of the major figures in the great reform movement of the last decade of the Ch'ing, had been born in 1859, a year after K'ang Yu-wei. He was a protégé of Li Hung-chang and had risen to prominence primarily as a specialist on military affairs. In the years following the Sino-Japanese War, Yuan had become the leading military reformer in North China and had created the most important of China's modern army corps. In these years he had also shown sympathy for K'ang Yu-wei's reform efforts and, as a result, the reformers had considered him a possible ally during the Hundred Days. However, out of what were apparently political rather than ideological motives, Yuan had supported the empress in the coup of September 1898. Therefore, after the reform movement, Yuan was quite popular among the conservatives, although he did not share their views. He continued his military work and in 1899 became a vice-president of the Board of Works.

Yuan's later policy in Shantung was foreshadowed in an important memorial which he wrote in the beginning of July 1899, in response to the German military expeditions to Jih-chao and Kao-mi.[138] This was Yuan's first memorial dealing with Shantung, and it was a factor in his appointment as governor.[139] With its emphasis on the use of administrative techniques and treaties to control the Germans and defend Chinese sovereignty, Yuan's memorial revealed an attitude which differed radically from the approach which Yü-hsien and the central government had adopted in the earlier crises.

Yuan began his memorial by discussing the nature of the German threat. He said that the Germans, who had long "coveted" Shantung, had now developed a way to take over the province. They planned to use the incidents caused by the missionaries and the engineers as "a pretext to send troops out from Kiaochow and to encroach on our sovereignty." Yuan pointed out that "the Jih-chao affair was hardly over when the Kao-mi incident began; they occurred successively and thus nearly amounted to a scheme to establish a regular practice. Such a practice would not only agitate the people, but, even worse, it would be sufficient to destroy our national fabric."

Yuan rejected a military solution to the German incursions. He did concede that "if we were to follow the accepted rules of international relations, since the Germans invaded our territory and attacked our people and so began hostilities, we would be justified in immediately attacking them." On the other hand, he pointed out, such a retaliatory policy would be inappropriate, because "the present situation is very difficult to judge; the court values foreign relations and cares for the overall picture; naturally it must be forgiving." This would seem to have been a polite and circuitous way for Yuan, the celebrated military expert, to tell the government that China simply was in no position to fight back.

The proper solution, he said, was "to manage things beforehand . . . so as not to supply pretexts" for the Germans. "This will gradually restore peace and hence enable us to defend our sovereignty." He then proceeded to make four specific suggestions as to how the Chinese might avoid future interventions. The first suggestion was, "Carefully select local officials." By this Yuan meant officials who neither hated the missionaries so much that they aroused the people against them, nor feared the missionaries so much that they favored them, thus arousing the people indirectly. Rather, he wanted officials who knew that the treaties specified that the proper procedure when a missionary acted badly or interfered was to remonstrate with him firmly and, if that failed, to report the matter to his consul or minister for action. "Selecting good officials," he concluded, meant "picking those who fully understand the terms of the treaties and are knowledgeable about current affairs."

The second suggestion, "Study the treaties," was related to the first. Yuan complained that local officials, in particular, were ignorant of the treaties. Therefore he urged the Tsungli Yamen to issue a book which would contain all the terms, laws, and precedents the local authorities needed in order to handle foreigners in the interior. He also said that the expectant officials in the province should be encouraged to learn the contents of this book in their course of study. Then, whenever an incident occurred, they could be dispatched to the scene as special commissioners.

The third suggestion was "Deploy a police force." According to Yuan this force should be stationed at the important towns near Kiaochow and also along the route of the railroad. "When a foreigner passes through an area, these troops can be sent to protect and care for him," Yuan said, and in this way incidents would be avoided. In addition, the possibility of

having to fight such troops might discourage the Germans from interven-
ing. Thus, he pointed out, "within the plan for protection, there is also
a secret technique for control."

The fourth suggestion was "Appoint an official to reside at Kiaochow."
Yuan said that this official should be responsible for dealing with all
questions which came up between the provincial government and the
administration of the leased territory. In particular, the official would be
responsible for negotiating regulations governing the movement of
foreigners in and out of the interior.

The renewed unrest at Kao-mi which greeted Yuan when he arrived
in Shantung provided the new governor with an immediate opportunity
to apply his views on defending Chinese sovereignty in Shantung to the
problem of establishing a policy for dealing with the German economic
activities in the province. The approach Yuan developed proved to be a
continuation of that begun during the reform movement and side-
tracked by Yü-hsien. Thus, Yuan decided to concentrate on making the
Germans negotiate the regulations required by the Kiaochow Treaty.[140]
According to Yuan, these regulations should allow China "(1) to regain
sovereignty over land, (2) to regain power over profit, (3) to control [the
Germans], (4) to bring advantage to the people." [141]

From the beginning of January Yuan informed the Germans that the
only way to settle the unrest at Kao-mi and to assure peaceful operations
in the future was to agree on the regulations.[142] He repeatedly urged
Hildebrandt to come to Tsinan to begin the negotiations; and, as the
Germans grudgingly admitted, for the next two months he "adeptly
used" the unrest at Kao-mi as "a lever" to force the railroad manager to
comply.[143] In so doing he temporarily took the diplomatic initiative away
from the Germans, creating for the first time a situation in which Chinese
officials acted in Shantung and the Germans reacted.

Although Yuan's strategic goal was to engage in broad negotiations
at Tsinan, his immediate objective was to end the unrest at Kao-mi. He
felt that such antiforeign violence was useless and, in addition, was
anxious to display good will toward the Germans and forestall any
military intervention on their part. When the SEG requested military
aid in the beginning of January, Yuan immediately sent 300 troops.[144]
By the end of February there were over 1000 Chinese soldiers on the
scene.[145] When the original troops arrived, Jaeschke sent the governor
formal permission for them to enter the neutral zone.[146] Yuan replied
that this was not necessary because China retained sovereignty in the
fifty-kilometer zone. When Jaeschke heard that more Chinese soldiers
were coming, he protested. However, Yuan sent the troops anyway,

stating that he had already received permission earlier and that, in any case, the status of the neutral zone could not really be settled until an additional set of regulations was drawn up to clarify the relationship between Kiaochow and the province of Shantung.

At first, the Chinese troops at Kao-mi did not fight the bands of villagers who were causing the trouble.[147] Yuan said that the unrest resulted from the "backwardness and stupidity" of the people and that therefore the situation should be treated differently from one involving bandits.[148] "Naturally," the governor wrote, "one should not use troops to attack and suppress" those concerned. This attitude was partially responsible for his mildness toward the peasants. In addition, Yuan's policy was influenced by the position of the central government. During this period the government was becoming increasingly ambiguous about the advisability of popular attacks on foreigners,[149] and its attitude was reflected in the orders sent to Yuan. At the end of January, for example, the governor received two decrees which urged him to stop the unrest but which stressed that he was "not to harbor the idea that nothing is possible unless troops are used." [150]

Yuan's troops began to move more vigorously against the peasants in early February, when the attacks on the railway had increased in scope and the Germans were about to send an expedition to Kao-mi.[151] As a result, several clashes broke out between the Chinese units and the village bands.

In addition to deploying troops, Yuan Shih-k'ai tried to end the disturbances by mediating between the Germans and the villagers.[152] When the attacks began, he posted proclamations in the district which assured the people that the railroad would not cause floods and that, if flooding should occur by accident, he would memorialize the throne to grant a tax rebate to the area involved. The governor also sent a number of officials, including the Teng-lai-ch'ing taotai and the prefect of Lai-chou-fu, to speak with representatives of the railroad company at Kao-mi.

Yuan reported that, as a result of these talks, the Germans had agreed to change the route of the railway. The company's version of the conversations was that the railroad's representatives had simply cleared up the misrepresentations about the route spread by the district magistrate and had told the Chinese negotiators that the SEG would naturally build bridges wherever they were needed to avoid blocking water courses.[153] When the talks concluded, the results were communicated to the village heads involved. By the end of February such methods had dissipated most of the unrest.

Throughout the disturbances and the discussions at Kao-mi, Yuan never lost sight of his primary goal, protecting China's interests with regard to the railroad. Even after it began to look as if the unrest was quieting down, and the Germans wanted to resume operations, they were told by the local officials that the governor had ordered that the "railroad work should temporarily not continue." [154] When they asked why, the Germans were informed that this was "because at present there is no treaty between Germany and China which regulates the matter." As soon as Yuan heard that the Germans had capitulated and Hildebrandt had finally left Tsingtao for Tsinan, he telegraphed that work on the line could begin again south of Kao-mi city. "The resumption of work further north" would be "dependent on the negotiations . . . in Tsinan." [155] It was clear, as Jaeschke put it, that the governor was "not playing all his trumps at one time."

While Yuan was pressuring the Germans to send a representative to Tsinan, he began to make preparations for the forthcoming negotiations. He drafted three sets of regulations for discussion.[156] The first dealt with the railway and the second with the mines. The third consisted of the regulations governing intercourse between Kiaochow and the province, which Yuan had originally suggested in July and which would have established a Chinese official in the leasehold. Yuan lacked the leverage to make the Germans seriously consider this last set. Nevertheless, it was significant that he hoped to use the unrest at Kao-mi not only to restrict the Germans in the interior but also to launch an assault on the independence of their colony.

At this time, Yuan also began organizing a Chiao-she-chü (Provincial Foreign Office) to deal with the Germans. Yuan's earlier proposal for the use of expectant officials as special assistants for foreign affairs indicates that he had been considering establishing some provincial agency for this purpose. The governor probably got the idea of a Chiao-she-chü from Manchuria, where an office with that name had been established to deal with the Russians and their railway.[157] His problems in Shantung were analogous to those of Manchuria, and the Chiao-she-chü is first mentioned in the regulations which the governor drafted for his negotiations with Hildebrandt. Shantung was apparently the second province to set up a Chiao-she-chü, an institution which later became a common feature of provincial government all over China.

The basic reason why Yuan Shih-k'ai's policy toward the Germans succeeded was that, by the time he took office, both the German government and the SEG had become more willing to negotiate about the railroad with high Chinese officials. Their change of heart was bolstered by Yuan's adept diplomacy and by the respect which the Germans felt for the new governor and his modern army.

The SEG relaxed its opposition to negotiations because it faced serious losses from any further delays in the work.[158] The company could not hope for any return on its investment until the railway was in operation. Furthermore, it was particularly crucial to meet the construction schedule for the early part of 1900, because the bridges and dams on the section to Kao-mi had to be completed before the spring floods. Finally, the value of the company's property, which was subject to damage when disturbances did occur, had reached 4,500,000 marks by the beginning of 1900. It is not surprising, therefore, that throughout the crisis the SEG emphatically stressed that the "most important" thing was to end the unrest in order to permit the "immediate resumption of work."[159]

In its eagerness to restore order, the company was willing to have either Chinese or German troops subdue the populace. Therefore, as soon as the disturbances began, it requested Yuan to send provincial forces to Kao-mi. Indeed, the company was so anxious for order that it declared that the presence of these troops in the zone was "no cause for worry," a sentiment not shared by the navy.[160] Shortly thereafter, the SEG asked for German troops to defend the line, arguing that this was absolutely essential to restore peace and would "prove as useful as had the expeditions to Jih-chao . . . and to Kao-mi."[161]

In addition to its requests for troops, the company also tried to strengthen the system of local control established by the July agreement. It urged the magistrate of Kao-mi to send someone to Tsingtao to collect the money which the railroad owed to landowners along the route. It also got him to exhort "the peasants about the benefit of the railroad" and explain how "they could get a little work if they wanted."[162] At the same time, the SEG pointedly referred to the scale of indemnities which would be collected for any damage to the line and threatened to impose a new fine of $1000 for each day of delay, which would be deducted directly from the price of the land.[163] The company also willingly participated in the conciliatory discussions organized by the officials whom Yuan had sent.

The naval administration at Tsingtao was also more sympathetic toward negotiations, because it was no longer so willing as it had been in July to send German troops to put down unrest in the interior. Tirpitz' attitude was primarily responsible for this new restraint. Although Jaeschke was probably less reluctant to use German military power than the naval secretary, his letters now echoed his commander's arguments against the precipitous use of force.[164] The presence of Yuan's troops in Shantung, too, may heve helped to convince Jaeschke that Tirpitz' fear of war with China was justified. He pointed out that the possible result of German "military measures is now less clear than in the first Kao-mi expedition" [165] and explicitly said that "one cannot do anything with the one or two hundred men we can now spare for such purposes against the modern troops which Yuan Shih-k'ai has brought to the province." [166]

The navy's anxiety about the presence of Chinese troops in the neutral zone did, to some extent, counteract its reluctance to use German troops to defend the work there. Tirpitz, with his respect for Chinese military strength, was particularly concerned about the security problem posed by having Chinese troops so close to the border of the leasehold.[167] Jaeschke also felt that the presence of Chinese soldiers who were reluctant to use force might tempt the populace to attack the railroad.[168]

As a result of Jaeschke's newly acquired caution, the use of German troops was limited throughout the crisis. In the beginning of January he decided that his forces were not needed at Kao-mi because Yuan had sent provincial troops as the SEG had requested.[169] Even later in the month, when the Chinese soldiers appeared unwilling to fight the peasants, Jaeschke wrote that he was still not sending troops, "despite the request" for them by the railroad men on the scene.[170] Instead, he asked the German minister, von Ketteler, to have the Tsungli Yamen authorize Yuan to take strong action against the villagers.

It was not until early February, when the attacks on the construction headquarters reached their climax, that Jaeschke finally decided to use troops.[171] However, the expedition, which consisted of 120 marines, only advanced as far as Chiao-chou, which was about 18 miles short of Kao-mi, and it did not see action of any sort during its stay there. Its purpose was primarily to ensure that the unrest did not spread further into the fifty-kilometer zone in the direction of the leasehold and to force the Chinese troops at Kao-mi to move more vigorously against the peasants.[172] The marines may also have been sent to provide Hildebrandt with some leverage in his negotiations with Yuan, since they were definitely kept at Chiao-chou for that purpose once peace had been restored.[173] The troops finally withdrew on March 10, after Yuan made their departure one of the preconditions for the resumption of railroad construction north of Kao-mi.

Given their situations, the company and the navy had little choice but to comply with Yuan's demand for negotiations. Both Hildebrandt and

Jaeschke, as the men on the scene, realized this and quickly decided that Hildebrandt should go to Tsinan to meet with the Chinese governor.[174] They told Berlin that Yuan was intent on negotiating the regulations called for in Section II, Article 3, of the Kiaochow Treaty; and they maintained that, while this might create problems for the SEG, it was the only way to get peace for the railroad.

The SEG's directors in Berlin were, of course, equally disturbed about the construction delays. However, they still hoped to end the crisis without conceding expanded Chinese administrative influence over the railroad. From their vantage point in Germany, they still believed that "the relation between the German mines and railroad and the Chinese government should not be settled by a general agreement . . . but should be handled case by case." [175] The directors were particularly hostile to sending a representative of the company to Tsinan. Such a negotiator, they claimed, would "not have the weight" of a government representative and would be in a weak position in relation to Yuan Shih-k'ai. The company felt that, if negotiations proved unavoidable, they should take place at a governmental level in Peking, where presumably the Chinese side would be in the inferior position.

Minister Ketteler played a decisive role in convincing the Berlin office to allow Hildebrandt go to Tsinan. From his contacts with the Tsungli Yamen, the minister was convinced that the Chinese had no real desire to negotiate the regulations called for in the treaty. He reported to Berlin that Hildebrandt and Jaeschke had misinterpreted Yuan's request.[176] He claimed that Yuan only wanted to discuss ways of ending the disturbances in Shantung and pointed out that the authorities in Peking had "never orally or in writing" asked for regulations although they had had "an excellent opportunity to do so after giving the permission for the railroad materials to come in tariff free." Therefore, the minister recommended without reservation that Hildebrandt be sent to Tsinan. The Foreign Office agreed with him, and Bülow put pressure on the company to begin negotiations.[177]

Later, when Ketteler's interpretation of Yuan's demands proved to be incorrect, the company complained that the Tsungli Yamen had played a "double game" by not informing the minister of the governor's real goals.[178] It is more likely, however, that the Yamen simply did not appreciate what Yuan was trying to achieve, for at this time, of course, the central government did not have strong feelings about the need for regulations in Shantung. Indeed, it never mentioned them, even in dispatches to Yuan, until negotiations had already begun in Tsinan.[179] The

Yamen, therefore, probably felt sincerely, as it told Ketteler, that the restoration of order was the only goal which China sought, and it did not purposely mislead him about Yuan's intentions.

At the end of January the company finally authorized Hildebrandt's trip to Tsinan. However, it emphasized that he was only to seek a way to reopen work, adding, "The German minister does not think the Chinese government wants to settle Article 3. Do not negotiate on it." [180] When these orders reached Tsingtao, Hildebrandt and Jaeschke realized that they could not be carried out. As Jaeschke wrote, "It is clear that the negotiations in Tsinan will be worthless if Hildebrandt obeys his orders and refuses to negotiate the regulations as the governor wants." [181] He complained that the directors of the company in Berlin did "not at all understand" the German position in Shantung. "They feel," he wrote, "that they can press forward the railroad and mining work without any further concessions to the Chinese. Those times are past. The Chinese have had their bristles up since the treaty of concession. Unless the desires of the officials are met, they will continually create difficulties to prevent the treaty's implementation and bring the enterprises to a halt." [182]

Hildebrandt and Jaeschke, therefore, decided that Hildebrandt should go to Tsinan and submit the results of his negotiations to the company afterwards.[183] Just as he was about to depart, however, the unrest at Kao-mi reached its peak. The two Germans, therefore, began to have second thoughts about beginning the talks while the disturbances continued and work on the railroad was still halted.[184] They felt that this would provide Yuan with too much leverage. However, Yuan continued to maintain that there would be no further work without negotiations, thus leaving the Germans little choice.[185] Hildebrandt left Tsingtao on February 17, accompanied by Captain von Buttlar, whom Jaeschke had appointed to represent the government and act as Hildebrandt's military attaché. Jaeschke seemed to realize that the Chinese side had already won a diplomatic victory, for on the very day Hildebrandt set out for Tsinan, the governor wrote, "Our standing with the Chinese will suffer serious damage if we let their pressure force us into these negotiations." [186]

The directors in Berlin were dismayed when they learned what had happened. As they complained to Bülow, "We never expected that Hildebrandt was entering into negotiations after we explicitly instructed him not to do so." They pointed out that "we only sent him to Tsinan" to obtain the "speediest end of the unrest" current in Shantung[187] and added that it was particularly "damaging to our interests" that "negotiations began in Tsinan before the unrest was put down." They did not authorize Hildebrandt to negotiate regulations until it became clear to them that there was no other way to resume work and that the talks were well under way. But, even then, the company still "left it open completely to disavow" the regulations which emerged and to do so because of Hildebrandt's "violation of instructions in entering into negotiations." [188]

Hildebrandt and Buttlar arrived at Tsinan on February 27. Although the details of the negotiations are not available, real bargaining apparently took place, and each side had to make compromises.[189] Yuan had sent to Tientsin for Yin-ch'ang, a noted German specialist, because he wanted him to handle the negotiations for the Chinese side. The Germans liked Yin but reported that he was a skilled negotiator who got the best terms possible for his side.[190]

The crux of the negotiations was the question of how much authority the provincial government would exert over the railroad. Yuan reported that at first Hildebrandt tried to limit the scope of the new regulations to that of the July 2 agreement, but that this was rejected. Eventually, the governor wrote, the German agreed to "more than half" of the Chinese demands.[191] Among the stipulations which Hildebrandt refused were those which implied that the concession for the line was just being granted, and those which called for a tax on the company's profit. The regulations, consisting of 28 articles, were formally signed on March 21, and both sides seemed satisfied with the results.

The Germans were pleased because they gave up very little in order to secure peace for the line. The regulations only granted a modest amount of control over the railroad to the Chinese and did not alter the operation of the enterprise to any appreciable degree. Yuan was satisfied because, by merely signing the regulations, the company had acknowledged that the line was under Chinese jurisdiction. The powers which the province did receive, and the controls which the company accepted, also served to emphasize the fact that, outside the leasehold itself, the railroad operated under Chinese sovereignty.

The regulations themselves referred only briefly to the general status of the railway.[192] However, they did state explicitly that Chinese sovereignty prevailed along the line and provided, for the first time, for further agreements to determine when and under what conditions the Chinese government might take over the railway in the future. The agreement also reiterated that the line was to be controlled by a joint Sino-German company which would sell shares to both sides. The possibility of Chinese participation in the management of the firm was recognized by a stipulation which said that the company should "half-yearly notify the Chiao-she-chü at Tsinan of the number of shares purchased by Chinese. As soon as the amount of such shares has reached 100,000 taels, the governor of the province of Shantung shall delegate a Chinese official for cooperation" in the management. However, the regulations acknowledged that "for the present" the line would remain "exclusively under German management."

On the whole, the regulations retained the system of purchasing land established in the agreement of July 2, although the company was now considerably more restricted with regard to what land it could legitimately buy. The regulations required that "officials or respectable citizens" be "consulted upon the location of the railway, in order to take . . . into consideration the interests of the population." Furthermore, the railroad was not permitted "to damage or cut through city walls, fortifications, public edifices, and important inhabited places"; and, in so far as possible, it was to avoid houses, farms, villages, temples, and graves. In addition, the SEG was forbidden to buy "more land than necessary for the railway enterprise, and future extensions thereof." The regulations specified the maximum amount of land which could be bought for any single purpose. An official appointed by the governor was to be one of the Chinese representatives in the negotiations over the precise location of the line, and the agreed-upon route was not to be considered final until a detailed map had been sent to Tsinan for approval. In addition, the province received the right to collect taxes on the land owned by the railroad. However, this provision was somewhat vitiated by the stipulation that the taxes would be levied at the same rate as those charged for the land of the most favored railway in China.

In those articles concerning the security of the line and its personnel, Yuan was able to achieve some of his primary goals. Both Yuan and Chang Ju-mei had been worried about the problem of protecting railway employees who moved casually about the province. The regulations included a provision obliging such employees to carry the proper passes, a requirement which was strengthened by the added disclaimer that "Chinese local authorities cannot assume responsibility if such a passport is not produced." However, Yuan's greatest triumph was contained in the stipulation which said, "Troops eventually necessary for the protection of the railway will be stationed by the governor of the province of Shantung. Therefore, outside the 100-li [50-kilometer] neutral zone, no foreign troops shall be employed for this purpose . . . Development of trade and communications being the only purpose of the railway, no transport of foreign troops and their war materials shall be allowed on it." The company further agreed to pay part of the cost of the Chinese troops which were used to defend the railroad.

The articles dealing with the construction of the line were specifically designed to solve some of the problems which had already caused trouble. For example, they stipulated that "whenever watercourses are met, sufficient flow has to be provided by building bridges and culverts so that agriculture may suffer no damage." In addition, they repeatedly mentioned the obligation of the workmen on the line to treat the local population well and emphasized that no Chinese employee could enjoy extraterritorial privileges. Finally, the regulations included three separate articles which were meant to ensure that "the natives of towns and villages near the railroad shall be, as far as possible, engaged as workmen and as contractors for the supply of materials."

Additional regulations placed mild obligations on the actual operations of the company. The SEG promised that "freightage for foodstuffs and clothing to be distributed amongst the distressed during famines and floods shall be reduced . . . and when troops are dispatched to suppress rebellions, the same is to be applied to the fares for soldiers and to the freightages for their war materials." The company also agreed to help the customs service collect tariffs along the route. Finally, it promised to publish a detailed schedule of compensation for any accidents it might cause.

One notable omission in the regulations was the important question of the status of German and Chinese troops in the neutral zone. This issue was avoided probably because the navy did not want to bring it up. When Yuan had sent the second detachment of troops to Kao-mi, he had said that he had already obtained permission from Jaeschke and added that the status of the zone could not be settled finally until regulations were written concerning the relationship between the province and Kiaochow. The Germans were adamantly opposed to discussing such regulations. Therefore, they maintained that Yuan had given de facto recognition to the principle that German permission was required for Chinese troops to enter the zone, and they decided not to push the issue further.[193] Nevertheless, the navy remained unhappy about the Chinese troops stationed in the neutral zone,[194] a concern which may not have been completely unjustified. Yuan had no offensive plans in mind for his forces in the zone and the surrounding districts. However, he did feel that they were there not only to protect the railroad but also to deter the Germans from "too lightly considering entering the interior," and perhaps to oppose them if they did.[195]

The railroad agreement worked effectively throughout the spring of

1900.[196] Yuan nominated a taotai to act as railroad commissioner and also increased the number of troops guarding the work. In April, when it seemed as if trouble might break out again, the commissioner and the troops acted swiftly to repress the incipient unrest before it could seriously interfere with the railway construction. One of the measures taken by the Chinese authorities was to arrest the local leaders, Sun Wen and Li Chin-pang. The railroad work proceeded smoothly, and both Hildebrandt and Jaeschke concluded that their decision to negotiate regulations with Yuan had been fully justified.[197]

Mining

The same syndicate which was building the German railway in Shantung also received the mining concession there. In 1898 and 1899 the history of the mining enterprise and of the Chinese response to it closely paralleled that of the railway. The chief difference between the two during this period was that mining did not really advance beyond the preparatory stage.

On June 1, 1899, when the German government gave the railway concession to the syndicate, it also granted it a separate one for the mines.[198] The group was given the "exclusive right" for five years "to prospect for coal and other minerals as well as petroleum, and to claim mining fields by reason of finds made within an area extending thirty li to either side of the railway lines." At the end of that time the government could grant concessions to other groups. The government also reserved the power, under certain circumstances, to pre-empt any fields which the syndicate claimed but was not working.

The rest of the concession was similar to that for the railroad. It spelled out only the relationship between the concessionaire and the German government and completely ignored the Chinese authorities. As with the railroad, the syndicate hoped to keep the mines as free as possible of Chinese administrative control. The only reference to China in the mining concession was again the stipulation that the syndicate would organize a Sino-German company in which Chinese stockholders could participate. The concession gave administrative control of this company to Germans. It also established a scale of taxes which the firm would pay to the government at Tsingtao. In addition, the mining concessionaires were "bound when called upon . . . to satisfy out of the coal produced by them in the first instance the requirements of the imperial navy," and to sell this coal at "5 per cent below market price."

On October 10, 1899, the syndicate organized the Schantung Bergbau

Gesellschaft (Shantung Mining Company, or SBG) to exploit its concession.[199] The company was founded with a base capital of 12,000,000 marks. Its headquarters were in Berlin, but it established a branch office at Tsingtao, with Hermann Michaelis, a mining engineer with experience in China, as the field director.[200] Just as it had done with the railroad, the syndicate planned to use its own capital to develop the mining enterprise. Although the government and the firm paid some lip service to the need for including Chinese investors in the SBG,[201] during its early years no effort was made to sell stock to Chinese.[202]

Prospecting for promising locations had, of course, begun before the syndicate received its concession. However, after the SBG was organized, the other firms which were active in Shantung turned their mining operations over to it. During 1898 and 1899 German mining activities were centered on Wei-hsien, the coal area closest to Tsingtao, which the railroad would reach first.[203] It was here that Schmidt began prospecting shortly after the Kiaochow Treaty was signed. By early 1900 several seams of good-quality bituminous and anthracite coal had been discovered. However, their size and practicability for mining had still to be ascertained. Elsewhere the German engineers were not ready to begin test borings.

The local population was, on the whole, far less hostile toward the mines than toward the railway. During the early years there were no disturbances at Wei-hsien because of them. Even the local magistrate, who had objected to Schmidt's presence, reported that the German paid "a fair and just price" for the land which he purchased, and that the Chinese sellers were "satisfied." [204] The situation at Wei-hsien remained quiet even after a major accident occurred in which the large wooden derrick used for the test borings collapsed, injuring several Chinese workmen.[205] At I-chou, where there was less actual mining activity, the German engineers were, of course, caught up in the disturbances of early 1899, but these were not aimed primarily at them.

The Germans maintained that the SBG had no trouble with the local population because mining activity was nothing new in Shantung and the people were used to it.[206] This was probably true, and, in fact, at both Wei-hsien and I-chou Western machinery had been employed before the Germans arrived.[207] Another reason for the good relations was simply that, during the unstable years from 1898 to 1900, German mining operations were on a relatively small scale.

The same fluctuations in policy manifested themselves in the behavior of the Tsinan government toward German mining as toward the railroad. Thus, Yü-hsien's arrival marked the abandonment of Chang

Ju-mei's concern with the miners. The only action Yü may have taken with regard to them was his attempt to ban the activity of all German engineers in retaliation for the Jih-chao episode.

During Yü's tenure, however, Chang Ju-mei's appeal to Chinese merchants to open mines finally met with some response. In the fall of 1899 two Wei-hsien merchants reported that, in answer to the earlier appeal, they were investing 12,000 taels to reopen an old coal mine at Fang-tzu, less than a mile from the spot where the Germans were carrying out their tests.[208] This mine, known as the Ting-chia-ching, had originally been established in 1890 by a former governor, Chang Yao, and had been closed because of difficulties with the local population rather than because its ore had given out. It still contained some modern equipment which, however, was not in working order. By 1900 the mine was back in partial operation.

Except for the Ting-chia-ching group, very few people, if any, responded to Chang's appeal. One of the merchants at Wei-hsien probably pinpointed the cause of this apathy when he complained that it was difficult to raise capital for mining in Shantung because "the atmosphere" of the province was "unenlightened" and the people there did not appreciate the value of modern mines.[209] In general, at least until 1905, nationalistically oriented officials were more concerned about German economic encroachments in Shantung than were the local gentry or merchants; and, in contrast to the situation in a number of other provinces, these officials led the fight to restrict the foreigners and to protect Chinese interests.

In addition, while Yü was governor, a significant initiative to keep the valuable mine field at I-hsien under Chinese control was taken by an outside group. I-hsien was perhaps the most important coal field in Shantung which had not been included in the original German concession; but it was now threatened by the proposed route of the Tientsin-Chinkiang line. In 1879 Li Hung-chang had begun a mining enterprise there which had been operated jointly by local officials and the viceroy's office. In 1896 Li Ping-heng closed the mines, using as a pretext a serious accident which had occurred. In 1899 the former managers reopened the work in order to forestall a German move into the field. To guarantee that the Germans would have no excuse for interference with the enterprise, it was incorporated into a new company, the Sino-German Restoration Mining Company, which was capitalized at 2,000,000 taels. Although 40 per cent of the stock was officially set aside for Germans and 60 per cent for Chinese, the company was and remained a purely Chinese enterprise. No shares were ever offered for sale to Germans, and the "German" director of the company turned out to be Li's old assistant, Gustav Detring.[210]

When Yuan Shih-k'ai became governor in late 1899, he decided to force the SBG to agree to mining regulations. He repeatedly mentioned the need for such regulations when he urged Hildebrandt to come to Tsinan in early 1900. However, since the Germans were more concerned about the railway and the unrest at Kao-mi, they tended to ignore these parts of Yuan's notes. Thus it would appear that when Hildebrandt set out, he did not fully realize that Yuan was also interested in discussing mining regulations.[211]

There are indications that the Germans had tried earlier to make the same sort of limited and local agreement for the mining as they had for the SEG.[212] Nevertheless, when Yuan presented the draft of his mining regulations to Hildebrandt, the director agreed to discuss them on behalf of the SBG. This decision seems to have been almost a matter of course. Once the Germans decided to yield to Yuan on the question of railway regulations, they probably considered a similar accommodation on mining a logical extension of their decision. The mining regulations, which consisted of twenty articles, were also signed on March 21.[213] They were not considered final, however, until Michaelis approved them for the SBG.[214]

The regulations were essentially the same as those for the railway and, for the most part, were couched in the identical words. The same rules were established for eventual Chinese participation in the enterprise, for the security of the work and its personnel, and for the protection of the interests of the local population. Perhaps to balance the company's pledge to sell coal cheaply to the German navy, the Germans also agreed to sell it at reduced prices to persons living near the mines.

The system for the purchase of land was also similar to that of the railway, though some elaborations were introduced to adapt it to mining. The key addition was the stipulation that "the surface land above subterranean works need not be purchased by the company" and that "no compensation" would go to a landowner "for coal and other minerals raised by the mining company" so long as his land was not disturbed.

The regulations also contained several clauses dealing with the status of Chinese mines which already existed within the thirty-li zone. There were several crucial differences between the Chinese and the German texts of these sections of the agreement.[215] According to the German text, Chinese mines in the zone were entitled to continue work but were not permitted to alter or modernize their mode of operations. If an existing

Chinese mine endangered a German shaft, the SBG was authorized to buy it, and if the owners refused to sell, the company could "appeal to the district magistrate for intervention." The SBG was also allowed to purchase any other mine within the zone which the Chinese owners were willing to sell. If they wanted, the owners were "at liberty to ask for shares of the Shantung Mining Company" as payment. The Chinese text omitted the clause saying that Chinese mines within the zone could not alter their mode of operation. In addition, the Chinese text was highly ambiguous about the status of Chinese mines which were close to German ones. It was not clear whether the Chinese owners could ever be compelled to sell such mines, even if the Germans claimed that their operations endangered a shaft of the SBG.

The textual discrepancies represented an attempt on Yuan's part to protect Chinese mining enterprises within the thirty-li zone, such as the reopened operation at Fang-tzu. Yuan may also have had a broader goal in mind. For, in later years, the differences between the Chinese and German texts provided a perfect, legal basis for the Chinese drive to get rid of the German monopoly in the thirty-li zone.

While the SBG prepared to exploit the mining concessions which the Germans had received in the Kiaochow Treaty, another German syndicate made a determined effort to use the Reich's position in Shantung to expand these privileges.[216] In the spring of 1899 the important commercial firm of Arnhold, Karberg and Company, acting on behalf of the new group, petitioned the K'uang-lu-chü for the exclusive right to search for minerals in five large zones not included in the original concession. The five zones were as follows: (1) the half of I-chou Prefecture which lay to the east of the I River, (2) a circle around the town of I-shui with a 36-mile radius, (3) the triangle of territory formed by a line from Tsingtao to Chu-ch'eng to Jih-chao, (4) a circle with a radius of 15 miles in the southwestern part of Wei-hsien, (5) a semicircle with a 21-mile radius centered on Chefoo.

Arnhold, Karberg and Company asked the K'uang-lu-chü to grant it the right to survey the areas for a year and to extend this time limit automatically if that should prove necessary. The company wished to retain the sole right to search for mining sites in the five zones while it was prospecting, though existing mines could continue to operate. Although the Germans promised to include Chinese shareholders in the enterprise so that the regulations established by the K'uang-lu-chü would not be violated, the bureau rejected the German request.[217]

Shortly thereafter, the K'uang-lu-chü, an institution which remained comparatively loyal to the spirit of the reform movement which had established it, strengthened China's position against the German demands by issuing four supplemental mining regulations.[218] The regulations were probably not promulgated simply because of the new German demands in Shantung, although they did deal with the problems posed by these requests. Two of them strengthened the requirements for Chinese participation in mining operations. The other two were even more directly related to the new German demands, for they set definite limits on the scope of future mining concessions.

One regulation pointed out that previously when companies had wanted mining concessions, they had "only vaguely" indicated their desire for "such-and-such prefectures, or such-and-such districts of a province, without indicating clearly certain places in certain districts." In the future, therefore, "each applicant for permission to conduct mining operations must specify a certain place in a certain district, and will not be allowed to indicate several places at the same time, or to indicate vaguely a whole prefecture or a whole district." The other regulation described how companies had formerly sought indefinite and monopolistic control over large pieces of territory by obtaining permission to mine them, but then they had not actually begun operations. The new rule attacked this practice by specifying that once a company had received permission to mine a certain site, it would have to start work within ten months. "If this period is exceeded without operations having begun, the sanction given shall be canceled," the regulation concluded.

After it had failed to obtain the mining concession which it wanted, the syndicate asked the German government for support. In August, Ketteler forwarded the request of Arnhold, Karberg and Company to the Tsungli Yamen.[219] The Yamen said that, as they stood, the company's plans violated the new regulations and could not be accepted.[220] However, its position was not so firm as that of the K'uang-lu-chü, and it held out the possibility that some arrangement might be reached which would grant the syndicate a more limited concession in accord with Chinese law. Negotiations over the German demands then began between Ketteler and the Tsungli Yamen and the K'uang-lu-chü.[221] The Chinese appeared willing to let Arnhold, Karberg and Company select one zone and examine it for ten months. Only if this site proved unusable could the Germans pick a second area and investigate it for the same length of time. The Chinese negotiators also wanted assurances that the operations would not be under foreign control. On his side, Ketteler sought to obtain for the syndicate the immediate, long-term, and exclusive right to the five zones. Despite the considerable distance between the two bargaining positions, the negotiations were making progress when they were broken off without a final agreement in June 1900 because of the Boxer Rebellion and the death of the German minister.

During this period the syndicate did not begin any operations in Shantung. However, in April 1900 the group felt that the discussions had made sufficient headway for it to organize the Deutsche Gesellschaft für Bergbau und Industrie im Auslande (German Company for Foreign Mining and Industry, or DGBIA) to take up the concession when it was obtained.[222]

The Boxer Rebellion

Just as the agreements between Tsinan and the SEG and the SBG went into effect, the Boxer Rebellion reached its peak in North China. The government's support for the Boxers represented the ultimate triumph of militant conservatism. Within Shantung, however, primarily because of Yuan's basic opposition to this point of view, the impact of the events of the neighboring provinces was comparatively slight both in terms of lives lost and property destroyed. Nevertheless, Shantung was not entirely spared, and the unrest which did occur had a significant impact on the German position in the province.

After his arrival in Shantung in late 1899, Yuan Shih-k'ai had managed to suppress the Boxer movement there. He did this by tightening the systems of local control, using moral suasion, and, where necessary, military force; and his success, even against so fervent an antiforeign movement, is a further indication of the influence which high officials could have on this type of local disorder. Suppressed in Shantung, Boxers began to appear in Chihli and other neighboring provinces to the north and west. By the spring of 1900 they were active in many parts of the countryside, killing Christians and destroying Western property. At the same time the militant faction in Peking was becoming more and more sympathetic to them.

By the end of May, the uprising reached its critical phase. On May 28 the foreign diplomats in Peking, fearful of the Boxer bands surrounding the capital, sent for additional marines from the coast to act as legation guards. The marines arrived on June 3. On June 10 a major expedition of about 2000 men set out from Tientsin for Peking under the British admiral, Seymour. In response, the Chinese government began to support the Boxers openly, and the crisis quickly escalated. Bands of Boxers entered Peking and Tientsin, the foreign ships on the coast fired on and took the Taku forts, and government troops helped the Boxers drive

Seymour back to Tientsin. On June 20, Minister Ketteler was killed in Peking, and the famous siege of the legations began. The next day China declared war on the powers. In the meantime, the antiforeign rampage in the countryside continued, and by August a large number of Chinese Christians and missionaries had been killed, many of them in Shansi where Yü-hsien was governor.

The powers responded to the crisis by preparing a relief force on the coast to raise the sieges of Tientsin and Peking and to quiet the unrest. On July 14 Tientsin was taken, and on August 14 the allied forces entered Peking. The empress dowager and the emperor fled to Sian, and the height of the Boxer crisis was over. However, foreign troops continued to arrive, and by late 1900 there were about 45,000 of them in North China, in addition to the Russian forces which had occupied Manchuria.

Shantung remained calm well after the violence in the north had broken out.[223] When the diplomats requested marines at the end of May, Ketteler asked Berlin to send the German contingent from Tsingtao.[224] Foreign Secretary Bülow agreed, noting that the Germans had successfully "restored order to what concerns us the most, the province of Shantung," and that therefore troops could be spared for use in the north even though Germany had few interests there.[225] On May 29 a detachment of 51 marines left Tsingtao. They arrived in Peking with the other reinforcements in the beginning of June and remained there throughout the siege of the legations.[226]

For most of June Shantung remained quiet, and the Germans continued to feel that it was safe to contribute troops from Tsingtao to the allied expedition in Chihli. On June 8, 25 additional marines from the garrison were sent north, followed by 240 more on the nineteenth. As late as June 23, Jaeschke could still note that the quiet in the province was evidence that the system of security established in the spring was a success. "If Yuan Shih-k'ai keeps the peace so well even in this troubled period," the Kiaochow governor wrote, "then one must say he is . . . in favor of upholding the railroad regulations." [227]

Yuan himself was, indeed, doing his utmost to keep order in Shantung. In June, Peking repeatedly asked him to send soldiers north to help fight the foreigners. Yuan declined to send more than token forces, arguing among other things that he needed his troops to prevent violence against the German activities in Shantung.[228] The governor's response was primarily an effort to keep from becoming involved in the fiasco which the conservatives were brewing. However, Yuan's argument also reflected an accurate understanding of the dangers which would arise if unrest again broke out against the Germans in the interior or even against Kiaochow itself.

The tranquillity of Shantung was shattered in the last week of June. In various parts of the province missionaries were threatened and some even assaulted. At Wei-hsien both the American Presbyterian mission and the German mining activities were attacked. At Chiao-chou and Kao-mi there was renewed violence against the railroad. These disturbances were the most serious experienced by the German enterprises. Not only was work disrupted, but employees of the two companies, both Chinese and German, were physically assaulted. Hildebrandt, who was in the Kao-mi area when the unrest began, was himself attacked by a local armed band.[229]

Neither the Boxers nor any other outside group incited the renewed violence in these areas. Rather, it was organized by local people whose longstanding antiforeign grievances provided a motive for action in response to the news that the conservatives were in power in Peking and were beginning an onslaught against Westerners. The center of the violence against the German activities was once again in the Kao-mi region, where the rising was led by the followers of the imprisoned Sun Wen, who had organized the earlier anti-German movement there.[230] Occasionally, as in a few instances at Kao-mi, provincial troops made common cause with the local population. But, on the whole, the Chinese military forces remained under Yuan's control. The governor's basic method for handling the unrest was first to ensure the safety of the foreigners by getting them out of the interior and then to protect the Western property left behind and deal with the local ringleaders.[231]

The immediate German response to the renewed outbreaks was to rush to the aid of the Westerners who were endangered. On June 26 a group of about thirty naval and civilian volunteers left Tsingtao to rescue the missionaries and mining engineers at Wei-hsien.[232] On June 28, Jaeschke also sent the Chinese company toward Wei-hsien and the next day followed it with troops from the III Marine Battalion. Yuan immediately asked Jaeschke to halt the advance of these troops at Chiao-chou since their presence farther inland might exacerbate the unrest.[233] The Chinese governor promised to defend all foreigners with his own troops. At the same time he urged Jaeschke to have the SEG and the SBG suspend their operations and evacuate their personnel to the leasehold until peace was restored.

Jaeschke, trusting in Yuan's "goodwill," ordered his troops to remain at Chiao-chou for the time being. At the same time, and upon orders from home, he made it clear to Yuan that the Kiaochow administration was concerned not only about the fate of German citizens in the immediate vicinity of the leasehold but also about that of every Westerner in the province. For a short time Jaeschke also tried to convince Yuan that it would be best if foreigners stayed in the interior under Chinese protection. He argued that if the Westerners came to the coast their work would be delayed and their property destroyed. Yuan responded that the primary goal was to save lives, and only if the foreigners withdrew could he guarantee their safety and probably even save their property. However, Yuan stressed, he did not have the forces to protect normal business operations, and he implored Jaeschke to make the Germans stop work and go to Tsingtao. Convinced by Yuan's argument, on July 1 Jaeschke ordered the SEG and the SBG once again to suspend their activities beyond Chiao-chou and to have their employees return to Kiaochow. He also told missionaries to come to Tsingtao if they felt threatened. Meanwhile, the German troops remained at Chiao-chou in order to preserve order on the borders of the leasehold and to be ready to move farther if the need arose.[234]

The missionaries and engineers at Wei-hsien had been planning to leave even before they heard from Jaeschke.[235] On July 2 they reached Chiao-chou safely, escorted by provincial troops and the German volunteers whom they had encountered en route. The railroad workers from beyond Chiao-chou also headed for the leasehold, and soon missionaries from all over the province began to arrive at Tsingtao.[236] Apparently, during the summer of 1900 not a single foreigner lost his life in Shantung.[237] In comparison with the events in the north, therefore, the disruption and inconvenience suffered by the Westerners in Shantung was rather mild.

Once the railway and mine workers had withdrawn, Yuan began to carry out his promises to Jaeschke. Chinese troops were sent to guard the abandoned installations.[238] In the Kao-mi region the provincial forces began to round up the local groups which had caused the unrest. Sun Wen, already in jail, was executed, and Li Chin-pang and some of the other leaders of the uprising were exiled.[239] Nevertheless, the disturbances in the Kao-mi area continued.

The third suspension of railroad construction in a year began to convince the Germans that the work would never be able to progress without interruptions unless it was under the protection of German troops. In a letter which Hildebrandt wrote to Jaeschke after the governor had told the SEG to suspend operations, the director, who had negotiated and championed the agreement of March 21, launched a strong attack on

Yuan and the dependability of his troops.[240] Hildebrandt began by saying that Yuan's request for a work stoppage amounted to an "empty evasion" of the real problems; he then proceeded to ridicule the effectiveness of the Chinese governor's guarantee to protect foreigners traveling to the coast and to defend the property left behind. Hildebrandt said that at Kao-mi the troops "not only did not defend our engineers but actually participated in the plundering of them and . . . in the attacks" upon them. Referring to his own experience, Hildebrandt continued sarcastically, "If Governor Yuan again telegraphs that what he most fears is that lives are endangered, we would like to ask him, how could the luggage of the engineers be attacked only two kilometers from Kao-mi on the same day on which it was being accompanied by 20 soldiers and while there were 500 well-armed troops back in Kao-mi? Why did these troops do nothing to protect us, despite the fact that two hours earlier we had asked the yamen in Kao-mi for protection? And why did our escorts shoot at our men . . . and then that night in Kao-mi divide up 3000 taels of silver which they had stolen?" The director demanded that Jaeschke send an "exemplary punitive expedition against the town of Kao-mi and the villages involved" and that railroad work be reopened immediately under the protection of naval troops. These were the only actions, he claimed, which would keep the Germans from losing face and enable construction to proceed without hindrance.

In Berlin the directors of the SEG made similar demands on the navy and the Foreign Office.[241] They emphasized that unless work resumed, the SEG would have to avail itself of the escape clause in its concession which gave the company the right to postpone the completion of the line if unforeseen circumstances arose. This was a potent way to get the naval administration to help the line, since Tirpitz felt that the economic potential of Kiaochow could not be realized until the railroad was built.

Although Jaeschke was more reluctant to use German troops than was Hildebrandt, it was clear that the renewed violence had removed some of his inhibitions. When the unrest in Shantung began, Jaeschke requested the return of the troops he had sent north so that they would be on hand to defend the leasehold and protect German interests in the interior.[242] He insisted that Yuan was doing his utmost to put down the unrest, and he continued to mention Tirpitz' warning against the precipitous use of force in the interior.[243] However, he wrote to the naval secretary that the current unrest, "the third and most serious disturbance to the work," was "a great blow" for the colony and would "set back its development." [244] He said that he hoped to rely on Yuan to defend German interests but added, "If the governor's goodwill does not continue, or his power is insufficient to put down the unrest, there will be no choice left to me but to move against the disturbed areas with all the strength at my command." [245] Since Yuan had made it clear that he could not protect the railroad's normal operations, Jaeschke's position was rather ambiguous.

As the violence continued, Jaeschke also became increasingly worried about the presence of Chinese troops in the neutral zone. In his letter to Tirpitz the governor described his fear that the Chinese forces in the zone "would immediately make common cause with the rebels against us" if Germany sent troops into the interior. A few days later he reported that "Yuan increases his troops at Wei-hsien and Kao-mi and is making preparations to send them toward Kiaochow. He could be doing this to stop the spread of the rebellion, but I cannot trust him and must consider the possibility that he is marching his troops up quietly in order to attack us overwhelmingly with the soldiers and the people." [246]

Because of his concern for the railroad and for the security of the neutral zone, in early July Jaeschke agreed to let naval troops protect the construction work between the borders of the leasehold and Chiao-chou. [247] The detachment based at Chiao-chou began patrolling the area, and on July 10 work on this section resumed.

Significantly, Tirpitz did not try to dissuade Jaeschke from helping the company in the interior. In addition, later in the month he himself wrote the directors of the SEG in Berlin to say that the navy was eager to do everything possible to make certain that the railroad work proceeded smoothly. [248] The admiral even gave the directors confidential military information about German troops headed for China which might be used to defend the line if necessary. The SEG continued to urge more massive action [249] and, perhaps to keep up the pressure on the navy, notified the government in early August that the firm would not be able to finish the railroad on time because of the continued interruptions. [250]

The navy adopted a more militant policy in Shantung not only because of the situation there but also because it was forced to do so in order to withstand the pressure for an even more aggressive position which developed in Germany during the summer of 1900. The Boxer Rebellion and the murder of Ketteler aroused many Germans to demand vigorous action against China. One outcome of this was the decision to send a great punitive expedition to China to form part of the allied forces. Eventually about 10,000 German troops went to China under the overall command of Field Marshal von Waldersee, although rather embarrassingly neither the field marshal nor his troops arrived in China in time to take part in the march to Peking.

The proponents of strong action in China discovered that the sphere of influence in Shantung constituted one of the ideal arenas for Germany's revenge; for there, retribution against the Middle Kingdom could be combined with the support and expansion of German interests.[251] The kaiser himself was one of the most fervent advocates of responding massively to the Boxer Rebellion and of doing so on a large scale in Shantung. Toward the middle of July, when the Berlin government became afraid that the German expeditionary force might get involved in a Russo-Japanese confrontation in Chihli, Wilhelm contributed the suggestion that the expedition be diverted from Chihli to Shantung, where it could "busy itself with the complete cleansing and subjugation of Kiaochow and its hinterland." [252] Bülow went along with the kaiser's proposal to send the forces to Tsingtao.[253] The army also agreed and made plans to have Kiaochow declared in a state of war in order to maximize the colony's effectiveness as a base for military operations.[254] Shortly afterwards, the kaiser spelled out his idea more specifically by calling for a grand "expedition into the interior" of Shantung "which would bring the engineers and missionaries back and which would restore peace and order to the hinterland by the energetic punishment of those who caused trouble, as well as by the occupation of the most important places, such as Tsinan." [255] Many of the kaiser's arguments for such action were of the sort calculated to appeal to Tirpitz. Wilhelm stressed how many troops Yuan Shih-k'ai had in Shantung and the threat which these forces posed for Kiaochow. He also pointed out that if Germany did not live up to its obligation to protect the Steyl Mission, the government "would lose the Catholic voices of the Center which are fairly certain for us on external matters now and whose support is needed for appropriations next year."

Tirpitz, however, did not share the hysteria which seemed to grip the kaiser and the other advocates of a punitive adventure in China. Indeed, he was one of the few German military leaders who questioned the whole idea of sending a large expeditionary force to China[256] and, after it arrived, worked to keep the influence of it and its commander on Shantung to a minimum. Though Tirpitz was willing to undertake military action to protect the railroad and pacify the neutral zone, he was opposed to any broader adventures in the province and tried, on the whole with success, to thwart them. Naturally he was opposed to the kaiser's proposals.[257] He was particularly concerned about the damage a major military expedition in the province might do to Germany's long-term economic interests there. For example, he used this argument to combat the plan to declare Kiaochow in a state of war. "One could expect," he wrote, "a complete paralysis of the flowering commerce of the colony for whose growth the government and private persons have for years sacrificed much. Until now, in agreement with the Foreign Office, I have done all in my power to indicate to . . . business and commercial interests that everything would be done to avoid having the current crises in China result in deleterious influences on the peaceful economic development of the colony," which, the admiral stressed, "was, after all, the real reason for its acquisition." He warned that if Kiaochow was declared to be at war, experience showed that "the economic stagnation would not only last during the military operations but . . . also for a long time afterwards, and that other competing commercial centers on the China coast would make use of the situation." [258] In order to prevent the adoption of an aggressive policy in Shantung, Tirpitz stressed how peaceful the province was and how good Kiaochow's relations were with Yuan Shih-k'ai, an assessment which the kaiser, certainly aware of the navy's activities on the scene, considered "definitely too optimistic and not in accord with reality." [259]

With the belated support of Bülow,[260] the navy's position prevailed, and the calls for expansion in Shantung which continued to come from military and colonialist groups had no effect. Many of the troops from the German expeditionary force did land in Tsingtao on their way north, but they apparently did not take part in the navy's actions in the interior.

These actions increased as the summer progressed. In August and September naval troops circulated freely around the districts near the leasehold, patrolling the railway and moving against suspected concentrations of "Boxers." The Germans continued to hold Chiao-chou and, temporarily, occupied Chi-mo, whose magistrate was not considered to be sufficiently energetic in suppressing antiforeign activity in his area. In early September there were a few clashes between German troops and local people. However, on the whole, the districts of Chiao-chou and Chi-mo, where the Germans were, remained peaceful, and the railroad work proceeded without difficulty. There was some continued unrest at Kao-mi. But even there, perhaps because the foreigners were gone or because of the efforts of the Chinese troops, it was comparatively quiet. Nevertheless, construction work on the railroad did not resume beyond Chiao-chou.[261]

By early October, Jaeschke decided to use German troops to reopen the work in the rest of the neutral zone and at the same time to estab-

lish formally German military control over the area.[262] Jaeschke's immediate decision was probably stimulated not only by the progress of the
railroad construction in the areas near the leasehold but also by Waldersee's arrival in China. Jaeschke went to Tientsin to see the field marshal,
and it was "in agreement" with him that the plans for action in the
zone were completed.[263] These called not only for protection of the railroad and the long-term occupation of Chiao-chou and Kao-mi but also
for punitive expeditions against the villages which had been involved
in the unrest.[264] It was just such reprisals that the SEG had demanded
and Jaeschke had previously rejected. Punitive expeditions were to become Waldersee's hallmark in Chihli, and he may have helped to convince Jaeschke that they were a good idea.

On October 7, Jaeschke telegraphed Yuan from Tientsin announcing
that the railroad work in Kao-mi would resume immediately under the
protection of German troops.[265] He declared that the fifty-kilometer zone
would henceforth be under German military control and requested the
Chinese governor to remove all his forces from the area by October 12.
Jaeschke further stated that the Germans wanted to reopen mining operations at Wei-hsien as soon as possible, although he indicated that
there, beyond the zone, the Chinese authorities could provide security.

In the fall of 1900 China's fortunes were at their nadir, and Yuan had
no way to resist Jaeschke's demands. Therefore, he quickly telegraphed
compliance.[266] On October 10, Chinese troops began to withdraw from
Kao-mi and the zone. These changes in the military status of the zone
took place without any real negotiations. However, the navy decided that
Jaeschke's exchange of telegrams with Yuan constituted a further "agreement" [267] between the provincial government and the Germans, which,
by clarifying the status of the neutral zone, perfected the agreement of
March 21 but did not violate it. When Yuan reported the matter to
Peking, he took the same position, perhaps because he was not eager to
underline the fact that he had made a concession or that his earlier success had not been complete. The governor glossed over the difference
between the fifty-kilometer zone and the leasehold by reporting that the
Germans were reopening work "within the borders" under the protection
of German troops, but that "in the interior" he would continue to provide security for the German activities.[268]

In the middle of October a strong detachment of naval troops arrived
at Kao-mi and also began to patrol the roadbed of the SEG where construction work had been resumed.[269] In late October and early November
the German forces began to move against the villages accused of having
been implicated in the earlier violence.[270] The Germans disarmed the

inhabitants and razed the village walls. Several places offered resistance and had to be taken by force. The efforts of the peasants to defend themselves resulted only in a one-sided slaughter. Between 200 and 400 Chinese lost their lives, while the German casualties consisted of only a few injuries and no deaths.[271] After the pacification campaign ended, the Germans continued to occupy Chiao-chou and Kao-mi, which remained their chief bases for the control of the fifty-kilometer zone and the protection of the railroad.

The navy had not been planning automatically to extend the protection of the railway line beyond the zone. However, in view of the difficulties which had plagued the work, a strong possibility existed that it might have to do so. To provide for this eventuality, the navy and the SEG directors reached an agreement on the future military protection of the line.[272] In the settlement the SEG promised to construct all the larger stations on the route to Tsinan in a way which would enable them to be used to quarter troops and be easily defended.

The Boxer episode officially came to an end in Shantung in early 1901 when Yuan Shih-k'ai concluded the formal arrangements for indemnifying the foreigners in the province. The indemnities to the Germans, while certainly inflated, turned out to be considerably lower than had been expected. This was because Yuan had been surprisingly successful in keeping his promise to protect foreign property. The SEG and the SBG received a total of 120,000 taels and the German missionaries something over 40,000 taels. In order to spare the provincial treasury and to punish the gentry and population for their actions, Yuan apparently collected the money for the reparations directly from the areas involved in the unrest.[273]

V. The Disintegration of the Sphere of Influence

The Bases of Disintegration

In the years from the acquisition of Kiaochow to the Boxer Rebellion, the Germans had considerable, though not unmixed, success in their efforts to obtain economic and political power in Shantung. However, between 1900 and 1907 it became clear that Germany would never achieve the goals it had originally sought in Shantung, and, indeed, during these years the province ceased to be a German sphere of influence. This occurred partially because international and domestic pressures kept the German government from pursuing its claims. Equally important, China, increasingly nationalistic after the Boxer Rebellion, strove to eradicate Germany's influence in the province.

In the years after 1900 the overall international situation directly curtailed German activities in Shantung because the growing diplomatic isolation of the Reich meant that Germany could not afford to antagonize other powers unnecessarily. In particular, as Germany's international position deteriorated and, especially, as her portentous split with Great Britain widened, Berlin feared that any attempt to exclude other nations from Shantung would invite retaliation elsewhere in China. Germans had extensive business interests throughout China, and they became particularly concerned lest a stress on Germany's special position in the relatively poor province of Shantung lead to the loss of privileges elsewhere, particularly in the rich Yangtze Valley where England predominated. The Foreign Office had generally been more willing than the navy to subordinate Germany's goals in Shantung to the Reich's broader interests in China and elsewhere. Therefore, first the Wilhelmstrasse and then the government as a whole not only denied that Ger-

140

many had a special position in Shantung but also came to believe that Germany could no longer treat the province as its sphere.

During the Boxer Rebellion there were some important early signs of these new attitudes. Both Tirpitz and Bülow, in opposing extreme German countermeasures in Shantung, argued that an overly aggressive policy in the province might result in the break-up of China and, hence, endanger German interests in the Yangtze. This fear was shared by some of the major figures in the Foreign Office, including Holstein, who had originally used the same argument to oppose the whole idea of obtaining a German sphere of influence in Shantung.[1] It was partially for this reason, therefore, that during the summer of 1900 Holstein suggested that the Reich should reach an understanding with England which would ensure German access to the Yangtze Valley regardless of the eventual effect of the rebellion on Chinese unity.

The result of Holstein's proposal was the so-called Yangtze Agreement of October 1900.[2] This treaty committed Germany and England to maintain the open door for "all Chinese territory as far as they can exercise influence." The Germans signed the agreement because they sought to guarantee their access to the Yangtze; and the English were willing to give this assurance because in exchange they hoped to win German support against Russia's annexationist moves in North China. The text did not mention Shantung, and neither side was primarily concerned about the relationship between the agreement and Germany's privileges in the province. Nevertheless, the treaty was a harbinger of the future.

Early 1902 marked the first crucial turning point in the evolution of the new German approach to Shantung. For at this time both the Foreign Office and the chancellor began to move significantly closer to a public renunciation of a German sphere of influence in the province. In addition, it was during this period that the Wilhelmstrasse, with its tendency to de-emphasize Shantung's importance, triumphed in a drive to take the control of German activity in the interior away from the navy.

The Anglo-Japanese Alliance, signed on January 30, 1902, was primarily responsible for precipitating these changes. The alliance was not directed against Germany but against Russia.[3] Nevertheless, by underlining the fact that England had selected another country rather than Germany as her main ally in the Far East, the alliance symbolized the growing tension between England and the Reich. The early part of 1902 also witnessed a surge of anti-German feeling in Britain, highlighted by a great press campaign against the Reich. The hostility in England was the result of a number of issues, including the naval race and the Boer

War, as well as the failure of the efforts of the two nations to form a united front against Russia in the Far East. The German claims in Shantung constituted one of the readily available targets for the British, and the press campaign included articles attacking Germany's dominance in the province. The issue even reached the floor of Parliament, where the foreign secretary was quizzed about the fact that "the German government" was "endeavoring to secure exclusive administrative and commercial privileges in the Chinese province of Shantung." [4]

Such attacks coupled with the general British hostility toward the Reich caused considerable anxiety in Berlin over the possibility that Germany might be excluded from the Yangtze Valley. As a result the Foreign Office initiated a campaign to convince England, the United States, and the other trading powers that Germany had re-evaluated its special claims in Shantung and did not plan to enforce them.[5] For example, in February the Foreign Office presented the United States with an important memorandum which subscribed to the open door in Shantung in a broader and more precise form than Germany had done before.[6] In March, Chancellor Bülow, upon the suggestion of the Foreign Office, devoted part of a major speech in the Reichstag to discussing the government's position with regard to the Anglo-Japanese Alliance and its relation to Germany's role in Shantung and the Yangtze Valley.[7]

In his address Bülow sought to emphasize Germany's position as a trading power with interests all over China and to denigrate her role as the owner of a sphere of influence. He pointed out that Germany had one overriding interest in China and that was "to develop our commerce as securely as possible." Therefore the German government welcomed the alliance, whose aim was to preserve the integrity of China, and at the same time was pleased to note that the agreement of 1900 with Britain was "in effect without change." This agreement, Bülow pointedly emphasized, had "guaranteed German trade and shipping free access to the Yangtze and guaranteed our economic equality in the Yangtze Valley and on the coast of China." The chancellor then alluded to the reports in the English press that Germany desired exclusive privileges in Shantung and said that he wanted to "grab this chicken by the throat as fast as possible . . . Germany only wants the open door in Shantung, that is, the same freedom of economic activity which we do not oppose for other powers in Shantung and elsewhere in China." Since Germany did not want any impediments to the activities of its citizens in the Yangtze Valley, this statement hinted that Bülow was giving up Germany's special claims in Shantung. As if to underline this implication, the chancellor added that all Germany desired in Shantung was the specific concessions it had already obtained, and in describing these privileges his tone was apologetic. "Though we secured from the Chinese government certain concrete railway and mining concessions for our entrepreneurs in Shantung . . . we only did what other powers were doing for their citizens in other parts of China — and furthermore, this happened three or four years ago in 1898 and 1899, and it is out of the question that something like this is going on now or ought to go on now."

Actually, in 1902 neither the Foreign Office nor the chancellor had probably yet become reconciled to limiting German claims in Shantung to the extent implied by Bülow's statement.[8] Nevertheless, such views increasingly influenced German policy as Anglo-German relations continued to deteriorate and as the importance of the Yangtze Valley to German interests grew.[9] In addition, because the Foreign Office had succeeded in a campaign to wrest control of German activities in Shantung from the navy, the new attitudes came to have a more direct impact on German behavior in the province. As might be expected, it was Tirpitz, with his particular sensitivity to political and economic realities, who recognized fairly quickly that the navy's plans for Shantung were no longer feasible and so yielded control to the Foreign Office more readily than did the naval officers in Kiaochow.

Prior to the Boxer Rebellion the Foreign Office and its diplomatic personnel in China had made comparatively little effort to control Sino-German relations in Shantung. The German ministers had occasionally complained that, in view of Jaeschke's frequent negotiations with Tsinan, the Kiaochow governor was not living up to the agreement of January 1898 in which the navy had promised to leave matters in the province to the Wilhelmstrasse; but the issue was not pressed.[10] However, in late 1900, as the Foreign Office began to lose interest in the sphere of influence, it also began to contest the navy's role in Shantung.[11]

In January 1901 the new minister to China, Mumm von Schwarzenstein, suggested that the Foreign Office send a consular representative to Tsinan to watch over the interests of the Foreign Office there.[12] The issue of establishing such a consulate developed into the focal point of the struggle between the Foreign Office and the navy. The death of Governor Jaeschke at the end of January brought about a temporary truce which lasted until June, when Jaeschke's successor, Captain Oskar Truppel, arrived. Truppel had served briefly at Kiaochow in 1898, and after his return to the colony in 1901, he remained there as governor, except for a few furloughs, until 1911. He was a capable and intelligent administrator of the colony and, in the long run, proved able to accommodate himself to the changes in the German position in Shantung and to establish harmonious relations with the Foreign Office and the provincial government. At the beginning of his tenure, however, he resisted the diminution of the navy's influence in the province.

On his arrival, Truppel quickly made it plain that he felt the governor of Kiaochow should remain the dominant figure in dealings between the German and Chinese officials in Shantung. During the summer of 1901, for example, he tried hard to establish a close relationship with Governor Yuan. Soon after he reached Tsingtao, Truppel decided to send a large delegation to Tsinan to present his greetings.[13] Truppel hoped that his representatives would be able to re-establish the warm and friendly relationship which he felt had existed between Yuan and Jaeschke and, at the same time, forestall Mumm's plans for a consulate in the provincial capital. Without consulting the legation in Peking, the German governor also began negotiations with Tsinan on a number of issues, including the status of German troops in the interior.[14] By September, Truppel's activities and, in particular, his independent negotiations over the troops had so exasperated Mumm that the minister stressed to Berlin that these events "showed once again that establishing a consulate in Tsinan was desirable." [15] The Foreign Office agreed with Mumm, and the consular representative, Lenz, arrived at Tsinan in early November.[16]

The debate over the establishment of the consulate occasionally revealed the existence of a bureaucratic rivalry between the Foreign Office and the navy, as, for example, when the Wilhelmstrasse complained to the chancellor about "the drive of the governors of Kiaochow to exclude the legation from any role in Shantung." [17] However, it was clear that the basic issue was the emphasis which Germany would place on Shantung in the future. The Foreign Office admitted that it was "hard to show direct proof" that the domination of the navy in Shantung had "materially disadvantaged German interests" in the province.[18] Nevertheless, it stressed that for "dealings with Chinese officials, including those in Shantung," it was "better to use the consular or diplomatic organs provided for by international law" rather than the governor of Kiaochow; for the latter gave these relations an extraordinary and even "military" character.[19] If there was a consul, the Foreign Office asserted, "we would obtain a very crucial benefit for our overall policy, namely, that our position in Shantung wouldn't look different from that of any other power in any other part of China." This was an extremely desirable goal because it would "protect" Germany "from any blame for violating the open-door principle" in Shantung "and would, thus, take away from other powers any pretext to strive for special privileges elsewhere." The Wilhelmstrasse pointed out that the governor of Hong Kong was not permitted to deal with Chinese officials in the neighboring province of Kwangtung, and it suggested that this was the proper model for the relationship between the governor of Kiaochow and the interior of Shantung.[20] England, of course, did not claim a sphere of influence in Kwangtung.

Basically, the navy opposed a diplomatic representative in Tsinan because it believed that a consul would hurt "the position and influence of the governor of Tsingtao with the Chinese" and, thus, would be a "detrimental influence" on German "economic and political interests in Shantung." [21] In one of his letters to Mumm, Truppel assured the minister that his desire to remain in control of relations in the province "did not spring from a belief that in Shantung the governor of Kiaochow could or should take over the business of the Foreign Office." Rather, he said, "practical points of view and facts" were involved. "If the next politico-colonial goal of our acquisition of Kiaochow is a recognition of the fact that Shantung should be opened economically and that Tsingtao should serve as its major port for commerce and communications, then all the efforts to achieve this goal must be centered in the government of Kiaochow . . . The governor of Shantung must also be made to serve this work of development, and the surest way to achieve this is through a suitable personal relationship on his part, based either on fear or respect, with the governor of Tsingtao, whom the Chinese must view as the decisive figure in questions involving Shantung." [22] To bolster such arguments both Truppel and Tirpitz stressed how smoothly and successfully Jaeschke had advanced German interests in Shantung through his negotiations with Yuan. Thus, Tirpitz insisted, a consul was unnecessary because "the governor of Kiaochow and the Chinese governor were at a point where, when faced with disagreements . . . they could settle them between themselves, without involving the Chinese government or our minister, or even having to let them know." [23]

In the beginning of 1902, Berlin's uneasiness over the Anglo-Japanese Alliance caused Tirpitz to reconsider his opposition to the consulate and to reconcile himself to the fact that the viewpoint of the Foreign Office concerning Germany's position in Shantung would have to predominate.[24] Nevertheless, although Tirpitz' position was changing, Truppel remained adamantly opposed to the presence of a diplomatic representative in Tsinan.[25] Lenz was having difficulties in some negotiations concerning German mining concessions, and Truppel demanded the "recall of the consul" at "the first good opportunity." Only then, he wrote, could "the real drama which we want to see in Shantung resume its course, namely, the development of our colony with the aid of the province and the development of the province through Tsingtao." Truppel even threatened to make the dispute over the consulate public by warning: "The Reichstag memorandum on Kiaochow covering this year . . . will have to say that in the 'first part of 1902 relations between Kiaochow and the province, which were begun last year and which were doing extremely well, have come to a complete halt because a mission sent by the legation . . . forced the administration to break off all relations with the provincial governor.'" Truppel summed up his case bluntly by saying that he should be in control because everyone, Westerners and Chinese, felt that "Shantung will have to gravitate to the German administration" at Kiaochow because "in Shantung the German governor is lord." [26]

Mumm countered Truppel's arguments with a clear reiteration of the viewpoint of the Foreign Office. He admitted that there might be advantages for Germany's position in Shantung if the governor of Kiaochow handled matters in the province, but he pointed out that such a situation would be bad for Germany's overall position in China.[27] As he wrote to the chancellor attacking Truppel's "opinion that there can be only one lord, only one king in Shantung, namely the governor of Kiaochow," the "care of German interests in Shantung . . . must, in my opinion, be handled by the authority which also has the responsibility for the maintenance of relations between Germany and China." [28]

In the spring, Truppel, apparently on his own initiative, began to take action to bolster his position in the battle for influence in Shantung. He acquiesced in a newspaper campaign at Tsingtao directed against the consulate in Tsinan.[29] The Tsingtao press revealed the existence of the debate between the navy and the diplomats and took the navy's side, arguing that the consulate would inevitably encourage other countries to send consuls to Tsinan and would thus contribute to undermining the German monopoly over Shantung.

Another, and a rather quixotic, step undertaken by Truppel was his cooperation in a scheme to bring a new governor to Shantung. In March 1902 the governor of Anhwei, Wang Chih-ch'un, contacted Truppel through the editor of the Chinese newspaper at Tsingtao. Wang said that he wanted to leave Anhwei and that Prince Ch'ing, the leading Manchu official, would support him for the governorship of Shantung if the request were to come from the Germans. In return for Truppel's help in getting him the appointment, Wang promised that he would follow the German governor's lead in handling matters at Tsinan and would comply with every German desire in the province. Wang invited Truppel to Shanghai to meet with him secretly in order to coordinate their plans. It is difficult to learn what lay behind Wang's clever scheme to capitalize on Truppel's rivalry with the diplomats, a rivalry which was, of course, public knowledge in the Tsingtao press. It may have been simply the product of an ambitious and unprincipled official's attempt for a promotion, or it may have had broader political implications involving, perhaps, the machinations of a clique opposed to Yuan Shih-k'ai. Amazingly, Truppel accepted the bizarre invitation to go to Shanghai. He went incognito in the attire of an adjutant, accompanied by the newspaper editor and Schrameier. Truppel met Wang secretly in a Chinese restaurant, and there Wang repeated all his promises directly to the German governor. No further meetings took place, however, and the whole scheme came to an abrupt end. This was partly because the German diplomats got wind of what Truppel was doing and exerted pressure to stop it.[30]

This sort of episode probably confirmed Tirpitz' growing feeling that the Wilhelmstrasse would have to handle matters in Shantung. In any case, the Foreign Office realized soon afterwards that Tirpitz had come over to their side and decided to tell him that "the only way to solve the situation" was to order Truppel to obey the agreement of 1898 and "to abstain completely from dealing with Chinese officials on economic, let alone political, matters." [31] Tirpitz apparently complied with the request of the Foreign Office; for, within a few months, the legation triumphantly notified the German consuls in Shanghai, Chefoo, and Tsinan that Truppel had "expressly recognized that 'the province of Shantung outside of the leasehold is the domain of the German legation.'" [32]

The competition between the diplomats and Truppel never entirely subsided, and their differing views on the importance of Shantung occasionally surfaced in later years. Nevertheless, the basic victory of the Foreign Office in the fight for control of German policy in Shantung remained completely secure; and the effect of this victory on the status of the sphere of influence was permanent.

As a result of the Russo-Japanese War of 1904–05, the diplomatic isolation of Germany reached an even more critical stage, and it was in this period that the German government finally set about giving up the sphere of influence entirely. This occurred primarily because the war, by revealing the weakness of Russia, paved the way for the end of the Anglo-Russian rivalry in East Asia.[33] The rivalry had been the basic factor which had given the Reich a bargaining position in the Far East and had limited the pressure that England could apply to Germany there. In addition, Japan's victory and her obvious military power raised the possibility that the Japanese, who had become very important in the economic life of Shantung, would contest the continuation of German dominance there.[34]

As in 1902, Germany's dilemma was highlighted by a surge of anti-German feeling in both Britain and Japan. In part this was the result of the accumulated antagonisms of the previous years. However, the hostility also stemmed from the fact that the Reich had shown some partiality for the Russians during the war. In addition, the Wilhelmstrasse believed that the anti-German outbreak in England was a manifestation of Britain's desire to expel the Germans from the Yangtze, where they were flourishing.[35] Once again, in both England and Japan, there ensued a major campaign against the Reich by the press, which repeatedly attacked Germany's ambition to dominate Shantung.[36]

As early as January 1905, Bülow responded to the situation by writing to the kaiser that the war would necessitate a major overhaul of German policy in China.[37] The chancellor predicted correctly that, after the war, Russia and England would become reconciled and that this would give England the freedom to fulfill her desire to expel the Germans from the Yangtze. "A variety of articles in the English press . . . appear to be a preparation for carrying out" such plans, he suggested, for they "complain, on the one hand, of the penetration of German economic influence in the Yangtze and, on the other hand, allude to our position in Shantung and claim we want to turn the whole province into a colony." Therefore, in order to safeguard its position in the Yangtze, he said, the Reich should "repress every manifestation of German expansionist drives in Shantung." At this time, the Germans may not have thoroughly appreciated how fully they would have to surrender their claims in Shantung. For example, in his letter to the kaiser, Bülow had reassured the monarch by telling him that the new policies in Shantung did not necessarily mean that Germany would have to give up its special position in the province; nevertheless, in the ensuing two years this was what occurred.

After 1900 the deteriorating international situation was not the only element which contributed to the German government's hesitation to pursue a vigorous policy in Shantung. In this period the support within Germany for such a policy was also much reduced. The primary reason for this was that the Center Party became increasingly disillusioned with the policy of *Weltpolitik* and formed a parliamentary coalition with the Progressives and Social Democrats to oppose German policy in the non-Western world.[38] This bloc was particularly hostile to any military activities in support of colonial adventures. Because the Center was a crucial prop for Bülow until 1907, the attitude of the party exerted considerable leverage on the government to act moderately overseas.

Naturally, such parliamentary pressures hobbled the government's capacity to conduct an activist policy in China. The Boxer intervention had not been popular at home, and in the following years the Foreign Office was extremely chary of taking any action in China which might lead to conflict there, either with the other powers or with China. In 1904, for example, the Wilhelmstrasse notified the kaiser that there was an "absolute feeling of antipathy in our Reichstag to any East Asian undertaking," and therefore the nation was "not in a position to take up any obligations which could require us once more to use land forces in China." [39] After the great revolts in Germany's African colonies which began in 1903, the hostility in the Reichstag toward adventures in the non-Western world reached its climax. This parliamentary dissatisfaction was particularly effective in influencing German policy in China, because it became especially intense just as Germany's diplomatic position was deteriorating and China's own drive to expel the Germans reached a new level.

The culminating factor in ending the sphere of influence was that Chinese actions directed against the German position in Shantung complemented the international and domestic pressures. What amounted to a concerted Chinese campaign against the German sphere evolved after 1900, the result of an extremely significant development in Chinese attitudes and policy. For it was in these years following the Boxer Rebellion that a nationalistic outlook like that which had earlier characterized K'ang Yu-wei and the reformers spread to broad segments of Chinese society and government and permeated the highest levels of the bureaucracy. This was the era of the great reform movement of the late Ch'ing, which by 1909 had implemented political reforms that went beyond even those advocated by K'ang Yu-wei in the late '90s. In addition, the old mainstream approach to foreign policy was abandoned, and the new nationalistic goal of sovereignty became the norm.

In Shantung the impact of the central government's nationalistic orientation revealed itself primarily in the appointment as provincial governors of talented men, embracing or at least influenced by the new attitude. These men not only initiated policies aimed directly at reducing German power and regaining Chinese sovereignty but were also willing and able to carry out institutional reforms with the same purpose. New institutions in Peking, such as the Ministry of Foreign Affairs and other specialized bureaus created after 1900, as well as new national laws and regulations, helped the governors to implement their plans in Shantung. After 1905 they also received growing support for their efforts from the local gentry, who, like the bureaucracy, were becoming increasingly nationalistic.

Yuan Shih-k'ai remained governor until November 1901. In the spring of that year his mother died, and Yuan would normally have had to retire from office in order to undertake two years of mourning. However, Peking allowed him to remain at his post and limit himself to one hundred days of token mourning.[40] While a dispensation of this type was not unusual, it was, nevertheless, indicative of the government's increasingly high opinion of Yuan and of its desire to keep an official of his caliber in Shantung. In the decree absolving Yuan of his filial obligations, the government stressed that his presence in Shantung was essential in order to continue the "excellent management" of the "extremely difficult foreign relations" of the province. When Yuan finally left Shantung in November 1901, it was to become governor general of Chihli, the most important provincial post in China and a position for which he was virtually the unanimous choice of the bureaucracy.[41]

On the day Yuan received his appointment as governor general he wrote to Sheng Hsuan-huai, expressing doubts about accepting the new post.[42] Signs of hesitation were part of the prescribed etiquette for an official offered a higher post; nevertheless, Yuan's main argument revealed his concern about the future of the relations with the Germans in Shantung after he had gone. After briefly pleading the stereotyped excuse of bad health, Yuan continued, "If I go, Shantung will certainly fall into chaos like Mukden," where Russia's power in its sphere of influence was growing stronger. "How can Chihli look after itself, if both Shantung and Mukden are in turmoil? My departure from Tsinan can only mean harm to the delicate situation."

Yuan's worries were shared by other officials and, perhaps because of his hint to Sheng, a movement sprang up to keep Shantung under Yuan's control even after he was transferred.[43] For example, Chang Chih-tung urged that an old position, viceroy of Chihli and Shantung (Chih-shan tsung-tu), be revived in order to assure that Yuan could continue to handle the Germans in his former province.[44] The court sympathized with the movement, though apparently not with Chang's plan for establishing a new viceroyship. It appointed a relatively minor figure, Chang Jen-chün, the director of grain transport, to be the new governor of Shantung.[45] At the same time, it was decided that Yuan would continue to oversee matters in the province.[46]

This arrangement quickly proved unsatisfactory, for it evidently was too difficult for Yuan to maintain the necessary contact with the "delicate situation" in Tsinan from his distant and heavy duties in Chihli; and Chang Jen-chün, while apparently a fairly capable man, was not able to conduct affairs with the high degree of competence expected of the governor of Shantung.[47] At the end of May 1902, Chang was transferred, and the practice of sending an especially competent official to Shantung to run the province independently was re-established.

Chang's successor was Chou Fu, who at the time was treasurer of Chihli, one of the outstanding officials of the last decades of the Ch'ing dynasty.[48] Chou was born in 1837 and, like Yuan Shih-k'ai, rose to power in the entourage of Li Hung-chang, a fact which ensured that Yuan would still have some influence in Shantung. Chou had been one of Li's most important lieutenants and had handled such projects as military finance, defense, and the construction of telegraphs and railroads for the viceroy. He had also assisted Li in the difficult negotiations over the Boxer settlement and had thereby gained the reputation of being a particularly skillful diplomat. As governor of Shantung, a post which he held until the end of 1904, Chou demonstrated that he was sympathetic to the nationalist approach to foreign affairs, and he played an important role in reducing German dominance in the province. However, Chou was not so fully or consciously nationalistic as men like K'ang Yu-wei and Yuan Shih-k'ai. He still conceived of his mission somewhat in terms of the old mainstream goal of keeping foreigners under control and did not show the delicate sensitivity of more thoroughgoing nationalists to theoretical infringements of Chinese sovereignty and independence. Nor did Chou employ the rhetoric of nationalism in an obvious way. One reason for these differences was certainly that Chou was from an earlier generation than that represented by K'ang and Yuan. They had been born in the late 1850s, whereas Chou was twenty-five years their senior and more likely to have assimilated earlier views on foreign relations. It is indicative of the mood of the bureaucracy that in 1905, despite his good record in Shantung, Chou was impeached (but quickly exonerated) for having been too acquiescent toward the Germans.[49]

In October 1904, Chou was transferred to the crucial post of governor general of Liang-kiang. For two months Hu T'ing-kan, who had held several high provincial posts at Tsinan, served as acting governor of Shantung.[50] In January 1905 the appointment of the new governor, Yang Shih-hsiang, showed that Peking intended to maintain the high standards for the office which had been set by Yuan Shih-k'ai and Chou Fu. Yang was from the coterie of Yuan Shih-k'ai and had had a meteoric rise in the bureaucracy similar to Yuan's.[51] Born in 1860, he became governor of

Shantung when he was only forty-five years old. His treatment of the Germans showed the same fervent and explicit commitment to nationalism as that of Yuan, and he went beyond Chou Fu in firmly opposing every infringement of Chinese sovereignty in Shantung, no matter how slight. In 1907 when Yang left Shantung, it was to become viceroy of Chihli. He owed his appointment to this high post not only to his close relation to Yuan Shih-k'ai but also to his skill in liquidating the German position in Shantung.

An indication of just how little political influence the Germans wielded in Shantung was the fact that they had nothing to do with the removal or selection of any of these governors. Each time the governorship changed hands, rumors circulated along the China coast that the Germans were somehow involved; however, these allegations were completely without foundation. When Chang Jen-chün replaced Yuan Shih-k'ai, the Germans had no idea who would be appointed until the day the decree appeared.[52] Soon after Chang arrived at Tsinan, press reports were published saying that the Germans were not pleased with the new governor's performance and that Mumm was pressuring Peking to have him transferred.[53] These reports constituted a part of the anti-German campaign of early 1902. In actuality, though the German legation was somewhat unhappy about Chang, it did not try to oust him, to a considerable extent because Mumm feared that such an act "would cause a great uproar in the diplomatic community" and would "give new nourishment to the voices in the English and American press . . . according to which we strive for 'exclusive rights' in Shantung and view this province as our domain." [54] Another reason for Mumm's reluctance to agitate against the governor was that Truppel was particularly hostile to Chang, and the latter's removal would have signified a victory for the navy in its contest with the Foreign Office. The only German initiative against Chang was Truppel's own bizarre flirtation with Wang Chih-ch'un, an episode which apparently never became public.

When the Chinese government decided to replace Chang, it neither forewarned the Germans nor consulted them about the selection of Chou Fu. Mumm was apparently surprised by the decree announcing the change, for he had not even reported earlier that Peking was considering the removal of Chang.[55] Similarly, in 1904 the Germans played no role in the Chinese decision to transfer Chou Fu and, indeed, had little premonition that Chou, whom they liked, was leaving.[56] Once again, the accusation that the Reich had had a hand in the selection of the new governor cropped up, this time in the anti-German press campaign of early 1905.[57] As a matter of fact, the Germans had no influence whatsoever over the appointment of Yang and, again, did not even know he would be nominated until the official decree appeared.[58]

In addition to the pressures generated by the provincial government, another source of opposition to the German position in Shantung was the growth of nationalism among the gentry of the province. Widespread gentry participation in the struggle against German privileges did not begin until after the Russo-Japanese War, which stimulated similar local manifestations of nationalism all over China. There was no basic difference between the attitudes of the Shantung gentry and those of the nationalistic governors, although the patriotic rhetoric of the local people sometimes tended to be more explicit and bitter. At the same time, the gentry were particularly concerned with blocking German investment, something which could hinder their own economic activities. In 1905, for example, they instigated a major campaign against the German privileges in Shantung and, in particular, against the loan for the Tientsin-Chinkiang Railway.[59] The Germans were vociferously maligned, and accusations were even leveled against Governor Yang for being too gentle with the foreigners. Such grass-roots pressure encouraged the governors to maintain and intensify their opposition to the Germans. Nevertheless, it must be stressed that at least up to 1907 the local gentry were less active in Shantung than they apparently were in many other provinces, and the bulk of the activity and leadership in the struggle against the German sphere continued to come from the provincial government.

Significantly, despite the growing patriotic fervor in Shantung, there were no serious missionary cases in the province after 1900. This is one of the most striking confirmations of the fact that the anti-German feeling which arose after the Boxer Rebellion had nationalist and not conservative roots. For, of course, the missionaries were not particularly disliked by nationalists unless they served as a wedge for incursions against Chinese sovereignty and economic autonomy. After 1900 the Germans never considered using the Steyl missionaries for such purposes, and the Chinese, therefore, lost interest in the missionaries' activities. Indeed, missionaries virtually disappear from the official record after the turn of the century.

One reason for the success of the provincial officials in translating their nationalistic spirit into an effective onslaught on the German position in Shantung was their willingness and ability to make institutional changes which would permit the government to deal effectively with the Germans. One important example of this was the establishment of new governmental organs in Tsinan which served the double function of countering the Germans and stimulating Chinese development. The governors' readiness to experiment with the administrative structure of the province openly testified also to their nationalistic approach. For their efforts were imbued with the same spirit as that which had stimulated K'ang Yu-wei to recommend changes in the hallowed nature of the central government in order to save China and which was now behind the Peking government's own innovations. No doubt because of the German presence, the new institutions were among the first of their type to be established by a provincial government.

The first of the new bureaus was the Chiao-she-chü, which Yuan had established during the railroad and mining negotiations of March 1900. Later in the year it was expanded and renamed the Yang-wu-tsung-chü (Bureau of Foreign Affairs). The sphere of activity of the Yang-wu-tsung-chü was extremely broad, and it was responsible for carrying out most of the policies designed to contain the Germans in Shantung.[60] Thus, it not only handled negotiations aimed at blocking any further concessions to the Germans but also endeavored to limit the scope of existing concessions. At the same time it directed the government's efforts to protect China's interests by encouraging Chinese development and economic competition.

The tasks of the Bureau of Foreign Affairs were probably too wide, and so in October 1901 Yuan organized a second new institution, the Bureau of Commerce. It gradually absorbed all the activities of the Bureau of Foreign Affairs which had been concerned with Chinese economic development. In early 1903 Chou Fu organized a third new institution, the Bureau of Railways and Mines. It relieved the Bureau of Foreign Affairs of the responsibility of controlling the existing German railway and mining concessions.

The administrative structure established in 1903 functioned essentially unchanged until 1906, when Yang Shih-hsiang organized the K'uang-cheng-tiao-ch'a-chü (Bureau of Mine Supervision). In a sense the new department symbolized the successful containment of the Germans, for it handled everything to do with mining, including negotiations over requests for new concessions, relations with the SBG, and the control and encouragement of Chinese mining. By giving all these responsibilities to one bureau, Yang was indicating that the provincial government no longer intended to treat German mining activities as special political or diplomatic issues but would deal with them simply as if they were a normal "commercial matter" like concessions held by Chinese entrepreneurs.[61]

An important institutional change of another type which had a significant effect on protecting Chinese independence in Shantung was the decision, made in 1904 after the completion of the railway, to turn Tsinan, Chou-ts'un, and Wei-hsien into "self-opened marts" (*tzu-k'ai shang-pu*). The creation of self-opened marts was one of the important innovations of late Ch'ing policy; however, since it has so far escaped scholarly attention, comments on it must remain somewhat tentative.

Apparently, the idea of self-opened marts was first conceived in 1898, and the new institution was meant to serve a double purpose. Initially the establishment of the marts was intended to prevent the monopolization of an area by a single power by opening the locale to all nations. Thus, the first three self-opened marts, Yochow, Chinwangtao, and Santuau, were created in March 1898 when the battle for concessions was at its height. Because Peking had reason to fear that the towns might be seized by one or another of the powers, it decided to place them "under the protection of quasi-international guarantee" by opening them.[62] Within a short time self-opened marts were also seen as a way of recouping Chinese sovereignty, as it quickly became axiomatic that in the marts foreigners were to have far fewer privileges and be under considerably more Chinese authority than in a treaty port. Therefore, they were preferable to the treaty port as a method of opening an area to foreign residence. It is significant that the Hundred Days of reform, with their nationalist approach to foreign affairs, apparently played an important role in developing this second purpose for self-opened marts.[63]

Five years later, in 1903, China again used self-opened marts in order to block one power from dominating an area, as well as to minimize all foreign privileges there. In April Russia demanded that China promise not to establish any new treaty ports in Manchuria or admit any additional foreign consuls, a demand which in itself demonstrates the importance an imperialist power placed on keeping an area closed to others.[64] The United States and Japan exerted strong pressure on the Russians and succeeded in forcing Saint Petersburg to drop its demands. At the same time, the United States suggested to the Chinese government that, in order to reduce Russian influence in the future, three places in Manchuria, including Mukden, be opened as ports. Peking eventually agreed to the idea, and in the commercial treaties of that year the three towns were opened. However, they were designated self-opened marts rather than treaty ports. The Ch'ing government was, in fact, never again to establish a treaty port. Every place opened after 1903 was designated "self-opened," testimony to the significance of the new institution in the nationalistic foreign policy of the late Ch'ing.[65]

The three towns in Shantung were the next self-opened marts to be created after those in Manchuria. In October 1903, Lü Hai-huan, who had been responsible for negotiating the treaties of that year, had the government request the provincial governors to recommend "strategically vital and commercially rich" places within their jurisdiction which might be made into self-opened marts.[66] One reply to the government's decree came from Chou Fu and Yuan Shih-k'ai. On May 4, 1904, immediately after the completion of the railroad, they recommended that Tsinan, Wei-hsien, and Chou-ts'un should be designated self-opened marts. "Now, because of the configuration of the two railways," they said, referring also to the Tientsin-Chinkiang Railway, which was being negotiated, Tsinan "has become strategically important, and the commercial activity there will become profitable." Therefore, China "should certainly open a mart" in the town and in the other locations "on the basis of the precedent set at Chinwangtao, Santuau, and Yochow." [67] Though Chou and Yuan did not explicitly mention the German threat, the history of self-opened marts and the precedents which the two officials cited made the purpose of opening the towns clear; and no one questioned that the move was intended to protect Chinese interests and restrict German influence in the area.

The Chinese authorities, as was their custom when making administrative decisions in Shantung, did not consult the Germans before they decided to open the towns.[68] Moreover, the provincial government took pains to inform the Germans that they would have no special role in determining the nature of the marts. Thus, the German consul in Tsinan reported that shortly after the announcement the provincial government had told him "with particular firmness" that China could set up whatever form of regulations it liked in the three places because the towns were opened voluntarily and, therefore, "were not in the same category as treaty ports, but rather were places under pure Chinese administrative control." [69]

Nevertheless, apparently because they had so firmly and independently taken a step which they considered a direct attack on German interests in the province, the Chinese officials evinced some "anxiety" about the attitude of the Germans. For example, shortly after the decision to open the marts became public, the Wai-wu-pu (Chinese Ministry of Foreign Affairs) ordered the Chinese minister in Berlin, Yin-ch'ang, to learn if Germany intended to oppose the step and told him "if the Germans inquire about the move" to "answer it is because China now wants to encourage trade." [70]

In reality, the Chinese fears proved ungrounded, for the German reaction was almost completely passive. Although the Germans at Kiaochow were troubled by the move, they had little influence over the diplomats, who, by 1904, no longer considered Shantung a place where Germany should or even could protest such Chinese actions. The Germans had guessed earlier that Tsinan might be opened. In late 1903 when Truppel first suspected the possibility, he is reported to have let Mumm know several times that "it would not be beneficial to Tsingtao if open places were established in Shantung," for it would "disturb the natural development" of the leasehold.[71] At the same time, the merchants in Tsingtao sent a protocol to the legation expressing similar views and pointing out that "Russia firmly opposed the opening of treaty ports in her sphere" and that Germany should also.[72] However, when the marts were opened, Truppel made no serious effort to have the legation object, no doubt because he realized there was little chance of receiving a favorable response.

If so, he was not wrong. When Prince Ch'ing told Mumm of the plan, the minister reported the matter home in a tone of diffident dissatisfaction. "This news came as no huge surprise, since I always took it for granted that the opening of Tsinan was bound to occur fairly soon and would go hand in hand with the unlocking of the province by the Shantung railway." He added that "we would be acting most intelligently if we came to terms with the opening . . . and did so without any protest." For it was "absolutely impossible" to keep Shantung closed to others, especially "in view of the open-door principle we have so often proclaimed and because of the American, English, and Japanese influences" in the province.[73] Shortly thereafter Mumm expressed similar feelings when he stated that although the opening would "smooth the way for foreign competition," there was no way of blocking the action. A German protest, he said, would "only raise up mistrust and the darkest sort of suspicions . . . without any tangible gain." And the Reich would "end up like the Russians in Manchuria, who, despite their far more favorable position, were forced to yield to the pressures of the powers and to acquiesce in the opening of Mukden, etc."[74] At Truppel's request, Mumm did ask Hart if the IMC planned to place customs houses in the towns, something which the German governor felt would destroy the growing commerce at Tsingtao. Hart replied that there were no such plans.[75] It is difficult to judge if Truppel's fears were justified, but, in any case, China had little reason to undermine the customs system at Tsingtao since it was coming under her control anyway.[76]

Germany's passive acceptance of the Chinese action came as something of a surprise to other Westerners. When the opening of the marts was announced, the *North China Herald* wrote, as if anticipating German opposition, that if the Reich's "intentions" in Shantung were "more commercial than political" she should "welcome" the arrangement.[77] From Shanghai, the German consul general wrote that "all shades of public opinion" expected the Germans to object because everyone felt that the move was intended "to block German efforts toward the annexation of Shantung," and "no one can be talked out of the idea that Germany is pursuing such efforts." [78] The Germans' acquiescent attitude earned them the approbation which they sought from the commercial powers. Mumm reported that the English and American ministers were "very pleased" and "gave us high praise for not placing any difficulties in the way of the opening of Shantung to trade, as did the Russians in Manchuria." [79] On the other hand, from Shanghai, the consul concluded his report with the rather plaintive information: "The Russian military attaché recently asked a German, 'What are you going to do to oppose the opening of the three towns?' And when he heard, 'Apparently nothing,' he answered, 'Then you are the biggest fools in the world.' " [80]

The Containment of German Military Power in Shantung

In 1900 the navy believed that the military occupation of the neutral zone was essential for both the protection of the railway and the security of the leasehold. Moreover, there was a real possibility that German military power would extend even farther into the interior if German economic activities there were endangered. This threat never materialized, however; and by 1907 Chinese policy and Germany's reluctance to preserve its dominance in Shantung had deprived the Germans of any military role in the interior. Indeed, the Germans were so fearful of appearing to harbor military designs in Shantung that by the end of the decade they had limited the military strength of the leasehold itself.

In the years after the Boxer Rebellion, construction work on the railway was by far the most likely source of trouble which might lead to German military intervention in Shantung. The mines of the SBG had never presented so serious a security problem as the railroad, for they had never experienced real difficulties with the population except during the unrest stimulated by the Boxer uprising. The railroad, on the other hand, had repeatedly aroused local opposition and, therefore, seemed destined to draw German troops into the interior as its construction progressed. The basic Chinese policy which averted this military threat was simple — to guard carefully against all violence to the line. This policy proved so successful that when some outbreaks did occur during the construction of the railroad the German officials blamed them not on the populace but rather on the SEG and its personnel.

At the end of 1900 when the railroad work resumed under German military protection, the line had almost reached the borders of the neutral zone, and Hildebrandt claimed that the construction could not possibly proceed unless the troops followed the work into the interior.[81] However, in early 1901, when operations actually crossed the border, Yuan Shih-k'ai took immediate action to ensure that the German forces did not follow.

Yuan sent a large contingent of infantry and cavalry forces to guard the work. In order to provide maximum security, the troops were spread along the roadbed in groups of 100 to 150 every ten or twenty kilometers.[82] At the same time Yuan made certain that local officials cooperated with the SEG in following the Agreement of 1900 concerning the purchase of land. When the company reached a given locale, the magistrate and the local notables met with its representatives and determined the average price per *mou* of land for the area. At the same time they drew up a scale of indemnities for damaged crops and for moving graves and houses. The Germans then delivered the money for the area to the district magistrate, who distributed it promptly to the landowners.[83] The cooperation of the local officials together with the Chinese military presence successfully prevented any disruptions in the work, and German troops did not advance beyond the borders of the neutral zone, which, however, they still occupied.

Hildebrandt was soon satisfied with the Chinese ability to provide security, and by the summer of 1901 he felt there was no longer any need for German troops in the interior or even for a private Chinese police force organized by the railway. In September he wrote to the Berlin office about his pleasure at the "ideal situation" which had developed along the line. "Yuan's cavalry protects our men wherever they go and shows itself to be tractable and friendly," he said; therefore "it would be bad to introduce a foreign element into the situation." Furthermore, he noted, "the Chinese troops also fulfill the task of protecting the railroad in a fully satisfactory manner and, except for modest tips, do so for free." [84]

At the end of 1901 the construction had reached Wei-hsien. By then there were about 2100 infantry and 230 cavalry strung out along the line between that town and the borders of the neutral zone.[85] In June 1902 the SEG met the terms of its original concession and opened the line for use as far as Wei-hsien. The good security which the provincial government provided after the Boxer Rebellion enabled the company to make up the time it had lost in 1899 and 1900.

Chou Fu continued Yuan's effort to provide good security for the

SEG. The work on the line proceeded on schedule and was completed on time. In April 1903 the railroad was opened to Ch'ing-chou (I-tou), 144 miles from Tsingtao, and by September of the same year to Chou-ts'un, 181 miles into the interior.[86] In March 1904 the entire 247 miles to Tsinan had been completed, and the branch line between Chang-tien and Po-shan was opened a few months later.[87]

Soon after Chou became governor he tried unsuccessfully to have the SEG contribute to the cost of the troops which were guarding the line.[88] He based his endeavor on the clause in the regulations of 1900 which said that the company would pay some suitable share of the cost of its own protection. However, the SEG refused to pay anything, maintaining that in the same regulations Tsinan had "agreed to defend the line in an effective way and with the required number of soldiers." The company also argued that since the line was being built without any cost to China, it was not unreasonable to ask the provincial government to pay for security, noting that "the protection" would become of "direct value to the people" of the province, who would "obtain the greatest benefits from the increase of commerce and trade in Shantung" brought by the railroad.[89]

At the time Chou had no way to bring pressure on the company, for no German official supported his request. Naturally, he could not threaten to withdraw any of the troops guarding the railroad as this would have risked the basic goal of his policy, the prevention of German military intervention. As the construction progressed, Chou continued to ask for assistance.[90] In time, however, the issue lost some of its urgency, for Chou found that the maintenance of a tolerable level of peace on the line did not require the original density of troops along the roadbed. By the end of 1903 there were not many more troops guarding the almost-completed railroad then there had been in 1901.[91]

Chou's desire to obtain German financial support for the Chinese troops stands in contrast to the attitudes of Yuan Shih-k'ai and those later adopted by Yang Shih-hsiang on this matter and is a significant indication of the fact that Chou's sense of nationalism was less developed than theirs. Yuan had considered asking for German financial assistance and had, therefore, included provisions for such aid in the regulations. However, after 1900 he evidently rejected the idea of having the Germans cover even part of the cost of the provincial government's police operations, and he made no effort to enforce the pledge of support. Yang followed his example. These two governors did not want any German financial assistance because they believed that such aid would represent a slight to Chinese sovereignty which would outweigh the financial gains.

On the other hand, Chou, in this and a number of other cases, was less willing to spend money in order to make what amounted to a purely theoretical demonstration of Chinese independence. Of course, like them, Chou was quite prepared to make a financial sacrifice in order to block an actual increase of German power in Shantung.

In late 1903 Chou decided to replace the troops defending the railroad with a specially trained police force which was intended to become the line's permanent security guard.[92] To head the new force Chou appointed a German named Sterz, who had earlier helped to modernize Tsinan's constabulary. Although Chou does not appear to have selected Sterz on account of pressure from the Germans, the appointment is of interest because it is another example of an act which the younger and more uniformly nationalistic governors Yuan and Yang would not have performed.[93] For, while Chou was willing to hire Germans if it was not dangerous and might be appropriate and effective, the other two made it a matter of principle not to do so, lest it bolster the German position in the province.

Despite Chou's overall success in protecting the railroad construction, the work was not entirely free of trouble. The difficulties consisted of two types of incidents: repeated small-scale clashes between the railway personnel and local residents, and a rash of thievery from the road just as the line was nearing completion. These problems were not serious in themselves but were significant because, in the disputes which they engendered, the German officials consistently favored the Chinese side over that of the SEG. This revealed the success of Yuan and Chou's efforts to defend the construction work and neutralize the railroad as a military threat, as well as the growing desire of the German authorities for good relations with their Chinese counterparts.

The reasons for the clashes between the railroad workers and the local population were essentially the same as they had been in 1899 and 1900. Disturbances occurred because of the fear and resentment aroused when the massive and disruptive operations of the railroad suddenly broke into the isolated existence of the population. In particular, the presence of workers from other areas helped to precipitate conflicts. Moreover, there may have been a new element contributing to the railroad's troubles. After the Boxer period a rather "colonialist" attitude seems to have developed temporarily among the German personnel of the SEG.[94] This attitude manifested itself in a feeling of superiority toward the Chinese and a tendency to treat them insensitively. It may have been a result of the earlier violence, or perhaps it had always existed and only became evident when the attitudes of the German officials changed.

In any case, the representatives of the German government did not choose to blame the clashes on the Chinese authorities. Instead, the German officials and Chou Fu formed what was virtually a common front against the SEG. Both naval and diplomatic personnel stressed that the disturbances were basically the result of "brutal acts against the Chinese" and "unjustified interference" in local affairs by Chinese and German railway workers. In particular, the German officials said, a major source of tension was the "brazen behavior" of Chinese employees from other provinces who "commit their abuses under the protection" of the railroad company.[95] Furthermore, these authorities pointed out, the German railroad men displayed "rude behavior to the Chinese people and officials" and thus "seriously hurt" themselves and all German interests.[96] Truppel, in one attack on the company, summed up the new position of the German officials when he wrote, "I have the impression that, especially with regard to the cliquish way in which the railroad director now protects his personnel and the interference with Chinese justice which doing this involves, that a situation has been created along the railroad in which the line's management plays the same role as the Catholic missionaries did during the Boxer Rebellion." [97]

Whenever an incident occurred, the German officials tried to get the SEG to meet Chinese desires.[98] Chou Fu appreciated such efforts. In 1904, for example, after referring to a rather serious case in which he had opposed the SEG, Chou commented, "I have been in Shantung for nearly two years, and in all this time I have always been so reasonably supported by all German officials that we have had no major differences between us. However, there have been many inconsiderate acts by German businessmen and entrepreneurs." [99]

The other difficulty, the robberies, became an issue in 1904 when there was a sudden rise in the disappearance of fishplates, screws, and other equipment from the line. Chou Fu insisted that his security system was not at fault and that most of the thieves were actually railroad workers. He said that they stole because the SEG had cheated many of them out of their pay and because laborers from other provinces were left stranded when the construction was finished. Those robbers who did not work directly for the railroad, he claimed, were mostly men who had been cheated either by the contractors whom the SEG used or by the railroad company's own subordinates.[100]

Hildebrandt retorted that the robberies were occurring primarily because the Chinese security system was inadequate.[101] He said that, while Chou could cite very few cases to back up any of his charges about fraud, "there was a whole chain of complaints" by railroad "personnel and workers against the Chinese for thievery, breaking and entering, not living up to contracts, etc. . . . We knew very well what sorts of problems we would have building a railroad here; and so," he added bitterly, "we have always tried to solve such problems by turning, in all good will and without complaints or recriminations, to the German officials." [102]

While there was certainly some truth in what both men claimed, Hildebrandt's side of the story was probably more correct. By late 1903 the Chinese system of security was showing signs of decay; and one of the main reasons behind Chou's decision to have railroad police replace the troops which guarded the line was that the soldiers had gradually become inefficient and ineffective.[103] When the first detachment of the new police was rushed out to deal with the robberies in early 1904, it was able to put a stop to them with little difficulty. Moreover, despite Chou Fu's assertions, there do not appear to have been many local people who felt cheated by the SEG. For after the line was completed, when all Chinese who had outstanding claims against the company were encouraged by the provincial officials and by the Germans to come forward to settle, practically no one did.[104]

The probability that Hildebrandt had a better case than Chou makes all the more striking the fact that when the director appealed to the German officials for redress, they were completely unsympathetic and unanimously sided with the Chinese governor. For example, the consul in Tsinan wrote that "the difficulty of guarding the railroad" was "the fault of the railroad personnel themselves," because the robberies were the result of a "great hatred" for the SEG and "especially of its subordinate personnel." The "basic reason for this hatred," he explained, "is the sad but well-known fact . . . that among many subordinate officials of the line a regular squeeze is collected, on the Chinese model." [105] Truppel also exonerated Chou from blame and agreed with the Chinese governor that "the robberies, especially those of rails, are done mostly by Chinese railroad workers or former employees . . . other Chinese don't even have the necessary tools"; and, he added, workers from other provinces were particularly to blame.[106] It is interesting to note that when the same sort of equipment was stolen in 1899, the German officials did not claim that ordinary Chinese were technically unable to perpetrate the crimes. Truppel suggested that the SEG might solve its problems by meeting Chou's long-standing demand for financial assistance to help cover the cost of the forces along the line, especially since these troops were protecting the company against its own employees.[107]

By blocking the need for German military action while the railroad was being built, the Chinese authorities had successfully weathered the period when the likelihood of such intervention was most probable. Much of the violence along the line was connected with construction work, and the longer the railway was in operation in an area the more secure the line became. In addition, after 1904 the heightened pressure on the Germans to limit their sphere in Shantung contributed to transforming the earlier Chinese success in avoiding German military intervention into a situation where it was essentially no longer possible for German troops to penetrate into the interior on behalf of the railroad or any other German interest.

The history of the successful Chinese drive to make the Germans leave the neutral zone, where the Kiaochow Treaty had specifically allowed the passage of German troops, clearly illustrates how this new situation developed. In September 1901, Yuan Shih-k'ai made the first request to the Germans to withdraw from the zone.[108] Yuan felt justified in doing this because by this time it was obvious that he could maintain peace in the interior. The timing of the governor's request was prompted both by the fact that the Germans were beginning to build permanent facilities for the troops at Chiao-chou and Kao-mi and by the signing of the protocol which settled the Boxer Rebellion.

Truppel rejected the request virtually on his own, though at the time no German, including Mumm, would have seriously considered removing the troops.[109] The Germans still believed that peace had only been tenuously established in the zone and, as Truppel told Yuan, if the troops left, "thievery from the railroad would immediately become prevalent again and other disturbances would follow." [110] Moreover, the soldiers were not there only to guard the line but also, and more importantly, to provide security for Kiaochow by keeping Chinese forces away from the border of the leasehold. Finally, in 1901 the Germans still felt comparatively little pressure from the other powers to reduce their military position in Shantung. Thus, the *North China Herald* supported the German stand and reported Yuan's request in a manner which showed an understanding of the new Chinese approach to foreign affairs. "There is a feeling about among the Chinese official class," the paper said, "a feeling which may grow into serious danger, that any foreign action which may impair in any way the sovereignty of China, must be withstood by force if necessary." The Germans should not give in, the paper added, lest a preposterous Chinese attitude be encouraged.[111]

Yuan quickly realized that he could not remove the Germans from the zone, and he agreed to allow them to remain "temporarily." However, in his letter of acquiescence to Truppel, the Chinese governor made it clear that the presence of the forces was a completely gratuitous safe-guard, maintaining, "Since I have been in Shantung I have protected the citizens and property of other nations as if they were my own. It certainly would not be hard for me permanently to provide whatever protection the railroad work needs." And, he concluded pointedly, "since your excellency is also imbued with a disposition for peace, please find a way to remove the troops soon." [112]

In spite of Yuan's requests, the navy continued to build the troop facilities in the zone and within a year or so had constructed a substantial complex of barracks and training areas.[113] In 1902 the Germans added a cavalry company to the III Marine Battalion and stationed it at Kao-mi.[114] Despite these developments, Chou Fu did not press the Germans to evacuate the zone during his first two years as governor, perhaps because he did not put so high a priority on German withdrawal as had Yuan. However, as the railroad neared completion, Chou began to hope that his success in maintaining security during the construction as well as his good relations with the Germans might encourage them to withdraw from Chiao-chou and Kao-mi. Therefore, in early 1904 he asked them to evacuate the zone, and he continued to urge this upon them as long as he remained governor.[115]

The Germans still did not accede to the request, though in 1904, unlike 1901, they were beginning to feel that there was no reason to continue occupying the neutral zone and that something might be gained by withdrawing. In June, for example, Truppel told an official of the German legation that the troops in the zone "were no longer absolutely necessary either for the security of the colony or of the railroad." Indeed, the governor added, the whole neutral zone was "not a very successful creation" and had never given "any sort of benefit" to Kiaochow. Therefore, he suggested, it might be ended altogether in exchange for extending the borders of the leasehold.[116] The diplomats were, naturally, less antagonistic to removing the troops than they had been earlier, for it was an important step toward the increasingly more desirable goal of limiting the German presence in Shantung.[117]

Nevertheless, in 1904 the Germans were not quite ready to terminate their military presence in the zone. In a sense, this was simply the result of inertia and, in particular, of the feeling that Germany would suffer a serious loss of face if the troops left after so many years of occupation and after having given their presence such an aura of permanence.[118] Such a loss of face, it was felt, would threaten all German interests in Shantung. In addition, the Germans did not wish to withdraw because they believed that the Russo-Japanese War might cause unrest in Shantung, unrest which the continued presence of German troops in the zone might avert.[119] This indicates that the Germans still felt they could intervene militarily in the rest of the province under certain circumstances. For troops in the zone could have no effect in the interior unless they threatened to advance.

After becoming governor in early 1905, the young and nationalistic Yang Shih-hsiang proved very anxious to have the German forces withdraw. He wrote that the Germans had occupied the neutral zone for seven years and that each time they were asked to leave they "procrastinated by saying they were protecting the railroad." This assertion was false, he maintained, for the German occupation of the zone was nothing but "the oppression of an area by foreign troops," whose real result was that it "frightened the people, hurt commerce, and destroyed autonomy and sovereignty." [120]

Therefore, from the moment he arrived in Shantung, Yang consciously strove to impress the Germans with the efficiency of the railway police outside the zone, while simultaneously "struggling to regain control" of the police powers within it.[121] In the spring of 1905 he reorganized the police force and increased its size. At the same time, he improved the training of its members and issued strict regulations to guide them in protecting the line. As part of the reorganization Yang placed a Chinese police specialist at the head of the force and deprived Sterz of all real authority. Yang's efforts evidently made the already good security on the line still better, and he received praise from the Germans for the improvement in the police. Only Sterz, for obvious reasons, criticized the new system and said Chou's had been better. Yang accompanied his police reforms with repeated requests for the Germans to withdraw from the neutral zone.

Yang's campaign succeeded. By the summer of 1905 it was clear that a German military presence in the interior was no longer tenable in the face of the economic and political dangers which the Russo-Japanese War had created for Germany. Even before the war was over, the Germans realized that they would have to withdraw. The anti-German press in England and Japan continually alluded to the Reich's desire to dominate Shantung militarily and referred to the occupation of the neutral zone as proof.[122] Similarly, German military ambitions became a popular target of the Shantung gentry's increasingly verbal and nationalistic campaign against the Germans.

One of the first German responses to these attacks was to cancel a projected map-making expedition in Shantung by the German army in early 1905. Mumm decided that this would be a provocative act, and the project was postponed.[123] In June the War Ministry complained to the Foreign Office that the surveying was of "the most urgent importance" and that there was "no good reason to give in to the pressures in the Japanese and English press" by delaying it further.[124] The Wilhelm-strasse, with Tirpitz' agreement, continued to oppose the plan on the ground that "the political objections" were too serious to warrant the possible gains.[125] As a result, despite continued pressure from the army, plans for the survey were permanently dropped.[126] Similar considerations interrupted naval surveying along the coastline of southern Shantung.[127] Things had indeed changed since 1899 when marines had landed in the same area to burn villages.

In August the peace negotiations confirming Russia's defeat finally convinced the German diplomats that the neutral zone would have to be evacuated as soon as possible. As Mumm wrote to the chancellor, "I have . . . always argued against withdrawing our troops before because I feared it would have a bad influence on our prestige. But the political situation has been completely altered by the final result of the Russo-Japanese War . . . China's self-consciousness has been greatly increased and it has found a powerful prop in Japan." As a result "we must draw a practical conclusion from this, and that now means the withdrawal of our garrisons." Mumm added that Germany could no longer ask anything in return, such as the territorial adjustments which Truppel had suggested the year before. "No matter how carefully we suggested our desires," he said, "the Chinese would blaze the news abroad, whereupon the Anglo-Japanese press would fall upon us." Mumm concluded that Germany had no choice but "to make the best of a bad job and with-draw in as amiable and harmless a way as possible"; for there was no evading the basic fact that "the so wonderfully dumb Chinese have finally become clever enough to realize that we can't stay permanently in a place to which we have no right." [128] In another letter the minister emphasized that German interests were particularly threatened because both Chinese and foreigners were hostile to the Reich. He alluded to the new "weapon" unveiled in the anti-American boycott of 1905 and warned that if the Germans hesitated to leave the neutral zone in the face of international pressure and nationalistic agitation, a boycott could be used against them. The "goodwill of the foreign merchants," he lamented, "which is guaranteed to the Americans . . . will, unfortu-nately, be rather hard for *us* to win, and we will have to battle alone against outraged public opinion." [129]

The naval administrators of Tsingtao were the only German officials who were not eager to withdraw. Their hesitations appear to have been primarily a reaction against the rapid decline of Germany's position in Shantung during 1905. Truppel, for example, reversed his views of the previous year and again insisted that there were some military advantages in the occupation, claiming that he "did not see any need to have the troops withdraw." [130] Truppel was on leave in the latter half of 1905, but his deputy, von Semmern, expressed similar doubts about the advisability of evacuating the zone.[131] He was particularly worried about the strength of Yang's police force, which, when coupled with the Chinese governor's obvious hostility to Germany's special position in Shantung, might make the police a kind of "veiled military" threat that should not be permitted near the colony.[132] However, the reservations emanating from Tsingtao received no support in Berlin and were quickly abandoned.

In October, Chancellor Bülow made the final decision to negotiate the immediate withdrawal of the troops. In his letter officially notifying the kaiser of the government's decision, Bülow summed up the reasons for leaving Kao-mi and Chiao-chou: "It is clear that the two garrisons are on Chinese soil without any tenable justification. Their presence there gives our enemies a welcome way of constantly keeping Chinese mistrust of us alive, and especially of doing so by means of the East Asian press . . . Until now the only problem has been to find a way of withdrawing which would not reduce our prestige in Chinese eyes. A satisfactory solution to this difficulty is now available to us because we can cite the restoration of peace in East Asia as the reason why we are giving up the two places." [133]

In November, negotiations began in Tsinan between von Semmern's representatives and the provincial government over the termination of the German occupation. On November 28 a set of agreements was signed which arranged for the German withdrawal.[134] These agreements stipulated that the German troops at Chiao-chou were to leave immediately, together with one quarter of the forces at Kao-mi. The rest of the troops at Kao-mi were to go within four months, after they had put the buildings and other installations in good repair.

Even though there was no longer any particular danger to the line, the chief issue in the negotiations was the question of how the railroad would be protected in the future. This issue was critical to the Chinese side because, according to Yang, it involved the most crucial "points relating to Chinese sovereignty." [135] It was also vital to the Germans because they still feared the presence of Chinese troops near the leasehold. Therefore, von Semmern tried to obtain a system of security for the railroad which would involve both German and Chinese forces, while

Yang's basic goal was to "put the maintenance of order" along the line "fully into the hands of the Chinese authorities."[136]

The final agreement on security was a major victory for the Chinese. It stipulated that in the future the "railways within the surrounding zone shall be completely under the supervision and protection of Chinese local authorities and police officers." Naturally, von Semmern was not pleased with this clause and wrote that he had wanted it "eliminated or essentially changed" but that "no bargain was possible on this point" with the provincial officials.[137] The Germans' inability to obtain any satisfaction on the crucial issue of security revealed how weak their position in Shantung had become by the end of 1905, especially since their negotiating posture had the basic advantage to be gained from the fact that they were removing their troops.

The only important restriction on Tsinan was that it would have to limit the number of police guarding the railroad in the neutral zone to what was needed to protect an equivalent stretch of line elsewhere. This amounted to 250 men, which was sufficient to establish a reserve force at Kao-mi of about 100 men, as well as to station one man per li along the roadbed.

Von Semmern suggested several other plans which would have preserved some German control over the Chinese police in the zone, but Yang rejected all of them.[138] Among von Semmern's suggestions were one to have Tsinan notify the Germans each time it sent police into the zone and another to let the SEG cover part of the cost of the Chinese forces. Chou Fu, of course, had tried to induce the Germans to help pay for the police guarding the line, and in late 1904 there had been indications that the German officials were becoming rather receptive to the idea. Thus, in view of the Germans' desire to ingratiate themselves, Yang could probably have obtained the financial assistance Chou had sought, not only in the neutral zone but for the whole length of the line. Nevertheless, Yang's nationalism was too strong for him to accept such aid. In describing the reasons why he had rejected von Semmern's offer he wrote, "though I clearly knew that our treasury was especially low, I also knew that if they helped with the cost, sovereignty would not be in our hands. So I absolutely could not agree."[139]

Once Yang had won his basic point concerning the independence of the railroad police, he was willing to make concessions concerning the disposal of the German installations in the neutral zone. At first von Semmern suggested that the Germans keep control of these installations; but this suggestion was probably only a bargaining point on his part[140] and was, in any case, quickly rejected. The final agreement evaluated the installations at $470,000, which Yang considered high. Nevertheless, he was willing to spend money if it served to underline Chinese independence, and he noted that "it was extremely important to buy them back," despite the depleted treasury, "in order to protect our sovereignty." [141] Yang also agreed, though apparently not sincerely, that he would convert the installations into a school of railroading, mining, and engineering which would employ the German language and use German teachers. The province was allowed to keep $70,000 of the cost of the buildings to establish the school. Von Semmern evidently inserted these provisions to make certain that the extensive installations were not used for military purposes. However, once the Germans left, there is no indication that the buildings were turned into a school.

The Chinese police moved into the neutral zone as soon as the agreement was signed. In the spring of 1906 there were about 900 policemen and officers stationed along the line from the borders of Kiaochow to Tsinan.[142] At the beginning of April the last occupation troops withdrew from the interior, and German forces were never again to venture beyond the borders of the leasehold.

In addition to renouncing military interference in the interior after 1905, the Germans also restricted the increase of military power within the leasehold itself, partially in order to avoid arousing the suspicions of China and the powers. Tirpitz had always stressed Kiaochow's role as a commercial center rather than as a strategic military base. Nevertheless, until 1906 there was a steady, though moderate, expansion of the colony's military power.

The first significant reinforcements came in 1902. In that year the navy added a company of cavalry to the III Marine Battalion. It also reinforced the Naval Artillery Detachment with an additional company. These new forces, as well as some further miscellaneous additions, increased the colony's garrison by about 300 men to a total of 1850.[143] In 1905 the navy added two more companies to the artillery detachment, raising the total force to 2300.[144] By 1905 the navy had also built two permanent sets of gun emplacements on Bismark and Iltis mountains and a number of smaller batteries elsewhere.

Shortly after the Russo-Japanese War, Mumm wrote a letter to the chancellor in which he argued that the new pressures on the Germans created by the conflict meant that it would be best to avoid further troop increases at Tsingtao.[145] The letter, oddly prescient in many ways, was concerned with the question "what is the impact of Japan's victory on our policies?" It said in part: "We must force ourselves to practice *great caution* in East Asia, and especially to do so with regard to our colony. Germany is militarily weaker than *Japan* in the Far East; against *China,* alone, Tsingtao might be held for a rather long time; but it is important to remember that such an attack by China would have the approval and support of Japan. In view of the position Japan is trying to win in East Asia, and the goals she has in China, she would consider a strong German fortress and naval base on the coast of Shantung as a provocation. In any case, increases in troops, new batteries, or warships there would definitely sharpen her present opposition. If Japan threatened Indochina, France is so engaged that she would *have to* fight for her colony. We are still not so deeply engaged at Kiaochow that, if complications did arise, they could not still be handled in a *peaceful* and honorable way. The more Germany arms Kiaochow, the more she becomes obligated to defend it militarily . . . Only the future can tell if we are going to have a conflict with Japan — she certainly has cause: 1895 (Shimonoseki), 1898 (Kiaochow), . . . and the opposition of her ally, Britain, to German world trade — all these make a conflict *possible;* arming ourselves heavily in East Asia makes it *probable"* [emphasis in original].

In the letter Mumm confided to Bülow that he was worried that the navy, and especially Truppel, did not seem cognizant of these problems or of "the needs of Germany's overall policy." However, such concerns were just the sort to appeal to Tirpitz, both because of his commercial goals for Kiaochow and his aversion to conflict. Therefore, after 1905 the strength of the Kiaochow garrison did not increase further, and the navy did not make any important additions to the fortifications there.[146]

The Limitation of the Original
Railway and Mining Concessions

The specific railway and mining concessions granted in the treaty of 1898 were probably the most important privileges in the interior of Shantung which Germany received. The railroads were expected to spread German influence over much of Shantung, and the mining monopoly in the thirty-li zone to give the Reich a grip on the best mineral resources in the province. However, the Germans did not attain these goals. They were able to exploit only part of the concessions and then only for the most narrowly circumscribed economic purposes: railroading and mining.

The Railway Concessions

It was in a sense through preventive action that the provincial authorities succeeded in keeping the Germans from utilizing the SEG as a base for the expansion of Germany's position in Shantung. Thus Tsinan, by providing security, neutralized the railroad's potential for extending German military influence and, by opening the three self-opened marts, gave other powers a stake in preventing German political and economic domination over the route of the line. The Germans, however, did try to pursue some activities connected with the railroad which threatened Chinese sovereignty and usurped Chinese sources of revenue. In particular, between 1900 and 1905 the Germans developed extensive postal and telegraph systems along the route between Tsingtao and Tsinan. However, even this limited exercise in expanding German power through the use of the railroad could not be sustained in the face of Chinese opposition.

In the early years virtually every German official took it for granted that "in order to advance German interests in Shantung" the Imperial German Postal Administration, which operated the mails at Kiaochow, would establish post offices along the line and would handle mail traveling on the trains.[147] The first German post office was opened at Wei-hsien in 1902, and as the railroad progressed, others were established in the important towns, including one in Tsinan itself in 1904.[148] These post offices, which served both Chinese and Germans, accepted and delivered mail, sold stamps, issued money orders, and, indeed, carried out a full range of normal postal activities. Special railway cars, staffed by employees of the Imperial Post, transported and processed the mail on the railroad. The operations of the system reinforced the idea that the railroad operated under German sovereignty as far as mail was concerned. For example, as the navy proudly noted, the mail cars were "marked with the insignia of the Imperial Postal Administration," just as in Germany.[149] Moreover, though the Germans were willing to carry mail for the Chinese customs post, they treated this mail essentially like freight, charging a fee and refusing to let Chinese postal employees handle it on the trains.[150]

In much the same way as the German government tried to take over the postal system along the railroad, the SEG attempted to dominate telegraph service. At the same time the railroad was being built, the company constructed a telegraph line which paralleled the tracks. At first it appeared that the line would only serve the railroad and would not be available for public use. In early 1903, however, when the telegraph line reached far enough into the interior, the SEG organized a telegraph agency and began to accept commercial telegrams as a sideline to its railroad operations. These services, like those of the post, were available to both Germans and Chinese.

The Chinese officials strongly opposed these additional activities along the railroad. When the German postal service began in 1902, Tsinan notified the Germans that they had "absolutely no right to open a branch office in Wei-hsien," which "seriously hurt the Chinese post through its competition." [151] As the mail service expanded, the recriminations continued. One German reported that Chou Fu was particularly incensed at the slur to Chinese sovereignty manifested by the fact "that on the railway cars and also on the stations the Chinese words 'German Post' appeared . . . despite all the treaties and despite all of his protests." [152] The Chinese government similarly decried the initiation of the telegraph service, complaining that the SEG was "daring to send commercial telegrams," thus "stealing the profit of the Chinese Telegraph Bureau." [153]

In addition to protesting, the Chinese authorities tried to eliminate the German post and telegraph by competing with them. By 1905 the Chinese mail service in Shantung had become quite efficient, and its success was one reason why the Germans were eventually willing to give up their own post offices. Similarly, the Chinese worked to improve their telegraph line between Tsingtao and Tsinan, lowering its rates to match those of the Germans.[154]

Significantly, one of the main opponents of the German postal and telegraph operations was Ohlmer, the director of customs at Tsingtao. His attitude and the tone of his advice to the Chinese officials on this issue are striking manifestations of the fact that at Tsingtao Ohlmer was a genuine representative of the Chinese Customs Service and government and not a tool of the Germans. In 1903 Ohlmer sent Chou Fu an important report in which he urged the governor to put a stop to the extracurricular activities along the railroad.[155] He said that this was urgent, not only because of the immediate need to protect the revenues of Shantung, but also because the SEG was setting a bad precedent for other foreign railroads in China. "In my opinion," Ohlmer wrote, "telegraphs and post are a great source of profit for a nation; so regulations should be drawn up" to define the relationship between these activities and railways. Ohlmer suggested the regulations stipulate that foreign railroads would have to provide special railroad cars for the Chinese mail and would "carry this mail for nothing." They should also make it clear that the Chinese Telegraph Bureau had the right to string an extra wire along a railroad telegraph and that "all commercial telegrams would be handled by the bureau and not by the railroad." Where a railroad already existed, Ohlmer continued, China "should establish laws to get back such rights," and every future concession should contain a clause concerning these questions "in order to prevent foreign plundering."

In the summer of 1903 the SEG's activities and also, apparently, Ohlmer's suggestions stimulated the Chinese Telegraph Bureau to draft a set of six regulations for the control of railway telegraphs. The regulations, which were quite detailed and strict, stressed the basic concept that "the right to operate a telegraph in Chinese territory or to grant to others the permission to operate a telegraph lies solely with China." According to the rules a railroad would not be permitted to handle commercial telegrams unless there was no available Chinese line, and then only with special authorization from Peking. If China gave such permission, the railroad could send the telegrams only as far as the nearest Chinese office, charging the same rate as the Chinese service. Moreover, all profits from such commercial telegrams would have to be turned over to China. The regulations further stipulated that if the Telegraph Bureau desired, it could string wires on the telegraph poles of a railroad and establish its own offices in the railroad stations. In each case the bureau was to pay for the facilities it used, but the railroad was obliged to grant it the privileges.[156] In 1904 these rules became China's national regulations on railway telegraphs, and the Chinese telegraph authorities began to press the SEG to obey them. No similar regulations dealing with the relations between the post and foreign railways appeared in 1903 or 1904, though this may have been because such regulations already existed on the books of the IMC.[157]

In any case, none of the Chinese efforts before 1905 stopped or reduced the German mail or telegraph services. Indeed, when Tsinan tried to match the prices of the railway telegraph, the SEG cut its rates, and a minor price war apparently resulted.[158] By 1904, however, some of the German diplomats had begun to reconsider the advisability of continuing these activities since they conflicted with the Wilhelmstrasse's growing desire to reduce Germany's role in Shantung. When Goltz, the first secretary of the legation, was in Tsinan for the celebration of the railroad's completion, he reported that Chou "complained bitterly over the action of the German Postal Administration opening post offices all over the interior and relentlessly trying to compete with the Chinese post." Goltz mused, "One is astonished as to why the German post office carries on this endless competition . . . for doing so only arouses bitterness among the Chinese officials." [159]

Friction over the telegraph and post continued into early 1905. In March, however, von Semmern reported that the Imperial Postal Administration was beginning to consider abandoning its services in the interior.[160] Five months later, Mumm wrote that as part of their plans to take account of the "new developments in East Asia" the Germans had decided to adopt "the most accommodating view toward the Chinese wishes . . . in connection with the German post and the railway telegraphs." [161]

Negotiations over the post offices began between Chinese postal officials and the Germans in the summer of 1905. By November they had reached an agreement which specified that the Germans would stop putting German mail cars on the line and would halt all their postal activities in the interior.[162] The two sides also set up rules governing the SEG's treatment of the Chinese mail. In 1907 the Chinese post received the further right to attach its own mail cars, manned by Chinese personnel, to the trains, thus marking the total integration of the SEG into the Chinese postal system.[163]

Although there are indications that the SEG had already curtailed its telegraph business, formal negotiations on the issue were not initiated until early 1906.[164] The negotiations were long and complex because they also involved several other outstanding questions concerning German telegraphs in China.[165] However, in early 1907 both the SEG and the German government signed agreements with the Chinese Telegraph Bureau. The railroad company agreed to stop its telegraph activities permanently and to comply essentially with the regulations laid down by the bureau in 1904.[166]

Thus by 1907 the net result of Germany's original railway concessions in Shantung was the construction and operation of the line from Tsingtao to Tsinan. None of the potentialities which the railroad possessed for extending German influence inland had materialized. This was primarily because China effectively used a combination of pressure on and cooperation with the Germans to exploit the Reich's inability to pursue an activist policy in Shantung. However, not every technique which the Chinese authorities devised to obviate the dangers presented by the railway proved successful.

The most important of these failures was the provincial government's attempt, for a short time after 1900, to obtain direct influence over the SEG by purchasing its stocks. The Kiaochow Treaty had granted Chinese citizens the right to purchase shares in the SEG, and the Agreement of 1900 had reaffirmed that right. In late 1901 the provincial Bureau of Commerce suggested that the province actually develop a plan to buy shares. In a report to the governor the bureau warned, "if Chinese don't buy shares of the railroad . . . we will not be able to participate in the affairs of the company. We will be at its beck and call in all matters, and it will not obey us." On the other hand, if Chinese did own shares, the bureau predicted that "all things which involve the management of the railroad will be discussed with the proper bureaus and placed before the governor for his opinion." The report listed some concrete concessions which might be obtained from the SEG by the ownership of stocks and also pointed out that such shares would provide revenue for the province.[167]

Governor Chang Jen-chün agreed with the report and, as soon as he took office, began to collect money to purchase shares, mainly by using revenue produced by special taxes which Yuan Shih-k'ai had instituted to finance projects for modernization in Shantung.[168] At the same time, Chang approached Hildebrandt to find out how to obtain shares.[169] Hildebrandt apparently had doubts about the advisability of selling stock to Chinese.[170] However, both the Berlin office and the German government supported the plan. From the point of view of the SEG, the sale of shares was evidently a sound financial move, and the company decided to sell them not only in Shantung but elsewhere. In addition, both the SEG and the Foreign Office felt that local notables would be more inclined to cooperate with the line if they had a financial interest in it.[171] There was never any question of selling enough shares to give the Chinese shareholders, or indeed the general public, a real voice in the company. In July, 15,000 shares were offered to the public in Tsingtao, Shanghai, and Tientsin; they were worth 15,000,000 marks, or about 20 per cent of the capital of the firm.[172]

When the stock became available, Chang decided to see if the local inhabitants would invest in the railroad. Instead of using the money he had collected, the governor established a procedure for prospective buyers to obtain their shares through their district magistrate.[173] However, no private individuals purchased stock.[174] This may have been due to the "backwardness" of the Shantung gentry, about which the provincial officials so frequently complained prior to the Russo-Japanese War. It may also have been, as the Germans suggested, that the wealthy people were wary of purchasing stocks which the government pushed.[175] The performance of earlier officially sponsored projects for investment had been disappointing; bonds, for example, had been sold to cover foreign debts and had never paid any interest. An additional reason for the lack of response was probably that the SEG stocks were not a particularly desirable investment. Not only were the shares a failure at Tsingtao, but they also did not do well with either foreigners or Chinese in the other ports, and most of the stocks were apparently returned unsold to Germany.[176]

When Chou Fu arrived at Tsinan, he implemented the original plan to have the provincial government purchase the stocks, though he still hoped to sell them to the public later.[177] In October, using 125,000 taels of the money which Chang had collected, Chou bought 300 shares.[178] The governor lacked the funds to buy more, but he did write to the important viceroys, Liu K'un-i, Chang Chih-tung, and Yuan Shih-k'ai, asking them to "buy a few shares, no matter how many," and pointing out that though China could not hope to control the railroad, it could "join in so as to influence it." [179] None of these pleas met any response.[180] Nevertheless, Chou himself continued to feel that buying shares in German firms might be an excellent way to control their activities; for, at the time he bought the SEG stock, he began to inquire about the possibility of obtaining shares in other German enterprises.[181] However, Chou did not purchase any other stock at the time, probably for lack of money.

According to the Agreement of 1900, after Chinese had bought 100,000 taels' worth of stock in the SEG, they were entitled to make an appointment to the management. As soon as he received the shares, therefore, Chou dispatched his representative to Tsingtao and, at the same time, attempted to get still more influence in the direction of the enterprise. In December 1902 he asked the company for the right to send several representatives to act as directors in addition to the one guaranteed by the regulations.[182] Chou planned to name a government official and a merchant, the former to be "responsible for relations with Chinese government officials" and the latter "for purely business matters." [183] Chou also hinted that in the future Tsinan might have to appoint even more representatives. The SEG did not seriously consider the governor's requests and in January rejected them bluntly by saying, "as far as we know, the relationship between the Chinese representative and our railway directors has developed in a completely satisfactory manner. Therefore, we do not see any reason why this situation should be altered by increasing the number of Chinese representatives." [184]

Once in possession of the shares Chou also began to press the company for some specific concessions. It was at this time that he initiated his unsuccessful campaign to have the company cover part of the cost of protecting the line. He also sounded out the SEG about the possibility of paying other taxes.[185] The company, whose concession included a most-favored-nation clause with regard to taxes, ascertained that there were other railroads in China which did not pay taxes, and so it rejected the governor's request.[186]

Chou, therefore, gained very little from owning stock in the railway. The purchase of shares had evidently been something of an experiment in influencing the Germans by obtaining some direct control of German

enterprises. It was an experiment which failed initially and never became successful. Thus, Chou abandoned his original plan to buy more
shares of the railroad or other companies. The shares of the SEG purchased in 1902 remained the only German stocks held by the province.

In addition to the railway from Tsingtao to Tsinan, the SEG's original
concession had given the company the right to construct railroads from
Tsinan to the border of Shantung, from Tsingtao to I-chou, and from
I-chou to Tsinan. However, the Germans never built any of these. The
I-chou–Tsinan line was rendered superfluous by the Tientsin-Pukow
Railway (formerly the Tientsin-Chinkiang Railroad), and the Germans
did not construct the other routes partly because the Tsingtao-Tsinan
line showed only a moderate profit. What is significant, however, is that
even if they had been extremely eager to do so, in the years after 1905
the Germans could not have extended their railway in Shantung without
full cooperation from the Chinese; and such Chinese support was no
longer available for any German or foreign railroad construction.

The opposition of the provincial government to any expansion of
the SEG beyond its initial line became clear shortly after the railroad
reached Tsinan. At that time both the Germans and the Chinese officials
felt that it would be a good idea to extend the railway a mile farther to
reach the Hsiao-ch'ing-ho Canal, which linked Tsinan to the Gulf of
Pechihli.[187] The SEG wanted to build the extension as part of its own
line. Chou, however, strongly opposed the company's plan. Ultimately
the governor managed to get the Germans to agree to build and operate
the route for the provincial government, which would finance the line
and receive all the profits. At first the SEG was not pleased with the
settlement since it endangered its right to build other extensions, but it
finally decided to go along with the governor because of the economic
importance of getting the connection to the canal built.

After the line to the canal was completed at the end of 1904, the Germans asked for permission to construct a similar extension to Lo-k'ou,
Tsinan's port on the Yellow River system. Yang Shih-hsiang, who had
become governor in the meantime, refused, for as usual he was unwilling to make even the moderate compromises which Chou had allowed.[188] In this instance, Yang's veto on the further expansion of the
SEG was supported by the local gentry, who were particularly hostile to
further German investment in Shantung.[189] Eventually the governor
asked a Chinese group to build the line.[190] Shortly before Yang left the
province, he even refused to let the SEG survey the proposed route of
the Tsingtao–I-chou railroad.[191]

In any case, by 1913 the Germans had not built the other lines and in that year formally gave up the right to do so.[192] In exchange, they received the privilege of providing Peking with loans to build Chinese railways with similar but somewhat longer routes. These were to go from Kao-mi to I-chou and then on to the Tientsin-Pukow line, and from Tsinan across the border of Shantung to the Peking-Hankow line. Ending the German railroad concession in return for a loan did, of course, represent a success for China. Nevertheless, the loan was the only privilege the Germans ever received in exchange for giving up a right they had obtained earlier in Shantung. Indeed, the loan concession stands out sharply as the only significant new privilege of any sort which the Germans got in Shantung after 1900. As such, it may actually indicate that the Chinese government in the early Republican period was less able to resist imperialist pressure than it had been in the last years of the Ch'ing.

The SBG

The Chinese success in limiting the German mining privileges was, if anything, even more impressive than the elimination of the dangers posed by the railway. For, in a sense, containing the threat of the railroad amounted to limiting the activities of the SEG to the company's basic economic function. On the other hand, the most serious threat presented by the SBG was contained in the company's monopoly over the thirty-li zone, which included some of Shantung's best mine fields. To regain economic freedom in these areas, therefore, the Chinese authorities had to violate the German concession directly. The basic strategy which the provincial government used to accomplish this goal was to encourage Chinese mining within the zone while at the same time parrying the considerable efforts of the SBG to preserve its monopoly.

It was Yuan Shih-k'ai's careful wording of the Chinese text of the Mining Agreement of 1900 which provided the Chinese officials with a theoretically legal basis for undermining the thirty-li zone. The Chinese text, as opposed to the German, had stated that existing Chinese mines in the zone could continue to operate, and it omitted the clause of the German text which limited Chinese mines to using traditional modes of operation. In practice, these discrepancies in the text of the regulations permitted Tsinan to justify the establishment of new Chinese mines of any type anywhere in the zone. There were many small Chinese companies already mining throughout the zone, and a liberal interpretation of the Chinese text allowed these companies to expand freely or improve their operations. Indeed, a Chinese entrepreneur could open a new mine by using the name of a defunct company which had once operated in the zone. Naturally the loopholes in the Chinese text would have remained nugatory if the Germans had not lost the power to enforce their own concept of the thirty-li zone. The Germans' belief that they had a monopoly in the zone was considerably closer to the spirit of the Kiaochow Treaty than was the interpretation which the Chinese asserted through their manipulations of the regulations of 1900.

In late 1900 the SBG resumed work at the Wei-hsien field, and the operations proceeded without disturbance thereafter.[193] In 1902 the mine there began producing coal. Intensive work at the Po-shan field began in 1902, and a mine was in operation there in 1907. At the same time the SBG reopened operations at Wei-hsien, Yuan Shih-k'ai renewed his drive to encourage local entrepreneurs to open mines in the zone. By August 1901 the *North China Herald* could note that Yuan "placed heart and soul" into the drive to open mines in Shantung and "had shown readiness to make considerable sacrifices for their accomplishment. The incentive is a good one from a patriotic point of view," the paper pointed out, "for Governor Yuan is determined not to let the Germans get ahead of him and take away rich mines from Chinese control." [194] In practice, however, neither Yuan nor his successor, Chang Jen-chün, got much of a response to their efforts to encourage Chinese mining; and in the early years after the Boxer Rebellion the SBG did not yet feel that Chinese mines presented a threat to the company's privileges in the thirty-li zone.

However, even in these early years Yuan's policy achieved at least one success which showed what the province was prepared to do in order to encourage and protect Chinese mining in the zone. In 1899 a Chinese company had reopened the Ting-chia-ching mine in the Wei-hsien field. Just as it began producing coal in 1900, the company had run into financial problems which, together with the Boxer Rebellion, forced it to suspend operations.[195] When the Ting-chia-ching closed, the SBG approached the owners and asked to purchase the mine. According to Taotai Hung Yung-chou of the provincial Bureau of Commerce, the Germans wanted the Ting-chia-ching because its coal was "good and abundant" and was much easier to work than at the nearby site where the Germans were boring. The owners refused to sell, however, and the Germans then demanded that the mine be closed because it was "only two li from the company mine and, therefore, dangerous." Tsinan, on behalf of the owners, repulsed this demand, maintaining that according to Article 17 of the Chinese text of the Agreement of 1900 whoever was working in an area first had priority there, whether Chinese or German.

By this argument the province temporarily succeeded in warding off the German threat. However, because of financial problems the Chinese mine owners were still unable to recommence operations, and in early 1902 they petitioned the province for a subsidy of 20,000 taels to enable them to reopen the mine. Taotai Hung was sympathetic to this request and urged Governor Chang to grant the subsidy. Hung pointed out that since the SBG still "lusted" after the excellent coal at the Chinese mine, the owners might be tempted to sell out either because they needed the money or because they "feared coercion" by the Germans. If, on the other hand, the province granted the subsidy, this not only would keep the mine in Chinese hands but also, by setting a precedent for resistance to German pressure, would "contribute to preserving China's power over profit in all of Shantung." Hung stated that though the Germans would "not be pleased" if the subsidy were given, their objections could be ignored. Governor Chang agreed with Hung and ordered the Bureau of Commerce to assist the enterprise by investing 30,000 taels in it.

When the SBG learned of the subsidy, it decided not to protest, because the Ting-chia-ching had been in existence prior to the regulations of 1900. However, the company did notify the Wilhelmstrasse of the case and warned that it might be the harbinger of a wider assault on the thirty-li zone, an assault which would probably rely on the ambiguities in Article 17. The company maintained that such a campaign was likely because the railroad would open up growing numbers of potentially profitable locations for mining in the zone and would, therefore, increasingly "turn the attention of Chinese businessmen toward mining operations." It pointed out that although the company had not yet striven to start a "theoretical discussion of the meaning of the clause" in question because there was no reason to raise a hypothetical issue, the Foreign Office should be prepared to exert pressure in the future to uphold the SBG's monopoly in the thirty-li zone.[196]

When Chou Fu became governor in the middle of 1902, he enthusiastically supported his predecessors' policies with regard to the SBG. Soon after his arrival Chou wrote that Chinese should claim as much mining territory as possible as quickly as possible in order to thwart the expansion of the German company. Chou's cavalier attitude toward the sanctity of the thirty-li zone was evident when he said that Chinese could easily get mining territory away from the company because the rights of the SBG only embraced a strip one-half-li wide on either side of the railroad.[197]

During Chou's term of office the provincial effort to encourage Chinese mining in the thirty-li zone gradually began to receive a more favorable response from private individuals. As the SBG had predicted, this was partially because the railroad made mining a more attractive investment. It was also due to the growing patriotism of the provincial elite. Since most of the new mines were small enterprises using traditional techniques, it is difficult to discover precisely how much the Chinese mining activities in the zone increased. However, by 1904 the mining bureau had encouraged at least three new mines in the Po-shan field which used simple modern machinery, such as pumps, and one large traditional-type enterprise in the Wei-hsien field.[198]

As the Chinese activities in the zone increased, they began to meet the active opposition of the SBG. For a time the protests of the company received backing from the German officials, but this support soon ebbed. The diplomats were never so critical of the SBG as they were of the SEG, for in its disputes with the Chinese authorities the mining company was only trying to obtain something guaranteed in its concession. Nevertheless, the German officials did not feel able to give the SBG the assistance it wanted, and for this reason the company eventually lost all hope of preventing Chinese from mining freely in the zone.

The SBG began its first concerted effort to stop the Chinese mining in early 1903 when the company sent protests to Chou Fu and Lange, the German consul in Tsinan.[199] Lange felt that the company's complaints were justified, and he interceded on its behalf with the governor. In the ensuing debate the basic argument of the Germans was that the Chinese mines operating in the zone violated "the sense of the Kiaochow Treaty and the wording of the Mining Agreement of 1900." [200] In particular, the Germans insisted, the Chinese enterprises were obviously illegal according to the German text of the agreement, which, they argued with little justification, was the "decisive" one because "it was written first and the Chinese was translated from it." [201]

Chou Fu responded by admitting that the two texts did not agree, but at the same time he asserted that "the regulations cannot be changed" and that the Chinese mines were legal "according to the Chinese text." [202] However, Chou was not content with defending the Chinese mines in the zone on the basis of discrepancies in texts. He also hinted that it would be advisable for the Germans simply to abandon the idea of a monopoly in the thirty-li zone. Since there was plenty of mineral wealth for all, he wrote Lange, "I hope Chinese and foreigners can open mines together." [203] Naturally, Chou made no move to curtail the Chinese activities in the zone.

Sporadic protests by the Germans continued, and in the second half of 1904 the SBG embarked on what proved to be its most intensive drive to preserve its monopoly in the thirty-li zone and to stop the Chinese mining. This campaign, too, ended in complete failure. For the diplomats, who had been willing but unable to enforce the company's rights the year before, had become less willing to pressure China and, in any case, had no real means available for doing so. The company's campaign against the Chinese enterprises began in the early summer and was precipitated by the completion of the branch line to Po-shan, which went through the best mining areas on the Tsingtao-Tsinan route. According to the SBG, as soon as the branch was completed, Chinese enterprises in the area began "to increase considerably." The company, therefore, decided that the time had come to make certain that its rights would be respected. Otherwise, it felt, the Chinese seizure of many excellent mining locations would be confirmed, and similar losses would occur in the future.[204]

Mumm and the consul in Tsinan, Betz, showed little interest in the company's new drive to enforce its monopoly. Betz in particular seemed unwilling to pressure Tsinan and, partly for this reason, quickly became the bête noire of the SBG directors at Tsingtao.[205] However, perhaps because of the legality of the SBG's position and the fact that it was just defending its concession, the Foreign Office in Berlin continued to back the company. In response to petitions from the directors in Berlin, the Wilhelmstrasse urged Mumm in August to investigate the complaints of the SBG and, if they proved legitimate, "to support the company firmly in its drive against the establishment of new Chinese mines and the expansion of old ones" in the thirty-li zone.[206]

Mumm was still loath to make a major case out of the company's complaints, for he felt that it would be very dangerous for Germany to coerce China in order to preserve a monopoly in Shantung. Although the minister did raise the issue with the Wai-wu-pu after Berlin ordered him to do so, he told the SBG he could do little in the capital and urged the company to settle the matter by working more closely with Betz in Tsinan.[207] This was rather hollow advice, and by November the SBG had accomplished nothing. Therefore, it decided to insist that Mumm "initiate the most serious sort of protest" in Peking in an effort to reach an "unambiguous interpretation" of the regulations of 1900 which would protect the SBG's monopoly in the zone.[208]

In essence, the SBG wanted the minister to open a major round of negotiations aimed at formally amending the regulations. In its letter to Mumm, the firm recapitulated the need for such amendments.[209] When the SBG originally agreed to Article 17, the company wrote, it had done so simply "to let Chinese mines already in existence die quietly."

This should have happened quickly, the company pointed out, for Chinese mine shafts did not have a life-span of more than five or six years because their technology, particularly in regard to water control, was poor. However, the Chinese had interpreted Article 17 in such a way as "to negate completely" the intentions of the company. This was because they claimed: "Mines which were formerly opened by Chinese can be reopened," and, "Concerns may change their locale whenever they consider themselves one and the same firm." Since the zone was covered with "thousands of old mine shafts," it was impossible to prevent unlimited Chinese infiltration. Finally, since the Chinese text also did not prohibit the use of Western equipment by Chinese mines, some of the illegal Chinese enterprises even had modern machinery, which enormously increased their efficiency.

The company submitted to Mumm four clauses which it wanted him to have added to the regulations. The first clause would have forced existing Chinese mines using Western machines to close, for it said that "within the thirty-li zone only the SBG is permitted to set up and use machines to mine." The company insisted that such a retroactive stipulation was fully justified because in 1900 there had been no Chinese mines in the zone using Western equipment, and therefore all those in existence in 1904 were illegal. The company was not particularly concerned about shutting down the traditional mines which had encroached upon the zone because they would die of their own accord. However, the remaining three clauses, which explicitly stated and restated the company's right to a monopoly in the zone, would have guaranteed that no mine of any sort could operate against the wishes of the company and, hence, take or keep a desirable location. The second article stipulated: "Chinese shall be allowed to continue mining where they are, but only in the Chinese manner and on the former scale, without machines." The third said, "If the SBG plans to open a mine . . . the governor of Shantung will be responsible for making certain that within two years all Chinese mines within fifteen li of the spot will be closed." The final amendment stated: "Chinese officials can make no objection to the SBG's use and location of machines within the thirty-li zone."

When it submitted its demands to Mumm, the SBG suggested a number of arguments which the minister might employ in his negotiations with the Chinese government. The company said one of the main points Mumm should stress was that the mining concession in the Kiaochow Treaty clearly envisioned a German monopoly in the thirty-li zone. In addition, the firm suggested, the minister could defend the sanctity of the zone on the basis of the "most-favored-nation clause" in the treaty.

For in 1902 the I-hsien coal mine had received a concession which stipulated that no mine using Western machines could open within one hundred li of its site, and no mine of any type could open within ten. Finally, the SBG reiterated its position that the German text of the Agreement of 1900 was decisive because it had been written first.

The SBG summed up the need for the amendments by saying, "We must have the Chinese officials recognize fully and without reservation the illegality of any further entrance of Chinese mines into the thirty-li zone and, equally important, the fact that such mines must be closed at our demand . . . Article 17 must be fixed clearly so that no further debates are possible and so that it is clear that Chinese mines in the zone are illegal if *we* feel they are harmful in any way . . . There is not a single Chinese mine in the thirty-li zone . . . founded prior to the Mining Agreement of 1900 and in uninterrupted operation since. We must, therefore, clearly contest the right of such mines to continue operations."

Despite the company's obvious desire for a serious effort to save its monopoly, Mumm made only token obeisance to the firm's wishes and did this only because of his orders from Berlin. At the same time, the minister endeavored to persuade the Foreign Office to discontinue its support of the SBG. Mumm sent a very pessimistic answer to the SBG's letter.[210] He pointed out that "experience" had shown that the Chinese government could be "moved only with great difficulty to agree to theoretical changes in settled texts," and therefore the central government would "not be very friendly to an initiative" in Peking aimed at changing the regulations of 1900 in favor of the company. Mumm admitted that the arguments which the SBG had presented with regard to the intentions of the Kiaochow Treaty were persuasive, and he also agreed that the privileges granted to the I-hsien mines might be cited to support the company's position. However, the minister pointed out, the only argument the company had suggested which related directly to the text under dispute was fallacious; for the archives proved that "the regulations of 1900 were first written in Chinese and only then translated into German." Therefore, he insisted, "the above considerations show that negotiations over the interpretation of the regulations would not be useful with the Wai-wu-pu" but should be held "with the officials who originally agreed to the regulations, that is, the provincial government." He again told the company to work with Betz and promised to ask the Wai-wu-pu to have the deputy governor, Hu T'ing-kan, enter into negotiations about the four amendments. If by any chance the Wai-wu-pu itself "should show some sympathy" for the SBG's position, Mumm assured the company he would "certainly work to negotiate with them with the greatest energy."

Mumm did pass on the company's requests to the Wai-wu-pu as he had promised,[211] and he asked the board to order Hu to negotiate with the SBG about the four clauses. In his letter the minister stated the company's case fairly but did not put any pressure on the Chinese officials to accept the four amendments. Indeed, there was nothing in Mumm's note which suggested why the Chinese should yield on the matter except for the fact that they were in the wrong.

The day after he wrote to the Wai-wu-pu, Mumm sent a letter to Bülow explaining why he was giving so little assistance to the SBG and suggesting that Berlin also withdraw its support from the company.[212] The minister admitted that the SBG was "fully justified" in a legal sense in desiring to maintain its monopoly over the thirty-li zone. "Nevertheless," he stressed, without real justification, "I think that it is necessary to consider the fact that the SBG received undreamed-of concessions in the Agreement of 1900 whose range the provincial officials did not appreciate at all at the time." Therefore, he said, "to move now with any sort of coercion against the Chinese in the zone might hurt the general interest of the Germans in Shantung." Mumm's argument, together with the growing danger of pursuing a seemingly aggressive policy in Shantung, evidently convinced the Foreign Office to change its position on the company, and by the end of 1904 the Wilhelmstrasse had stopped urging the minister to support the SBG.

The Chinese authorities rejected the suggested amendments and, in doing so, practically made an open declaration that they no longer believed the Germans had any special rights in the thirty-li zone. The Wai-wu-pu notified Deputy Governor Hu of Mumm's request. However, instead of ordering Hu to negotiate the four clauses, the board told him that they "violated the original regulations" and that he should oppose them on that ground.[213] In early January 1905, after the appropriate bureaus in Tsinan had submitted reports on the issue,[214] the Wai-wu-pu in Peking and Hu in Tsinan officially notified Mumm and Betz that the Chinese would not consider negotiating any amendment to the Agreement of 1900.

In Peking the Wai-wu-pu concentrated on defending the status quo and argued that there was no legitimate reason to change the regulations. The board said that, since the Chinese text was just as valid as the German, the SBG was actually requesting new concessions which would violate the earlier agreement. The board further pointed out that the company had no claim whatsoever to the privileges enjoyed by the

Chinese mines at I-hsien, for the origins and the status of the two enterprises were totally dissimilar. Finally, the board rejected each of the four amendments in turn, stressing in each case that the new stipulation was either redundant or illegal.[215]

The provincial government went even farther. Its response all but ignored the four points and instead launched a direct attack on the idea that the Germans had a monopoly or even a right of priority in the thirty-li zone. Tsinan said that the Chinese activities were perfectly legal according to Article 17. In addition, the provincial government continued, "Chinese are free to open mines wherever they choose so that the Chinese people will be assured of profit." Tsinan also asserted that Chinese could use modern machinery wherever they liked as long as it did not endanger a company mine already in existence and, moreover, insisted that the SBG could not begin work at any spot which would threaten an existing Chinese mine.[216]

After receiving these negative replies the German officials decided "to let the matter die" and made no further move to induce Peking or Tsinan to negotiate the four points.[217] Indeed, after Mumm's initial letter, the diplomats apparently never again formally mentioned the demands to Chinese officials. The reason for Germany's reticent policy was, of course, to avoid any controversy over a German monopoly in Shantung. However, even Mumm's patently half-hearted presentation of the company's demands proved to be extremely embarrassing to the Reich. The Chinese authorities apparently leaked the contents of the minister's letter to the press, which seized upon the SBG's demands and used them, in a considerably exaggerated form, in the anti-German drive then in progress.[218] In April 1905, for example, the German ambassador to the United States reported that an article on the demands was causing a stir in Washington.[219] The Wilhelmstrasse ordered the ambassador to rebut the charge that Germany was seeking a monopoly in the thirty-li zone and to do so by pointing out that there were a "large number of Chinese mines within the zone" which "not only continue undisturbed but which have recently installed modern machinery." [220] The Foreign Office did not indicate to the ambassador that it considered this situation in the zone unfortunate but, rather, seemed to regard it proudly as proof of the fact that Germany had no special claims in Shantung, not even in the thirty-li zone.

The SBG, thus, had to reconcile itself to the fact that its major attempt to save its monopoly in Shantung had failed and that it could no longer claim some of the best mining spots there.[221] After early 1905 the company abandoned any large-scale effort to stop Chinese infiltration into the thirty-li zone, and the sporadic protests which did continue had little effect.

Yang Shih-hsiang, of course, vigorously continued the policies of his predecessors and encouraged Chinese entrepreneurs to open mines in the zone, with the result that Chinese mining, particularly in the richer Po-shan field, rose sharply after he became governor. Yang's most significant action in stimulating the development of Chinese mines was the establishment in 1906 of the Bureau of Mine Supervision, one of whose activities was evidently the systematic subversion of the German monopoly in the zone. Shortly after it was founded, for example, the bureau opened a branch office in the Po-shan field itself in order to assist the Chinese mine owners there.[222] In 1906, when the SBG was looking for a spot for its second Po-shan shaft, it had to pass up some promising locations because they were too close to existing Chinese mines.[223]

The bulk of the growing Chinese mining in the zone continued to be carried on primarily by traditional methods, although such simple machines as pumps were often used. The absence of modern heavy equipment, however, does not appear to have been the result of any pressure from the Germans. Rather, it was probably due to the ability of the primitive Chinese mines to produce coal more cheaply than the large German establishments.[224] Thus, the Chinese mines could compete very successfully with the Germans. In 1907 a German observer noted that it was "astounding in what large quantities" the Chinese mines in the vicinity of the SBG could produce their "frequently excellent" coal, and as a result their output was depressing the price of the German product.[225] The SBG never became a financial success, in part because of the strong local competition which it encountered.

While Governor Yang was bringing about the de facto termination of the thirty-li zone, he also initiated the process which eventually led to its formal dissolution. In the first place, by disregarding the existence of the zone he began to convince the German diplomats that it represented a meaningless privilege which not only did not benefit the SBG but injured the amicable relations the German government was working to develop in Shantung. Furthermore, Yang began a campaign of harassment against the activities of the company.[226] This harassment was not only intended to destroy the thirty-li zone but was also an element in Yang's overall drive to limit and contain every German activity in Shantung. Because of the harassment, the SBG grew more sympathetic to the idea of renouncing its nonexistent monopoly in exchange for good relations, which might put an end to Yang's obstructionist tactics.

The forms of harassment which Yang employed ranged from attempts to establish likin stations around the German mines to efforts to prevent the Germans from exploring new mining possibilities within the zone. However, Yang's most effective measure proved to be his refusal to let the company undertake any other activities besides extracting ore, no matter how closely related to mining. In 1905 the SBG began to construct a coal wash and briquet factory at its mines in Wei-hsien. These facilities were considered essential for the efficient operation of the mining enterprise and were clearly an integral part of it. Nevertheless, Yang mounted an offensive against these additions, maintaining that the German concession did not include the right to engage in industry.[227]

By 1906 the directors of the company in Tsingtao were prepared to surrender many of their prerogatives in the thirty-li zone in order to improve relations with Tsinan. In May the SBG representative in the provincial capital, with the warm support of the diplomats, let the local mining officials know that the company would allow traditional Chinese mines to open anywhere in the zone as long as they did not impinge on mines of the SBG already in existence.[228] In exchange, the SBG wanted the Chinese authorities to allow the company to pursue its activities without hindrance. The general feeling about the plan among the Germans in China was expressed by the SBG representative when he wrote, "It would be a completely worthwhile exchange in return for the right to open the briquet factory . . . especially since our protests against new Chinese-style undertakings in the Po-shan field have had no effect anyway." [229] Yang was sympathetic to the proposal, though he probably did not take seriously the company's apparent desire to prohibit Chinese mines in the zone from using pumps.[230]

Nevertheless, an agreement might have been reached had not the directors of the SBG in Germany brought the negotiations to a halt by sharply vetoing any plan to compromise the existence of the thirty-li zone. The Berlin directors were apparently too distant from the scene to appreciate the rapid deterioration of the German position in Shantung, and they could not understand why the directors in Tsingtao, who only a year earlier had demanded that the zone be strengthened, were now willing to give it away. Thus, when they were informed of the discussions in Tsinan, the Berlin directors complained to the German government in a tone which would have seemed appropriate a year earlier but already sounded far out of date. They wrote, "While our directors in Shantung hope to solve the problems of Article 17 through a special agreement with the Chinese and report that the minister and the consul share this view, we do not feel that such a goal can be reached through the sort of compromise which seems to be floating in front of their eyes."

The "loss of rights . . . involved in permitting all traditional Chinese mines to open freely in the thirty-li zone," the company said, was an "unconscionably great concession" to make in exchange for nothing but good relations. Indeed, Yang's campaign of harassment was "simply an empty scheme to create problems" for the company in connection with "rights granted by treaty and by the regulations." [231] Therefore, the directors ordered their officers in Tsingtao not to negotiate "under any circumstances." [232]

The German diplomats in China were extremely displeased with the attitude of the SBG in Berlin. During the summer of 1906 they endeavored to have the Wilhelmstrasse force the directors to "accommodate themselves to the changed nature of the times" and become "more willing to meet Chinese desires." [233] They pointed out that it was foolish for the company to cling to its supposed privileges, because they were being ignored anyway as the Chinese "continued to reopen mines" in the zone and "to outfit with new machines those which only used traditional methods." [234] By October the government's pressure had had an effect on the Berlin directors, who wrote the Wilhelmstrasse, "We are now willing to come to an understanding with the local Chinese officials to solve, in as friendly a way as possible, the problems which exist." [235] The directors said they would approve of an agreement similar to, but somewhat less compromising than, the one proposed in the spring.

However, no agreement was signed in 1906. This was partially because the SBG in Berlin was still not willing to compromise quite so much as their directors in Tsingtao had wanted. Moreover, even the terms proposed by the directors would have required further negotiation to win Chinese approval. In addition, Yang himself may have lost interest in negotiating on the basis of the earlier plan. During the summer Merklinghaus, the German consul at Tsinan, reported that the provincial government was taking an "increasingly aggressive stance" toward the SBG [236] and that the local officials were saying the passage of time would put the Chinese in a better bargaining position in relation to the Germans.[237] The consul may simply have forwarded this information in order to convince the Berlin directors to negotiate. However, it apparently reflected Yang's actual position, for about the time the company agreed to talk, Merklinghaus wrote that Tsinan was no longer pushing for negotiations.[238] Yang may have changed his mind when he realized that the proposed agreement on the zone might reinstate some formal restrictions on Chinese mining, which was doing quite well under the old arrangements.

In the following years the Chinese mines in the zone continued to flourish.[239] In 1911, China finally succeeded in obtaining an agreement formally abolishing the thirty-li zone on the Tsingtao-Tsinan line, on the railroads which had not been built, and on the Tientsin-Pukow route.[240] By this agreement German mining privileges were limited to the area immediately surrounding the existing German shafts at Po-Shan and Wei-hsien and to the vicinity of the Chang-tien and Chin-ling stations, where the company was prospecting for iron. The rest of the zone was abolished, though a few restrictions remained on Chinese mining within its former boundaries. In exchange, China agreed to pay the company $280,000. This may have been a high price for eliminating a German privilege which was essentially meaningless anyway, but it was typical of the extravagance which nationalistic officials tended to display when any question involving China's sovereignty arose.

The Chinese success in abolishing the thirty-li zone was the result of steady pressure on the German mining monopoly. Yet it was also partially attributable to the poor financial returns of the SBG, which meant that the company, like the SEG, had little reason to expand. However, unlike the railroad, the disappointing performance of the SBG was partially due to the Chinese competition. Indeed, the fact that the SBG was unable to stop Chinese mining, which seriously hurt the company financially, even though that mining had originally been stimulated by the German railroad, was testimony to the decline of Germany's influence in Shantung after 1900.

Nullification of Germany's Rights of Priority

In 1898 the Germans expected that their sphere of influence in Shantung would enable them to obtain wide-ranging opportunities for investment in the province in addition to the specific concessions granted by the Kiaochow Treaty. They also hoped to monopolize the right to supply foreign advisers to the provincial government and to predominate in Tsinan's commercial dealings with foreigners. The Germans planned to attain these goals partially through the specific clauses in Article 3 of the 1898 treaty which granted the Reich priority privileges, and also through their general influence in the province. In practice, however, the German hopes were to remain unfulfilled.

In 1900 the Germans were on the verge of obtaining two additional economic concessions: one to finance the northern half of the Tientsin-Chinkiang Railway and the other to allow the Deutsche Gesellschaft für Bergbau und Industrie im Auslande (DGBIA) to mine in five large zones in Shantung. After the Boxer Rebellion the Germans sought confirmation of these two concessions so that work on them could begin. The difficulties encountered by the DGBIA in its attempt to confirm its concession illustrate why the Germans were unable to obtain new economic concessions in Shantung after 1900, let alone to invest freely in the province. It took years of negotiation before China was willing to recognize the DGBIA's claims, and then it did so in a different form and on a vastly reduced scale.

In 1901 the Germans reopened the negotiations over the DGBIA, which had been interrupted by the Boxer Rebellion. The case was presented to Yuan Shih-k'ai and the Wai-wu-pu as one which had been "settled" earlier and in which only "details" remained to be decided.[241] The German description of the state of negotiations prior to the rebellion was only partially correct, however, for the Tsungli Yamen had never "definitively approved" [242] the five zones, as the Germans claimed. Nevertheless, the discussions of 1900 had reached the point where details were being negotiated, and so the Chinese had opened themselves to the charge that they had agreed to the concession in principle.

At first, Peking and Tsinan refused to grant the request for confirmation of the concession. However, in 1901 the German diplomats were still willing to exert considerable pressure to strengthen the German sphere in Shantung, and they displayed what the Chinese authorities considered to be a "very coercive" attitude with regard to the DGBIA.[243] For example, Mumm wrote the Wai-wu-pu, "If you don't order this case settled soon, then I have no alternative but to report to my government that the normal methods of negotiation do not suffice to obtain concessions which have already been promised. This will cause a rupture in our normal pattern of relations, something which you certainly do not want." [244] The Germans even threatened that if China did not agree to recognize the just claims of the DGBIA, the company would simply begin mining without an agreement.[245]

Such pressure proved quite effective, for at this early date China was not yet able to parry a determined German effort to obtain something which had already been agreed upon. Moreover, the central government had not totally recovered from the Boxer Rebellion and still had to reconstitute the legal and institutional structure for dealing with foreign mining demands.[246]

Therefore, in January 1902, after almost a year of negotiations, the Germans were on the verge of success. Peking gave the Germans the right to begin exploring for minerals in the zones.[247] At the same time, in Tsinan, Governor Chang Jen-chün came to an agreement with the Germans on a set of twenty-one draft regulations confirming the DGBIA's concession and establishing the rules for the company's operations in Shantung.[248] The regulations were based partly on the Chinese national mining regulations of 1899 and partly on the SBG regulations of 1900. The Germans were not completely satisfied, for they had wanted the regulations for the DGBIA to be exactly like those of the SBG. Nevertheless, they accepted the draft agreement, probably because it did fulfill their primary objective, official confirmation of the concession.[249]

However, in February, when the Wai-wu-pu received the draft regulations for approval, it decided to reject them.[250] For by then considerable progress had been made in Peking toward reconstructing China's ability to pursue a nationalist policy on foreign mining.[251] In January the government re-established the K'uang-lu-tsung-chü, and by early February the bureau was drawing up newer and stricter national regulations on mining. One reason why Peking acted so quickly on these matters was the case of the DGBIA itself, as well as the increased pressure from the Russians for new mining concessions in Manchuria.

In its rejection of the draft regulations the Wai-wu-pu said that the DGBIA would be permitted to mine in Shantung only if the company were willing to abide by the Chinese national regulations. This would have meant, for example, that the Germans would have had to pay mining taxes called for in the new regulations, which included both a 5 per cent tax on production and a 25 per cent tax on profits. It would also have meant that the territorial extent of the German concession would have been severely reduced. After the Wai-wu-pu rejected the draft regulations, the Germans again resorted, for a short time, to the use of threats to obtain confirmation for the concession and even tried to use the board's refusal as a pretext for changing the draft regulations themselves.

Toward the end of February, however, the Chinese officials began to report that the Germans were becoming "exceedingly friendly and agreeable"[252] on the matter of the DGBIA, and by the middle of March the Germans had completely suspended their efforts to have the concession confirmed. The reason for the new policy was the wave of anti-German sentiment which accompanied the Anglo-Japanese Alliance. The demands of the DGBIA for five huge zones had probably done as much as any other single German claim to stimulate the charge that the Reich was seeking total economic control in Shantung. It was, for example, an attack on the DGBIA in the British press which prompted Foreign Minister Richthofen to ask Bülow to deliver the speech in which he publicly disclaimed that Germany had a sphere of influence in the province.[253]

The Germans reopened the question of the DGBIA in September, after Chou Fu became governor; and for the next three years they continued to try to persuade the Chinese authorities to confirm the concession.[254] The Germans were again willing to accept the draft agreement which they had signed with Chang Jen-chün, and occasionally they even offered compromises which indicated that they might be willing to yield somewhat more than they had to Chang. The Chinese rejected every German offer, however, maintaining that the DGBIA would not receive its concession unless it was willing to obey the Chinese mining regulations and surrender its claim to special privileges. The stalemate continued until 1905.

During these years the company hunted for suitable mining spots within the five zones, for Peking did not rescind the permission it had granted in early 1902 to undertake such surveys. As a result, the failure of the DGBIA to obtain its concession was not a disaster for the company. However, the Chinese officials were careful to make certain that the firm did not actually begin to mine. Although the surveys and tests apparently did not come up to the Germans' original expectations, the DGBIA did find enough promising locations to encourage it to continue the quest for its concession. Since it had not yet obtained the concession, the company naturally did not have the monopoly which it had demanded and, therefore, had no power to prevent Chinese from mining in the zones. One reason for the DGBIA's difficulty in finding suitable sites may have been that Chinese mines already occupied or were occupying the best locations. However, in contrast to the situation in the thirty-li zone, the provincial government does not appear to have made a concerted effort to encourage Chinese mining in the five zones. Probably this was because the DGBIA had no monopoly and no prospect of obtaining one.

Throughout most of 1905 the Germans continued to seek the terms contained in the draft agreement with Chang. Then, toward the end of the year, they suddenly became more willing to compromise. In November the company wrote the Wai-wu-pu to announce that the DGBIA was prepared to make a major "concession" and to agree, among other things, to pay the taxes specified in the Chinese mining regulations. "What we want to do," the Germans said, "is to give you proof that we are eager to use a friendly approach to compromise this long-standing case."[255]

An important factor in the DGBIA's decision to compromise in late 1905 was that the company was ready to begin actual operations at Mao-shan, and perhaps elsewhere.[256] Therefore the firm needed confirmation for its concession. Even in 1899 the SBG had found it impossible to mine in Shantung without the acquiescence and cooperation of the Chinese government, and this was even more true in 1905. Furthermore, the DGBIA feared that if it did not give in, it might lose its concession completely. As was the case with all German activities in Shantung, Chinese opposition to the enterprise was growing while the support of the German Foreign Office was diminishing.

The most important of the new pressures on the DGBIA came from the gentry of Shantung, who wanted to force the company to obey the Chinese mining regulations or to cancel the firm's concession altogether.[257] Indeed, the gentry, both those resident in Shantung and those in service elsewhere in the bureaucracy, were more hostile to the German attempts to confirm those earlier concessions which had not yet been implemented — the DGBIA and the Tientsin-Chinkiang loan — than to any other German initiatives after 1900. This is significant, for it is an indication of the opposition which would have built up if the Germans had tried to obtain entirely new concessions. In addition, it underlines the particular hostility the gentry felt toward German activities that might hamper their own opportunities for investment.

An excellent illustration of the gentry's attitude was a memorial written by Hsü Hui-feng, the president of the Board of War, who was a native of Shantung.[258] Hsü's basic point was that the Germans were violating Chinese sovereignty by using diplomatic pressure to demand mining rights in Shantung which did not accord with Chinese regulations. In order to "stop disaster and defend sovereignty," Hsü said, China ought "immediately to reject" the new German demands and "completely cancel" the concession.

Hsü's memorial presented an historical sketch of the DGBIA negotiations, which indicated how sensitive the Chinese elite had become by 1905 to slights to China's economic and political independence. It began by pointing out how unusual the whole situation was, for "in every other country . . . the natives administer the financing and control of railways and mines . . . and I have never heard of a foreign ambassador or consul in any other country interfering on behalf of his nationals and turning a common business deal into a diplomatic case." Hsü praised the Railway and Mining Bureau, which, he claimed, had originally rejected the demands of the DGBIA in the spring of 1899 "because the zones were too broad and violated regulations." According to Hsü, the turning point in the case occurred "in the summer of 1899 when Minister Ketteler unexpectedly interfered" on the company's behalf with the Tsungli Yamen, thus turning a "normal commercial case" into a diplomatic issue. Since in 1899 diplomatic pressure to obtain a commercial concession in

China, particularly in a sphere of influence, could hardly be termed "unexpected," Hsü's choice of words is an interesting indication of how widespread the nationalists' conception of China's rights had become.

Significantly, Hsü severely attacked the comparatively conservative Tsungli Yamen of that time and made a sharp distinction between its policies and those of the K'uang-lu-tsung-chü. He claimed that the Yamen "did not investigate the case or the action of the Mining Bureau and hence did not immediately reject" the minister's demand. "Rather," he said (without complete justification), the Yamen "just split hairs . . . without saying a word about how the huge zones of several hundred li should be . . . dismissed because they violated the regulations." Therefore, he continued, after the Boxer Rebellion the Germans could claim that China had agreed to the concession, and their arguments sounded plausible simply because the Yamen had not "explicitly" rejected the demands but had, rather, reacted in a way which could be construed as having given "tacit approval" to them. Hsü also criticized Chang Jen-chün, who, though he "made a few changes, had only some plans to ameliorate the situation and so did not clearly reject" the German demands. As a result of Chang's mistake, Hsü lamented, "the Germans again falsely considered the concession to have been confirmed . . . and the harm of allowing a purely commercial matter to become a diplomatic issue became very clear."

Hsü went on to praise the Wai-wu-pu and Governor Chou, who, from 1902 onwards, had understood the real issues involved in the case and had therefore insisted that the concession could not be granted unless the Germans followed the Chinese regulations. Furthermore, because the board and the governor had been "stubborn and had maintained fixed principles," China was "in a position to recoup the situation" completely and reject the concession. "If we act firmly," Hsü concluded, "the Germans will have no basis for interfering. This will allow the merchants and other people of Shantung to control the mineral wealth of the province themselves. It will avoid a great disaster and will regain sovereignty; both Shantung and our overall situation will be greatly benefited."

Yang Shih-hsiang basically agreed with the local gentry about the DGBIA; and Hsü Hui-feng, for example, praised him as a man who "studies earlier mistakes and firmly upholds principles." Nevertheless, Yang felt that it would "be extremely difficult" to annul the concession.[259] A surer and perhaps even more effective way to defend the essential principles at stake, he believed, would be to recognize the concession but to treat the company exactly like a Chinese firm. The most powerful program for recouping the situation now, he contended, "is to reach a further understanding with them, clearly saying that this is a commercial venture, and that they should follow the commercial regulations. This would include a plan to reduce the size of the mining zones, to have them pay a production tax, and in every way preserve our mining profit and protect our sovereignty." In order to guarantee that the DGBIA would retain no vestige of any special privileges, Yang did not even want to draw up a set of detailed regulations for the concession. He hoped instead to reach an agreement with the company which would bind the DGBIA to follow the Chinese regulations.[260]

Yang implemented this policy with great success. Negotiations over the concession were resumed in Tsinan in early 1906 between representatives of the DGBIA and the provincial Bureau of Mine Supervision. Yang's desire to emphasize the routine nature of the DGBIA concession permeated even the structure of the talks, for the main responsibility of the K'uang-cheng-tiao-ch'a-chü was the supervision of Chinese mines in Shantung. At one point during the negotiations the DGBIA representative, Baer, broke off the talks and went to Peking to appeal to the Wai-wu-pu on a number of disputed points. The board, however, was in complete accord with Yang's position, and Baer's visit to its office only resulted in a considerable loss of face for him and the company. The German raised one substantive point after another, only to have the board refuse to discuss any of them. Every time Baer mentioned a particular issue, the Wai-wu-pu replied, "This is basically a commercial matter and should be discussed between the company and the local officials," or "Even if you talk to us, the negotiations for the agreement must still be done in Shantung with the Bureau of Mine Supervision," or "If you will just negotiate in a friendly commercial way, then Governor Yang will be glad to help you." Baer quickly returned to Tsinan.[261] One of the reasons the Chinese were able to deal so cavalierly with the DGBIA in 1906 was that the German diplomats themselves did not want to make the case into a diplomatic issue and took virtually no part in the negotiations.

In the late spring of 1906 the DGBIA finally obtained confirmation of its concession, but on Chinese terms. The agreement[262] between the company and the Bureau of Mine Supervision did give the firm the right to begin mining, but the constant reiteration of the unexceptional nature of the company and its concession effectively put the DGBIA in the position of a Chinese enterprise. The agreement, whose definitive text was to be the Chinese one, began by annulling all earlier special regulations and stating explicitly that the company "will operate only according to normal commercial practices, for its activities bear no relation to any international diplomacy and are entirely unlike the mining carried out in the thirty-li zone which developed as a result of the Kiaochow Treaty."

The company agreed to comply with the most recent Chinese mining regulations, those of 1904, for all important matters, including taxation. Since in 1906 Chang Chih-tung was in the process of drafting new mining regulations, the agreement also bound the company to obey these when they appeared. The company was placed under the supervision of the provincial Bureau of Mine Supervision except where the national regulations specified the Ministry of Commerce in Peking. Moreover, the DGBIA was explicitly enjoined from turning to German officials for assistance in the future, an extraordinary stipulation in the era of extraterritoriality. Indeed, one of the most striking examples of the fact that the company's status approximated that of a Chinese firm was a clause stating that the DGBIA had to inform the Bureau of Mine Supervision whenever the company opened a branch office, even if the office was in a treaty port.

By placing the company under the Chinese mining regulations the agreement considerably reduced the size of the German concession. The company was given two years to select seven mining spots within the five zones. After that time it could not expand or choose any new locations. The seven mining sites had to conform to the dimensions specified by the Chinese regulations of 1904; each would have to be a continuous piece of territory which could be no more than four times as long as it was wide and whose total area could not exceed thirty square li. Once the DGBIA had selected a spot, the company would have to begin full-scale operations there within six months or else forfeit its claim.

Although the DGBIA could only select mining locations within the five zones, the company did not receive a monopoly over the zones. The agreement specified that the DGBIA could not take any spot where Chinese were mining or where they had "temporarily stopped but not completely closed their operations." This clause, based on the experience in the thirty-li zone, gave the Bureau of Mine Supervision and local Chinese entrepreneurs the power to block the company from obtaining any area of real value, for such a place would almost certainly be occupied by some sort of Chinese mine which could be reactivated. Furthermore, the agreement specified that any Chinese could request permission to open a new mine in the zone, and the company then had two months to decide if it wanted the spot as one of its seven. This clause opened the door to all sorts of additional restrictions on the Germans' choice.

Yang was overjoyed with the agreement, for, on the whole, it had resolved "the most fundamental issue in the whole case" just as he had hoped, by treating the DGBIA "exactly like a mine run by Chinese merchants." The governor was also proud of the fact that the company was forced to follow the Chinese regulations even though this meant that its concession was altered. "The total area of the five zones originally designated by the company was 120,000 square li and more. Now they have been permitted to designate . . . only a total of 210 square li, more than 570 times less." [263]

Peking also approved of the agreement but did not officially confirm it until August 1907, when the new Chinese mining regulations appeared.[264] The Shantung gentry were not pleased with the arrangement, however, and urged Peking to disavow it.[265] The government responded that the agreement protected China's basic rights and recovered so much from the DGBIA that added complications were not worthwhile.

By 1909 the two-year option granted to the DGBIA was nearing an end, and the company was not thriving.[266] It was only mining at Maoshan and even there was doing poorly. Therefore, two months before the agreement expired, the DGBIA offered to leave Shantung and to sell its assets to the province. Tsinan realized that this offer was really an attempt by the DGBIA to recoup some of the losses it had incurred in its decade in Shantung. Nevertheless, the provincial officials, never chary of spending money if they thought it might end foreign privileges, decided to negotiate with the company.

At first the Germans demanded 2,500,000 marks, a sum which may have been close to what the company had spent. However, they eventually agreed to settle for 340,000 marks. At the last minute the provincial gentry initiated a vigorous campaign against paying the company anything to liquidate its position. The officials countered by saying that if the DGBIA was totally rebuffed and given nothing for its equipment, the company might drag out the case and cause difficulties. It was worth some financial sacrifice to dissolve the concession neatly and rapidly. The officials prevailed and the deal was closed, thus terminating the DGBIA's venture in Shantung.

The other concession which the Germans received prior to 1900 and which was not implemented for many years was the loan for the northern half of the Tientsin-Pukow Railway. The draft agreement for the loan had been concluded in 1899 when the line was still known as the Tientsin-Chinkiang Railway; however, the final settlement was not made until 1908. The complex negotiations over this concession were not solely concerned with Shantung and did not particularly involve Tsinan.[267] However, the final concession for the loan was evidently delayed for a decade because of conditions similar to those which stymied the efforts of the DGBIA. That is to say, China was increasingly unwilling to agree to terms as favorable as those granted before the Boxer Rebellion, and the foreigners were no longer able to pressure China so effectively.[268]

As a result, when the concession was finally confirmed, its terms were far different from those of the preliminary agreement of 1899 and were, indeed, the most generous ever granted Peking for a railway loan.[269] The accommodating attitude of the foreign financiers evidently came mostly from the German side rather than the British, and, as a confidential Whitehall memo noted of the history of the negotiations, "the German demands, from being extremely exacting at the outset, assumed in the end the character of concessions to the Chinese which the British negotiator was inclined to view with a feeling of alarm." [270] The most important change from the preliminary agreement was that control and operation of the line were taken away from the foreign concessionaires and placed under the Chinese Railway Administration. The significance of this alteration was noted by the American chargé in Peking when he wrote that "the placing of the entire ownership and control of the road in the hands of the Chinese Government marks an important departure from the lines followed by the preceding railway agreements"; and he added that this "provision was made necessary by the outcry against foreign control of railways and, in view of the awakened national spirit, will likely be copied into all future railway agreements." [271] The other significant change in the concession was the improvement of the financial terms, which, among other things, no longer provided the concessionaires with a possibility of gaining control of the line if there were difficulties in repaying the loan. All in all, as one author has noted, " 'Tientsin-Pukow Terms' became a synonym for undue leniency and insufficient care for the safety of foreign investors." [272]

Between 1900 and the end of the Ch'ing the Germans obtained no economic privileges in Shantung other than the confirmation of the DGBIA's concession and the Tientsin-Pukow loan. Thus Shantung never became the field for investment which had been dreamed of in 1898. However, it is difficult to learn whether or not Germany still theoretically retained some right of priority for foreign investment in railroads and mines in Shantung. After 1902 the Germans repeatedly declared that they had abandoned that privilege. Nevertheless, no other foreign country received a major mining or railway concession in the province. In all probability this was because the Chinese officials were so successful in using Chinese competition and applying administrative controls that they did not have to limit German power by granting concessions to other foreigners, a technique which became extremely unpopular after 1905.

In any case, the provincial authorities did not hesitate to ignore the German rights of priority in those fields where there was no other way of limiting Germany's influence. Tsinan used other foreigners to prevent Germans from getting control over the right to supply foreign advisers to the province and to monopolize commercial transactions between the provincial government and foreign firms. As a result, by 1907, Germans not only had no monopoly in these areas but did not even predominate in them.

Yuan Shih-k'ai initiated the effort to avoid hiring German personnel. In 1901 when the governor established a modern provincial college, he appointed an American missionary, Watson Hayes, as its president. Yuan told Peking that he was selecting Hayes not only because the American was competent, but also because the United States had always been "peaceful" in its relations with China.[273] In addition, Yuan may have hired some Japanese teachers, but he apparently did not engage a single new German.[274] Nevertheless, the Germans did not protest. Even at this early date they had realized that they could not hope to enforce the right of priority for every type of personnel, and they decided that they would only insist firmly that all military instructors used in the province should be German.[275] They would have been pleased, of course, if Yuan had employed Germans in other fields, and the navy would certainly have allowed naval personnel to work for the provincial government and might even have subsidized German civilians whom Yuan hired. This would have allowed Tsinan to obtain highly trained and expensive specialists at a considerable saving. Yuan's refusal to use German advisers represents yet another example of the nationalists' willingness to make financial sacrifices for the sake of asserting Chinese independence.

Chou Fu ignored Yuan's policy and began to hire Germans for both civilian and military jobs. He continued to employ other foreigners, but he evidently had no qualms about using the inexpensive and talented Germans as well. For example, when Chou established a modern hospital in Tsinan in 1903, he asked a German naval doctor to be its head.[276] Since Chou was not compelled to use German civilians, his willingness to do so must be attributed to his less firmly developed sense of nationalism.

On the other hand, there was German pressure on Chou to hire German military personnel. In early 1903 the governor first began to consider employing some new foreign military instructors. The German consul told him, and the legation stressed to the Wai-wu-pu, that the Kiaochow Treaty specified that all such instructors would have to be Germans.[277] Chou, therefore, did hire two "Germans," one of whom turned out to be an Austrian.[278] Since the Germans' use of pressure to discourage the choice of other foreigners as military instructors was more than just a theoretical attack on Chinese independence, it appears that in this area Chou did try to avoid hiring Germans; for basically he was also concerned about the danger of German influence in Shantung. Chou's selection of an Austrian may actually have been an attempt to circumvent the German demands. In addition, the governor hired some Japanese who, Mumm said, "did jobs very similar to those of military instructors" but about whom the Germans could not complain because they were officially called teachers.[279]

German influence at Tsinan did not increase because of the Germans Chou appointed. This became clear by 1904 when Seckendorff, the German military instructor, wrote to Truppel to ask if some of the military students at Tsinan might go to Tsingtao for training. Seckendorff pointed out that such students had formerly been sent to Germany but that since this had become too expensive, they were being trained in Japan instead. "These measures have greatly weakened the influence and effectiveness of the German instructors," Seckendorff claimed, "especially since the most talented and best students are being sent." Seckendorff pointed out that if the students could go to Tsingtao instead, it would bolster Germany's power in the province.[280] Truppel denied the request, saying that he did not have sufficient personnel to handle the training of Chinese cadets.[281] Since Tsingtao could easily have absorbed a few top Chinese military students, Truppel's negative reply indicated that even the navy had given up trying to obtain power by influencing the military in Shantung.

Yang Shih-hsiang resumed Yuan's practice of not hiring Germans, and he had no difficulty in extending it to the field of military personnel as well. In 1906 the consul at Tsinan reported that the Germans had become the nationality with the "least prospects" for employment by the provincial government; and, he noted, "the few who still hold jobs here have them thanks to the previous governor of Shantung, Chou Fu. No new appointments can be expected from the present governor." The consul added that "the Chinese are quite frank about the fact that they find it uncomfortable to hire Germans because they fear this might lead to an expansion of German influence in Shantung." He also said that Yang was turning increasingly to Japanese when he wanted to hire foreign specialists.[282] By the end of 1906 the German military instructors had lost their jobs, presumably to be replaced by Japanese.[283] It would appear, therefore, that by 1907 the Germans not only did not predominate among the foreign advisers in Tsinan, but that, as a result of their former claims in Shantung, they actually got fewer appointments — given German competence, especially in military affairs — than they would have otherwise received.

There is little information about Germany's right of priority over the commercial transactions of the provincial government. However, it is unlikely that this privilege had much effect, especially after Tsinan was opened, for it would have denied that freedom of commerce so crucial to the trading powers. The available evidence seems to indicate that this privilege was treated in roughly the same manner as that for German personnel. Thus, Yuan evidently made a special effort not to purchase German goods or equipment, and he tried to deal with other countries.[284] Chou, on the other hand, perhaps under some pressure, had no compunctions against doing business with Germans when it was convenient.[285] Yang Shih-hsiang, however, once again turned away from German firms as a matter of principle, and the Germans did not object.[286]

The End of Tariff Autonomy at Tsingtao

As German power in Shantung declined, the navy jealously guarded the independence of Kiaochow. The administration was successful in maintaining the complete political and legal autonomy of the colony, and the Germans easily rebuffed every attempt by the provincial authorities to obtain administrative influence over the Chinese in the leasehold.[287] However, there was one area in which the independence of Tsingtao was compromised far beyond anything that had been anticipated when the Germans took the leasehold. For by the end of the first decade of the occupation the colony was no longer a free port but had become an integral part of the Chinese customs system. The naval administration consented to this fundamental change in Tsingtao's status because the tariff system negotiated in 1898–99 proved to be incompatible with the navy's main goal for Kiaochow, commercial development. Nevertheless, the Germans were reluctant to alter the system and refrained from doing so for as long as possible.

The Imperial Maritime Customs proved to be one of the earliest opponents of the original customs system. The IMC's main objection to this arrangement was that it encouraged smuggling across the long border between the free territory of Kiaochow and the interior.[288] According to one estimate, by 1901 smuggling was so prevalent that, although 80 per cent of the goods shipped into Tsingtao were destined for the interior, duty was paid on only 40 per cent of them.[289] In order to solve the problem, the Maritime Customs proposed in 1901 that an entirely new customs system be established. It suggested that, with the exception of a small free zone at the docks for the transit trade, Tsingtao cease to be a free port. The tariff revenue on those goods which were destined to remain in the leasehold would go to the German administration in the form of a fixed percentage of the yearly customs intake.[290] This plan was eventually adopted, but not until 1905.

In order to persuade the Germans to integrate Tsingtao into the Chinese customs system, the IMC tried to keep the navy aware of the dangers and disadvantages of remaining apart. For example, the IMC could always threaten to place a cordon of customs houses along the frontier, a situation which would have seriously hampered Kiaochow's dealings with the interior. In 1902 Ohlmer wished to write in his Decennial Report that "all goods and produce from the hinterland enter the German territory free of duty." Hart told him not to do this, so that the IMC would not lose any of its leverage over the Germans. "Our present *practice*," Hart stressed, "is to await export before touching what comes from the hinterland, but the convention has not given up China's right to tax such produce at the frontier, on or before entering German territory, and so it would never do for the Commissioner's Decennial Report to give it away." [291]

The IMC also refused to allow ships to undertake inland steam navigation to and from Tsingtao. Through regulations established in 1898 and revised in the Mackay Treaty of 1902, China's closed waterways and ports had been opened to foreign steamers.[292] The ships involved in this traffic were under the special supervision of the customs station of the treaty port in which they were based and were licensed by this station. The issue of whether the inland regulations applied to Tsingtao was raised at the end of 1902 when a German company decided to begin manufacturing silk in Kiaochow and planned to obtain some of its raw silk from southern Manchuria. When the firm asked the customs at Tsingtao for permission to use steamers to carry cocoons from the unopened ports on the mouth of the Yalu directly to Tsingtao, the IMC refused. The customs argued that under the 1899 system Tsingtao represented foreign waters, and steamships which operated under the inland regulations were not permitted to sail to foreign waters or to set out from foreign waters for China. This argument was a pointed reminder of the disadvantages of keeping Tsingtao outside the Chinese customs system.[293]

In addition to the IMC, another group which wanted to revise the customs system was the Chinese merchants at Tsingtao. They were primarily involved in trade with the interior and felt that the existing tariff structure enormously hampered this commerce. These Chinese merchants began urging a change in the system in 1901, and they became increasingly vociferous after 1902, when the railroad first opened service to the interior.[294]

The case of the Chinese merchants against the 1899 system was clearly presented in a petition which a group of firms submitted to the naval administration in 1903.[295] In it the merchants pointed out that the "European firms import goods free of customs and then sell them to major Chinese companies, who in turn sell them to large and small specialized merchants. If the goods then go into the interior, it is the last group which must pay the toll in Tsingtao. It is clearly from this circumstance that most of the problems arise." For, the petition continued, "at present instead of one large company paying the toll, it must be met by hundreds of small Chinese merchants. In this way smooth transactions become impossible, there are delays all along the line, and business piles up. Furthermore, the Chinese merchants are utterly ignorant about the system and the way it works and, therefore, have the greatest difficulty until their goods have passed the customs house successfully. When they reach the border, there is a further delay in the form of the customs check points there." Besides the complexity of the system, the merchants noted, another serious problem was that the "unavoidable" smuggling which it encouraged was "not only injurious to the customs but to the whole of the honest portion of the merchant community."

According to the petition, the weaknesses of the customs particularly affected Chinese businessmen because they worked on a profit margin so small that any setback was ruinous. Therefore, the existing structure tended to drive Chinese merchants out of the colony. Indeed, the petition pointed out, "in the areas directly on the border of the leasehold, commerce concentrates itself on distant Chefoo. This makes it clear that as the railroad grows, no large change in affairs will occur, for all these places are already much easier to reach from Tsingtao than from Chefoo. The Chinese prefer the inconvenience of the longer but unhindered trip to Chefoo to the difficulties which are tied up with exports at Tsingtao." The petition even claimed that "the millions which are paid to coolies for the public works" in Tsingtao "are not turned into goods here but go directly into the interior" in cash, because the workers from the surrounding area preferred to buy merchandise brought from Chefoo rather than to purchase items in Tsingtao for which they would have to negotiate customs.

The Chinese merchants proposed a customs plan which was similar to that drawn up by the IMC. Their suggestion was to make Tsingtao into a "free harbor on the model of Hamburg . . . that is, transit goods go free, so that foreign trade can be easily attracted and duty on goods meant for the interior is paid on the spot by the importer." Under this system the importer would add the tariff to the cost of the merchandise, and from then on the trade would be free.

The German business community was split over the desirability of retaining Tsingtao's status as a free port. The small merchants, who relied chiefly on supplying goods for the needs of the colony, wanted to maintain the status quo. On the other hand, the large import houses, which, like the Chinese, were primarily interested in the growing trade with the interior, sought an end to the free port.[296] At first the smaller concerns dominated Tsingtao's commercial circles. By 1903, however, the number of larger firms had increased to the point where their views prevailed, though some debates continued. In that year the Chamber of Commerce, which represented the European trading community, sent a petition to the navy calling for a new system similar to those proposed by the IMC and the Chinese merchants.

Until 1903 the naval administration opposed a revision of the customs system.[297] Any further integration of Tsingtao into the Chinese customs would have constituted a serious setback to the navy's dream of keeping the leasehold a totally autonomous colony like Hong Kong; and, as far as customs were concerned, such a move would have simply reduced Kiaochow to the status of a treaty port under German control. Even Schrameier, who felt it was necessary to change the 1899 system, admitted that any alteration in it would mean "without a doubt" that "the colony would have to give up some of its priority rights." [298] Another reason for the administration's hesitation was its desire to remain on good terms with the foreign community of Tsingtao, which until 1903 was dominated by the small German merchants.

In 1903 the navy itself began to recognize the economic and political disadvantages of maintaining Tsingtao as a free port, and the administration became more sympathetic to the pressure for a new system. For example, the navy answered one of the merchants' petitions by saying, "If it can be maintained that Tsingtao is strong enough within itself to reach an assured size independent of the interior through its own natural position and through the creation of its own commercial possibilities, then, like Hong Kong, whose huge transit trade can never be diverted, it can isolate itself consciously against the interior." But "if, on the other hand, Tsingtao sees its blossoming in the exploitation and utilization of the economic power of the Chinese province, it would be advisable . . . as far as possible to destroy and overcome all limitations which are placed in the path of a natural commercial expansion by way of the tariff." Since the naval administration had always stressed Tsingtao's economic connections with the province, it suggested that limiting the free zone to the harbor might have as beneficial an effect as at Hamburg and Bremen when these towns had joined the German customs system under "careful preconditions and with guarantees for their sovereignty." [299]

Nevertheless, the administration moved slowly to implement its new position and did not open negotiations with the IMC in 1903 despite the growth of the railroad and the increasing economic necessity for a change in the customs system. No basic reform was made in 1904 either. After the railway was completed, Chou Fu told Truppel that the time had come to revise the settlement of 1899.[300] The German governor replied that the system was part of the "special customs position of Tsingtao," and he made no effort to encourage negotiations. However, the navy did sign a special agreement with the IMC in 1904 dealing with inland steam navigation at Tsingtao.[301] In return for increased authority for the customs house at the port, the IMC allowed ships under the inland regulations to use Tsingtao as a base. This agreement seemed to indicate that the IMC appreciated the navy's more accommodating attitude toward the customs at Kiaochow, and it was also a sign that the navy was willing to grant the IMC a larger role in the leasehold in order to obtain economic benefits.

In February 1905 the navy finally asked Mumm to begin negotiations in Peking with Hart to end Tsingtao's tariff autonomy. The request was primarily the result of the accumulated pressure of the previous years. Its timing, however, was certainly a product of Germany's general tendency to seek accommodations with China in 1905. Schrameier called the decision a "declaration of Germany's policy in Shantung" and compared it favorably to Russia's hostility toward the IMC in Manchuria.[302] In addition, the growing drive in the Reichstag for economies in the administration of the colonies probably contributed to the navy's desire to negotiate; for closing the free port at Tsingtao would provide customs revenue for the leasehold. Mumm said that the Kiaochow government had asked him to act for two reasons: "First, the creation of a lucrative income for the administration, which will help the colony to come closer to the goal of self-sufficiency," and second, "freeing traffic to the interior from tariff." [303]

Because of the fundamental concession it was making, the navy hoped to obtain extremely favorable terms from the IMC. However, the negotiations, which lasted almost a year, apparently involved considerable compromise on both sides.[304] The final agreement was signed on December 1, 1905, and went into effect on January 1, 1906.[305]

Essentially, the new agreement transformed Tsingtao's customs status as a free zone into that of a treaty port. In exchange for the duties which the IMC collected on goods consumed in the leasehold rather than the interior, the IMC agreed to pay the naval administration 20 per cent of the customs received. This figure represented a compromise between a German demand for 30 per cent and a Chinese offer of 10 per cent. Articles for public or military consumption as well as capital equipment for industry in Tsingtao were exempt from duty. A small free area was established at the harbor to accommodate transit trade. The authority of the Tsingtao customs house to enforce the system and prevent fraud was substantially increased, although the German administration was responsible for prosecuting anybody who violated the rules of the IMC.

It was particularly difficult to establish the tariff for goods manufactured in the leasehold, and the problem was not settled until 1907, when a compromise agreement was finally signed.[306] According to this settlement, any item made in Tsingtao from products brought from the interior was, upon export, subject only to the duty on the raw materials. In addition, the duties on imported raw materials would be refunded if the finished product went out by sea. However, when an article manufactured in Tsingtao entered another Chinese port, it was subject to the full import duty.

The IMC and the Wai-wu-pu were pleased with the new customs system. Hart reported that he approved of it,[307] and Ohlmer said that the "new arrangement has inspired confidence in the stability and future of the port." [308] When China negotiated with Japan over the establishment of the customs in Dairen in 1907, the goal of the IMC was to get a system like the one at Kiaochow.[309] However, the Japanese apparently were in a stronger position than the Germans, for the system eventually set up was closer to that of 1899 than to that of 1905.

The Kiaochow authorities were satisfied with the economic benefits of the new system; and the navy made no effort to revise it in 1910 when the agreement would have permitted the naval officials to suggest changes.[310] However, they remained aware of the fact that they had made a concession which seriously impinged on the independent status of the leasehold. Thus, in his final analysis of the "worth of the agreement," Schrameier emphasized the navy's statesmanship in putting economic rationality above all other goals and giving the IMC so much power in the German colony. To prove his point, Schrameier quoted with great pride a long section from an article in a London *Times* of 1906 which praised the new tariff agreement as a "German Object Lesson in China." Among other things the article said, "The Germans have recognized that an illegal trade is a poor foundation upon which to build a colony; and, thus, have proven themselves to be more understanding and better colonists than their three rivals (England, France, and Russia) and, we must admit, than the new Japanese owners of Port Arthur and Dairen. Instead of keeping the Chinese financial officials far from themselves or even hindering in carrying out their just activities within the German borders, the Germans have invited the customs house into Kiaochow . . . Now in the place of partial control, full tariff control has been given to the Chinese customs." [311] Since the *Times* had normally been hostile to Germany's special privileges in Shantung, its commendation of the new agreement testified to the fact that the tariff settlement represented a major element in the abolition of those privileges.

VI. The Germans and Development in Shantung

The Success of the Naval Administration and the Reaction of the Reichstag

The Germans eventually lost their claims to special privileges in Shantung. Nevertheless, they did make a contribution to development within the province. This contribution was limited in scope and affected, for the most part, only the leasehold itself and, to a lesser degree, the areas surrounding the roadbed of the SEG. Still, what was accomplished is not only an intrinsic and important part of the history of the sphere of influence in Shantung but is also of interest because of the insights which it provides into the impact of imperialism on China. The Reich's activities were no more advantageous to Germans than to other foreigners and the Chinese, who profited from the German efforts without having to finance them. Indeed, because of the inherent difficulties of economic development in China, Germany did not, on the whole, benefit from its involvement in Shantung.

Since the center of German endeavors in Shantung was at Kiaochow, an important element in Germany's role as a modernizing force within the province was its effective administration of the leasehold. The navy's original goal with regard to the problem of governing Kiaochow had been to make the territory into a model colony and a focus for commercial growth. In the years which followed, the navy's administrative system contributed significantly to the attainment of these objectives and, hence, to the development of Tsingtao. In China both Chinese and foreigners were struck by the success of the German efforts, and in Germany this success was underlined by the fact that, among all the German colonies, Kiaochow was singularly popular with the Reichstag.

Tsingtao's population grew steadily after 1900. By 1907 the population of the port had reached 35,000. This included 31,000 Chinese and 1,650 European civilians.[1] Almost all the foreigners were German. By 1913 the town had grown to 55,700 people, of which about 53,000 were Chinese and the rest European civilians.[2] The 1,855 Germans still vastly outnumbered the other nationalities; however, the percentage of non-Germans had grown considerably. Among the more important groups were the Japanese with 316, and the Americans, British, and Russians with about 50 each. As a result of the development of Tsingtao, the population of the rural areas of the leasehold also grew. Although it is difficult to learn the precise size of the increase, it would appear that the population of the hinterland, which in the early years was about 80,000, had reached about 135,000 by the last years of the German presence.

As Tsingtao grew after 1900, the administrative structure which the navy had established proved able to cope efficiently with the problems of governing a larger community. The only important change affecting the European population came in 1908 when the navy established a separate court of appeals for cases originating in Tsingtao, which, by eliminating the need to appeal cases to the German consul general at Shanghai, made the colony's legal system more autonomous.[3] The story behind the establishment of this court reveals that the rivalry between the navy and Foreign Office extended even into Tsingtao itself; for the navy had wished to set up a separate court there as early as 1901 but had been prevented from doing so by the Wilhelmstrasse. The navy argued that the further development of Kiaochow necessitated a separate appeals court for the colony, while the Foreign Office claimed that the navy only wanted the court in order to increase Germany's commitment to Shantung and to reduce her role in other parts of China, particularly Shanghai. The Wilhelmstrasse successfully blocked the appeals court for six years, or until the battle between the two branches of the German government had long been settled in favor of the Foreign Office.[4]

The navy's administrative structure for the Chinese in the leasehold also remained more or less unchanged. After 1900 the most significant development in the urban zone occurred in 1902 when a Chinese committee was established to advise and assist the navy in governing the Chinese community.[5] This committee fulfilled the same function for Chinese residents as the advisory council, which the navy had appointed earlier, performed for the European community. The Germans claimed that as time passed the Chinese population of the urban zone became increasingly accustomed to German rule and increasingly impressed with its efficiency and justice.[6] Among other things, the absence of any unrest after 1900 would tend to support this claim. In the rural zone the Germans continued to govern according to the loose and effective system they had established earlier on the basis of Chinese methods of local government. However, the navy did try to rationalize some of these methods, particularly in the fields of education and taxation. There was also no unrest in the rural zone after 1900.

The navy's unique approach to the utilization and taxation of land contributed significantly to the smooth development of the leasehold. The system provided the colony with a steady supply of inexpensive lots for building and, in addition, raised some revenue for the administration. Indeed, the Germans claimed that Tsingtao was the only place on the crowded China coast which had escaped the evils of land speculation.[7]

The government continued to purchase land after 1900. By the end of 1901 it had obtained most of the real estate which was eventually incorporated into the town.[8] Thereafter, the administration bought land in different parts of the leasehold only as it was needed for special purposes. The acquisition of land on a large scale stopped in 1906; by then the government had about 6000 acres. Much of the territory which the administration owned was used for its soil reclamation and forestry programs, both of which were very successful. In the urban zone the government carried out a program of total land reclamation. By the end of the first ten years the navy had filled in gullies and other eroded areas and had covered the once barren soil with a variety of vegetation. The hills in and around the city were thoroughly wooded. In the rural zone the administration engaged primarily in forestry. It planted trees and also, by distributing saplings and providing various forms of assistance and advice, helped the Chinese residents to develop their own programs. The navy was especially proud of its success with land reclamation and forestry and claimed that these efforts were unique in China.[9] The navy may have been correct, for visitors to Kiaochow were amazed by the tree-covered hills which were such a "strange sight in China." [10] One visitor even proclaimed that Germany's greatest triumph at Kiaochow was the fact that "not less than a hundred square miles of country, where a tree had not been seen for a thousand years," were "clothed with verdant wood." [11] The program of land reclamation at Tsingtao made some impact elsewhere. The navy supplied the SEG and SBG with trees which the companies planted near their enterprises. The Germans also helped develop a forestry program for Chou Fu at Tsinan and for T'ang Shao-i at Mukden.

The sale of land to the public proceeded smoothly as Tsingtao grew. By 1906, Chinese had purchased about 50 acres and Europeans 540 acres in the urban zone. The government also continued to lease space to private individuals and companies. This consisted mostly of land used to build storage facilities at the harbor, as well as real estate bought by the navy and rented back to the original owners.

The revenue which the land system produced was a moderately important source of income for the administration. By 1906 the government had earned enough from land sales to cover the cost of all the real estate which it had purchased from Chinese landowners; and such income continued to come in thereafter. Of course, the increased value of the land which the navy held was primarily due to the government's own vast investments in developing Tsingtao. The administration also raised some revenue from the 6 per cent tax on land, though not from the profits tax on the sale of real estate. This latter fee was aimed primarily at preventing speculation, however, and was therefore considered a success. In 1913, the year in which the revenue raised locally reached its peak, the Kiaochow government received 380,000 marks from the sale and leasing of land and 200,000 marks from the land tax.[12]

The major change in the land system after 1900 was the integration of the Chinese rural zone into the tax structure of the colony. This development deserves attention not only because it is an example of the thoroughness of the naval administration but also because it provides an interesting insight into the possibilities which might have been open to the Chinese government to rationalize its own system of land taxes,[13] if it had had the desire and the power to do so.

The most serious problem with the existing Chinese tax system was that collection was completely in the hands of local collectors and go-betweens, who not only took out a substantial percentage for themselves but also tended to favor those with connections, which naturally included the larger landowners. An additional drawback of the traditional system was that the district magistrate received the land revenue in silver, while the landowners paid the collector in copper cash. By 1900 the price of silver had dropped considerably below what it had been when the tax quotas had been set. This resulted in a drop in revenue for the government without particularly benefiting the landowners; for the tax collectors did not reduce their collections of copper but simply bought the silver for the magistrates more cheaply, thus increasing their own percentage of the take.

Chinese officials had developed various complicated schemes for circumventing such problems. One was to add a bewildering number of special fees to the tax rate officially prescribed. Another was to establish an artificial exchange rate between silver and copper within a given locality or province. For example, while Yuan Shih-k'ai was governor of Shantung, he instituted a tax reform in which he set the value of an ounce of silver at 4800 cash, though its market price was really 2000 cash.

The Germans, from the start, had planned to rationalize the Chinese system in order to collect taxes in the rural zone. But it was not until the cadastral survey of the rural zone was finished in 1904 that they could effect any real changes. The German tax reform of that year was quite simple.[14] In the first place, the administration established a single tax rate, 200 cash per *mou*. This, the average rate prescribed under the old system, actually represented about one half of what had been collected. Secondly, the Germans eliminated the office of tax collector and made the village elders responsible for collecting taxes and bringing them to the German magistrates. In exchange for collecting and transporting the taxes, the elders were permitted to levy and keep a surcharge of 5 per cent of what they obtained from each landowner. Finally, the German magistrate calculated the tax in ounces of silver at whatever the real exchange rate was at the time of payment.

The new system worked extremely well. The amount of revenue which the government received in 1904 was three times what had been obtained under the old system. This was particularly impressive because of the low rate. The revenue obtained was negligible: $9,840. However, the purpose of the new system was to help make Kiaochow a model colony, not to produce income.

The navy proudly pointed out that its new tax system was almost identical in outline to a comprehensive plan for national tax reform which Robert Hart suggested to the Chinese government in 1904.[15] The two plans appeared at virtually the same time; Schrameier said that they were similar not because either had influenced the other, but because both aimed at rationalizing the same traditional system. Hart estimated that if his plan were implemented, the revenues of the Chinese government might rise from 80,000,000 taels to 400,000,000; and the Germans, on the basis of their experience at Kiaochow, agreed that this was a reasonable figure.

The growth of Tsingtao's population did not interfere with the German administration's success in eradicating the poor health conditions which had plagued the colony in its early years and which were the rule throughout China. The basic health problems at Tsingtao were solved within ten years, and, indeed, by 1907 the port was reputed to have the best public health record in China.

The improvement in health standards shows up clearly in the statistics kept on the German troops. In 1902 the rate of illness among the troops dropped to what the Germans considered an impressively low figure for China, 68 per 1000.[16] Nevertheless, as the navy was quick to admit, this figure was still double that for similar troops in Germany. However, it continued to drop steadily, and by 1907 the disease rate among the forces at Tsingtao, 36 per 1000, finally approximated the rate in Germany.[17] Detailed figures are not available for the rest of the population at Tsingtao, but the health of the civilians apparently improved along with that of the troops, though more slowly for the Chinese community than for the foreigners.

One reason for Tsingtao's relative lack of disease was that the government strictly enforced the zoning rules and building codes which had been established in the early years. As a result, the town developed in an orderly fashion unusual for the early twentieth century, especially on the China coast.[18] The master plan adopted in 1898 remained the basic guide, and as the city grew, new areas were integrated into the plan. In 1901, for example, the government established a third area for Chinese residence, located on the western side of Tsingtao, which it named T'ai-hsi-chen. Like T'ai-tung-chen, T'ai-hsi-chen was to be a planned community, and the navy leased land there to residents on the same basis as at T'ai-tung-chen. By 1902 virtually the entire population of the urban zone lived in new buildings which met the requirements of the building codes, for the government had razed most of the barracks and houses which had been built before 1898. In 1904 a commercial and residential area was opened near the new harbor. Eventually the open spaces between the various sections of Tsingtao disappeared, and the town became a single unit; but the navy continued to enforce the zoning regulations. These rules, however, did have one drawback: the stringent limitations on population density and land use tended to make rents at Tsingtao among the highest in China.

A further reason for the good health record was that the hygienic regulations at Tsingtao were carefully observed. A special wing of the police force was made responsible for enforcing them. Among their other duties, these policemen were supposed to teach modern health practices to the Chinese community. They checked up on vaccinations and even organized campaigns against flies, mosquitoes, and other pests. The health regulations governed the handling and sale of food, and in 1906 the government itself opened a new slaughterhouse which, like most of the navy's projects at Tsingtao, was a model of its kind. An awed observer claimed that it was "magnificently arranged with all the latest appliances in machinery, mechanical contrivances, refrigerators." [19]

It came to have the "best reputation" of any slaughterhouse in East Asia.[20]

The modern water and sewage systems which the navy constructed also contributed to Tsingtao's high health standard. By 1902 the navy had finished building a central water system which supplied the town with safe drinking water. The water came from artesian wells which the navy dug at the Hai-po Valley north of the city, pumped to a reservoir on the heights behind Tsingtao, and then piped into town. At first, the water was made available to the public at several locations in the European and Chinese sections of the city. However, beginning in 1904, water could be piped directly into houses in the European section; and this service became available to the Chinese in 1906. As Tsingtao grew, the government expanded the system and in later years built reservoirs elsewhere in the rural zone. In 1899 the government had begun to build a system of small storm sewers in Tsingtao. During the early years, however, private Chinese contractors, under the close supervision of the government, were responsible for removing sewage. Then, in 1903, the navy started to construct a sewage system, which went into operation in the European sections in 1905 and in the Chinese sections in 1907.

Both the Europeans and the Chinese in the leasehold enjoyed what appear to have been excellent hospital facilities. In 1900 the government established a modern and well-equipped hospital for Europeans. By 1907 this hospital had grown into a major medical center with a complex of buildings and a large staff. Attached to the hospital was a bacteriological research laboratory which, the navy proudly reported, made significant contributions to the understanding of local diseases. The medical center was in contact with doctors all over Shantung and sought to improve the health standards elsewhere in the province.

The navy and the missionaries cooperated in setting up hospitals for Chinese residents. The first modern hospital for Chinese at Tsingtao was opened by the Weimar Mission in 1901. By 1907 the Catholics were operating another one there, and the navy had established two in the rural zone at Li-ts'un and Hsi-fang. The Germans also set up hospitals for the local population of the neutral zone. The Weimar Mission opened one at Kao-mi, the Berlin Mission one at Chi-mo, and the navy one at Chiao-chou, which was turned over to the Weimar Mission when the German troops withdrew.

These hospitals were quickly accepted by the Chinese population, which contributed financially to their upkeep. In addition, the Chinese were stimulated by the Germans to open their own hospitals. In 1904, for example, the residents of T'ai-tung-chen built a modern hospital with the aid and encouragement of the missionaries and the navy. In the same year the navy helped Chou Fu open his new hospital in Tsinan.

One light-hearted tribute which the residents of the China coast paid to the salubrious atmosphere of Tsingtao was to flock to the town for the summer. In 1904 there were 500 tourists, and the figure rose steadily thereafter. One satisfied customer wrote that, after the Russo-Japanese War, "gradually the news spread about in Far Eastern ports that Tsingtao was the healthiest city in Asia and was a delightful summer resort," with the result that the summer months "found American, British, German, French, and Chinese residents of Hong Kong, Shanghai, Yokohama, and other Eastern ports all away from their sweltering climates and lounging comfortably about in innumerable beautiful little villas of Tsingtao . . . Each year saw the prestige of the colony in this respect rise." Eventually, he said, "Tsingtao became known as the 'Brighton' of the Far East." [21]

Probably the main reason for the navy's ability to administer Kiaochow so effectively and to perform the many other tasks required for the lease-hold's development was the fact that Germany spent tremendous amounts of money on the colony. The budgets for Kiaochow between 1898 and 1907 totaled 102,337,442 marks, and the actual expenditures were probably higher.[22] Discounting the cost of suppressing the great African uprisings of 1904–1906, more money had gone to Kiaochow by 1907 than had ever been spent on any other German colony. This was the case despite the fact that the African colonies were many times larger and had been receiving money since the 1880s.[23]

Only 3,517,000 marks of the total expenditure before 1907 came from revenue collected within the colony itself; the rest was supplied entirely by subsidies from the German government to the naval administration.[24] Kiaochow never came close to being self-supporting, though in its last years a growing percentage of its annual budget did come from local revenue. In 1913 the total budget for Kiaochow was about 16,800,000 marks, of which 7,200,000 marks were obtained locally.[25] Besides land, the other major sources of indigenous revenue for the leasehold in that year were the government shipyard, which produced 3,600,000 marks; the government utilities, which yielded 2,700,000 marks; the customs, 550,000 marks; and harbor fees, 155,555 marks.[26] By 1913 the German government had spent altogether about 200,000,000 marks on Kiaochow, of which about 36,000,000 had been obtained locally.[27]

During the first decade of Kiaochow's existence, despite the enormous amount of money which the colony consumed, it enjoyed unusual favor in the Reichstag. This support was the sort of approbation for which Tirpitz had hoped when he put Kiaochow under the navy rather than the Colonial Bureau of the Foreign Office, and it testified to the navy's success in administering and developing the leasehold. In later years the huge expenditures on Kiaochow came under attack in the Reichstag, but politicians did not question the fact that the colony itself was being extremely well managed and developed.

The most striking manifestation of Kiaochow's unique popularity occurred during the period from 1904 to 1906 when the opposition in the Reichstag to the German colonies reached its peak. This opposition consisted of the usual charges that the German colonial empire was a failure because the Colonial Bureau had administered the colonies poorly, had not tried to develop them economically, and had, therefore, simply wasted tremendous amounts of money. While these charges may not have been totally accurate, what is significant is that many of the Colonial Bureau's most vehement critics continued to praise Kiaochow at the same time they were attacking the other colonies.

In 1905, for example, when the controversy over the colonies was raging, the vote on the Kiaochow budget elicited nothing but a series of speeches praising the leasehold. A highly significant speech was that delivered by the deputy, Eickhoff, on behalf of Eugen Richter's Progressive Party, one of the most important parliamentary groups which condemned the other colonies.[28] The speech was applauded from both sides of the house. Eickhoff began by noting the "gratifying development" of Kiaochow and then said, "Certainly through the years we have granted a large amount of money for Kiaochow, but it was used in a rational way." The adjective "rational" was probably the highest compliment a Progressive could pay to any expenditure. Eickhoff continued with a pointed reminder of the differences between the ways the navy and the Foreign Office administered their colonies. "The navy has made a really workmanlike, German job of it. Our party has said this in past years, and our spokesman, Deputy Eugen Richter, therefore, added the suggestion that in the future all the colonies should be put under the Naval Ministry. (Very true! *from the Left.*) Gentlemen, I really believe that the Naval Secretary ought to be pleased about this. (*Cheering.*)" Eickhoff then launched into a sympathetic discussion of Kiaochow's problems and progress. At one point he referred to the health situation in the colony, something which had previously bothered the Progressives, by saying, "Gentlemen, I confirm joyfully that the pessimistic conception which I earlier . . . expressed about the climate of Tsingtao has fortunately not been confirmed by facts. (Hear! Hear! *from the Right.*) The state of health in Tsingtao . . . has improved from year to year, and the figures from this year's annual memorandum show that one can now say: Tsingtao can be considered completely healthy."

The representative of the Center Party, which had spearheaded the attack on the other colonies, devoted his speech to extolling the legal system of Kiaochow.[29] He also discussed the contribution which the navy was making to the entire field of German colonial law through its activities there and urged that it do even more. The Social Democrats generally opposed Kiaochow, but, perhaps because they recognized a difference between it and the other colonies, they did not speak at the session at all.

The criticism of the colonies in the Reichstag stimulated the colonial reform movement, which began in late 1906 under the leadership of Bernhard Dernburg.[30] It would be interesting to discover what impact the example of Kiaochow had on Dernburg's plans for the other colonies; for his most famous reforms, which were primarily intended to stimulate economic development, attacked just the kinds of problems which the navy had solved successfully at Kiaochow. Dernburg sought to reform each colony's administration, improve the legal system, better the treatment of the colonial peoples, and bring land speculation under control. His prescriptions for economic progress laid particular stress on the improvement of communications within each colony and the construction of good harbors on the coast.

Although Kiaochow never lost its reputation as a model colony, parliamentary opposition to it developed over the basic question of whether, in the final analysis, the whole undertaking was worth the cost. This campaign against Kiaochow reached a climax in 1908, with a broad attack on the leasehold in the Reichstag. The nature of this opposition is clearly revealed in a speech delivered by Mathias Erzberger, the Center deputy who had made his reputation in the earlier battle against the colonies.[31] Erzberger began by referring to that year's memorandum on Kiaochow and stating that he was very impressed by the colony's progress. "I acknowledge," he said, "that on the basis of all reports, both official and private, which we have received about Kiaochow, the money used there has accomplished very much and has been spent very skillfully." But, he stressed, "I miss one thing in this very interesting memorandum: everything is enumerated which concerns development and the growth of commerce. But there is one figure which is missing that would seem to concern us Germans quite a bit, namely the 110-million-mark subsidy." Erzberger continued with a jibe at Prussia by noting that although the development of Kiaochow was indeed remarkable, "I believe that if the 110 million had been spent in Germany, one could make the finest garden in the world even out of the Mark of Brandenburg. Very salutary cultural work could also be accomplished at home if 110 million were spent on an area smaller than an ordinary Prussian district, an area only as large as the Free City of Bremen. We must always keep this sum of 110 million marks in mind when we really want to evaluate the accomplishments of the naval administration, which I fully acknowledge."

This sort of attack, of course, struck not only at Kiaochow but at the supposed economic value of all imperialism. The navy responded by instituting economy measures at Kiaochow, and, in the remaining years, criticism of the cost of the leasehold abated. The amount spent on Kiaochow remained large, and the navy's economies apparently did not set back the development of the colony, for which the groundwork had already been laid. Nevertheless, the whole effort had lost its sheen; no matter how well the navy spent its money to improve Kiaochow, the basic question always remained, should the place be developed at all? It may have been for this reason that the 1909 annual memorandum to the Reichstag was the last of these lavish publications which the navy issued. This was a subtle sign of economy, as well as recognition of the fact that there was no point in stressing the wonderful "Development of the Colony of Kiaochow" each year unless it could be shown somehow that Germany was benefiting in an important way. This was hard to demonstrate because it was not true.

Transportation and Communications

The Germans transformed Tsingtao into a first-class port and connected the town to the interior by rail. These and other German contributions to the improvement of Shantung's transportation and communications were the necessary first step toward any economic development within the leasehold or the province.

The navy built and operated the port facilities at Tsingtao.[32] The main installation was the Large Harbor, located, as planned, where the village of Hsiao-chu-t'an had stood in the northwest section of Tsingtao. The Large Harbor consisted of a great semicircular dam three miles long with a 330-yard opening into Chiao-chou Bay. Inside the dam was an area of about 725 acres which had been dredged to a depth of 31 feet, deep enough for the largest ships. At the end of the dam was a flanged-out area, about 220 yards wide, where there were both a government and a private wharf. The railroad ran the length of the dam.

Jutting out from the shore into the Large Harbor were three large piers, two for general use and the other for petroleum. There were also several small piers and docking locations. Together, the two large general piers provided over a mile of modern docking facilities. The railroad ran the length of both piers, and loading and unloading were done directly between ships and railroad cars. The petroleum pier was connected by a pipeline to railroad storage tanks built by the Asiatic Petroleum Company and the U.S. Standard Oil Company. Space for the construction of godowns was provided by the surface of the piers as well as by land the navy filled in on the shore of the harbor.

The harbor was an expensive undertaking, and the navy was eager to publicize the massive feats of engineering, dredging, and construction which went into building the facility. Therefore, every annual memorandum submitted by the administration contained loving descriptions of the progress of the work, the amounts of earth moved, the types of construction undertaken, and the particular difficulties involved. The encircling dam and Pier I were completed and open for use in March 1904, just as the railway reached Tsinan. The second pier was ready for use in 1907 and the petroleum facility a year later.

To the south of the Large Harbor, the navy built the so-called Small Harbor with essentially the same facilities, although on a far smaller scale. The dredged-out area which the harbor dam protected was about 328,000 square yards, and the pier 116 yards long. The shoreline was filled in for godowns, and the railroad ran to both the pier and the areas on the shore. Originally, the Small Harbor, which was completed in 1901, was intended to provide a place for lighters to land in the period before the Large Harbor was completed and when ships still had to load and unload at anchor. Ultimately, it was meant to be used by small naval vessels and junks. The navy also established an excellent system of lights and other navigational aids for the port. These included a large lighthouse out at sea on Cha-lien-tao Island and a small one on the tip of the peninsula to mark the entrance to Chiao-chou Bay.

The navy was proud of the port facilities it had built at Tsingtao. They were considered to be among the finest anywhere and testified to the navy's dedication to the task of making Tsingtao a great port. "Tsingtao now has the safest and easiest facilities for loading and unloading in East Asia," boasted the navy in 1906. "Even in the older harbors, such as Hong Kong and Shanghai, the loading and unloading of large steamships must be done with the aid of lighters. At Tsingtao this can be done directly into the railway. The harbor itself is excellent and well marked, and it is safe all the year round in all weather." [33]

As usual, foreigners were equally impressed. During World War I a speaker in London, despite his contempt for "Prussian Aggression" in Shantung, admitted that the harbor at Tsingtao was "the finest in China, not even Dairen excepted." [34]

The navy also developed extensive communications facilities within the leasehold. The government paved streets in every section of Tsingtao and constructed what was apparently an extraordinarily comprehensive network of excellent roads in the rural zone.[35] The German Imperial Post established a postal system which was at first limited to the urban zone and later expanded to cover the entire colony.[36] The navy built and operated a modern telephone system in Tsingtao, laid telegraph cables to Shanghai and Chefoo, and set up a wireless station.

Besides the navy's work on the port of Tsingtao, the other major German contribution to the development of communications in Shantung was, of course, the SEG's construction of the railroad to Tsinan. Although the line contributed to economic growth, it did not prove to be a particularly good investment for its builders.

The actual construction of the railway revealed the same thoroughness and care which distinguished every German undertaking in Shantung.[37] As a result, the SEG received much commendation for the fact that the line was exceptionally well built and efficient.[38] Because of the dense population of Shantung and the total inadequacy of all other forms of land transportation, even for short hauls, the SEG built as many stations as possible.[39] There were in all fifty-six stations along the line, or approximately one every two and a half miles, many of them located in comparatively insignificant villages.[40]

About the time the line was completed, the rolling stock of the SEG consisted of 690 freight cars, 107 passenger cars, and 27 locomotives. The great majority of the freight cars were for coal. There were three classes of passenger cars rather than the four common in Germany at the time. The first class on the SEG was equivalent to the second class in Germany; however, the third class was more comfortable than the lowest class common in China, and the SEG boasted that it ran no open passenger cars such as were used, for example, on the Chinese railways in the north.[41] At Ssu-fang, north of Tsingtao, the railroad built a large machine shop to handle maintenance and repair for the line.

After 1905, though Germans still held the top jobs, the railroad came to be operated increasingly by Chinese, and eventually they formed the vast bulk of both the staff and the work force. Therefore, like other German activities in Shantung, the SEG contributed to economic development not only by carrying out its primary function but also by teaching modern skills to the local people. All Chinese employees in a responsible position with the SEG were trained at a special railroading school which the Catholic missionaries ran for the company in Tsingtao. In addition, the machine shop operated an apprenticeship program for Chinese which eventually supplied almost all of the shop's personnel. Thus, by 1907, an observer noted that "in the administration of the railroad there are Chinese secretarial assistants, and in the line's operations the Chinese have all sorts of jobs ranging from station masters to telegraph operators. On the trains they act as guards and conductors, and there are even some Chinese engineers." [42] In 1910 the company employed 55 Europeans and 768 Chinese on the staff and 1520 as laborers.[43]

The line made a tremendous improvement in the ease and cost of transportation along its route. The trip from Tsingtao to Tsinan, which had formerly taken twelve days, was reduced to twelve hours by local train and ten hours by express. To go from Tsinan to Shanghai had formerly required three weeks, but, with the railroad and the improved maritime connections made possible by the facilities at Tsingtao, it now took three days.[44] The price of a third-class ticket was two thirds of a cent per mile, or a little over four dollars for the entire distance. There are no reliable figures available on the cost of traditional means of transportation, but they must have been considerably more expensive. There were, however, tests made to determine the comparative costs of using the railroad or traditional means to carry freight, all of which showed that the line was cheaper. For example, according to one test of the cost of moving heavy items between Tsingtao and Wei-hsien, the railroad's charge of two and a half cents a mile per ton was about one fourth the price of traditional modes of transportation.[45] Occasionally, the SEG, like other railways, established preferential rates for goods it was trying to encourage.

The railroad attracted what the Germans and others considered a substantial amount of business, even though, after an initial upsurge, the use of the line did not increase very sharply, particularly for passenger traffic.[46] During its first full year of operations, in 1905, the line carried 803,517 passengers, and in 1913, 1,317,438. All but a tiny percentage of the passengers traveled third class, which meant that they were almost all Chinese. In 1905 the line hauled 310,482 tons of freight and in 1913, 946,610 tons. Since the most important items were coal and coke, rising coal production was an important factor contributing to the steady growth of freight tonnage on the line. In 1905 the SEG carried 158,115 tons of coal and 42,138 tons of beans, the second most important product.[47] In 1910 the tonnage of beans, still the second most important item, remained about the same, but the tonnage of coal had almost tripled.

Even if one ignores the fact that the Germans lost the railroad entirely in 1914, the line, because of the limited traffic which it could attract, was only moderately successful financially. In 1905 the SEG paid its first dividend, amounting to 3.25 per cent of the share capital.[48] By 1909 dividends had reached 6 per cent and remained there or a bit higher. The profitability of the line in terms of the ratio between net worth and net profits, perhaps a more important criterion of financial success, is more difficult to ascertain. However, it does not appear to have exceeded 10 per cent.[49] Both the dividends and the profit ratio indicate that, while the enterprise was not a financial loss, its profit was no greater than could be obtained in the West, and probably somewhat below what should have been expected in view of the greater risks involved in investing in China.[50]

An additional benefit of the railroad was that it stimulated the Chinese population to make some improvements of their own in the fields of transportation and communications. As was true of similar steps which the Chinese took in relation to other German undertakings, these improvements were made partially to take advantage of what the Germans were doing and partially to compete with them. Thus, there was a striking improvement in the networks of roads surrounding the railway stations.[51] Some of these roads were on the outskirts of important towns, but many, because of the numerous stops on the line, were in places which had formerly been almost totally isolated. The SEG itself built a few of the new roads, but most of them were the work of local Chinese businessmen and officials who readily appreciated the value of the line to their areas. It is interesting that in 1902, when the first sections of the railway were being opened, one of the questions on the provincial examination was "State the advantages of constructing railways in Shantung." [52]

Another major undertaking which the Chinese government initiated in order to profit from and compete with the railroad was the development of a postal system. Until the Germans arrived, there had been no postal system in central and western Shantung.[53] Then, in 1899, the Chinese post established a new postal district for the area. By 1901 the district had twelve post offices, ten on the proposed route of the Tsingtao-Tsinan line and two on the proposed line between Tsingtao and I-chou. In that year the district handled only about 23,000 pieces of mail.

As the railroad grew and the Germans began to establish post offices in the interior, the Chinese government expanded its own postal system and improved mail service. For example, shortly after the first German post office opened at Wei-hsien, the Chinese post reduced the cost of mail to foreign countries and also added a money-order service to match the one provided by the Germans. By 1905, when the Germans were just about to terminate their mail service, the Chinese had a total of 32 offices and agencies in the district.[54] The system continued to grow, and in 1910, the last year in which roughly comparable figures are available, there were 103 Chinese post offices and agencies in the area, handling about 2,000,000 pieces of mail.

In order to compete with the SEG, the provincial government also endeavored to improve the efficiency of the Hsiao-ch'ing-ho Canal, which connected Tsinan with Yang-chiao-kou on the northern coast of Shantung.[55] The purpose of these efforts, which began under Yuan Shih-k'ai, was to reduce the dependence of Tsinan on the railroad. Merchants from Chefoo contributed to the expenditures on the canal because goods which moved out of Yang-chiao-kou were generally transshipped at Chefoo and helped business there. However, the attempt to improve the canal was only moderately successful.

Industry

Both the navy and German businessmen invested heavily in a number of new industries in Shantung, and these investments, like those in the railroad and harbor works, contributed to development in the province. However, because of the difficulties involved in establishing modern industry in China, they were even less successful financially. As a result, the total number of German industrial enterprises remained comparatively small.

The most important such undertaking established by the navy was a large shipyard in Tsingtao, which served both naval and private vessels. The shipyard was opened on a small scale in 1901 in a temporary location; between 1905 and 1907 it was greatly enlarged and moved to a permanent site at the tip of the Large Harbor.[56] The establishment was apparently one of the most lavish enterprises of its kind in the Far East. It had about 1100 yards of docks and was carefully outfitted with all "the most modern appliances." [57] One piece of equipment which attracted much attention was a huge floating dock with a capacity of 16,000 tons, which could serve as a drydock for several ships at a time and was reputed to be the largest of its type in the world; another mechanical wonder gracing the shipyard was an electric crane with a lift capacity of 150 tons.

Most of the employees at the shipyard were recruited locally, only the top officials being naval officers. In order to train its Chinese employees the navy established a four-year apprenticeship program at the yard. The program gave the apprentices not only technical training but also instruction in German and other subjects. By 1907 the first two groups of apprentices, about 150 men, had finished the course; and there were about 1300 men enrolled in various stages of training. By 1913 the yard employed about 1550 Chinese and 65 Europeans.

The shipyard both built and overhauled ships. About 60 per cent of its business was with the navy, although some of this probably included the construction of ships which the navy planned to sell to others. By 1914 the yard had built twenty-two medium-sized vessels, several of which were sold to the Chinese government.

The navy had originally hoped that the shipyard would be a private operation, for the administration was eager to promote the image of Tsingtao as a lucrative field for German investment. However, the navy was unable to induce any private concern to undertake the project. This failure provides evidence not only of the uneconomic nature of the yard but also of the reluctance of German businessmen to invest in industry in Shantung.

Before the navy established the yard in 1901, it approached several firms, including Krupp, to see if they would like to build and own the facility.[58] In its request the navy stressed that the companies should welcome the opportunity to construct the shipyard for both economic and patriotic reasons. Nevertheless, the firms refused. In 1905, when the navy began to enlarge the yard, it again asked private companies to take over the enterprise. The navy promised that if the firms did so, the German government would extract a guarantee from the Chinese government to purchase a fixed number of ships from the yard. After carefully studying the economic feasibility of the facility, the companies again rejected the administration's request. In 1907 when the yard was operating at full capacity, the navy made a further attempt to get Krupp to purchase the undertaking. Once again, the navy tried to make its offer attractive and included promises of business from both the German and Chinese governments.

Krupp politely but rather firmly refused the request. In its answer to the government the company recapitulated the various offers the navy had made through the years and stressed that the company understood that the issue of buying the yard "was not one which touched only purely business matters" but also involved questions of politics and patriotism. Therefore, Krupp emphasized, it had given the request very favorable consideration and had commissioned several surveys to learn if the company could possibly take over the yard. The results of all these studies had been negative. The basic reason for this, Krupp wrote, was that the shipyard was simply too large and valuable for the limited business opportunities of the Far East. In addition, the firm pointed out, the navy's suggestion that the enterprise might become profitable if Peking was forced to buy ships was impractical and might harm Germany's relations with China. Therefore, "from an economic point of view" it was simply "not justifiable" for any private company to buy and operate the yard, no matter what other considerations might be involved.

Besides the shipyard, the navy operated several other industries in Tsingtao. The most important of these were the electric company and the slaughterhouse. As was the case with the shipyard, the navy probably ran these because private enterprise was unwilling to do the job. The navy actually persuaded a private company to build and operate the electric facilities for Tsingtao; however, the firm failed in 1901.[59] The government then had two large German companies use public funds to build bigger facilities and operate them on behalf of the government. The navy may have done this to show that a large electric company could be run profitably at Tsingtao. If so, it failed in its purpose, for the two companies withdrew from the undertaking in 1904.

The most important private German industrial enterprise in Shantung was the SBG. Although the company had a significant impact on the economic development of Shantung, it was a financial failure.

The SBG's mining activities took place at the Wei-hsien and Po-shan fields, each of which had two major shafts and a number of subsidiary ones.[60] The first shaft in the Wei-hsien field was begun in 1901 at Fang-tzu and was ready for operation within a year. In 1904 the SBG began Wei-hsien's other major shaft in a location closer to the Chang-lo-yuan railway station and finished it in 1907. The first shaft at Po-shan which was started in 1904 near the Tzu-ch'uan station was producing coal in 1907. In that year a second and larger shaft was begun nearer Hung-shan and was ready for use in about 1911.[61]

The SBG outfitted its enterprise in the usual German manner with "all the most modern equipment." [62] The most unusual piece of machinery at each field was a large automatic coal washer, which cleaned the coal and then sorted it into four grades. The installation of the first washer at Wei-hsien inspired Ohlmer to write that it was an "ingenious contrivance

. . . the only one of its kind in the Far East";[63] and the *North China Herald* ventured the guess that, because of its uniqueness, the washer would "give Germany an immense advantage in the coal trade" of the Far East.[64] Each field was also equipped with a briquet factory, which took the dust and small pieces of coal from the washer and turned them into fuel briquets.

As the German mining operations grew, they required increasing numbers of Chinese workers, and at first the SBG had trouble recruiting laborers. The basic problem was that the local people considered mining an extra occupation and always planned on leaving whenever they were needed for agricultural work. By 1905 the SBG decided that the only solution to the crucial and "delicate matter" of developing a steady work force was to "improve the treatment of the workers." [65] The company sought outside help and made a settlement with the provincial government in which the firm agreed to hire coolies only from Shantung, to set a higher pay scale for its employees, to improve their rates of accident insurance, and to establish a benevolent fund for them; in return, the province agreed to help the company hire workers. At the same time, the company also began "settling the Chinese workers and their families in special colonies near the mines to get secure hold of them and to break the influence of their villages." [66] The SBG claimed that these "colonies" were attractive, rent-free, and equipped with good health facilities. It is difficult to learn how much the working and living conditions of the miners actually improved as a result of the company's efforts; however, it does appear that the SBG had less difficulty in recruiting workers in later years. By 1911, when both the Wei-hsien and Po-shan fields were in full operation, the company employed about 8000 Chinese workers and 70 German supervisors.

The quality of the coal produced at Wei-hsien was not particularly good, primarily because it burned with too high a residue of ash and was therefore not suitable for trains and steamships. Moreover, the Wei-hsien coal was difficult to extract, for the veins did not lie well, and water seepage proved to be a recurrent nuisance, particularly in the later years. The coal from Po-shan, on the other hand, was of a uniformly high quality. It was "excellently suited" for all purposes and was said to be the equal of Cardiff coal.[67] In addition, the Po-shan field was easy to mine.

In the 1906–07 business year the SBG produced 179,083 tons of coal, with almost all of it still coming from the Wei-hsien field.[68] By 1913 the total had reached 613,000 tons, of which two thirds was the superior coal from Po-shan and the rest from Wei-hsien.

Despite the success of the SBG in developing its two fields, the firm never paid any dividends and, indeed, lost money steadily. Therefore, in 1913 the directors liquidated the company and transferred all its assets to the SEG in return for railway stock worth only 5,400,000 marks, less than half of the fully paid-up capital of the SBG. The railroad bought the mines primarily because their continued operation was essential to the line, whose chief cargo was, of course, coal.

The direct cause of the failure of the SBG was that by the time the company's coal reached the coast at Tsingtao or elsewhere, it had to be sold at too high a price to compete successfully with coal brought in by sea, especially from the Kaiping mines and from Japan. This situation existed primarily because it was comparatively expensive to transport coal by rail from the interior of Shantung to Tsingtao, and also because the SBG's production costs were unusually high. Therefore, the company sold much of its coal in the interior. This was no solution, however, for the SBG had built its large establishment with the prospect of selling its product throughout the Far East. The local trade was far less lucrative, because it served a smaller market and brought a lower price.

The government gave the SBG a rebate on the cost of carrying coal to Tsingtao to enable the company to sell at least some of its product on the coast and also to increase the business of the railroad. The rebate covered about 25 per cent of the transportation costs from Wei-hsien and 30 per cent from Po-shan. This subsidy, however, still did not allow the SBG to sell most of its coal at Tsingtao. In 1911, for example, of the 170,405 tons of coal produced at Wei-hsien, only 43,000 tons were sent to Tsingtao. The rest was sold in the interior to the local population and the railroad or was used by the SBG itself. Because of the poor quality of the coal only 5000 tons of the Tsingtao consignment were sold for bunker coal and 10,000 tons exported to other ports. The rest was used in Tsingtao. Po-shan produced 288,752 tons of coal, of which only 109,000 tons were marketed at Tsingtao; however, of this amount 53,000 tons were sold as bunker coal, 39,000 tons sold to the navy, and only 11,000 tons sent to other ports. Thus, for the SBG, the main effect of the government subsidy was not to enable the company to enter the market on the coast but only to sell some of its better-quality coal to naval and commercial vessels refueling at Tsingtao.[69]

Because of the large investment in the SBG the firm needed to break into the coastal market, and even if the company had been able to sell its coal at a profit in the interior, it still would not have been a financial success. What made the company's failure so striking, however, was the fact that it evidently could not produce coal so cheaply as its Chinese competitors and therefore had to sell much of its coal in the interior at a loss. The SBG's main competition in the interior came from the Chinese mines at Po-shan. Probably the best explanation for the SBG's failure to match Chinese production costs is that the German enterprise was simply too large and complicated, and that the Chinese mines, which were generally simple undertakings using little modern equipment but pumps, were better suited to the economic realities of Shantung. In its desire to establish a large modern enterprise, the SBG probably invested too heavily in expensive equipment when it could have used cheap labor and, at the same time, probably required more workers who were acclimatized to modern working conditions than the company could obtain efficiently.

In addition to the SBG, German businessmen also became involved in a number of other industrial enterprises in Shantung. What were probably the two most important of these undertakings also failed. One was the DGBIA. Since the company never actually began mining on a substantial scale, it is only of interest from the point of view of Sino-German relations and not in connection with the German economic activities in Shantung. The other enterprise, the Deutsch-Chinesische Seiden-Industrie-Gesellschaft (The Sino-German Silk Production Company, or DCSIG), however, became quite large before it, too, went under.

The DCSIG was founded in 1902 and capitalized at 1,800,000 marks.[70] The company planned to establish a modern factory in Kiaochow to process silk from the interior of Shantung and other parts of China. The firm set up its headquarters at Ts'ang-k'ou on the railway north of Tsingtao and was in operation by 1904. The production complex there centered on a large factory outfitted with the most modern equipment for spinning and throwing silk. The company also built extensive facilities for storage and transportation, as well as a residential colony for its workers. The DCSIG employed about 1500 Chinese. The silk which the company produced was considered to be an extremely fine product. However, the price was 40 per cent higher than average, chiefly because production costs were 25 per cent too high. As a result, the DCSIG failed. In 1909 the owners decided to suspend operations and the next year sold the assets of the firm to a Chinese combine.

The high costs of production were primarily due to the difficulties which the firm encountered in creating a competent and reliable work force. Like the SBG, the silk company found it hard to obtain workers who considered factory work a full-time occupation. In addition, the efficient operation of the company's sophisticated machinery required a particularly heavy amount of training. The firm apparently wasted inordinate amounts of silk because of its workers' technical inexperience.

In order to eliminate these problems, the company established a school to train Chinese foremen who would, in turn, train workers and supervise the factory. The curriculum of the school, designed to attract upper-class Chinese, included German, Chinese literature, mathematics, and geography, in addition to technical subjects. The company also set up a residential colony for its workers, which Ohlmer described as "a model of its kind" that could "bear comparison with any in Europe." [71] These efforts may have had some impact on reducing the DCSIG's difficulties, but they came too late to save the firm.

There were several other German industries which were considerably more successful, primarily because they were smaller and catered either to the market at Tsingtao or to a specialized clientele on the coast.[72] The most important of these was probably also the most profitable, and certainly the most *gemütlich*, German industry in Shantung. This was the beer company known as the Anglo-German Brewery Company. The firm was organized in 1904 by a syndicate composed of treaty-port denizens from several nations and capitalized at 400,000 marks. The company began selling its brew in 1905 under the brand name "Germania." The beer did very well and quickly became so popular on the coast that its only real competition came from European imports.[73] The firm expanded its facilities steadily and always paid a good dividend;[74] and the excellent light and dark "Germania" beer is said to have had a salutary influence on the outstanding quality of Japanese beer.

All the building trades, including related endeavors such as brick-making, flourished at Tsingtao because of the rapid growth of the town. The German contractors of the colony had a good reputation elsewhere in China and were frequently asked to put up German-style buildings in different parts of the country. Other small but successful local industries included a privately owned shipyard, a soap factory, a tannery, a pottery factory, a barrel company, a sausage firm, two small albumen companies, and a soda water company.

Chinese industrial activity in Shantung also increased to some extent as a result of the German presence. However, this development came about primarily through the expansion and adaptation of traditional industries rather than the introduction of modern methods. In general, traditional economic activities, not only in manufacturing but in other fields as well, did not suffer because of competition with the Germans' advanced technology. The Chinese enterprises showed great resilience and in some cases even grew as a result of the opportunities created by the foreigners.

The greatest growth took place in mining as a result of the campaign to curb German mining activities. Much of this expansion occurred in the thirty-li zone, particularly at Po-shan. By 1911 the Chinese mines there, using a combination of traditional techniques and pumps, were producing 200,000 tons annually.[75] Another coal field which the Chinese made a major effort to develop, partly in order to prevent German aggrandizement, was at I-hsien.[76] From 1899 to 1907, although the Chung-hsing company there remained nominally a Sino-foreign firm, it was, in fact, a completely Chinese enterprise. During these years, the provincial government considerably enlarged the operations of the company and built a very useful railroad from the mines to the Grand Canal. A foreign visitor reported that I-hsien was "simply a huge mine worked by native methods" and did not have "the fine modern works of the German mines" [77] at Wei-hsien or Po-shan. Perhaps for this reason the company was extremely successful. By 1908 its mines were producing 250,000 tons a year of top-quality coal and making a profit. In that year the firm dropped the fiction that it was partly German, probably because the dangers presented by German imperialism in Shantung had come to an end. The I-hsien mine continued to grow and eventually became one of China's most important and profitable mining enterprises.

The output of other important products manufactured near the railroad, such as silk and strawbraid, also increased. Silk was produced both in traditional-style factories and by cottage industry; strawbraid was made almost entirely by the latter method.[78] It is interesting to note, in view of the German difficulty in establishing modern industries, that one of the few similar attempts on the part of Chinese entrepreneurs also failed. Po-shan was a traditional center of glass-making, and in 1907, in order to capitalize on the railway, a Chinese company opened there a glass factory equipped with modern machines.[79] The concern remained in business for a number of years, but it never proved profitable. However, at least one modern Chinese factory, a paper mill in Tsinan using German machines, managed to prosper.[80]

Commerce and Finance

Commerce and related business activities grew spectacularly at Tsingtao and, to a lesser extent, along the railway to Tsinan. This was a great triumph for the navy, which had been primarily concerned with commercial development both in selecting Chiao-chou Bay and then in administering Kiaochow. However, the rise of trade affected German business groups quite unevenly. German industrialists were unable to use the Reich's position at Tsingtao to obtain a large share of the market in Shantung. On the other hand, German merchants and shipping firms, the groups which had originally been the most enthusiastic advocates of a colony in China, did quite well. Yet, since the open door prevailed at Tsingtao, whatever special advantages these German firms had in the colony were not actually institutionalized. As time passed, the German share of the business at Tsingtao approached what it was in other parts of China. In any case, the benefit to Germany from the commercial activities at Tsingtao was hardly commensurate with the Reich's outlay in creating the administrative, economic, and technical preconditions for such trade.

After the harbor and the railway were completed in 1904, Tsingtao's trade increased rapidly. By 1907, just ten years after the Germans had begun to develop Chiao-chou Bay, Tsingtao's customs receipts of 934,623 taels made the town the seventh most important port in China — after Shanghai, Canton, Tientsin, Hankow, Swatow, and Chinkiang.[81] The total value of Tsingtao's foreign imports amounted to 16,416,053 taels.[82] Shantung's capacity to absorb foreign goods, like that of China as a whole, rose only slowly, and a considerable portion of the growing import trade at Tsingtao occurred at the expense of Chefoo.[83] The most important imports were cotton products, which accounted for nearly half of the total and primarily consisted of 5,164,167 taels' worth of cotton yarn and 1,657,231 taels' worth of finished cotton goods.[84] The other important foreign imports were these: petroleum, worth 997,920 taels; sugar, 810,252 taels; dyes, 669,075 taels; wood, 566,192 taels; Japanese matches, 459,608 taels; and metals, 377,891 taels. The total value of goods of Chinese origin imported into Tsingtao was 7,134,099 taels. The principal Chinese products brought by steamer were these: cotton yarn, 1,439,751 taels; paper, 649,702 taels; and rice, 206,728 taels. The main staples of the junk trade were paper, 2,226,616 taels, and raw cotton, 331,051 taels.

Tsingtao exported 10,530,616 taels' worth of goods produced in Shantung. Since the growth of Tsingtao's export trade was not at the expense of Chefoo, whose exports rose along with those of the leasehold, it was the result of a genuine increase in production and trade in the interior. The most important item exported by steamer was 4,005,589 taels' worth of strawbraid. The braid was produced on the northern seacoast of Lai-chou-fu and in the lowlands extending southwards toward the leasehold; it was traded primarily at the town of Sha-ho, about a day's journey northeast of Wei-hsien.[85] Tsingtao's next most important exports were raw silk and silk waste at 1,728,242 taels, and silk pongees at 1,136,414 taels. Some of the silk was the famous Shantung "raw wild" silk, which was grown chiefly on the slopes of the mountains to the west of the leasehold and marketed primarily at Liu-t'uan, about 27 miles to the northeast of Wei-hsien.[86] Other important goods exported by steamer included 215,280 taels' worth of hides and 162,112 taels of black dates. The major junk exports were peanut oil, 852,672 taels, bean oil, 457,207 taels, and ground nuts, 93,495 taels.

The overall growth of trade at Tsingtao fulfilled all expectations. Nevertheless, the share of German goods in the import trade, the item which directly benefited the home country, was comparatively small. Accurate figurés on the origin of imported goods are impossible to obtain, but various contemporary estimates clearly indicated Germany's weak position. In 1907 Japanese goods apparently accounted for between 50 and 55 per cent of Tsingtao's imports, English for between 20 and 25 per cent, American for about 15 per cent, and German for something close to but less than the American.[87] Since German goods only pre-empted a little over 4 per cent of the entire China market, the Germans did have some advantage at Tsingtao.[88] In later years, however, Germany's position in Tsingtao's trade, as in other fields, increasingly approximated the German role elsewhere in China. The destination of the exports from Tsingtao did not particularly concern contemporaries, although Germany was of minor importance in this area as well. In 1909, the first year for which figures are available, France directly imported 1,558,000 taels' worth of Shantung products; then came England with 901,000 taels, Japan with 676,000 taels, Russia with 442,000 taels, and Germany with 323,000 taels.[89]

Since the basic commitment of the navy was to the development of Tsingtao itself, the administration was only moderately disappointed with Germany's small share of the leasehold's import trade. Instead, the navy rejoiced at the continuing increase in the volume of commerce at the port and boasted about this growth with great satisfaction in its annual memoranda. Thus in 1907 the navy described how Tsingtao's trade had grown since 1898.[90] It pointed out that, despite poor business conditions on the coast, commercial activities at Tsingtao had risen sharply even in the preceding two years, with cotton yarn and petroleum contributing mainly to the rise. Neither of these products was German, of course.

The administration stressed the sheer volume of trade partially because of the navy's particularly commercial orientation with regard to the leasehold. A large amount of business in itself benefited trading firms and shipping companies, the business groups with which the navy had the closest ties. Even more important, the rise in trade represented the ultimate proof that Kiaochow had been rationally and efficiently run and that the navy had indeed equaled Britain's touted ability to develop and administer a commercially valuable colony. Naturally, those who felt that Kiaochow was a poor place to spend German money, no matter how efficiently, found plenty of evidence for their case in the trade figures. In his attack on Kiaochow in 1908, Erzberger said, "I don't deny at all that imports and exports have risen sharply in the port, but this has not been to our profit. For all the money we have spent on Kiaochow has been spent entirely and completely for the benefit of the Japanese and the Chinese." [91]

Trade through Tsingtao continued to rise steadily even after the initial spurt had leveled off. This was considered to be a particularly impressive sign of how well planned the colony had been, for the years 1905–1912 were bad for business on the China coast, and the trade of other ports suffered severely.[92] In 1913 the customs revenue at Tsingtao reached 1,915,889 taels, placing the town ahead of Chinkiang as the sixth most important port in China.[93] The total value of foreign imports in 1913 had grown to 26,207,915 taels, some of which still represented trade being diverted from Chefoo.[94] The net value of Chinese imports reached 11,592,412 taels. By 1913 a substantial transit trade had also developed, and about 1,250,000 taels' worth of goods came into the leasehold for re-export to ports in the north which did not possess the harbor facilities of Tsingtao. The total value of exports had risen to 27,330,447 taels, again not at the expense of Chefoo. The German share of the goods imported in 1913 had declined to about 8 per cent.[95] This was only a bit above the percentage of German goods coming into China as a whole in that year.[96]

The influx of commercial firms to Tsingtao was both a cause and an effect of the port's increased trade.[97] At first, most of the companies doing business in Tsingtao were small Chinese and German firms. The Chinese merchants virtually monopolized the trade with the interior, while the Germans concentrated on goods consumed in Tsingtao, which during these early years were primarily things used by the government.

Once the main transportation facilities were built, many larger firms came to Tsingtao in order to trade with the interior. A significant number of these were Chinese. Many of the larger Chinese firms were those which had already established branches at Chefoo or had been involved in the junk trade at T'a-pu-t'ou. By 1907 the merchants of Kiangsu,

Anhwei, and Chekiang were sufficiently settled to build an impressive joint guild house at Tsingtao; and, in 1909, the Chinese firms at the port formed their own European-style Chamber of Commerce.[98]

Large foreign enterprises also came to Tsingtao. At first the Germans were virtually the only Westerners active there, and, together with the large Chinese companies, they monopolized the trade. By 1907, however, increasing numbers of other foreigners had begun to do business at Tsingtao; and by 1911 Ohlmer could report that "most of the large China firms — German, English, and French — have now established branch houses or have agents here." [99] The first foreign consul at Tsingtao was appointed by the United States at the end of 1906, and the other important nations followed.

The navy, very happy about the large number of trading firms which established themselves in Tsingtao, did not concern itself much about the relative role of German companies. In the earlier period, when the Chinese merchants dominated the commerce to the interior, the navy pointed out that "all experience of European trade in East Asia shows that the development of a place on the China coast is fundamentally dependent upon the participation of the native merchant community . . . Therefore, as the navy has always said, the development of a lively and wealthy Chinese merchant group at Tsingtao will be of clear benefit to German businessmen also." [100] Later on, when other foreigners began to do business in Tsingtao, the navy evinced pride in the arrival of "the most significant firms of the China trade" [101] and suggested that it was "a good sign of the growing economic importance of Tsingtao that more and more foreign capital participates in the developing commerce." This participation should "not be hampered in any way," the administration stressed, "but rather should be welcomed as a positive factor in the opening of the colony and its hinterland; for it will also indirectly serve the development of German commerce and industry." [102] There are even indications that the navy may have offered government business to foreign firms in order to attract them to Tsingtao." [103]

As the possibilities for trade at Tsingtao developed, the port became a regular stop for coastal steamers. Until 1901 only the small and reputedly unsatisfactory line of Diederichson, Jebson, and Company served the colony. In that year, however, the Hamburg-Amerika Line decided to expand its activities in East Asia and bought out Diederichson, Jebson. Hamburg-Amerika immediately increased service to Tsingtao, and, from then on, the company dominated shipping to the port. In 1903 the first non-German steamship lines, one Japanese and one English, began regular runs to Tsingtao.

Despite the fact that Japanese goods were already swamping the import trade at Kiaochow, Governor Truppel evidently helped encourage the Japanese steamship company, the Ōsaka Shōsen-kaisha, to begin service to Tsingtao.[104] The governor's activities were in line with the navy's tendency to foster increased trade at Tsingtao without making any special efforts to safeguard Germany's share of the business. Since German businessmen were facing rising Japanese competition elsewhere in China, Truppel's actions were attacked by the German diplomats as being "detrimental to German business" interests all along the coast.[105] Mumm, for example, wrote that "if the governor now wants a steamship line to Japan, the fault lies with an overemphasis on the development of our little colony, an overemphasis which has frequently overridden the general interests of German trade in China." [106] The Foreign Office officially requested Tirpitz to tell Truppel that "we can't block Japanese goods, but at least we shouldn't pave the way for them because of momentary benefits to the merchants of Tsingtao . . . in no case should we encourage direct steamship connections between Japan and Shantung." [107] It is difficult to determine whether the Kiaochow government continued to encourage foreign shipping at Tsingtao; nevertheless, the navy certainly continued to pride itself on the yearly increases in the variety of shipping available at the port and particularly on the growing number of foreign vessels which called there.

By 1907 regularly scheduled ships connected Tsingtao with Vladivostok, Newchang, Tientsin, Chefoo, Shanghai, Hong Kong, Kobe, and Nagasaki. There were as yet no scheduled runs direct to the Occident; however, the Hamburg-Amerika Line averaged about one steamer a month direct to Europe on an unscheduled basis, as did other companies less frequently. In 1907 a total of 982 ships with a tonnage of 1,108,913 entered and cleared Tsingtao.[108] About 57 per cent of the tonnage was German, 26 per cent English, 12 per cent Japanese, and the rest mixed. Since German ships comprised about 8 per cent of the tonnage in the rest of China, the Reich had a decided advantage at Tsingtao.[109]

Shipping to Tsingtao continued to grow in the later years. In 1908 a British firm inaugurated the first direct scheduled run to Europe, and other companies followed suit.[110] By 1911 Ohlmer reported that there were a variety of ships which "call regularly, competing for the export cargo and affording direct connection, for goods and passengers, with the large European and American ports and Japan." [111] Nevertheless, many of the exports from Tsingtao, like those from the other ports in the central and northern parts of China, were still transshipped at Shanghai.[112]

In 1913, 1,733 merchant ships with a tonnage of 2,679,319 entered and cleared Tsingtao. The German share of the tonnage was 43 per cent, while England had 31 per cent and Japan 18 per cent.[113] Thus, in contrast to the other areas of commercial activity, the Germans continued to enjoy an especially favored position at Tsingtao. An important reason for this was probably the great strength, on a world-wide basis, of the German shipping industry. The Hamburg-Amerika Line was the largest steamship company in the world, and the Norddeutscher Lloyd was one of the largest.

While Tsingtao was becoming an important port for steamships, the traffic of oceangoing junks at Chiao-chou Bay continued to flourish. There were large fluctuations from year to year in the junk trade, but between 1901 and 1907 its average annual value was about 4,700,000 taels, and from 1908 to 1913 about 16 per cent higher, 5,600,000.[114] There was a similar increase in the number of junks which participated in this trade. The intra-bay junk traffic also increased enormously in response to the growth of Tsingtao. Thus, in shipping as in industry, traditional elements of the economy were able to benefit from the German presence.

Despite the growth of the oceangoing junk trade, it did not shift its center of operations from the traditional junk ports within the bay to Tsingtao. The small junks and sampans which sometimes went to nearby places on the coast were attracted to Tsingtao. Larger junks, however, continued to dock at T'a-pu-t'ou and put their cargoes on the railway at Chiao-chou.

The navy was anxious to attract the junks to Tsingtao and, at one point, even considered closing T'a-pu-t'ou, but decided against it for fear of driving the junk trade away altogether. Instead, the administration tried various schemes to entice the traffic to Tsingtao. For example, the government did not collect docking fees on the side of the small harbor reserved for oceangoing junks. This policy evidently had some effect, for, in 1907, Ohlmer reported that "an important change, deserving of special record, is the fact that during the year twenty Foochow and Ning-po junks made use of the Tsingtao junk harbor for the first time . . . Their advent here marks a turning point of some importance in the development of the port and the colony, and is all the more satisfactory because it is not a dislocation of the Kiaochow [Chiao-chou] junk trade in favor of Tsingtao but a *bona fide* increase." [115] However, just as the junks began coming to Tsingtao, the navy, under pressure from the Reichstag to increase the revenue of the leasehold, decided to levy docking and other fees at the Small Harbor. As a result the junks stopped coming and did not return.[116]

Because the junk trade continued to thrive, inland steam navigation at Tsingtao made comparatively little headway. In 1904 the Germans obtained the regulations permitting such trade. The navy was anxious to begin inland steam navigation not only in order to obtain silk for the DCSIG but also to develop trade by steamer with the unopened ports on the eastern and southern coasts of Shantung, such as Hai-chou. When the regulations were promulgated, the Hamburg-Amerika Line began to run small steamships on a regular schedule along the coast of Shantung, but this service folded within a year.[117] Thereafter, inland steam navigation grew very slowly and not at the expense of junks.[118] Until the 1920s inland steamers remained comparatively unimportant not only at Tsingtao but all over China.[119]

Banking developed rather slowly at Tsingtao but managed to keep pace with the needs of the business community. The Deutsch-Asiatische Bank established a branch at Tsingtao in 1898, and for the first decade it was the only Western bank in the colony. In the early years many of the small Chinese businessmen ran banking shops on the side, but there were no modern Chinese financial institutions at the port until 1905. In that year a modern Chinese bank, the Kien Shun Bank (later Bank of Shantung) opened a branch at Tsingtao.[120] During the first decade the navy tried unsuccessfully to attract other Chinese and Western banks.[121]

In later years Tsingtao's financial community grew along with its commerce. By 1913 several important Chinese modern banks had set up branches in the port, as had at least one key bank from each of the countries involved in the trade.[122] Among the Chinese banks were the Kien Shun Bank, the Ta-ch'ing Bank (Bank of China), and the Yu-ta Bank; the foreign banks included the Deutsch-Asiatische Bank, the Hong Kong and Shanghai Banking Corporation, the Russo-Asiatic Bank, and the Yokohama Specie Bank.

The Germans managed the monetary system of the leasehold so that it too kept pace with the growth of business. As a result, Kiaochow quickly passed through the successive monetary changes which had taken place elsewhere on the China coast in the previous sixty years.[123] Prior to 1898 the only currency at Chiao-chou Bay was sycee silver and copper cash. When the Germans arrived, they introduced the Mexican dollar, which quickly became the primary medium of exchange for larger transactions.[124] The Germans, like other foreigners, did not like the Chinese cash, which were inconvenient and frequently scarce. Therefore, a motley and confusing assortment of subsidiary coinage sprang up in Kiao-chow similar to what prevailed in other places where the Mexican dollar was the dominant currency.[125] The smaller money included cash, coins, bits of silver, chits, and written checks, none of which bore any fixed relation to the dollar.

By the end of the first decade the economic development at Tsingtao had outrun this monetary system. The increased business activity required larger amounts of currency than could be met by the supply of Mexican dollars, whose availability was not controlled by the monetary needs of Tsingtao or, for that matter, of the China coast as a whole. In addition, the system of subsidiary coinage had become increasingly unmanageable as the town grew.

The navy successfully met the need for more currency by granting a concession in 1907 to the Deutsch-Asiatische Bank to issue bank notes at Tsingtao. These notes were to be in denominations of one, five, ten, twenty-five, and fifty Mexican dollars and were to be backed by assets held by the Deutsch-Asiatische Bank and the great German banks which supported it. The bank was responsible for exchanging the notes at face value in Tsingtao and at the current rate of exchange at other places on the coast. In order to encourage trade with the interior, the government also stipulated that the bank had to exchange the notes for face value anywhere in Shantung. In return for the concession, the bank agreed to pay the government at Tsingtao a yearly fee amounting to 1 per cent of the value of the paper in circulation. The notes were first issued in June 1907 and were readily accepted. To handle the problem of subsidiary currency, the navy in 1909 issued small nickel coins, which soon supplanted the other forms of small change.[126]

In addition to the growth of commerce at Tsingtao, business also proliferated along the SEG's right of way and the network of new roads which grew up around the railroad. New business centers with banks, shops, hotels, warehouses, shipping firms, and restaurants sprang up near the stations.[127] In the larger towns, these centers greatly increased the facilities for commerce, while at many of the smaller stations they provided the first opportunity for trade with more distant places. Farther from the stations, commercial life also quickened on the new roads surrounding the railway. Part of this activity represented the transport of goods to the railroad, and part consisted of the exploitation of the opportunities which the new roads presented for increased trade among local markets and villages. Wherever the impact of the railway was felt, the Mexican dollar became an accepted medium of exchange.

Because of the growing export market, as well as the expansion of local trade, agricultural production along the roadbed increased and became more diversified and commercialized. Many different groups contributed to these developments. The provincial government was involved in promoting agricultural changes.[128] Tsinan introduced the cultivation of cotton for export and sought to increase and improve the production of Shantung's major crops. Chinese and foreign merchants also encouraged similar developments, as did the SEG and the navy.[129] The impact of the navy's activities was primarily limited to the rural areas of the leasehold, where the administration established a particularly successful program of agricultural improvement.[130] The navy tested innumerable varieties of crops from all over the world in order to discover if they could be cultivated in Shantung and then distributed seeds and cuttings of the chosen plants. In addition, the program also experimented with high-class European livestock and supplied animals to the peasants to improve local breeds.

By 1911, as a recent statistical analysis has suggested, the structure of some of the local marketing patterns along the roadbed of the SEG provided excellent examples of early agrarian modernization.[131] To an eyewitness in that year the commercial progress, particularly in the export trade, provided "a striking illustration of what even a single line of railway can do in a few years to develop trade in a roadless country like Shantung. Produce which formerly could not bear the expense of the laborious cart journey to the coast new finds a ready market, and is produced in yearly increasing quantities. Prosperity is visible everywhere in the districts along the line and beyond, and the railway, at first bitterly opposed, is now pronounced a blessing." [132] Nevertheless, the commercial changes in the interior were essentially limited to the areas near the railway and did not extend deeper into the province because of the poor communications which still prevailed throughout most of Shantung.[133]

Education

The German presence at Tsingtao also contributed to educational development. At Kiaochow the navy and the missionaries succeeded in establishing a variety of schools both for Germans and Chinese; and, in the interior, German activities stimulated both the missionaries and the provincial government to expand and improve educational facilities.[134]

The educational facilities for Germans at Tsingtao, though limited in size, were considered to be among the best outside the homeland. Until 1902 the only school which served Westerners was the joint public and private institution founded in 1898. It was a combination grammar and middle school and did not provide a standard German higher school education. In 1902 the navy decided to transform the middle school into a *Reformrealgymnasium,* a secondary school which would be fully integrated into Germany's educational system. This was an unusual ambition, for, at the time, there was no other official school on this level anywhere outside Germany.[135] The navy maintained that it wanted to establish such a school at Kiaochow "not only for the needs of Tsingtao but also for the sake of German education all over East Asia." [136] In addition, of course, the navy felt that the establishment of the only Gymnasium abroad would further demonstrate how well the leasehold was being administered and the high level of development it had reached.

The navy assumed complete control of the old school. Girls were banished from the higher grades, and several licensed teachers were imported from Germany. At first the instruction was rather thin, and the school had only three middle-school grades, rather than the six required for a Gymnasium. Each year, however, the administration added new classes and brought more teachers from Germany, until in 1906 the highest and last grade was established. The school then received permission from the German Ministry of Education to confer upon the graduates the *Berechtigung zum einjährig-freiwilligen Militärdienst* (Right to only one year's service in the military on a voluntary basis). This authorization was official recognition that the school had become an official Gymnasium in the German system. The Gymnasium graduated its first class of five students in 1907. In that year the school had 92 pupils, including 15 girls in the lower grades and four English students. While the school was being developed, older girls were educated by the missionaries; however, in 1908 they were reintegrated into the Gymnasium. By 1913 it had 227 pupils, slightly more than half of them boys.[137]

The educational facilities which the Germans established for Chinese in the leasehold were also of high quality. Both the missionaries and the navy believed that the provision of good education for the Chinese would not only further the development of the leasehold but would also win support for the Reich in Shantung. Therefore, particularly after 1906, when China increased the pace of her own program of educational reform, the Germans tried to organize their educational activities in the leasehold so as to complement the Chinese efforts in the interior and to contribute to the development of the province. Unlike many other foreign groups, they seemed eager to make their own activities conform to the new Chinese educational plans and rules, rather than to oppose them.

The missionaries provided education for the Chinese inhabitants of Kiaochow at every level from grammar school to normal school. In addition, the missionaries offered an assortment of evening courses, kindergartens, and technical classes. They also prepared textbooks and other educational materials and ran at least one newspaper. The curriculum of the missionary schools was essentially secular; though some religious studies were included, their extent depending upon the mission involved. Purely religious training aimed at creating Chinese ministers and missionaries was restricted to a few theological seminaries.

Figures on the missionary schools in the leasehold are available for 1911.[138] In that year, in addition to the miscellaneous activities, the three German missions ran sixteen elementary schools for boys with a total of 285 pupils; two girls' schools with 95 pupils; one middle school for boys with 45 pupils; a middle school for girls; two teacher's seminaries which provided education for 167 men from the elementary level to that of an advanced normal school; a similar teacher's seminary for women; and two theological schools. The American Presbyterians established one middle school and a theological school.

The most important educational institution which the missionaries ran at Tsingtao was the normal school of the Weimar Mission, the Deutsch-Chinesisches Seminar. Its curriculum and activities provide an insight into the direction of the German educational efforts in the leasehold. After the provincial government had instituted its educational reforms, the navy encouraged the school to do all it could to further the Chinese efforts. As a result, among other things, the school reorganized its curriculum to accord with the educational requirements specified by the new Chinese regulations. The Deutsch-Chinesisches Seminar ran a three-year elementary school whose curriculum included Chinese reading and writing, Chinese classics, ethics, geography, mathematics, natural history, and German. Above the elementary school was a four-year middle school where the major subjects were German, Chinese, mathematics, science, and geography.[139] The highest level of the Seminar was a three-year normal school which primarily provided teacher training. In order to carry out its own work and to further education elsewhere, the Deutsch-Chinesisches Seminar produced texts and dictionaries; a number of these were written by the famous sinologist Richard Wilhelm, who headed the school for years. The school ultimately supplied many of the teachers in the leasehold.

It was the Chinese educational reform which first encouraged the navy itself to undertake the education of Chinese in the leasehold. In 1905 the navy opened two grammar schools, which it organized according to the requirements for grammar schools set down in the Chinese educational plans. Their curriculum was, therefore, similar to that of the elementary school attached to the Deutsch-Chinesisches Seminar, where many of the teachers had been trained. By 1911 the navy was running twelve grammar schools in the leasehold with 380 pupils.[140]

The navy's most ambitious educational undertaking was the establishment of a college at Tsingtao. The administration hoped that the school would serve as the "keystone" of education in the leasehold and would become one of the important educational institutions in China.[141] The navy pointed out that the school was necessary to offset Germany's relatively minor contribution to China's educational reform; it said that this diffidence was unfortunate "especially because China's study commission to Europe in 1906 particularly noted the preeminence of German educational methods." The navy maintained proudly that Tsingtao was a location "especially suited" to the establishment of a major school, because the colony provided a "rich variety of illustrative materials for training, both in technical installations, forestry, and health facilities, and in the organization of an administrative structure, etc." [142]

The school, the Deutsch-Chinesische Hochschule, opened in 1909. The province of Shantung agreed to subscribe 40,000 marks annually to help defray some of the expenses and, in return, received the right to send a representative to the school to keep Tsinan informed on developments and to supervise Chinese studies. The Chinese decision to cooperate with the Germans in running the Hochschule was an unusual one. The provincial government probably wanted to reap the educational and financial advantages of establishing an excellent school in Tsingtao which would cater to Shantung's needs. In addition, since the school was not located in the interior, it not only did not impinge on the independence of the province but actually gave Tsinan an administrative presence in the leasehold.

The Hochschule was divided into an upper and a lower school. The lower school was similar to a Gymnasium, and to enter it a student had to be thirteen years old and possess the equivalent of a Chinese higher elementary school education. It provided a five-year course of study with a curriculum consisting of Chinese, German, English, mathematics, history, geography, science, hygiene, technical drawing, physical education, music, and stenography. The upper school was essentially a college, and admission to it was limited to students who were over eighteen and had passed the graduation examination of the lower school. The upper school was divided into four faculties, law and political economy, natural sciences and engineering, forestry and agriculture, and medicine. The courses in law and agriculture took three years and those in sciences and medicine four. The school was equipped with libraries, laboratories, a museum, gymnasium, and a model farm. By 1913 the school was flourishing and had 368 pupils.[143]

It would appear that as a result of the German educational activities in the leasehold the proportion of the elite there who received some taste of modern education was not insignificant. According to a survey conducted by the German magistrate of the rural zone, there were originally about 3000 male students under the age of 20 in the leasehold who were receiving some form of traditional education.[144] The German schools enrolled approximately 1000 male students, in addition to the large number in the various training programs of the German economic enterprises.

Most of the German educational activities in the interior were carried on by the Steyl Mission, for none of the German Protestant groups had the facilities to expand their efforts beyond the leasehold and the neutral zone. Although the Steyl schools in the south and west of the province increased in number, this was not apparently a result of the German presence in the province after 1898. Nevertheless, the Catholics did open seventeen primary schools in the hsien bordering the colony and the Protestants about six.

The main contribution of the Germans to the advancement of education in the interior of the province came about through the opportunities which the railway opened up for the large American Presbyterian mission and other Protestant groups in Shantung. The first and most striking development attributable to the line was the formation of a union college at Wei-hsien by the Presbyterians and the English Baptists in 1905.[145] The missionaries had long wanted to establish a college in the center of Shantung, but such a move was not considered feasible until transportation within the province improved. The union college was later transferred to Tsinan and renamed Shantung Christian University (Cheeloo). It eventually became one of China's leading universities.

The Presbyterians also moved the general focus of their activities from the north and east of Shantung to the vicinity of the railroad.[146] The mission came to be considered "the largest in the world," [147] and part of its growth was certainly a result of the progress which accompanied the railroad. In 1917 the Presbyterians were running 150 primary schools in the districts along the railway and a wide variety of higher schools.[148]

The direct and indirect effects of the German presence on the modernization of Chinese education in the interior are difficult to assess, though the navy insisted that they were considerable. In any case, Shantung was one of the provinces which instituted educational reforms most successfully. In 1911 Ohlmer reported that there were 3,822 government schools in the province. These included primary schools, normal schools, colleges, and 90 industrial and handicraft schools. He said there were 4,613 teachers and 60,000 pupils. The level of the schools could not have been very high. Nevertheless, Ohlmer seemed to consider these educational developments "remarkable" and attributed them partially to foreign efforts in Shantung.[149]

Postscript: Japan Ousts the Germans

At least as early as 1905, the Germans had come to realize that Kiaochow, far from being a military asset, was really an isolated outpost, hostage to any nation with real power in East Asia which might decide to move against the colony. The most obvious threat seemed to be Japan, with its English alliance, burgeoning commercial interests in Shantung, and growing desire for power in China. Such German apprehensions were entirely justified, for when the outbreak of World War I gave Japan the opportunity to strike, Germany lost all its holdings in Shantung.

On August 3, 1914, Great Britain declared war on the Reich.[150] Within a week the Japanese government decided to enter the conflict on the Allied side and to begin hostilities by seizing Kiaochow and the German possessions in Shantung. On August 15, Tokyo issued an ultimatum demanding that Germany remove her warships from East Asian waters and turn Kiaochow over to Japan by September 15. The tone of this ultimatum was reminiscent of Germany's note in 1895 which had forced a humiliated Japanese government to return the Liaotung peninsula to China. The deadline for an answer was August 23, and when this date came without a response, Japan declared war.

The Germans, knowing that Kiaochow could not be defended, tried various schemes to forestall the impending Japanese take-over or at least to minimize German losses. The original Kiaochow Treaty had stipulated that Germany could, if she so desired, return Kiaochow to China and receive compensation for what had been spent on developing the leasehold. The German minister in Peking, therefore, hastily started negotiations aimed at returning the colony before Japan could seize it. Berlin also tried to cooperate with the United States on a plan to have foreign areas in China declared neutral of the conflict in Europe. Peking was sympathetic to such plans, but apparently because of pressure from Japan, nothing came of them.

As a result, by the end of August the Germans' only options were military. The German squadron at Kiaochow was sent away to avoid being bottled up in the harbor; and on August 27, when Japanese warships appeared off the mouth of the bay, there were only one disarmed Austrian cruiser and a German destroyer left inside. The few German troops in other parts of China were sent to the leasehold by rail, and those German civilians who were reservists were also mustered for the colony's defense. Munitions were collected, and work began on preparing Kiaochow's defenses for attack. In answer to the governor's assurance, "We are responsible for fulfilling our duty to the end," the kaiser telegraphed back, "God be with you! In the coming struggle I will think of you." [151]

Japan decided to launch the assault on Kiaochow from the land side, which was less well defended. On September 2 a large contingent of Japanese troops landed at Lung-k'ou on the northern coast of Shantung, about 150 miles from Tsingtao. At first it was unclear why these forces had landed so far from their objective. However, the reason soon became obvious as the troops moved, not only toward the leasehold but also westward along the SEG seizing the important towns on the route and eventually occupying Tsinan. In the middle of September additional Japanese troops landed inside the leasehold at Lao-shan Bay, followed a few days later by a token unit of British forces. By October, Tsingtao was surrounded by over 20,000 Japanese troops and a formidable array of artillery. Even counting the recently arrived reinforcements, there were still only about 3,500 German troops in the town, together with about 2,000 reservists.

The final assault began on October 31, and the Germans surrendered on November 7, twenty-seven years to the day after the kaiser's orders had gone out to the East Asian Squadron to occupy the area. An American observer witnessed the capitulation of the last German strongpoint, Iltis Mountain, and wrote: "With bayonets in front of them gleaming in the glow of the morning sun, just rising as a ball of fire from above the horizon of the Yellow Sea, the attacking force charged up the slopes . . . The surrender came at 7:05 a.m. As the white flag struck the top of its mast the air about the forts was suddenly rent by the 'banzaiing' of the victorious troops. For twenty minutes the cheering kept up, until at length it was replaced by the appearance of the Rising Sun flag floating from the peak of every fort and hill in the neighborhood. Thus had

Germany's dream of domain in the East come suddenly to an end." [152]

Japan's seizure of Kiaochow and the German holdings in the interior inaugurated one of the most important diplomatic issues created by the First World War, the so-called "Shantung Question." During the war Japan strengthened her claims to the German possessions, both by forcing agreements such as the Twenty-One Demands on the Chinese government, and by negotiating secret treaties with the Allied Powers. In 1917 China entered the war against Germany, partially in order to establish her case for regaining the German holdings once the Reich was defeated. The Wilsonian mirage of national self-determination and independence also encouraged China's expectations of ousting Japan from Shantung. However, the Versailles Peace Conference confirmed the Japanese position in the province. As a result, the Chinese delegation refused to sign the treaty, while in China the Shantung issue became the focus of the great wave of anti-imperialist and anti-warlord nationalism which began with the May Fourth incident of 1919. It was not until 1922 at the Washington Conference that Japan agreed, with suitable compensation, to return Kiaochow and the Tsingtao-Tsinan Railway to China and to turn the former holdings of the SBG over to a joint Sino-Japanese company.

While the international aspects of the Shantung Question have received much attention, far less has been given to Japan's activities as Germany's successor in Shantung. What becomes evident, even to the most casual observer, is that Japan did not simply replace Germany in the province but amassed far more power there than the Reich had ever had.[153] The SEG provides an excellent example of this. Japan opened telegraph and postal stations along the route and replaced almost all the Chinese employees of the company with Japanese. Japanese troops patrolled the line, and garrisons were maintained in Tsinan and elsewhere. Finally, and most important, Japan even established various forms of civil administration at the important places along the route. By 1907, of course, the Germans had been forced to renounce all their plans to use the railway concession for any purpose other than simply operating the line. Similarly, in other fields, Japan's domination over the province was consistently greater than Germany's had been. It is likely, therefore, that at least part of the Chinese bitterness over the Shantung Question resulted from the fact that the striking success of earlier years in containing imperialism in Shantung had been so decisively reversed.

VII. Conclusions

Within ten years after the Germans established themselves in Shantung, the imperialist threat which they posed had been completely contained. Most importantly, the German sphere of influence in the interior no longer existed. Furthermore, the leasehold at Chiao-chou Bay, while still in German hands, exerted no political influence on the province and had even suffered serious infringements on its own independence. The chief reason for the disintegration of the Reich's position was that China, whose foreign policy had become increasingly nationalistic after 1900, strove consciously to destroy every element of German influence and sovereignty in Shantung. This policy proved particularly effective against the Reich because Berlin, for diplomatic, political, and economic reasons, was unable to press its claims in the province. However, despite the failure of its imperialist ambitions in Shantung, Germany did make attributable to the colonial policy of the German navy. With its intense a contribution to development there, a contribution which was largely desire to make Kiaochow into a model colony, with its lavish expenditures and commercial orientation, the navy brought efficient administration and economic progress to the leasehold, and in so doing created what many considered to be Germany's most successful colony.

These specific findings concerning the German sphere of influence in Shantung can provide a basis for some broader and, in general, more speculative observations. These concern China's foreign policy and the defense of her independence in the last years of the Ch'ing, as well as the general nature of this era and its place in modern Chinese history. In addition, it is possible to use the evidence from Shantung to draw some inferences concerning the impact of imperialism on Chinese economic life.

Before discussing China's survival, it should be pointed out that at the end of the nineteenth century the Middle Kingdom may not have been in quite so much danger of being cut up into colonies as was generally felt at the time. Clearly the German sphere of influence did not represent the threat it was supposed to have been. This is evident in the light of the difficulties which the Reich had in pursuing a firm policy in Shantung, difficulties which quickly forced both the navy and the Foreign Office to retreat from the goals of 1898. In addition, the Foreign Office had never really been an ardent advocate of the venture in Shantung and had, to a considerable extent, supported it only because of the belief that China was going to be split up. This was a self-fulfilling prophecy which arose at the time of the Sino-Japanese War, came to a climax in 1898, and then gradually began to reverse itself as China remained intact. As a result, the Foreign Office, which dominated government policy-making after 1900, was not particularly enthusiastic about pressing Germany's claims in Shantung. Of course, Germany did not pose the only, or even the major, threat to China, and before any sort of definitive judgment can be passed on the seriousness of China's predicament, studies will have to be made of the other powers. The German case, though, suggests that it is important to discover in detail what the goals of each power were, to what extent its actions were imitative or reactive, and how they were affected by domestic and international pressures.

In any case, in 1898 Germany did want economic domination over Shantung and looked forward to exerting as much political influence there as possible; and it was the development of a new and nationalistic Chinese foreign policy which proved decisive in containing the German threat. The advent of this policy was clearly one of the most significant features of the Ch'ing response to the imperialist onslaught at the turn of the century, and it is probably a crucial factor in explaining why China as a whole was saved from foreign domination. Before extracting the chief features of this new foreign policy from its particular setting in Shantung, it should be noted that essentially it replaced two traditional alternative approaches to foreign affairs. One of these was what has been identified here as the mainstream approach, with its goal of maintaining sufficient control over foreigners so that they would not become a threat to China. The other approach, which I have called militant conservatism, was a highly ideological position that sought to preserve in as pure a form as possible the Chinese Confucian culture and way of life. When the mainstream began to fail even in its own terms in the late '90s, China opted for first the traditional alternative — militant conservatism — and then the new nationalist approach. Conservatism became highly influential from late 1898 through 1900, when it was discredited by its handi-work, the Boxer Rebellion. Nationalism predominated briefly during the Hundred Days reform movement of 1898 and then finally won out after 1900.

The most significant component of the new nationalist approach was that its basic goal was the retrieval and defense of full sovereignty for China. Since sovereignty implied a commitment to the complete au-tonomy of China as well as to her total equality with other nations, the new policy was extremely broad, opposing not only those imperialist acts which threatened to introduce foreign control but all those which infringed, even theoretically, on China's sovereignty. An equally im-portant aspect of the nationalist policy was the fervor and commitment which its adherents manifested. For an understanding of the modern sense of sovereignty implied and resulted in a sense of inferiority and even shame at the unusual position of China and engendered a deter-mination to end that inequality.

As a result of these basic characteristics, a further feature of the new approach was a willingness to make heavy financial sacrifices in order to curtail even theoretical infringements on Chinese sovereignty. At the same time it involved a commitment to change traditional governmental institutions and create new ones when this was required in the struggle for China's rights. Perhaps because of its traditional administrative com-petence, the success of the Chinese officialdom in making such institu-tional changes appears to have been noteworthy.

Another significant element in the nationalist policy was its emphasis on the economic development and autonomy of China. These were con-sidered important in the short run because the most immediate threat to the nation's sovereignty in the late Ch'ing came from the Western seizure of broad economic concessions. Not only were these privileges obtained by means which affronted China's sovereignty — political and even mili-tary pressure — but, once in existence, they were operated under special arrangements which violated the nation's rights. In addition, it was believed that if, in the long run, China was to attain the strength needed to regain and fully defend her equality as a nation, she would have to become a modern industrial state. This desire for economic development bore little fruit; overall, there was little significant economic growth in China during these years. However, the attempt to keep the nation's resources out of foreign hands seems to have been more successful.

A related aspect of the nationalist policy was an effort on the part of the government to involve private individuals, local gentry and mer-chants, in the struggle against the foreigners, especially in economic matters. This was done in order to enlist the skills and capital of private entrepreneurs in the task of economic development, as well as to pre-empt the possibility of foreign domination of China's economic resources. On the other hand, when the use of foreign advisers or foreign capital was advisable or unavoidable, the government's comprehension of the real meaning of sovereignty enabled it, apparently rather effectively, to prevent such relations from infringing upon the nation's inherent political rights. Thus it quickly became clear that what was most important was not excluding a foreigner from China but rather supervising his activities so that they did not violate China's national equality. This was frequently accomplished by making certain that foreign companies would follow the same regulations and submit to the same degree of Chinese government control as Chinese companies. As a result, one of the most common themes of the period was the insistence that foreign activities be purely "commercial" rather than "political" or "diplomatic." In Shantung, because of the need to liquidate a sphere of influence, nationalist officials were generally unwilling to use German assistance or capital under any circumstances. Nevertheless, this new attitude toward foreign investment is evident in the negotiations over the Tientsin-Chinkiang Railway and the DGBIA.

Another, and successful, element in nationalist policy was the effort to prevent the local attacks on foreigners which had long served as a pretext for the increase of foreign power in China. In particular, the new approach unambiguously opposed violence against missionaries, the group which had been the most common object of local hostility because of the breadth and ideological nature of its activities as well as its wide dispersal in the interior. Here, too, an appreciation of the concept of sovereignty allowed the government to focus effectively on the framework within which missionaries and other foreigners could reside in the country rather than on limiting their numbers or movement. It was the new approach, for example, which encouraged Peking to create self-opened marts, an innovation which, unlike the treaty ports, was intended to maintain China's sovereign rights instead of simply excluding or managing foreigners.

Concurrent with the attempt to prevent uncontrolled violence, another facet of the nationalist officials' policy was to develop modern military forces. It was hoped that the new armies would discourage foreign military intervention; it is also possible that some considerations was given to reasserting China's rights directly through the use of armed might. However, the Chinese government was probably unnecessarily restrained about employing open threats of military action to counter foreign pressures. After the Boxer Rebellion the major powers felt that military intervention in China was no longer a matter to be treated lightly, and the existence of the new Chinese armies was one reason for their position; as a result, the threat of force might, if applied selectively, have been rather effective. Apart from the dangers involved, the disinclination to follow this method may have been the result of the old mainstream bias against the use of violence in foreign policy. It is interesting that K'ang Yu-wei, in some respects closer to the militant conservative tradition than were most later nationalist officials, was comparatively willing to consider military resistance as a way of upholding China's rights.

A final important element in the new foreign policy was the government's skillful use of international rivalries in order to achieve its goals. Balancing off one foreign power against another was, of course, a technique characteristic of the old mainstream approach to foreign policy; however, it was now used to support China's sovereignty rather than simply to control the foreigners. This observation suggests an additional characteristic common to a number of the other features of the nationalist policy, namely, that they could be effectively developed and implemented because they were closely related to earlier techniques and approaches to foreign policy. For example, the interest in economic autonomy was related to the self-strengtheners' desire to protect China's li-ch'üan (power over economic resources) from foreign control. On the other hand, it should be stressed that the old techniques were transformed and took on a new significance from the new context in which they were placed: the drive for national equality.

Because the idea of sovereignty is central to my interpretation of late Ch'ing foreign policy, it was necessary to determine whether a commitment to and appreciation of the new concept was indeed a crucial variable in the last years of the dynasty. Therefore I made a count of the frequency with which the word "sovereignty" appeared in the Ch'ing-chi wai-chiao shih-liao, the major collection of foreign policy documents from the Kuang-hsü and Hsuan-t'ung reigns (1875–1911).[1] The results support my contention (see figure). The word was in use as early as the 1860s, but in the years from 1875 to 1894 it appeared on an average of only once per 100 pages. Then between 1895 and 1899 it was used more often, but still on an average of only 2.5 times per 100 pages. In the next discernible period, covering 1900 and 1901, there was a marked rise in usage, about 8.8 times per 100 pages. Finally, in the period 1902 to 1910 the frequency soared to about 22 appearances per 100 pages. The highest incidence in a single year occurred in 1909, when the word was

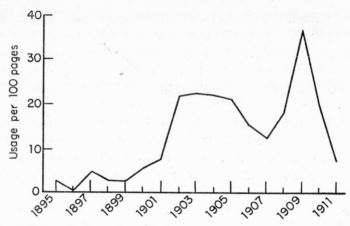

Number of times per 100 pages that the term "sovereignty" occurs, 1895–1911, in the *Ch'ing-chi wai-chiao shih-liao.*

used 37 times per 100 pages, or more than once every 3 pages; obviously, sovereignty was the prime topic of concern.

Although the Chinese ability to contain the Germans in Shantung was partly attributable to problems unique to the Reich, the striking success of the new nationalist policy in Shantung suggests that in the last decade of the dynasty the Chinese government made considerably more progress in its struggle against imperialism than has generally been believed. This conclusion is supported by the fact that China did remain intact, as well as by the evidence presented by recent studies of the late Ch'ing.[2] Overall success for the new nationalist policy did not, of course, mean equal success for all its aspects. In particular, little progress was made in economic development. However, though Peking felt that economic development was an essential prerequisite to resisting the West, the evidence from Shantung (not to mention the comparative success of China's moves against Western privileges from the 1920s onwards) suggests that this was not actually the case. Resistance to imperialism and economic development are apparently not interdependent; although related, they can and should be analyzed separately.

This revisionist approach, which emphasizes the comparative success of late Ch'ing anti-imperialism, cannot be more than a supposition until careful studies are made of Sino-foreign relations at the end of the dynasty and of the particular status of the powers in their own spheres. Yet, as one indication that the failure of Germany's hopes in Shantung was not exceptional, it is worth quoting an analysis of the reasons for the Reich's decline which was presented in a confidential British report on Kiaochow written in 1908. The memorandum said that in 1898

"China was considered to be on the verge of dissolution, and the Powers were working to strengthen their respective positions, in view of the approaching dismemberment of the Empire. Each was endeavoring to mark out for itself as large a sphere of influence as possible and intriguing to foil the designs of its rivals. It seems to have been overlooked at the time by the Western world that some day the Chinese people might shake off their lethargy and refuse to allow Europe to settle their destiny. Yet the outburst of 1900 was at bottom a patriotic protest against foreign aggression. The first Anglo-Japanese Alliance no doubt called a halt to the progress of the ambitions which aimed at the dismemberment of the Chinese Empire, and the convincing demonstration of Japan's power in the struggle with Russia compelled a decisive change in the attitude and policy of the Powers in the Far East. But the trend of events in China of late seems to show that, even without the stand taken by Great Britain and Japan, the hopes and aims founded on a belief in Chinese decadence would never have been realized." [3]

If it does prove true that, in the last decade of the Ch'ing, China made unsuspected progress in its drive against foreign power, it is quite possible that part of the fervor of the anti-imperialist movement after World War I was attributable not only to the steady accumulation of nationalist sentiment but also to the fact that, in the years after the Revolution of 1911, China lost ground in its struggle with imperialism. Japanese influence, which was on the ascendance even before the end of the Ch'ing, was clearly continuing to grow. It is significant, if only symbolically, that the Shantung Question played so large a role in the May Fourth movement, for Shantung provides a striking example of the re-emergence of foreign, and especially Japanese, influence. The new concessions which the Germans obtained after 1912 suggest a foreign resurgence, as does the power Japan amassed after replacing Germany in the province.

With regard to more general issues of modern Chinese history, the most important result of this examination of Shantung is to suggest a new approach to Chinese nationalism. The investigation of China's foreign policy has indicated that a fruitful way to understand the nature and, perhaps even more important, the impact of late Ch'ing nationalism is to consider it as an amalgam of positive elements rather than as a negation of traditional values; and, further, that, at least initially, it is best to investigate and analyze it in a manner which reveals its various concrete features, features that cannot be ascertained primarily through a priori deductions based on the general concept of nationalism. In addition, it is useful to reverse the common approach which tends to emphasize the difficulties that traditional attitudes presented for the development of a nationalist consciousness among the Chinese elite and to search instead for the many elements in the past which favored such a development.

Thus, nationalism in Chinese foreign affairs is best described as an understanding of and commitment to the modern concept of sovereignty and to the particular set of policies and attitudes which grew out of this understanding. The precise nature and importance of this facet of nationalism could not have been delineated without examining foreign policy in detail. In addition, its important elements could not have been described as the negation of traditional cultural universalism or of earlier views on foreign policy. Analysis shows that the new approach and the policy to which it gave rise had strong roots in the past, not only in the techniques of the traditional mainstream approach but even in the intense culturalism of the militants.

One task for future students of late Ch'ing China will be to delineate the positive elements which comprised the nationalist outlook in other fields. For example, it already seems clear that nationalism in internal matters, in political theory and action, meant a commitment to stimulating and unleashing the energies of the Chinese people, ending their atomization, and uniting them in the task of solving the nation's problems.[4] It seems likely that the understanding of the positive content of nationalism in foreign and internal policy can provide the key to probing its role in more specific matters, such as educational or military policy. However, each of these areas must be analyzed carefully and concretely in order to elucidate not only the actual impact of nationalism but also its connections and roots in Chinese tradition. For example, the ch'ing-i approach appears to have been of considerable importance not only in the origins of the nationalist approach to foreign affairs but also toward internal matters; it may, indeed, prove to be of unsuspected significance in the whole development of Chinese nationalism.

Although this study has analyzed Chinese nationalism in a particular way, it has supported the recent tendency in scholarship to emphasize the spread of nationalism as the most significant development of the last decades of the Ch'ing.[5] At the same time, it has suggested that a commitment to the new perspective was more influential in determining the nature of the actions of a member of the elite than was his particular role in society. Whether one was, so to speak, a "new person" or an "old person" ideologically was more important than whether one was in the government or outside it. This is obvious in Shantung, where officials carried out those nationalist policies which in other provinces were associated with the local gentry or merchants. It should also not be surprising, since the bureaucracy and the extra-governmental elite essentially came from the same class.

Although the importance of nationalism in the late Ch'ing has been underlined here, more than the usual weight has been given to the role of the reform movement of 1898 in the development and spread of nationalist attitudes. This seems clearly justified in the field of foreign policy and may prove to be true in other areas as well. K'ang Yu-wei and his followers, of course, supported a wide variety of new measures in many fields; and once the positive elements of Chinese nationalism are identified and these are compared with what the reformers advocated, their movement may occupy an even more pivotal position in modern Chinese history than it does today.

Placing late Ch'ing foreign policy and nationalism in a broader context, an approach to understanding the basic significance of the period following the Sino-Japanese War may now be indicated. It was in these years that important segments of the Chinese elite began to perceive China's problems and the solutions to these problems, not in traditional terms but rather within the framework of new ideas and categories derived from the West. Thus, in foreign policy, what most fundamentally differentiated the quest for sovereignty from earlier approaches is that it was derived from Western concepts of international relations. The same shift seems to have taken place in a host of other fields, ranging from political thought to educational policy. That qualitative changes in Chinese attitudes took place in the '90s was to be expected. First of all, it was in the '90s that the generation born in the late '50s and the '60s began to attain influence. This was, of course, the first generation which came to maturity when the presence of the West was already an integral part of the Chinese scene. Secondly, the Sino-Japanese War brought Japan and her successful response to the West to the attention of the Chinese elite; and any attempt to comprehend what had happened in Japan since 1868 would necessitate an understanding of Western ideas and methods.

It should be stressed that to suggest such a major change in Chinese attitudes is not to say that prior to the 1890s the West was not considered to be a very important problem for China, or that there was homogeneity in China's approach to her foreign and internal difficulties, or even that there was not a considerable attempt at reform. However, with the exception of a few intellectuals, the Chinese elite, from Lin Tse-hsü through Li Hung-chang, conceived of China's problems within some traditional framework, though clearly a different one for different men in different periods. This also does not imply that traditional values and modes of thought did not play a major role in shaping the selection of what was taken from the West in the '90s; indeed, as in the case of nationalism, once the nature of the new attitudes is clarified, their ties to the past will be more precisely understood.

This study has not focused primarily on economic matters. However, since the German sphere of influence in Shantung does present a useful case study of imperialism in action, events there should be related to the long-standing question of the foreign impact on Chinese economic life.[6] This can be done most precisely by noting that the evidence from Shantung lends support to the conclusions presented by Hou Chi-ming in his recent study, *Foreign Investment and Economic Development in China, 1840–1937*. In particular, the German experience in Shantung provides further illustrations of two of Hou's major themes: first, that on the whole the Western presence had a favorable impact on economic growth; and second, that, at least prior to the 1930s, it did not tend to harm traditional activities.[7]

China made little overall economic progress during the years covered by this study; even in Shantung, the effect of the German activities was limited to the leasehold and, to a lesser extent, to the areas surrounding the SEG. Nevertheless, the direction of the German impact was positive. Tsingtao, a tiny, isolated fishing village in 1897, had become a major port by the time the Germans left. It had an efficient administration and modern public services and schools. It also had up-to-date facilities for transportation, communication, and banking. As a result, commercial activities flowered, and there was even some industrial growth. It was German capital, skills, personnel, and international contacts which laid the foundations for this development. After 1914 Tsingtao continued to grow. By 1931, the last normal year before World War II, it ranked as the fourth most important port in China, after Shanghai, Tientsin, and Dairen.[8]

In the interior of Shantung, a province whose transportation facilities had been considered particularly poor even for China, the chief German contribution was the construction of the SEG from Tsingtao to Tsinan. The line was quickly connected to one major north-south trunk route, the Tientsin-Pukow, and in later years to the other, the Peking-Hankow. In its wake the SEG instigated a variety of changes, most notably the expanded commercial activity of the areas which it served. The other important German creation in the interior was the SBG, whose activities reached major proportions by 1914 and which eventually became one of China's most important mining enterprises.

Chinese actively participated in each area of development that grew

out of the German presence, though in the interior tı
the population involved was certainly small. Local peop
skills both from the training programs which the Germ.
established and from working on the new jobs themselves.
time, Chinese officials and businessmen expanded their ow
as a result of the German presence. This was done partially to
of what the foreigners had introduced, as exemplified by the   ot
Chinese entrepreneurs to Tsingtao and to newly created business locations along the SEG. It was also done in order to compete with the
foreigners, as in the case of the Chinese mining at I-hsien and in the
thirty-li zone.

The new developments in Shantung did not seem to have an adverse
effect on indigenous traditional economic activities. Neither the junk
trade, traditional mining, nor silk and strawbraid production suffered
reverses. Indeed, the new situation appears to have resulted in some
growth in these enterprises by providing better communications, larger
markets, and the stimulus of competition.

Although the Germans may, to some extent, have assisted in development within Shantung, it should be stressed in closing that this does not
necessarily imply a favorable judgment on their presence in the province.
Indeed, it is clear that an increasingly broad segment of the Chinese elite,
and perhaps of the general population as well, did not want the Germans
in Shantung and, especially after nationalist attitudes became prevalent,
felt demeaned and oppressed by the German presence. As a result they
were willing, quite consciously, to sacrifice even economic development
in order to resist foreign domination. Clearly if the Germans, despite the
spread of nationalism, had tried to carry out their original intentions in
Shantung, even those concerned solely with economic development, the
results would have been disastrous. This would seem to suggest a
principle which is still applicable now that nationalist attitudes have
become virtually universal. The effort to assist economic development
in a foreign country may be successful only if great concern is shown for
the rights of the nation involved; active intervention for the sake of
furthering political modernization or in order to achieve some political
system desired by a great power is still prone to disaster.

Appendix
Notes
Bibliography
Glossary
Index

Appendix: Maps

The three maps show the following areas as they appeared in the later years of the German occupation:

Map I. Shantung
Map II. Kiaochow and surrounding areas
Map III. Tsingtao

The places listed below are keyed as follows: those on Maps I and II, place name, map number, coordinates; those on Map III, place name, map number.

Arkona Island (Ch'ing-tao I.), III
Auguste Victoria Bay, III
Bismarck Mountain, III
Chang-ch'iu, I, C-c
Chefoo, I, G-b
Chi-mo, I, F-c; II, E-a
Chi-ning, I, B-d
Chiao-chou, I, F-c; II, B-b
Chiao-chou Bay, I, F-c; II, D-c
Chin-ling, I, D-c
Ch'ing-chou, I, D-c
Ch'ing-tao Bay, II, D-c; III
Ch'ing-tao Island (Arkona I.), III
Chou-ts'un, I, C-c
Chu-ch'eng, I, E-c
Chü-yeh, I, B-d
Fang-tzu, I, E-c
Hai-po River, III
Hsiao-ch'ing-ho, I, C-b
Hung-shan, I, D-c
I-chou-fu, I, D-d
I-chou-fu Prefecture, I, D-d
I-hsien, I, C-c

I River, I, D-e
I-shui, I, D-d
Iltis Bay, III
Iltis Mountain, III
Jih-chao, I, E-d
Kao-mi, I, E-c; II, A-a
Lai-chou, I, E-b
Lai-chou-fu Prefecture, I, E-c
Lai-wu, I, C-c
Lao-shan Harbor, II, F-c
Large Harbor, III
Li-ts'un, II, E-c
Ling-shan-wei, II, C-d
Liu-t'uan, I, E-c
Nü-ku-k'ou, II, D-b
Po-shan, I, C-c
Potato Island, II, D-b
Sha-ho, I, E-b
Sha-tzu-k'ou, II, F-c
Small Harbor, III
Ssu-fang, III
Ta-pao-tao, III
T'a-pu-t'ou, II, C-b

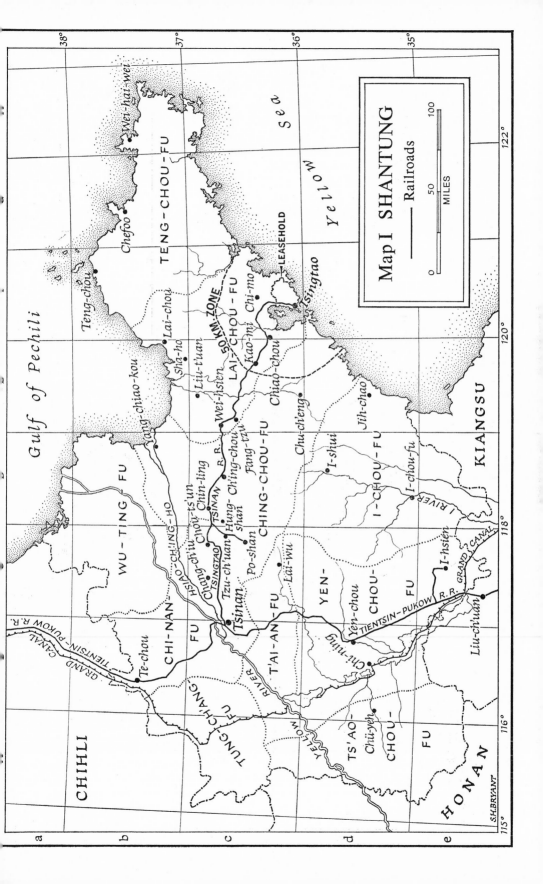

Map I SHANTUNG

—— Railroads

MILES
0   50   100

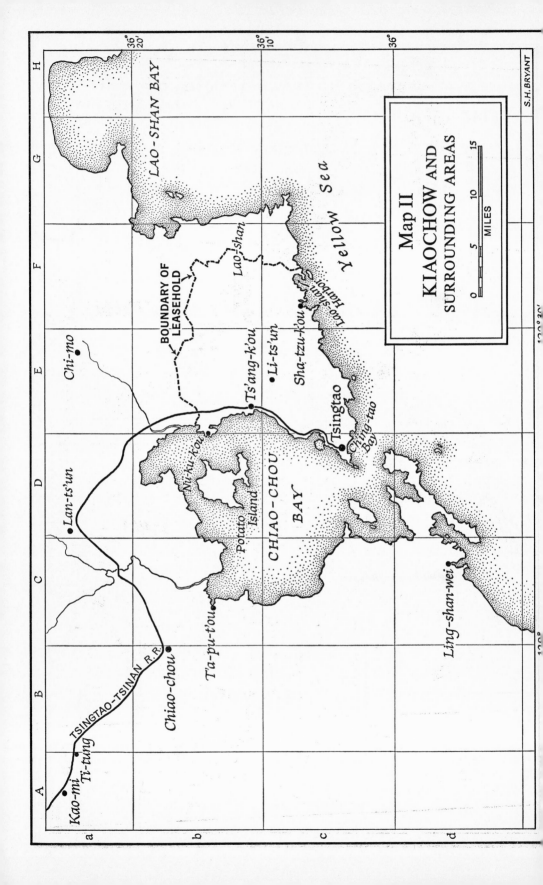

Map II
KIAOCHOW AND
SURROUNDING AREAS

MILES
0   5   10   15

S.H.BRYANT

LAO-SHAN BAY

Yellow Sea

BOUNDARY OF
LEASEHOLD

Lao-shan

Chi-mo

Lan-ts'un

Ts'ang-k'ou

Ni-ku-k'ou

Li-ts'un

Sha-tzu-k'ou

Lao-shan
Harbour

Tsingtao

Ching-tao
Bay-tao

Potato
Island

CHIAO-CHOU
BAY

T'a-pu-t'ou

Chiao-chou

TSINGTAO-TSINAN R.R.

Ti-tung

Kao-mi

Ling-shan-wei

36°
20'

36°
10'

36°

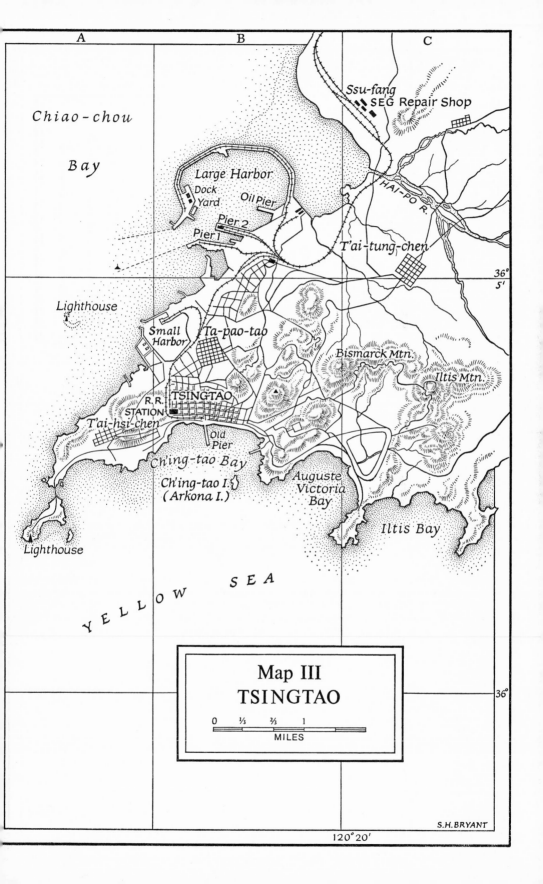

Chiao-chou

Bay

Large Harbor

Dock Yard

Oil Pier

Pier 2

Pier 1

Ssu-fang
SEG Repair Shop

HAI-PO R.

T'ai-tung-chen

36° 5'

Lighthouse

Small Harbor

Ta-pao-tao

Bismarck Mtn.

Iltis Mtn.

TSINGTAO

R.R. STATION

T'ai-hsi-chen

Old Pier

Ch'ing-tao Bay

Ch'ing-tao I. (Arkona I.)

Auguste Victoria Bay

Iltis Bay

Lighthouse

YELLOW SEA

Map III
TSINGTAO

0   ⅓   ⅔   1

MILES

36°

36°

S.H.BRYANT

120°20'

Notes

Abbreviations

AABK   Archives of the German Foreign Office, Dept. II (Auswärtiges Amt, Abt. II), file entitled "Bergwerkskonzessionen in China." *

AADE   Archives of the German Foreign Office, Dept. I, file entitled "Deutsche Eisenbahn-Unternehmungen in China."

AAKS   Archives of the German Foreign Office, Dept. I, file entitled "Kiautschou und die deutschen Interessen in Schantung."

AKV   Wilhelm Schrameier, *Aus Kiautschous Verwaltung* (Jena, 1914).

Denk.   Germany, Reichsmarineamt, *Denkschrift betreffend die Entwicklung des Kiautschou-Gebiets,* yearly publication, 1899–1910. (Each *Denkschrift* runs from October of one year to October of the next. The citations mention only the main year; e.g., the *Denkschrift* covering October 1898 to October 1899 has been cited as *Denk.*, 1899.)

DGSB   Archives of the German Legation in China (Deutsche Gesandtschaft in China), file entitled "Schantung-Bergbau-Gesellschaft."

DGSE   Archives of the German Legation in China, file entitled "Schantung-Eisenbahn."

DGSN   Archives of the German Legation in China, file entitled "Handelsniederlassungen in Schantung."

GP   *Die grosse Politik der europäischen Kabinette, 1871–1914,* ed. Johannes Lepsius et al. (40 vols.; Berlin, 1922–1927).

HFT   *Hai-fang-tang* (Archives on naval defense), ed. Wang Yü-chün et al., Academia Sinica, Institute of Modern History, Compilations of Source Materials on Modern Chinese History, no. 1 (5 vols.; Taipei, 1957).

IMC, *Decennial*   China, Imperial Maritime Customs, *Decennial Reports on Trade, Navigation Industries* . . . 1892–1901, 1902–1911.

IMC, *Returns*   China, Imperial Maritime Customs, *Returns of Trade and Trade Reports,* annual vols.

*See Bibliography for more detailed citations of archives and *Denk.*
The form used in my notes is this: AABK [or other archive], volume: document number. The number given is the basic one and does not include *zu, an,* or prefixes which cannot help to locate the document. Outgoing documents should be located by their date and incoming by their number.

KWT   *K'uang-wu-tang* (Archives on mining), ed. Wang Hsi and Li En-han, Academia Sinica, Institute of Modern History, Compilations of Source Materials on Modern Chinese History, no. 3 (8 vols.; Taipei, 1960).

MK   Archives of the German Imperial Naval Cabinet, file entitled "Kiautschou." (Note form: MK, volume, reel: frame number.)

NCH   *North-China Herald and Supreme Court and Consular Gazette* (Shanghai).

SL   *Ta-Ch'ing li-ch'ao shih-lu* (Veritable records of successive reigns of the Ch'ing dynasty; Tokyo, 1937–1938; reprinted Taipei, 1964).

STTL   *Shan-tung chin-tai-shih tzu-liao,* vol. III (Source materials on the modern history of Shantung), comp. Shantung Historical Association (Tsinan, 1961; reprinted Tokyo, 1965).

WCSL   *Ch'ing-chi wai-chiao shih-liao* (Historical materials concerning foreign relations in the late Ch'ing period, 1875–1911), comp. Wang Yen-wei and Wang Liang (Peiping, 1932–1935; reprinted Taipei, 1963).

I. The Acquisition of the German Sphere of Influence

1. Sino-German relations from their beginnings to 1895 are the topic of Helmuth Stoecker, *Deutschland und China im 19. Jahrhundert* (Berlin, 1958). This fine study, based on a wide range of German materials, has been the most important source for this introductory section. A good though brief discussion of the Chinese side of these early relations is to be found in Part I of Lee Kuo-chi, *Die Chinesische Politik zum Einspruch von Shimonoseki und gegen die Erwerbung der Kiautschou-Bucht* (Münster, 1966). An older but still useful work which gives some of the early history in an introductory chapter is Djang Feng-djen (Chang Feng-chen), *The Diplomatic Relations between China and Germany since 1898* (Shanghai, 1936).

2. An excellent work dealing with the social, ideological, and political ties between the German navy and the middle classes is Jonathan Steinberg, *Yesterday's Deterrent — Tirpitz and the Birth of the German Battle Fleet* (London, 1965); see especially part 1. Eckart Kehr, *Schlachtflottenbau und Parteipolitik, 1894–1901* (Berlin, 1930), is still a basic work with much to say on this topic. For the navy's early role in German imperialism see also Walther Hubatsch, *Die Ära Tirpitz* (Berlin, Frankfurt, 1955).

3. For some earlier contacts as well as the commercial developments discussed here see Djang Feng-djen, pp. 1 and 217–218, and Stoecker, pp. 37–39.

4. Stoecker, pp. 40–43.

5. *Ibid.,* pp. 42–48.

6. See *ibid.,* pp. 49–61, for the expedition to China and its background.

7. Lee Kuo-chi, p. 41.

8. Quoted in Stoecker, p. 60.

9. Stoecker, pp. 62–68.

10. *Ibid.,* pp. 69–84.

11. Quoted *ibid.,* p. 72.

12. John K. Fairbank, *Trade and Diplomacy on the China Coast: The Opening of the Treaty Ports, 1842–1854* (Cambridge, Mass., 1953), I, 276.

13. Stoecker, p. 73.

14. Lee Kuo-chi, p. 37.

15. *Ibid.,* pp. 42–45.

16. *Ibid.,* pt. I, sec. A.

17. Stoecker, chaps. 7 and 8.

18. Lee Kuo-chi, pp. 17–20; Stoecker, chap. 9.

19. Except as otherwise noted, the material on the expansion of the German role in China presented here is taken from Stoecker, chaps. 6, 12, and 13.

20. IMC, *Returns,* 1895, p. 20.

21. For Germany's military role, in addition to Stoecker see Lee Kuo-chi, pt. I, secs. A and B.

22. John L. Rawlinson, *China's Struggle for Naval Development* (Cambridge, Mass., 1967), p. 147.

23. The carefully presented and detailed information in Stoecker's discussion of German financial expansion (pp. 190–211) does not seem in accord with the overall interpretation which he gives to this information, namely that German financial circles were rather eager to invest in China. On the question of rates of return on investment in China, see Hou Chi-ming, *Foreign Investment and Economic Development in China, 1840–1937* (Cambridge, Mass., 1965), p. 112.

24. See IMC, *Returns,* 1895, p. 31, for both firms and individuals. Overall, there were more Americans and Frenchmen in China, but many of them were missionaries.

25. Except as otherwise noted, the material on the Steyl Mission comes from Stoecker, chap. 14.

26. Both the missionary and the government representative are quoted by Stoecker, p. 252.

27. Lee Kuo-chi, p. 139.

28. For a discussion of Bismarck's subordination of imperialist goals, during this period, to the wider concerns of foreign policy and especially to the desire for friendship with Britain, see Mary Townsend, *The Rise and Fall of Germany's Colonial Empire, 1884–1918* (originally published 1930; reprinted New York, 1966), pp. 110–115. When Caprivi became chancellor, he continued Bismarck's policy. See *ibid.,* pp. 160–165.

29. See Steinberg, pp. 61–71, for a discussion of the navy's attitudes in the period between the removal of Stosch as chief in 1883 and the rise of Tirpitz in the middle '90s.

30. Convenient descriptions of the bay are to be found in *Kiaochow and Weihaiwei* (handbook prepared under the direction of the Historical Section of the Foreign Office, no. 71; London, 1920), pp. 1–4; Georg Franzius, *Kiautschou: Deutschlands Erwerbung in Ostasien* (Berlin, 1898), pp. 98–111; and IMC, *Returns,* 1899, pp. 79–80.

31. For traditional Chinese maps of these two areas showing boundaries, see *Shan-tung t'ung-chih,* comp. Yang Shih-hsiang and Sun Pao-t'ien (1915). The maps precede chüan 2, pt. 2, p. 26, and chüan, 2, pt. 2, p. 28. Note that in this later period Chiao-chou had become a *chih-li-chou.*

32. IMC, *Returns,* 1899, p. 80, and IMC, *Decennial,* 1892–1901, p. 98.

33. T'an T'ien-k'ai, *Shan-tung wen-t'i shih-mo* (Shanghai, 1935), pp. 1–2; IMC, *Returns,* 1899, p. 83.

34. Exact figures on the junk trade are not available. This is an estimate based on the figures for 1899 and 1900 in IMC, *Returns,* 1900, p. 65.

35. IMC, *Returns,* 1899, pp. 83–85.

36. *Ibid.,* p. 79.

37. Ferdinand von Richthofen, *China, Ergebnisse eigener Reisen* (Berlin, 1877–1912).

38. See discussion of transportation in Shantung, *ibid.,* II, 258–266; the quotation is from IMC, *Returns,* 1899, p. 82.

39. Richthofen, II, 184, 199, 201, 210.

40. *Ibid.,* II, 262.

41. *Ibid.,* II, 265–266.

42. There is a discussion of this interest in T'an T'ien-k'ai, pp. 2ff. T'an also gives lengthy quotes from documents. These documents and others can, however, be found more easily and in full in *STTL.*

43. *STTL,* p. 62; the memorial which follows is on p. 51.

44. *Ibid.,* p. 52.

45. *Ibid.,* pp. 53–54.

46. *Ibid.,* p. 59.

47. See T'an T'ien-k'ai's discussion and *STTL,* p. 63.

48. Hsieh K'ai-hsün, *Erh-shih-erh nien lai chih Chiao-chou-wan* (Shanghai, 1920), p. 3.

49. Letter quoted in *NCH,* Nov. 21, 1900, p. 1084.

50. Chang Chih-tung, *Chang-wen-hsiang-kung ch'üan-chi* (1937 ed.; reprinted Taipei, 1963), 37:24 (July 19, 1895); hereafter referred to as *Works.*

51. Benjamin Ming-chu Bee, "The Leasing of Kiaochow, A Study in Diplomacy and Imperialism" (unpub. diss. Harvard University, 1935), p. 137.

52. *SL,* 377:9b (Nov. 22, 1895), and 377:12 (Nov. 27, 1895), show reluctance. Quotations are from the latter.

53. Except as otherwise noted, the opening part of this section, which relates the navy's role in China to material on the general connection among the navy, Tirpitz, and German imperialism, uses materials from Steinberg and from William L. Langer, *The Diplomacy of Imperialism,* 2nd ed. (New York, 1951), chap. 13.

54. Steinberg, pp. 202–203.

55. In addition to Steinberg, chap. 7, see Kehr, chap. 6, on naval politics and the liberals, and chap. 8 on the Center.

56. *The Holstein Papers,* ed. Norman Rich and M. H. Fisher (Cambridge, Eng., 1955–1963), IV, 245 (Jan. 11, 1902). Holstein refers to the seizure of Kiaochow and to the Jih-chao episode (see my chap. iv). This quotation is also cited by Steinberg, p. 151, to make the point about Tirpitz' coolness toward military confrontation.

57. Steinberg, pp. 150–151.

58. The most extensive study of the immediate background to the acquisition of Kiaochow, 1894–1897, is Bee. Lee Kuo-chi, Steinberg, and Langer are also very useful. All these have been used extensively in the rest of this section. I have, however, re-examined primary sources in order to understand the story in the light of the later history of Kiaochow. This has resulted in some reinterpretation of specific events, a greater emphasis overall on the split between the

navy and the Foreign Office, and somewhat greater stress on the role of Bishop Anzer. Particularly useful in uncovering the split between the navy and the Foreign Office has been Norman Rich, *Friedrich von Holstein* (Cambridge, Eng., 1965). I have cited the primary sources where I have used them, though it should be noted that some of the documents are also cited in the above secondary works.

59. *GP,* IX, doc. 2219 (Nov. 17, 1894).

60. The value of Germany's trade with China and Hong Kong was about 48,000,000 marks in 1895 (Stoecker, p. 240). In terms of either dollars or taels the figure is lower.

61. Bee, p. 50.

62. Rich, II, 437ff; note also that *GP* documents between the spring and fall of 1895 show no interest on the part of the Wilhelmstrasse in a base.

63. *GP,* XIV, doc. 3662 (Mar. 18, 1896).

64. *Holstein Papers,* I, 178.

65. *GP,* XIV, doc. 3646.

66. MK, 1.5:551ff. Precise date not given.

67. Townsend, chaps. 6, 7, and 8; J. Rubinstein, "Bernhard Dernburg: Colonial Reform and German Politics, 1906–1910" (unpub. seminar paper Harvard University, 1963; cited with author's permission).

68. Alfred von Tirpitz, *My Memoirs* (New York, 1919), I, 100–101.

69. For example, Holstein: see Rich, II, 555.

70. *GP,* XIV, doc. 3669, footnote with long excerpt from "Denkschrift des Auswärtigen Amtes" (Mar. 19, 1897).

71. The memorandum also suggests that the navy was pushing for a colony purely out of political motives. This does not seem to be true; rather, there was a congruence between what the navy wanted and what was politically helpful.

72. Bee, chap. 3, gives the details of the complicated story of what places were suggested and by whom.

73. *GP,* XIV, doc. 3656.

74. *GP,* XIV, doc. 3658.

75. *GP,* XIV, doc. 3656.

76. *GP,* XIV, doc. 3662.

77. *GP,* IX, doc. 2221; XIV, doc. 3662.

78. The material in the text on Chinese policy during and after the war and on the early German approaches for a base is drawn from Lee Kuo-chi, pt. II and pt. III, sec. A.

79. This famous trip is described in all the important secondary works.

80. Tirpitz, II, 92.

81. Steinberg, p. 104.

82. *Ibid.,* p. 103, and *Holstein Papers,* I, 180.

83. Julius Irmer, *Die Erwerbung von Kiautschou, 1894–1898* (Cologne, 1930), p. 28.

84. Large sections of Tirpitz' report are reprinted, *ibid.,* pp. 29ff.

85. Bee, chap. 4.

86. The history of the problems surrounding the convention are well summarized in a footnote in Bee, p. 145. Perhaps the prime argument which he

presents against the authenticity of the agreement is that no Chinese text was available. There is, however, a Chinese text in *Kuang-hsü-ch'ao tung-hua-lu* (Peking, 1958; 1st ed. in different format, 1909), IV, 3876 (Oct. 21, 1896). It is also mentioned in contemporary Chinese sources, for example, as a memorial by Li Ping-heng in *WCSL*, 124:14ff (Jan. 12, 1897). Despite this added evidence the status and even authenticity of the convention can still be questioned, and the whole issue is worthy of more investigation. The quotations given here are from the Chinese text mentioned above.

87. *GP*, XIV, doc. 3669. The navy's earlier rejection on economic grounds is contained in a footnote to this document on p. 45.

88. Bee, pp. 125ff, has the story of the final decision and its aftermath. There was still some debate in 1897 (Heyking, for example, wanted Amoy), but it was not significant.

89. Lee Kuo-chi, pt. III, sec. C, describes Heyking's efforts.

90. Bee, p. 130.

91. On these last steps see Bee, pp. 153ff. See also Langer, p. 445, for the broader international context of the Peterhof meeting.

92. *WCSL*, 125:8bff (Feb. 13, 1897). This is also discussed in Bee, p. 83.

93. *SL*, 406:13b.

94. Lee Kuo-chi, pp. 138–139, describes this incident and the kaiser's orders to use it as a pretext for action.

95. Bee, p. 166, says that the members of the band were simply robbers with no particular antimissionary feelings. Lee Kuo-chi, p. 139, says that they had antimissionary purposes, though he does not say directly that they were members of the Ta-tao-hui. The judgment given here is based on the most recent and detailed study of the incident, that found in *STTL*, pp. 30ff. This account uses a wide variety of local sources, many of which are quoted in full. Interestingly, the feeling among Westerners at the time was also that the murderers were anti-Christian secret-society members.

96. Rich, II, 560. The same basic secondary sources used in the last section have also been used here, supplemented again by primary sources as described in note 58 above.

97. *GP*, XIV, doc. 3689.

98. *Ibid.*

99. *GP*, XIV, doc. 3694, footnote p. 76, describes the bishop's efforts and cites documents which contain the two quotations below.

100. Bee, pp. 191ff.

101. Steinberg, p. 154.

102. *AKV*, p. 1.

103. Bee, pp. 182ff; Langer, p. 452.

104. Rich, II, 565; Steinberg, p. 155.

105. Tirpitz quoted by Steinberg, p. 155.

106. Holstein quoted by Rich, II, 565.

107. *GP*, XIV, doc. 3697.

108. Bee, p. 196.

109. *GP*, XIV, doc. 3701.

110. Langer, pp. 452ff; Bee, chaps. 6 and 7.

111. Bee, p. 178; Diedrichs to kaiser (Nov. 18, 1897), MK, 1.5:656.

112. Bee, pp. 327ff.

113. *WCSL*, 127:16b (Nov. 7, 1897).

114. *WCSL*, 127:17 (Nov. 10, 1897).

115. *WCSL*, 127:17 (Nov. 11, 1897).

116. *WCSL*, 127:18b (Nov. 17, 1897).

117. See chap. ii for a discussion of Li's policy.

118. Bee, pp. 200ff. See also *SL*, 411:13 (Nov. 16, 1897), and 411:15b (Nov. 17, 1897).

119. Bee, pp. 206ff.

120. *Ibid.*, p. 340.

121. *Ibid.*, p. 335; Lee, p. 148.

122. Bee, p. 337.

123. Tirpitz, I, 98; Bee, p. 362. Also see the border debate discussed in note 124.

124. Bülow to kaiser (Dec. 23, 1897) and its enclosures, MK, 1.5:722ff; Knorr to kaiser (Dec. 27, 1897), MK, 1.5:728ff. See also *Denk.*, 1898, pp. 574–576, for a discussion of the border.

125. *Denk.*, 1898, p. 575.

126. Quoted by Langer, p. 459.

127. Friedrich Behme and M. Krieger, *Guide to Tsingtau and Its Surroundings* (Wolfenbüttel, 1905), pp. 21–22.

128. Bee, p. 359.

129. *Ibid.*, pp. 376ff.

130. *Ibid.*, pp. 367–375, 378–380.

131. Text can be found in John V. A. MacMurray, comp. and ed., *Treaties and Agreements with and concerning China, 1894–1919* (New York: Oxford University Press, 1921), I, 112–116. This work is quoted by permission of the Carnegie Endowment for International Peace.

132. Wilhelm Schrameier, *Kiautschou, seine Entwicklung und Bedeutung* (Berlin, 1915), pp. 23–24. Key Chinese documents on the negotiations can be found in *WCSL*, chüan 134 and 135. They range in date from Sept. 5, 1898 (KH 24, 7, 20) to Oct. 24, 1898 (KH 24, 9, 10). The text of the final border treaties can be found in *WCSL*, 135:11bff. One possible explanation for the Germans' success in the negotiations which emerges from these documents is that the Chinese negotiators were comparatively ignorant of the area. They had been there for only two weeks before the borders were fixed. The Germans had been in the leasehold for nine months and had worked carefully to get a clear idea of the area and of the borders they wanted.

There was widespread dissatisfaction with the work of the Chinese negotiators as news of what had happened became public; on this, see documents cited above from *WCSL* and also, for example, *SL*, 425:6b (Sept. 9, 1898), 443:8b (May 31, 1899), and 444:13 (June 20, 1899).

133. Many documents on this campaign in late 1897 and early 1898 appear in Chang Chih-tung, *Works*, and in Sheng Hsuan-huai, *Yü-chai ts'un-kao* (originally published 1939; reprinted Taipei, 1963; hereafter referred to as *Collected Papers*). For Sheng's immediate reaction see his *Collected Papers*, 29:6

(Nov. 23, 1897); for Chang's see his *Works,* 30:3b (Jan. 26, 1898). For a description of their opposition see Wang Wen-shao's telegram to the Tsungli Yamen which he quotes to Chang in Chang, *Works,* 30:15 (Feb. 5, 1898).

134. *Kuang-hsü-ch'ao tung-hua-lu,* IV, 4040 (Feb. 11, 1898).

135. Chang Chih-tung, *Works,* 155:4 (Mar. 8, 1898).

II. The Chinese Response

1. For the information presented here on what I have called militant conservatism, see Lloyd Eastman, "Ch'ing-i and Chinese Policy Formation during the Nineteenth Century," *The Journal of Asian Studies,* 24.4:610 (August 1965); and Benjamin Schwartz, *In Search of Wealth and Power: Yen Fu and the West* (Cambridge, Mass., 1964), pp. 15–16.

2. This is a comment by Liang Ch'i-ch'ao quoted in John Schrecker, "The Pao-kuo Hui, A Reform Society of 1898," *Papers on China,* 14:51 (1960).

3. Wang T'ao was one, for example. See Paul A. Cohen, "Wang T'ao and Incipient Chinese Nationalism," *The Journal of Asian Studies,* 26.4:568–569 (August 1967).

4. Immanuel C. Y. Hsü, *China's Entrance into the Family of Nations* (Cambridge, Mass., 1960), pt. II.

5. Bee, pp. 276ff.

6. Wang Shu-huai, *Wai-jen yü wu-hsü pien-fa* (Taipei, 1965), pp. 147ff. See also telegrams in Sheng Hsuan-huai, *Collected Papers,* 29:27b–35 (Dec. 23, 1897–Jan. 10, 1898), and Chang Chih-tung's telegram to the Tsungli Yamen in his *Works,* 79:17 (Jan. 2, 1898).

7. Sheng, *Collected Papers,* 29:27b (Dec. 23, 1897). Wang Shu-huai feels that Liu tended to support the idea of exclusive reliance on England and Japan. This telegram would seem to indicate, however, that Liu evidently did not want simply to recreate the old Russian alliance using new partners.

8. Wang Shu-huai, pp. 155–156, 176ff.

9. On this point, in addition to Wang, see also Li Hung-chang's views in Sheng, *Collected Papers,* 29:31b (Dec. 30, 1897); even Li acknowledged that Russia had perhaps become the greatest threat, though he did not support a formal alliance with England.

10. Chang Chih-tung, *Works,* 79:26 (Jan. 21, 1898).

11. *Ibid.,* 79:27 (Jan. 21, 1898).

12. Sun E-tu (Zen), *Chinese Railways and British Interests, 1898–1911* (New York, 1954), chap. 1.

13. *SL,* 382:13 (Feb. 7, 1896), and 385:9b (Mar. 22, 1896).

14. Arthur W. Hummel, ed., *Eminent Chinese of the Ch'ing Period, 1644–1912* (Washington, D.C., 1943–1944), I, 407.

15. See, for example, Li's summary of the causes for the outbreak of violence against the Steyl Mission in the spring and summer of 1896 in *I-ho-t'uan tang-an shih-liao,* comp. National Bureau of Archives, Office of Ming and Ch'ing Archives (Peking, 1959), I, 3ff (Aug. 3, 1896). See also Lee Kuo-chi, p. 139.

16. *WCSL,* 124:14ff (Jan. 12, 1897).

17. Schwartz, p. 16.

18. *WCSL,* 127:21 (Nov. 18, 1897).

19. See *ibid.*, 127:18 (Nov. 15, 1897), for the original admonition of the Yamen. Li's rebuttal is at 127:21 (Nov. 18, 1897).

20. See Bee, chap. 9. There were moments during the negotiations when the Yamen considered breaking off the talks and fighting instead.

21. Chang Hao, "The Anti-Foreign Role of Wo-jen, 1804–1871," *Papers on China*, 14:21 (1960).

22. Bee, p. 405.

23. *Wu-hsü pien-fa* (The reform movement of 1898), ed. Chien Po-tsan et al. (Shanghai, 1953), II, 188ff (December 1897–January 1898).

24. Wang Shu-huai, pp. 162ff, gives considerably more weight to what he calls K'ang's "enthusiasm" for alignment with England in this period. Most of the evidence for this comes, however, from K'ang's *Tzu-pien nien-p'u* (Self-compiled *nien-p'u*), which was written after the reformer had fled China for Japan and when, in order to cultivate English and Japanese support, he had reasons for overstressing his earlier sympathies for the two countries. On the dating of the *nien-p'u* see Chaoying Fang's review of *Wu-hsü pien-fa* in *The Journal of Asian Studies*, 17.1:99–105 (November 1957).

25. *Wu-hsü pien-fa*, II, 197ff (Jan. 29, 1898).

26. Cited in Schrecker, "Pao-kuo Hui," p. 56.

27. *Ibid.*, pp. 60–61.

28. *Ibid.*, pp. 51, 60.

29. *Wu-hsü pien-fa*, II, 134.

III. The Establishment of the Leasehold, 1898–1900

1. The decree can be found in F. W. Mohr, *Handbuch für das Schutzgebiet Kiautschou* (Tsingtao, 1911), p. 6.

2. This statement is based on how the Germans treated Kiaochow. For a detailed discussion of the formal legal status of the leasehold under international and German law, see Ralph A. Norem, *Kiaochow Leased Territory* (Berkeley, 1936), chap. 2.

3. The legal position of the governor both at Kiaochow and in relation to the homeland authorities is discussed in Norem, pp. 99–106.

4. *Denk.*, 1898, p. 560.

5. Diedrichs cited by Norem, p. 105.

6. Quoted in Foreign Office to Bülow (Dec. 4, 1901), AAKS, 8:16447.

7. Norem, pp. 107ff.

8. Descriptions of the units and the complements come from Germany, Reichsmarineamt, *Marineverordnungsblatt*, 29:295ff (1898). The official complement of about 1500 was the number actually there in 1900: see Deimling, "Die Kolonie Kiautschou," *Abteilung Berlin-Charlottenburg der Deutschen Kolonial-Gesellschaft Verhandlungen, 1900/01*, II, 43–63.

9. Governor's semiannual report on troop activity at Kiaochow (May 16, 1900), MK, 4.6:686ff; Tirpitz to kaiser (Sept. 18, 1900), MK, 4.6:768ff; *NCH*, Mar. 20, 1899, p. 468.

10. Norem, pp. 107ff.

11. *Denk.*, 1899, p. 2830. On this council see also Norem, p. 108.

12. Norem, pp. 119ff; *Denk.*, 1898, pp. 563–564.

13. This can be roughly extrapolated from the health figures in *Denk.*, 1899, p. 2840, and Mohr, pp. 442–443.

14. *Denk.*, 1899, p. 2836; *Denk.*, 1900, p. 727; Norem, p. 107.

15. *Denk.*, 1898, p. 564; *Denk.*, 1899 p. 2836.

16. *Denk.*, 1899, p. 2836.

17. "Verordnung betreffend die Rechtsverhältnisse der Chinesen" (Mohr, p. 72).

18. *Denk.*, 1899, p. 2831.

19. *AKV*, p. 26; see also *Denk.*, 1899, p. 2838.

20. Germany, Reichsmarineamt, *Das deutsche Kiautschou-Gebiet und seine Bevölkerung, Kartenkrokis und statistische Tabellen* (Berlin, 1899), p. 56.

21. Reported in Jaeschke to Tirpitz (April 21, 1899), enclosed in AAKS, 4:7272.

22. For example, *Denk.*, 1898, p. 560.

23. Tirpitz to kaiser (Oct. 7, 1898), MK, 3.6:392.

24. Governor's semiannual report on troop activity at Kiaochow (May 16, 1900), MK, 4.6:686ff.

25. Tirpitz to kaiser (Sept. 18, 1900), MK, 4.6:768ff.

26. Mohr, p. 452.

27. These memoranda are the *Denk.* There was a close discussion of the *Denk.* at each budget debate, and the deputies frequently compared what the navy reported with what they had learned from newspapers and elsewhere. These other sources rarely contradicted the navy's facts. When the navy was criticized it was on broader grounds. For a discussion of the Reichstag and Kiaochow see the first section of chap. vi.

28. His major work on administration is *AKV*. Also useful is his *Kiautschou, seine Entwicklung und Bedeutung.*

29. *Denk.*, 1898, p. 560. I have used *AKV* and the *Denk.* generally. However, much of this material can be confirmed in IMC publications, various secondary works, and the *NCH*.

30. *AKV*, p. 1.

31. Mohr, p. 238.

32. *AKV*, p. 91.

33. *Denk.*, 1898, p. 560.

34. *WCSL*, 128:12 (Jan. 10, 1898).

35. *AKV*, p. 3.

36. *AKV*, pp. 3 and 90ff.

37. *AKV*, p. 90.

38. *AKV*, pp. 4–5. See also *WCSL*, 128:12, on these events.

39. *AKV*, p. 6.

40. *Denk.*, 1898, p. 560.

41. Quoted in *AKV*, pp. 6–7.

42. Quoted in *AKV*, pp. 7–8.

43. *AKV*, p. 6.

44. *Denk.*, 1899, p. 2832.

45. *AKV*, p. 108.

46. Mohr, p. 238, has the text.

47. *Denk.*, 1898, p. 561; *AKV*, p. 19.

48. *Denk.*, 1898, p. 561.

49. *AKV*, pp. 63ff. See also Harold Schiffrin, "Sun Yat-sen's Early Land Policy," *The Journal of Asian Studies*, 16.4:549–564 (August 1957).

50. *AKV*, p. 63. Schrameier was eager to emphasize, however, that practical considerations were more vital than theoretical ones in establishing the land system.

51. Schiffrin, "Sun's Land Policy."

52. *Denk.*, 1898, pp. 561ff.

53. *Denk.*, 1898, p. 565; see also *Denk.*, 1899, pp. 2840–2841.

54. *Denk.*, 1899, p. 2839.

55. *AKV*, p. 32.

56. *Denk.*, 1899, p. 2832.

57. *AKV*, p. 38.

58. Newspaper article quoted in *AKV*, pp. 39ff; *Denk.*, 1898, p. 562.

59. *Denk.*, 1899, p. 2832.

60. *AKV*, p. 25; *Denk.*, 1899, p. 2831.

61. *Denk.*, 1899, p. 2832; *AKV*, p. 42.

62. *Denk.*, 1899, p. 2845.

63. *AKV*, pp. 12–13.

64. This is the implication of *AKV*, p. 91, which says that the navy received no rural land tax until 1900. See also the story of the collection of the tax lists, discussed in the next paragraph of the text, which has the same implication.

65. *Denk.*, 1899, p. 2845; *AKV*, pp. 91ff.

66. Jaeschke to Tirpitz (April 13, 1899), enclosed in AAKS, 4:6674.

67. Jaeschke to Tirpitz (April 25, 1899), enclosed in AAKS, 4:7272. A translation of the poster is included in Jaeschke's letter.

68. The idea that the German colony in China should be a free port was taken for granted as early as Richthofen's day (see first section of chap. i). It was again assumed as certain in Tirpitz' crucial report on Chiao-chou Bay written in 1896. For a restatement in 1898 see *Denk.*, 1898, p. 560. See also *AKV*, pp. 154ff.

69. *Denk.*, 1899, pp. 2832–2833; *AKV*, p. 154.

70. *Denk.*, 1899, p. 2832.

71. *AKV*, p. 162. On the negotiations see also Hart's later report in *WCSL*, 188:13bff (April 27, 1905).

72. *Denk.*, 1898, p. 562.

73. For text see MacMurray, I, 198.

74. *Denk.*, 1899, p. 2833.

75. On these advantages see IMC, *Decennial*, 1892–1901, pp. 87ff, as well as the text itself.

76. *AKV*, pp. 159–160.

77. MacMurray, I, 198ff.

78. *AKV*, p. 189.

79. *NCH*, July 10, 1899, p. 53.

80. *NCH*, July 31, 1899, p. 221.

81. Knappe to Ketteler (July 14, 1899), enclosed in AAKS, 4:10851.

82. Hart in *WCSL*, 188:14 (April 27, 1905); Stanley Wright, *Hart and the Chinese Customs* (Belfast, 1950), p. 705. Schrameier plays down the doubts of the IMC. For more on this matter see the last section of chap. v.

83. *AKV*, p. 176, inadvertently shows this; see also S. Wright, p. 705.

84. S. Wright, p. 727, n. 92.

85. *Ibid.,* p. 706.

86. See this attitude, for example, in *AKV*, p. 176.

87. IMC, *Returns,* 1899, p. 90.

88. *AKV*, pp. 166–167.

89. Ohlmer to SEG (July 20, 1899), enclosed in AADE, 8:11203.

90. Gaedertz to Hohenlohe (Sept. 6, 1899), AADE, 8:11203.

91. *AKV*, p. 178.

92. IMC, *Returns,* 1900, p. 61; *Denk.,* 1899, p. 2834.

93. *Denk.,* 1900, p. 723.

94. IMC, *Returns,* 1899, p. 80.

95. *Ibid.,* p. 91.

96. *Ibid.,* p. 90.

97. *Denk.,* 1899, p. 2832.

98. All the early *Denk.* have a section of "Churches, Education, and Scientific Studies," but the best discussion is in *Denk.,* 1901, pp. 2893ff.

99. Samuel Couling, *The Encyclopaedia Sinica* (originally published 1917; reprinted Taipei, 1964), p. 47.

100. Kenneth S. Latourette, *A History of Christian Missions in China* (originally published 1929; reprinted Taipei, 1966), p. 576.

101. *Denk.,* 1899, p. 2837; 1901, p. 2893.

102. *Denk.,* 1898, p. 566; 1899, p. 2838.

103. Governor's semiannual report on troop activity at Kiaochow (May 16, 1900), MK, 4.6:686ff. See also *Denk.,* 1899, p. 2838.

104. Schrameier, *Kiautschou, Entwicklung und Bedeutung,* p. 37; *NCH,* June 26, 1899, p. 1159; *Denk.,* 1899, p. 2838.

105. *Denk.,* 1898, p. 566.

106. Governor's semiannual report (May 16, 1900), MK, 4.6:686ff.

107. *Denk.,* 1899, p. 2838.

108. *Ibid.*

109. This was especially true of liberals, such as the Freisinnige, who were opposed to the German colonies operated by the Foreign Office in Africa but were willing to see if the navy could run one better. See, for example, their contribution to the 1899 debate in Eugen Richter's speech in Germany, *Stenographische Berichte über die Verhandlungen des Reichstages,* 165:559 (Jan. 31, 1899), and to the 1900 debate in Eickhoff's speech, 169:4398–4399 (Mar. 2, 1900).

110. The quotations that follow are from *Denk.,* 1898, p. 566, and 1899, pp. 2839–2840.

111. *Denk.,* 1899, p. 2839; 1898, p. 566.

112. In addition to *Denk.* descriptions, see Mohr for texts of many such regulations.

113. *Denk.,* 1899, p. 2841.

114. Quotation from *AKV*, p. 26; see also *Denk.,* 1899, p. 2841.

115. *AKV*, p. 26.

116. *Ibid.*

117. *Denk.*, 1899, p. 2842; see also Deimling, "Die Kolonie Kiautschou."

118. *Denk.*, 1898, p. 562. The 1898 code can be found in Mohr, p. 206.

119. For example, "Verordnung betreffend Chinesenordnung für das Stadt-gebiet" (July 14, 1900), in Mohr, p. 22.

120. *Denk.*, 1899, p. 2841.

121. *Denk.*, 1898, p. 565; 1899, p. 2842.

122. *Denk.*, 1898, p. 564; 1899, p. 2836; 1900, p. 727.

123. For good examples of this see report of Admiral Diedrichs (Mar. 1, 1899), enclosed in AAKS, 3:4447.

124. Quotation from *Denk.*, 1898, p. 546. A number of surveys can be found as appendixes to the various *Denk.*

125. Germany, Reichsmarineamt, *Das deutsche Kiautschou-Gebiet und seine Bevölkerung.*

126. *Denk.*, 1899, p. 2837.

127. Germany, Reichsmarineamt, *Das deutsche Kiautschou-Gebiet und seine Bevölkerung,* is made up mostly of charts, each of which answers these questions.

128. *Denk.*, 1898, p. 566; 1899, p. 2843. See charts in the appendixes to these also.

IV. The Germans in the Interior, 1898–1900

1. In addition to the material on K'ang presented in chap. ii, see also Li En-han, *Wan-Ch'ing ti shou-hui k'uang-ch'üan yun-tung* (Taipei, 1963), pp. 14–17.

2. A. S. Jerussalimski, "Das Eindringen der deutschen Monopole in China an der Wende vom 19. zum 20. Jahrhundert," *Zeitschrift für Geschichtswissenschaft,* 8.8:1848–1849 (1960).

3. *Denk.*, 1900, p. 725.

4. *KWT*, II, doc. 509 (July 24, 1898); Newsclipping from *Das kleine Journal* (Jan. 20, 1899), enclosed in AAKS, 1:936.

5. *NCH*, Aug. 15, 1898, p. 292.

6. For a brief and not very enlightening biographical sketch see *Mi-hsien chih,* comp. Wang Chung and Lü Lin-chung (1924), 16:8.

7. Enclosed in *KWT*, II, doc. 592 (May 12, 1902); *NCH,* Aug. 15, 1898, p. 292. The proclamation is quoted briefly in the *KWT* enclosure and discussed in both items.

8. *KWT,* II, doc. 509 (July 24, 1898).

9. *Ibid.*

10. *KWT,* II, doc. 510 (July 26, 1898).

11. *KWT,* II, doc. 511 (Nov. 4, 1898).

12. *Ibid.*

13. *KWT,* II, doc. 513 (Nov. 11, 1898).

14. *KWT,* II, doc. 514 (Nov. 18, 1898).

15. *KWT,* II, doc. 515 (Nov. 22, 1898).

16. *KWT,* II, doc. 517 (Dec. 30, 1898). Both Chang and the Yamen wanted

the Germans to let Chinese officials know when they were coming so that they could be protected; on this point see also doc. 516 (Dec. 27, 1898).

17. Letter attached to *KWT,* II, doc. 517 (Dec. 30, 1898).

18. *KWT,* II, doc. 518 (Mar. 9, 1899).

19. Jerussalimski, "Das Eindringen," p. 1857, does mention one communication on this matter from the Chinese governor. He says the governor was Yü-hsien; but the date indicates that it was Chang, for the letter is dated April 2 and Yü did not arrive until April 8, though he was named earlier.

20. Newsclipping from the *Kölnische Volkszeitung* (Dec. 5–12, 1898), enclosed in AAKS, 2:2502. On the attack see also Anzer to Jaeschke (April 2, 1899), enclosed in AAKS, 4:7150.

21. *NCH,* Dec. 5, 1898, p. 1053; Rosendahl to Tirpitz (Jan. 3, 1899), enclosed in AAKS, 2:AS534; Heyking to Foreign Office (Jan. 15, 1899), AAKS 1:553.

22. Jaeschke to Tirpitz (Mar. 15, 1899), enclosed in AAKS, 3:5341.

23. *I-ho-t'uan tang-an shih-liao,* I, 16; *NCH,* May 16, 1898, pp. 829, 841; Cremer to Nottmeyer (Mar. 4, 1899), enclosed in AAKS 3:5341.

24. *I-ho-t'uan tang-an shih-liao,* I, 16.

25. Anzer to Heyking (Dec. 25, 1898), enclosed in AAKS, 2:2954.

26. This was even true of Chang Ju-mei: see, for example, *SL,* 418:3 (May 24, 1898).

27. The story of Anzer and the Stenz case and the quotations on it which follow are from Anzer to Heyking (Dec. 26, 1898), enclosed in AAKS, 2:2954. For Heyking's criticism of such intervention by Anzer, see Heyking to Hohenlohe (Feb. 2, 1899), AAKS, 2:3288.

28. Hosea Bellou Morse, *The International Relations of the Chinese Empire* (originally published 1918; reprinted Taipei, n.d.), III, 151. Morse speaks of and lists antiforeign outbreaks in the "spring and summer of 1898." There were not too many, and, more important, with the exception of one all occurred before or after the Hundred Days. This single case, referred to in Morse's note 70, was not a missionary case, however; see Great Britain, Foreign Office, "Blue Book," *China No. 1,* 1899, doc. 213, in *House of Commons Sessional Papers,* 1899, vol. CIX.

29. *Wu-hsü pien-fa,* II, 36.

30. Anzer to Heyking (Dec. 26, 1898), enclosed in AAKS, 2:2954; Cremer to Nottmeyer (Mar. 4, 1899), and Jaeschke to Tirpitz (Mar. 15, 1899), both enclosed in AAKS, 3:5341.

31. For an accurate German view of the meaning of the personnel change, together with some comments on Yü's anti-Christian past, see Heyking to Hohenlohe (Mar. 30, 1899), AAKS, 3:5698. For similar shifts in personnel on the district and prefectural level in late 1898 and early 1899 see Anzer to Jaeschke (April 2, 1899), enclosed in AAKS, 4:7150. For the comment on the depth of Yü's antiforeignism see Hummel, I, 207.

32. Heyking to Hohenlohe (Jan. 17, 1899), AAKS, 2:2954, and its enclosure, Anzer to Heyking (Dec. 26, 1899); Rosendahl to Tirpitz (Jan. 3, 1899), enclosed in AAKS, 2:AS534; Heyking to Hohenlohe (Feb. 17, 1899), AAKS, 3:4206, and its enclosure, Rosendahl to Heyking (Jan. 30, 1899).

33. See newsclippings from *Kölnische Volkszeitung* interspersed in AAKS in early 1899; also Tirpitz to Jaeschke (June 27, 1899), enclosed in AAKS, 5:8587.

34. Anzer to German consul in Tientsin (approx. Jan. 1, 1899), enclosed in AAKS, 2:2954.

35. Anzer to Jaeschke (April 2, 1899), enclosed in AAKS, 4:7150. If Anzer is correct, this would be the second recorded use of this motto and would indicate that it was widespread earlier than is sometimes believed. On the issue of dating this motto and its importance for the history of the Boxer movement, see Victor Purcell, *The Boxer Uprising* (Cambridge, Eng., 1963), pp. 209ff, esp. pp. 216–219.

36. Anzer to Heyking (Dec. 26, 1899), enclosed in AAKS, 2:2954.

37. This is the case, for example, in Yü's memorials from this period in *I-ho-t'uan tang-an shih-liao.*

38. Tirpitz to kaiser (March 11, 1899), AAKS, 2:2916.

39. *Ibid.;* see also Jaeschke to Tirpitz (Mar. 15, 1899), enclosed in AAKS, 3:5341.

40. Jaeschke to Tirpitz (April 5, 1899), enclosed in AAKS, 4:6674. The note which Jaeschke had presented to the Jih-chao magistrate when the German troops took the town (see story later in text) indicates that the governor was probably telling the truth about not knowing that the Stenz case had been settled.

41. Heyking to Foreign Office (Mar. 16, 1899), AAKS, 2:5607.

42. Jaeschke to Tirpitz (April 5, 1899), enclosed in AAKS, 4:6674.

43. Heyking to Hohenlohe (Mar. 30, 1899), AAKS, 3:5698.

44. Heyking to Foreign Office (Jan. 15, 1899), AAKS, 1:553; note the kaiser's comment in the margin, "Must not happen!"

45. Lenz to Heyking (January 1899), enclosed in AAKS, 2:2956.

46. *NCH,* Jan. 30, 1899, p. 169.

47. *NCH,* Feb. 20, 1899, p. 288.

48. Bülow to Tirpitz (June 20, 1899), AAKS, 4:7150.

49. Jaeschke to Tirpitz (Mar. 29, 1899), enclosed in AAKS, 4:6674; *Denk.,* 1899, p. 2844 (source of quotation).

50. Jaeschke to Tirpitz (Mar. 29, 1899), enclosed in AAKS, 4:6674. The letter also tells of Heyking's acquiescence.

51. Tirpitz to kaiser (Mar. 11, 1899), AAKS, 2:2916; Tirpitz to Bülow (Mar. 16, 1899), AAKS, 2:AS585 (source of quotation).

52. Lt. Hannemann to Jaeschke (Mar. 27, 1899), enclosed in AAKS, 3:5645.

53. *Ibid.*

54. Lü Hai-huan to Bülow (April 22, 1899), AAKS, 3:4797.

55. For example, a year later Sheng Hsuan-huai said the incident proved the Boxers were useless against foreign soldiers; see his *Collected Papers,* 160:4 (June 7, 1900).

56. Jaeschke to Tirpitz (April 5, 1899), enclosed in AAKS, 4:6674.

57. Heyking to Tsungli Yamen (Mar. 31, 1899), enclosed in AAKS, 4:6274.

58. Foreign Office to German ambassador in U.S. (Mar. 29, 1899), AAKS, 2:AS693. This document also includes the similar telegrams sent to other countries.

59. Hannemann to Jaeschke (April 7, 1899), enclosed in AAKS, 4:6674.

60. Jaeschke to magistrate of Jih-chao (Mar. 13, 1899), enclosed in AAKS, 3:5341.

61. Jaeschke to Tirpitz (April 21, 1899), enclosed in AAKS, 4:6674.

62. Heyking to Foreign Office (April 10, 1899), AAKS, 3:4227.

63. *Ibid.;* Jaeschke to Tirpitz (April 12, 1899), enclosed in AAKS, 4:6674.

64. Jaeschke to Tirpitz (April 20, 1899), enclosed in AAKS, 4:7150.

65. *Ibid.*

66. *Ibid.*

67. Jaeschke to Tirpitz (May 26, 1899), enclosed in AAKS, 5:8761.

68. Jaeschke to Tirpitz (June 26, 1899), enclosed in AAKS, 5:10500.

69. The figure is in a memorial of Yü-hsien (July 17, 1899) in *I-ho-t'uan tang-an,* I, 21. Anzer's notification to Jaeschke is spoken of in Jaeschke to Tirpitz (June 26, 1899), enclosed in AAKS, 5:10500.

70. Decree (April 1, 1899) in *I-ho-t'uan tang-an,* I, 21. Documents on the Jih-chao case continue through p. 32.

71. *Ibid.,* p. 21.

72. *SL,* 439:20b (April 1, 1899).

73. Reported in Foreign Office to Heyking (April 3, 1899), AAKS, 3:AS739.

74. Chinese Legation to Foreign Office (April 10, 1899), AAKS, 3:4232.

75. Chinese Legation to Foreign Office (April 6, 1899), AAKS, 3:4102.

76. Chinese Legation to Foreign Office (April 10, 1899), AAKS, 3:4233.

77. Jerussalimski, "Das Eindringen," p. 1857; Yü-hsien report (July 6, 1899) in *HFT,* V, doc. 223, suggests that he may have tried to stop the engineers in April.

78. Yü-hsien report (July 6, 1899), *HFT,* V, doc. 223.

79. See Tirpitz' views on the episode discussed at the end of this section.

80. *SL,* 439:24 (April 6, 1899). The words used in the text could conceivably mean "to quell the unrest"; but the context of the sentence and the dispatches which follow show clearly that they refer to the Germans.

81. Yü-hsien memorial (April 30, 1899) in *I-ho-t'uan tang-an,* I, 23. There is no evidence to indicate that such talk was for form only; for good evidence that it was not, see, for example, Yuan Shih-k'ai's admonition against the use of force described in the next section.

82. *Ibid.*

83. *SL,* 441:6b (May 1, 1899).

84. Kuo T'ing-i, *Chin-tai Chung-kuo shih-shih jih-chih* (Taipei, 1963), II, 1045–1046; Shen Tsu-hsien and Wu K'ai-sheng, *Jung-an ti-tzu-chi* (originally published 1913; reprinted Taipei, 1962), 2:10ff.

85. *NCH,* June 5, 1899, p. 1002.

86. Foreign Office memorandum (May 12, 1899), AAKS, 3:5635.

87. For the German quotation see *ibid.* The *NCH* quotation is from the issue of May 15, 1899, p. 862.

88. There was heightened defense planning following the incident; see, for example, orders to Yü-hsien (May 26, 1899), *SL,* 443:2b, and other items on defense in this chüan of *SL,* which covers early June 1899.

89. See next section.

90. *I-ho-t'uan tang-an,* I, 31 (July 17, 1899).

91. Tirpitz to Foreign Office (April 6, 1899), AAKS, 3:AS758; Tirpitz to Foreign Office (April 15, 1899), AAKS, 3:4453.

92. Tirpitz to Jaeschke (June 27, 1899), enclosed in AAKS, 5:8587.

93. *Denk.*, 1899, p. 2835; Jerussalimski, "Das Eindringen," pp. 1850ff; *Ostasiatischer Verein Hamburg-Bremen, zum 60 jaehrigen Bestehen,* issued by the Verein (Hamburg, 1960), pp. 188, 216.

94. MacMurray, I, 240ff, gives the text of the concession.

95. Jerussalimski, "Das Eindringen," pp. 1850ff. This approach to the railroad is also clear in *Denk.,* 1898, p. 563.

96. The material on the railroad's early construction work on the next few pages of text comes, except as otherwise noted, from *Denk.,* 1899, p. 2835, and 1901, pp. 2901ff.

97. Stoecker, p. 233.

98. IMC, *Returns,* 1900, p. 89.

99. *Ibid.; NCH,* Feb. 7, 1900, p. 235.

100. Hans Weicker, *Kiautschou: Das deutsche Schutzgebiet in Ostasien* (Berlin, 1908), p. 157.

101. *Denk.,* 1900, p. 721.

102. *Denk.,* 1901, p. 2903.

103. Jerussalimski, "Das Eindringen," p. 1858; Ketteler to Hohenlohe (Feb. 13, 1900), AAKS, 6:4052.

104. For example, Hsü Ching-ch'eng and Wang Wen-shao (who was heading the K'uang-wu t'ieh-lu tsung-chü, now subordinate to the Yamen but still more committed than the latter to the policies for which it had been established).

105. Jerussalimski, "Das Eindringen," pp. 1851–1852; two communications from the German Legation to the Tsungli Yamen (June 24, 1899, and June 25, 1899) in *HFT,* V, docs. 220 and 221.

106. Jerussalimski, "Das Eindringen," p. 1852. Except for the word "details," which Jerussalimski quotes from Urbig's orders, the quotation here contains the words of Jerussalimski, who examined the orders and paraphrases them.

107. Jaeschke to Tirpitz (June 21, 1899), enclosed in AAKS, 5:9453; Capt. Mauve to Jaeschke (June 27, 1899), enclosed in AAKS, 5:10169; *NCH,* July 10, 1899, p. 71.

108. Capt. Mauve to Jaeschke (July 11, 1899), enclosed in AAKS, 5:13311.

109. *Ibid.*

110. Jaeschke to Tirpitz (June 21, 1899), enclosed in AAKS, 5:9453.

111. Yü-hsien to Jaeschke (June 23, 1899), enclosed in AAKS, 5:10169; Chinese Legation to Foreign Office (July 18, 1899), AAKS, 5:8731; memorial of Yuan Shih-k'ai (April 1, 1900), *WCSL,* 142:12bff.

112. Jaeschke to Tirpitz (June 21, 1899), enclosed in AAKS, 5:9453.

113. *Ibid.*

114. Jaeschke to Tirpitz (June 26, 1899), and Jaeschke to Tirpitz (July 1, 1899), both enclosed in AAKS, 5:10169; Capt. Mauve to Jaeschke (July 11, 1899), enclosed in AAKS, 5:13311.

115. A token force remained till August; see Kiaochow governor's office to Naval Ministry (Aug. 25, 1899), enclosed in AAKS, 5:12098.

116. Subprefect of Chiao-chou to Jaeschke (June 29, 1899), and Jaeschke to Tirpitz (July 1, 1899), both enclosed in AAKS, 5:10169.

117. Chinese Legation to Foreign Office (June 26, 1899), AAKS, 4:7758.

118. *SL*, 445:3 (June 25, 1899).

119. *Ibid.*, 446:1 (July 8, 1899).

120. Jaeschke to Tirpitz (July 1, 1899), enclosed in AAKS, 5:10169.

121. *Ibid.*

122. Subprefect of Chiao-chou to Jaeschke (June 29 and June 30, 1899), both enclosed in AAKS, 5:10169.

123. The text of the July 2 agreement is enclosed in AAKS, 5:10169.

124. Jaeschke to Tirpitz (June 20, 1899), enclosed in AAKS, 5:10169.

125. Proclamation of the magistrate of Kao-mi (June 26, 1899), attached to Capt. Mauve to Jaeschke (June 27, 1899), enclosed in AAKS, 5:10169.

126. Jaeschke to subprefect of Chiao-chou (July 7, 1899), enclosed in AAKS, 5:10169.

127. *Ibid.;* Jaeschke to Yü-hsien (July 7, 1899), enclosed in AAKS, 5:10169.

128. Text in MacMurray, I, 266–267.

129. For material in this paragraph see Richthofen report to Bülow (April 10, 1899), AADE, 6:AS743, and its enclosures; Deutsch-Asiatische Bank (Berlin) or Foreign Office (sender unclear) to Urbig (April 19, 1899), enclosed in AADE, 7:AS801; Heyking to Foreign Office (April 23, 1899), AADE, 7:AS852; two memorials of Hsü Ching-ch'eng and Chang I (both May 22, 1899), *WCSL*, 138:29ff and 138:30bff; Percy Kent, *Railway Enterprise in China* (London, 1907), pp. 148–152.

130. Text in MacMurray, I, 694ff.

131. Jaeschke to Tirpitz (Jan. 2, 1900), enclosed in AADE, 8:1991; P. Hildebrandt (brother of Heinrich) to SEG (Tsingtao) (Jan. 10, 1900), and Jaeschke to Tirpitz (Jan. 22, 1900), both enclosed in AADE, 8:3368; Jaeschke to Tirpitz (Feb. 20, 1900), enclosed in AADE, 9:4629; Jaeschke to Tirpitz (Dec. 29, 1899), enclosed in AAKS, 6:1743; Yuan Shih-k'ai memorial (April 18, 1900), *WCSL*, 142:22ff.

132. Yuan Shih-k'ai memorial (April 18, 1900), *WCSL*, 142:22ff; *STTL*, pp. 91–98.

133. This is the viewpoint of *STTL*.

134. Quote is from IMC, *Returns*, 1899, p. 89. The causes of the unrest come, except as otherwise noted, from the same sources as the description of it.

135. *NCH*, Feb. 7, 1900, pp. 235–236; IMC, *Returns*, 1899, p. 89. The eventual agreement took much care to specify that workers should be local people (see end of section in text).

136. P. Hildebrandt to Jaeschke (Jan. 22, 1900), enclosed in AADE, 8:3891; Jaeschke to Tirpitz (Mar. 4, 1900), enclosed in AADE, 9:6467; Jaeschke to Tirpitz (Feb. 25, 1900), enclosed in AAKS, 6:4788.

137. For a biography of Yuan in English see Jerome Ch'en, *Yuan Shih-k'ai* (Stanford, 1961); Yuan's life through 1899 is covered in chaps. 1–3.

138. *I-ho-t'uan tang-an*, I, 27ff (July 4, 1899).

139. Ch'en, p. 65.

140. *WCSL*, 142:12bff (April 1, 1900).

141. *Ibid.*, 13a.

142. Jaeschke to Tirpitz (Jan. 15, 1900), enclosed in AADE, 8:3367.

143. Report of Capt. Buttlar (April 9, 1900), enclosed in AADE, 9:7578.

144. Jaeschke to Tirpitz (Jan. 2, 1900), enclosed in AADE, 8:1991.

145. Ketteler to chancellor (Mar. 7, 1900), AADE, 9:5092.

146. See *ibid.* for the story of the correspondence.

147. P. Hildebrandt to SEG (Tsingtao) (Jan. 10, 1900), enclosed in AADE, 8:3368; Yuan memorial (April 18, 1900), *WCSL*, 142:20ff.

148. Yuan memorial (April 18, 1900), *WCSL*, 142:24b.

149. Purcell, p. 208.

150. Two decrees to Yuan Shih-k'ai (Jan. 20 and Jan. 21, 1900), *I-ho-t'uan tang-an*, I, 61.

151. Yuan Shih-k'ai memorial (April 18, 1900), *WCSL*, 44:22a; Jaeschke to Tirpitz (Feb. 20, 1900), enclosed in AADE, 9:4629.

152. *Ibid.*

153. Jaeschke to Tirpitz (Feb. 25, 1900), enclosed in AAKS, 6:4788.

154. Report of results of talks at Kao-mi (February 1900), enclosed in AADE, 9:4629.

155. Jaeschke to Tirpitz (Feb. 25, 1900), enclosed in AAKS, 6:4788.

156. Yuan Shih-k'ai memorial (April 1, 1900), *WCSL*, 142:12bff; report of Capt. Buttlar (April 9, 1900), enclosed in AADE, 9:7578.

157. H. S. Brunnert and V. V. Hagelstrom, *Present Day Political Organization of China,* trans. A. Beltchenko and E. Moran (originally published 1912; reprinted Taipei, n.d.), p. 389.

158. SEG (Berlin) to Foreign Office (Mar. 26, 1900), AAKS, 6:3805; Jaeschke to Tirpitz (Feb. 5, 1900), enclosed in AADE, 8:3891.

159. SEG (Berlin) to SEG (Tsingtao) (Feb. 7, 1900), AAKS, 6: unnumbered (precedes doc. 1743).

160. P. Hildebrandt to SEG (Tsingtao) (Jan. 10, 1900), enclosed in AADE, 8:3368.

161. Jaeschke to Tirpitz (Jan. 15, 1900), enclosed in AADE, 8:3368; quotation is from SEG (Berlin) to Foreign Office (Jan. 23, 1900), AADE, 8:964.

162. P. Hildebrandt to SEG (Tsingtao) (Jan. 10, 1900), enclosed in AADE, 8:3368.

163. *Ibid.*

164. For example, Jaeschke to Tirpitz (Jan. 22, 1900), enclosed in AADE, 8:3368.

165. *Ibid.*

166. Jaeschke to Tirpitz (Mar. 4, 1900), enclosed in AADE, 9:6467.

167. Tirpitz to Foreign Office (Mar. 15, 1900), AADE, 8:3368.

168. Jaeschke to Ketteler (Jan. 19, 1900), enclosed in AADE, 8:3368.

169. Jaeschke to Tirpitz (Jan. 15, 1900), enclosed in AADE, 8:1991.

170. Jaeschke to Tirpitz (Jan. 15, 1900), enclosed in AADE, 8:3368.

171. Jaeschke to Tirpitz (Feb. 20, 1900), enclosed in AADE, 9:4629.

172. *Ibid.*

173. Jaeschke to Tirpitz (Feb. 25, 1900), enclosed in AAKS, 6:4788.

174. Jaeschke to Tirpitz (Jan. 15, 1900), and Jaeschke to Tirpitz (Jan. 19, 1900), both enclosed in AADE, 8:3368; SEG (Tsingtao) to SEG (Berlin) (Jan. 22, 1900), enclosed in AADE, 8:964.

175. SEG (Berlin) to Foreign Office (Jan. 23, 1900), AADE, 8:964.

176. Ketteler to Foreign Office (Jan. 24, 1900), AADE, 8:1022.

177. Bülow to SEG (Berlin) (Jan. 28, 1900), AADE, 8:964.

178. SEG (Berlin) to Bülow (Mar. 5, 1900), AADE, 8:2856.

179. For example, the dispatches in *I-ho-t'uan tang-an,* I, 61–63.

180. SEG (Berlin) to SEG (Tsingtao) (Jan. 29, 1900), enclosed in AADE, 8:1363.

181. Jaeschke to Tirpitz (Feb. 20, 1900), enclosed in AADE, 9:4629.

182. Jaeschke to Tirpitz (Mar. 4, 1900), enclosed in AADE, 9:6467.

183. Jaeschke to Tirpitz (Feb. 5, 1900), enclosed in AADE, 8:3891.

184. Foreign Office to Ketteler (Feb. 15, 1900), AADE, 8:1939; Jaeschke to Tirpitz (Feb. 20, 1900), enclosed in AADE, 9:4629.

185. Jaeschke to Tirpitz (Feb. 20, 1900), enclosed in AADE, 9:4629.

186. Jaeschke to Ketteler (Feb. 17, 1900), enclosed in AADE, 9:4629.

187. SEG (Berlin) to Bülow (Mar. 5, 1900), AADE, 8:2856.

188. SEG (Berlin) to Foreign Office (Mar. 10, 1900), AADE, 8:3047.

189. Governor's office (Tsingtao) to Tirpitz (April 3, 1900), enclosed in AADE, 9:6467; Yuan's memorials (April 1 and April 18, 1900), *WCSL,* 142:12bff and 142:22ff.

190. Report of Capt. Buttlar (April 9, 1900), enclosed in AADE, 9:7578.

191. *WCSL,* 142:14 (April 1, 1900).

192. Text in MacMurray, I, 236ff.

193. Ketteler to Foreign Office (Mar. 19, 1900), AADE, 9:5794.

194. Governor's office (Tsingtao) to Tirpitz (Mar. 19, 1900), enclosed in AADE, 9:6467.

195. Yuan Shih-k'ai, *Yang-shou-yuan tsou-i chi-yao,* comp. Shen Tsu-hsien (1937; reprinted Taipei, 1966), 4:3 (May 12, 1900); cited hereafter as *Selected Memorials.*

196. SEG (Tsingtao) to SEG (Berlin) (May 8, 1900), enclosed in AADE, 9:13102.

197. *Ibid.;* see also last section of this chapter.

198. MacMurray, I, 252ff.

199. For the founding rules of the company see *ibid.,* 254ff.

200. SEG to Foreign Office (Oct. 7, 1899), AAKS, 5:11927.

201. *Denk.,* 1900, p. 724.

202. Li En-han, p. 42.

203. *Denk.,* 1900, p. 725; IMC, *Returns,* 1900, p. 58; *NCH,* June 13, 1900, p. 1065.

204. *KWT,* II, doc. 509 (July 24, 1898).

205. *KWT,* II, doc. 511 (Nov. 4, 1898); *NCH,* Nov. 7, 1898, p. 858.

206. Report of Capt. Buttlar (April 9, 1900), enclosed in AADE, 9:7578.

207. Alexander Armstrong, *Shantung* (Shanghai, 1891), p. 58; *NCH,* Aug. 1, 1898, p. 204.

208. Petition of Taotai Hung Yung-chou (May 12, 1902), *KWT,* II, doc. 592, and its attached documents: petition of Wei-hsien magistrate (Jan. 20, 1900), and petition of Chang Yü-chu (May 10, 1900).

209. Petition of mining investors (n.d., but latter half of 1899) with history of their efforts, attached to *KWT,* II, doc. 592.

210. See Li En-han, pp. 121–122. He does not explicitly say that the establishment of the Restoration Company was aimed at forestalling the Germans; however, the date of the founding and the fact that the firm was a fictitious Sino-German company make such an eventuality highly probable.

211. Note that no representative of the SBG accompanied Hildebrandt, and the casual comment that Yuan seemed also to want to negotiate mining regulations, in SEG (Berlin) to Foreign Office (Mar. 10, 1900), AADE, 8:3047.

212. Yü-hsien to Jaeschke (June 23, 1899), enclosed in AAKS, 5:10169; it mentions mines also. SEG (Berlin) to Foreign Office (Mar. 10, 1900), AADE, 8:3047, seems to indicate that the SBG had prepared some regulations earlier.

213. Text in MacMurray, I, 248ff.

214. Yuan memorial (April 1, 1900), *WCSL*, 142:12bff.

215. Chinese text is in *WCSL*, 142:17ff. The discrepancies are noted in comments appended to each clause.

216. The so-called "Magnaten Syndicat" mentioned by Jerussalimski, "Das Eindringen," p. 1849.

217. Wai-wu-pu to Yuan Shih-k'ai (April 22, 1901), *KWT*, II, doc. 522, and its attached letter from Ketteler (Aug. 7, 1899).

218. For a discussion of the regulations see Li En-han, pp. 16–17; the text is in W. W. Rockhill, *Treaties and Conventions with or concerning China and Korea, 1894–1904* (Washington, 1904), pp. 372ff.

219. Ketteler letter (Aug. 7, 1899) attached to *KWT*, II, doc. 522.

220. Yamen letter (Aug. 24, 1899) attached to *KWT*, II, doc. 522.

221. Seven letters (Oct. 12, 1899, to May 23, 1900) attached to *KWT*, II, doc. 522.

222. *Kiaochow and Weihaiwei,* p. 27.

223. Purcell, pp. 246ff.

224. *GP,* XVI, doc. 4511.

225. *Ibid.*

226. *Ibid.*, note; *Denk.,* 1900, pp. 718–719.

227. Jaeschke to Tirpitz (June 23, 1900), enclosed in AADE, 9:13102.

228. Yuan Shih-k'ai, *Selected Memorials,* 4:18a (June 19, 1900).

229. *NCH,* July 4, 1900, pp. 4, 11, 27, and *NCH,* July 11, 1900, pp. 54, 64–65; Yuan Shih-k'ai, *Selected Memorials,* 5:2ff (June 28, 1900); Hildebrandt to Jaeschke (July 1, 1900), enclosed in AADE, 9:11557.

230. *STTL,* pp. 95–98.

231. Yuan Shih-k'ai, *Selected Memorials,* 9:13ff (May 27, 1901). Here Yuan states what he tried to do, and his actions during the unrest bear him out.

232. Jaeschke to Tirpitz (July 3, 1900), MK, 4.6:720ff; *Denk.,* 1900, p. 719; *NCH,* July 4, 1900, p. 4, and *NCH,* July 11, 1900, p. 64.

233. Jaeschke to Tirpitz (July 3, 1900), MK, 4.6:720ff.

234. *Ibid.*

235. *Ibid.; NCH,* July 11, 1900, p. 65.

236. Jaeschke to Tirpitz (July 20, 1900), MK, 4.6:736ff; *NCH,* July 18, 1900, p. 120, and *NCH,* July 25, 1900, p. 182.

237. *The Boxer Rising* (originally published by *The Shanghai Mercury,* 1901; reprinted New York, 1967), pp. 115ff, has list of deaths.

238. Jaeschke to Tirpitz (July 14, 1900), MK, 4.6:730ff.

239. *STTL,* p. 97.

240. Hildebrandt to Jaeschke (July 1, 1900), enclosed in AADE, 9:11557.

241. Foreign Office to Tirpitz (July 8, 1900), AADE, 9:8441; Tirpitz to Bülow (July 12, 1900), AADE, 9:9318.

242. Jaeschke to Tirpitz (July 2, 1900), enclosed in AADE, 9:11557; Jaeschke to Tirpitz (July 3, 1900), MK, 4.6:720ff; Jaeschke to Tirpitz (July 14, 1900), MK, 4.6:730ff.

243. Jaeschke to Hildebrandt (July 2, 1900), and Jaeschke to Tirpitz (July 2, 1900), both enclosed in AADE, 9:11557.

244. Jaeschke to Tirpitz (July 2, 1900), enclosed in AADE, 9:11557.

245. *Ibid.*

246. Jaeschke to Tirpitz (July 14, 1900), MK, 4.6:730ff.

247. *Ibid.;* Jaeschke to Tirpitz (July 23, 1900), MK, 4.6:747ff; *NCH,* Aug. 15, 1900, p. 337.

248. Tirpitz to SEG (July 21, 1900), enclosed in AADE, 9:9605.

249. SEG to Jaeschke (Aug. 9, 1900), enclosed in DGSE, 2:549/00.

250. SEG to Hohenlohe (Aug. 14, 1900), AADE, 9:11176.

251. See *Holstein Papers,* IV, 195–196; Alfred Vagts, *Deutschland und die Vereinigten Staaten in der Weltpolitik* (New York, 1935), II, 1066.

252. *GP,* XVI, doc. 4558.

253. *GP,* XVI, doc. 4559.

254. War Ministry to kaiser (July 12, 1900), MK, 4.6:705–706.

255. *GP,* XVI, doc. 4585.

256. Vagts, II, 1068.

257. *GP,* XVI, doc. 4585.

258. Tirpitz to War Ministry (July 18, 1900), MK, 4.6:706ff.

259. *GP,* XVI, doc. 4585.

260. *GP,* XVI, doc. 4582. The result of the debate over the declaration of war was that Waldersee carried with him the power to institute it, but he never did so.

261. *Denk.,* 1900, p. 719; Jaeschke to Tirpitz (Sept. 22 and Sept. 27, 1900), both enclosed in AAKS, 7:16893; Naval Ministry to Foreign Office (Sept. 13, 1900), AADE, 9:13102; *NCH,* Sept. 12, 1900, p. 563, Sept. 19, 1900, p. 600, and Sept. 26, 1900, p. 656.

262. Mumm to chancellor (Oct. 8, 1900), AAKS, 7:16869; Jaeschke to Tirpitz (Oct. 10 or 11, 1900), enclosed in AAKS, 6:14573.

263. Jaeschke to Tirpitz (Oct. 10 or 11, 1900), enclosed in AAKS, 6:14573.

264. *Ibid.*

265. *Ibid.;* Yuan Shih-k'ai to Jaeschke (Oct. 7, 1900), enclosed in AAKS, 7:16744. Yuan quotes in part Jaeschke's telegram of the same day.

266. Yuan to Jaeschke (Oct. 7, 1900), enclosed in AAKS, 7:16744.

267. *Denk.,* 1900, p. 719.

268. Yuan Shih-k'ai, *Selected Memorials,* 7:4 (Nov. 3, 1900).

269. *NCH,* Oct. 24, 1900, p. 871.

270. Jaeschke to Tirpitz (Oct. 25, 1900), enclosed in AAKS 7:15299; Mumm to Foreign Office (Oct. 27, 1900), AAKS, 7:15386; Jaeschke to Mumm (Oct. 29, 1900), DGSE, 2:1962/00; *STTL,* pp. 96–98.

271. Mumm to Bülow (Dec. 5, 1900), AAKS, 7:1585.

272. Tirpitz to Foreign Office (Nov. 13, 1900), AAKS, 7:16491. The text of the agreement, dated Oct. 22, is enclosed.

273. Yuan Shih-k'ai, *Selected Memorials*, 9:13aff (May 27, 1901); on amount of damage see report of mining director Michaelis on the resumption of work (December 1900), enclosed in AAKS, 7:861.

V. The Disintegration of the Sphere of Influence

1. Rich, *Holstein*, II, 619ff; *Holstein Papers*, IV, 195 (Aug. 23, 1900); Vagts, II, 1069ff.

2. On the Yangtze Agreement, in addition to the sources in note 1 above, see Langer, pp. 700ff. Quotations are from text of the agreement in Langer, p. 702.

3. On the alliance and the state of Anglo-German relations in this period, see Vagts, II, 1139ff, and Langer, chaps. 22 and 23.

4. Great Britain, Foreign Office, "Confidential Print," *Further Correspondence respecting the Affairs of China*, March 1902, F.O. 405/119, doc. 17, p. 24.

5. In addition to examples which follow, see Vagts, II, 1132ff.

6. For text see MacMurray, I, p. 117.

7. Richthofen to Bülow (Mar. 1, 1902), AAKS, 9:3448. The speech is to be found in Germany, *Stenographische Berichte über die Verhandlungen des Reichstages*, 183:4527 (Mar. 3, 1902).

8. See, for example, Foreign Office to Mumm (Mar. 13, 1902), AAKS, 9:2977.

9. On the rising importance of the Yangtze see Vagts, II, 1252–1253.

10. Foreign Office to Bülow (Dec. 4, 1901), AAKS, 8:16447.

11. Letters on the issue begin to appear in October 1900 in AAKS, vol. 7.

12. Mumm to Bülow (Jan. 21, 1901), AAKS, 8:3529. Mumm repeats here a request he says he originally made on Jan. 3.

13. Truppel to Mumm (Sept. 8, 1901), enclosed in AAKS, 8:16447.

14. Mumm to Foreign Office (Sept. 14, 1901), AAKS, 8:13301; Mumm to Bülow (Oct. 2, 1901), AAKS, 8:16416.

15. Mumm to Foreign Office (Sept. 14, 1901), AAKS, 8:13301.

16. Lenz to Goltz (Nov. 9, 1901), enclosed in AAKS, 8:971.

17. Foreign Office to Bülow (Dec. 4, 1901), AAKS, 8:16447.

18. *Ibid.*

19. Foreign Office to Tirpitz (Dec. 4, 1901), AAKS, 8:16447.

20. The quotations are from Foreign Office to Bülow (Dec. 4, 1901), AAKS, 8:16447; see also Mumm to Foreign Office (Mar. 5, 1902), AAKS, 9:5947.

21. Foreign Office to Mumm (Nov. 1, 1901), AAKS, 8:15411.

22. Truppel to Mumm (Sept. 8, 1901), enclosed in AAKS, 8:16447.

23. Tirpitz to Foreign Office (Nov. 17, 1901), AAKS, 8:16447.

24. Arguments from him against a consul stopped in early 1902, and by April the Foreign Office was beginning to view him as something of an ally against Truppel; see Foreign Office memorandum (April 18, 1902), AAKS, 9:5959.

25. Truppel to Mumm (Feb. 17, 1902), enclosed in AAKS, 9:5947; Truppel to Mumm (Mar. 17, 1902), enclosed in AAKS, 9:8303.

26. Truppel to Mumm (Mar. 17, 1902), enclosed in AAKS, 9:8303.

27. Mumm to Truppel (April 4, 1902), enclosed in AAKS, 9:8303.

28. Mumm to Bülow (April 8, 1902), AAKS, 9:8303.

29. Truppel denied that he sympathized with the campaign or that he helped it, but this seems highly unlikely. For the story see Truppel to Mumm (Mar. 20, 1902), enclosed in AAKS, 9:8303; Mumm to Bülow (April 6, 1902), AAKS, 9:8301; Foreign Office memorandum (April 18, 1902), AAKS, 9:5959; *NCH*, Mar. 19, 1902, p. 517.

30. Truppel to Mumm (Mar. 20, 1902), enclosed in AAKS, 9:8303; Knappe to Mumm (Mar. 21, 1902), enclosed in AAKS, 9:8302.

31. Quotation is from Foreign Office memorandum (June 8, 1902), AAKS, 9:8943; see also Foreign Office memorandum (April 18, 1902), AAKS, 9:5959.

32. Truppel to Goltz (Sept. 30, 1902), DGSE, 2:3879/02. Quotation is from Goltz to consuls in Shanghai, Chefoo, and Tsinan (Oct. 6, 1902), DGSE, 2:3879/02.

33. For a discussion of the war and its impact on diplomacy in East Asia see Vagts, vol. II, chap. 11, pt. 6; see also Rich, vol. II, chap. 47.

34. Mumm to Bülow (June 3, 1905), AAKS, 15:14104.

35. In addition to my account, see Vagts, II, 1251ff.

36. Newsclippings can be found in AAKS, vol. 13 and 14.

37. Bülow to kaiser (Jan. 22, 1905), AAKS, 13:781.

38. Townsend, pp. 231ff.

39. *GP*, XIX, appendix to doc. 6264, cited in Vagts, II, 1251.

40. *Kuang-hsü-ch'ao tung-hua-lu*, IV, 4676 (June 16, 1901); see also Sheng Hsuan-huai's request for such a decree in his telegram to Jung Lu, Wang Wen-shao, etc., in his *Collected Papers*, 55:16b (June 16, 1901).

41. Ch'en, pp. 73–74.

42. Quoted *ibid.*, p. 74.

43. *Ibid.* The Germans who liked Yuan were sympathetic to this movement; see, for example, Chang Chih-tung, *Works*, 175:9b (Nov. 16, 1901).

44. Chang Chih-tung, *Works*, 175:9b (Nov. 16, 1901).

45. For a brief biographical note see Mumm to Foreign Office (Nov. 11, 1901), AAKS, 8:15922.

46. Ch'en, p. 75, implies that this was done through a formal arrangement, though no source is given. Goltz to Foreign Office (Nov. 27, 1901), AAKS, 8:16835, would imply it was done informally.

47. Mumm to Foreign Office (May 29, 1902), AAKS, 9:10437; note also his difficulties in handling the DGBIA negotiations, discussed in a later section of this chapter.

48. For biographical information see Mumm to Foreign Office (May 29, 1902), AAKS, 9:10437, and Stanley Spector, *Li Hung-chang and the Huai Army* (Seattle, 1964), p. 317.

49. Chou Fu, *Chou-ch'üeh-shen-kung ch'üan-chi* (originally published 1922; reprinted Taipei, 1966), *nien-p'u*, 2:10bff (hereafter cited as *Complete Works*); Chang Chih-tung's report acquitting Chou in Chang, *Works*, 64:25ff (Sept. 7, 1905).

50. For biographical information see Mumm to Bülow (Nov. 17, 1904), AAKS, 13:178.

51. For biographical information see Mumm to Bülow (Jan. 18, 1905), AAKS, 13:3913; also Deputy Governor von Semmern to Tirpitz (June 29, 1905), enclosed in AAKS, 15:14883.

52. The decree appeared November 7. Note Mumm's report of the appointment in Mumm to Foreign Office (Nov. 8, 1901), AAKS, 8:15771.

53. *NCH,* Jan. 29, 1902, p. 188, and Feb. 26, 1902, p. 359; Mumm to Foreign Office (March 5, 1902), AAKS, 9:5947.

54. Mumm to Bülow (Mar. 20, 1902), AAKS, 9:6819.

55. Mumm to Foreign Office (May 29, 1902), AAKS, 9:10437. The decree appeared May 28.

56. Mumm to Bülow (Nov. 17, 1904), AAKS, 13:178. The decree appeared October 31.

57. Mumm to Bülow (Jan. 18, 1905), AAKS, 13:3913.

58. *Ibid.;* decree appeared January 10.

59. See newsclippings from the Chinese press enclosed in AAKS, 14a:13580 and 15:18843, as well as doc. 18843 itself (Mumm to Foreign Office, Aug. 30, 1905).

60. Contemporary bureaucrats took a knowledge of the administrative structure at Tsinan for granted. Hence, the founding dates and the functions of the new bureaus described here have been obtained by comparing and collating a large number of German and Chinese documents which were concerned, on the whole, with other matters. More examples of the activities of the bureaus appear in the later sections of this chapter.

61. Quotation is from Yang Shih-hsiang (May 1, 1906), in *KWT,* II, doc. 629; see also Goltz to Bülow (Aug. 16, 1906), AABK, 1:26227.

62. *Kuang-hsü-ch'ao tung-hua-lu,* IV, 4602–4063 (Mar. 24 and Mar. 26, 1898); Morse, III, 157 (Morse's dates are somewhat unclear because they do not differentiate between the opening of the port and the establishment of the customs house). The quotation is from Morse. The three ports were still officially called "Treaty Ports" (*T'ung-shang k'ou-an*) when they were opened, but were soon recognized to be in a different category and came to be given a different name. See IMC, *Returns,* 1899, pp. 157, 426; Wright, p. 896; and note how the three ports were used as a precedent in later years.

63. See memorial of Ch'en Pao-chen of June 14, 1898, in *Wu-hsü pien-fa tang-an shih-liao,* comp. National Bureau of Archives, Office of Ming and Ch'ing Archives (Peking, 1958), p. 385; and decree in *SL,* 422:9a (Aug. 10, 1898).

64. Morse, III, 421–425.

65. See chart in S. Wright, pp. 895–896.

66. Quoted by Yuan Shih-k'ai and Chou Fu, *WCSL,* 182:13 (May 4, 1904).

67. *Ibid.* For an explicit statement that the move was aimed against the Germans see, for example, Chou Fu, *Complete Works,* introductory chapter, 5b.

68. Mumm to Bülow (May 26, 1904), AAKS, 12:11293.

69. Betz to Mumm (July 16, 1904), DGSN 1:3846/04. Tentative regulations are enclosed.

70. Mumm to Bülow (June 6, 1904), AAKS, 12:11984. The quotations in

the last sentence are enclosed; they are from Wai-wu-pu to Yin-ch'ang (May 22 and June 6, 1904); Mumm did not disclose how he got these documents.

71. Mumm to Bülow (May 26, 1904), AAKS, 12:11293.

72. Quoted *ibid*.

73. *Ibid*.

74. Mumm to Truppel (July 25, 1904), enclosed in AAKS, 13:14840.

75. *Ibid.*, and Truppel to Mumm (July 1, 1904), enclosed in AAKS, 13:14840.

76. See last section of this chapter.

77. *NCH,* May 27, 1904, p. 1094.

78. Knappe to Bülow (May 25, 1904), AAKS, 12:10755.

79. Mumm to Bülow (May 26, 1904), AAKS, 12:11293.

80. Knappe to Bülow (May 25, 1904), AAKS, 12:10755.

81. Jaeschke to Tirpitz (Dec. 4, 1900), enclosed in DGSE, 2:2401/00, and its enclosure, Capt. Schoeler to Jaeschke (Dec. 1, 1900).

82. *NCH,* June 26, 1901, pp. 1222–1223; SEG (Tsingtao) to SEG (Berlin) (Sept. 16, 1901), enclosed in DGSE, 2:4?01/01 (film blurred).

83. *Denk.,* 1901, p. 2903; SEG to Mumm (Mar. 15, 1901), DGSE, 2:1090/01 and its enclosures.

84. SEG to SEG (Sept. 16, 1901), enclosed in DGSE, 2:4?01/01.

85. Report on Chinese troops (Nov. 1, 1901), enclosed in DGSE, 2:4540/01.

86. A convenient chart showing the distance of each station from Tsingtao is to be found in Tahara Tennan, *Kōshū-wan* (Dairen, 1914), pp. 437ff.

87. There are a number of documents in AAKS and DGSE for this period which describe the colorful opening ceremonies of the line.

88. Yin-ch'ang to SEG (Dec. 29, 1902), enclosed in DGSE, 3:1139/03; Chou Fu to SEG (no date, approx. December 1902 or early January 1903), enclosed in DGSE, 3:1732/03.

89. SEG to Yin-ch'ang (Jan. 23, 1903), enclosed in DGSE, 3:1139/03.

90. See, for example, when line was almost done, Lange to Mumm (Nov. 18, 1903), DGSE, 3:4281/03.

91. Report on police (Mar. 24, 1906), enclosed in DGSE, 5:1532/06.

92. Lange to Mumm (Nov. 18, 1903), DGSE, 3:4281/03; Wedel to Mumm (Feb. 6, 1904), DGSE, 3:1067/04.

93. Goltz report on trip to Tsinan (June 12, 1904), enclosed in AADE, 13:12667.

94. This attitude especially affected Hildebrandt. See, for example, his views in the Haussner murder case (which is the subject of many documents of the spring of 1903 in vols. 2 and 3 of DGSE). As a result Yuan and Chou developed an intense dislike for him; see report in Deutsch-Asiatische Bank (Tsinan) to Deutsch-Asiatische Bank (Berlin) (Oct. 17, 1904), enclosed in DGSE, 4:5753/04.

95. Truppel to Mumm (Mar. 27, 1903), DGSE, 3:1087/03.

96. Mumm to Foreign Office (Feb. 25, 1904), AADE, 12:6214.

97. Truppel to Tirpitz (May 5, 1904), enclosed in DGSE, 3:2644/04.

98. For a statement of this policy see Mumm to Hildebrandt (April 25, 1904), DGSE, 3:2267/04.

99. Chou Fu to Mumm (May 3, 1904), DGSE, 3:2621/04.

100. *Ibid.;* transcript of discussion between Chou and Truppel (April 28–29, 1904), enclosed in AAKS, 12:11296.

101. Wedel to Mumm (Feb. 6, 1904), DGSE, 3:1067/04; Hildebrandt to Mumm (May 13, 1904), DGSE, 3:2272/04.

102. Hildebrandt to Mumm (May 13, 1904), DGSE, 3:2272/04.

103. Report on police (Mar. 24, 1906), enclosed in DGSE, 5:1532/06.

104. Betz to Mumm (July 22, 1904), DGSE, 3:3891/04; Hildebrandt to Mumm (Aug. 8, 1904), DGSE, 3:4165/04.

105. Wedel to Mumm (Feb. 6, 1904), DGSE, 3:1067/04.

106. Truppel to Tirpitz (Mar. 17, 1904), enclosed in DGSE, 3:1848/04.

107. Truppel to Tirpitz (May 5, 1904), enclosed in DGSE, 3:2644/04.

108. Truppel to Mumm (Sept. 7, 1901), enclosed in AAKS, 8:16416.

109. *Ibid.;* Mumm to Foreign Office (Sept. 14, 1901), AAKS, 8:13301; Tirpitz to Foreign Office (Sept. 17, 1901), AAKS, 8:13384.

110. Telegram quoted in Truppel to Mumm (Sept. 7, 1901), enclosed in AAKS, 8:16416.

111. *NCH*, Sept. 18, 1901, pp. 533–534.

112. Yuan to Truppel (early October 1901), enclosed in AAKS, 8:17059.

113. See governor's semiannual reports on troop activity at Kiaochow, found in MK, vol. 5, reels 6 and 7.

114. Tirpitz to kaiser (Sept. 26, 1901), MK, 5.6:813ff; decree of kaiser (March 29, 1902).

115. Transcript of discussions between Chou and Truppel (April 28–29, 1904), enclosed in AAKS, 12:11296; Mumm to Foreign Office (Nov. 5, 1904), AAKS, 12:20472.

116. Goltz report on his talk with Truppel (June 20, 1904), enclosed in AAKS, 12:12665.

117. See, for example, Knappe to Bülow (June 22, 1904), AAKS, 12:12473.

118. Mumm to Bülow (June 3, 1905), AAKS, 15:14104; Mumm to Bülow (Aug. 14, 1904), AAKS, 15:17084.

119. Truppel to Chou (Sept. 29, 1904), enclosed in AAKS, 13:12072; Mumm to Foreign Office (Nov. 5, 1904), AAKS, 13:20472.

120. Yang memorial (April 26, 1906), *WCSL*, 196:17bff.

121. *Ibid.;* on Yang's efforts and German response discussed here see also memorial of Yang and Yuan Shih-k'ai (Dec. 27, 1905), *WCSL*, 195:13ff; Betz to Mumm and its enclosures (including new police regulations) (June 23, 1905), DGSE, 4:3628/05; *NCH*, Oct. 27, 1905, p. 182; report on police (March 24, 1906), enclosed in DGSE, 5:1532/06.

122. In addition to the following account, see clippings and translations from the English, Japanese, and Chinese press for the first half of 1905 in vols. 13, 14, and 14a of AAKS.

123. Mumm to Foreign Office (April 15, 1905), AAKS, 14:9259.

124. War Ministry to Foreign Office (June 20, 1905), enclosed in AAKS, 14a:10775.

125. Quotation is from Foreign Office to Tirpitz (July 5, 1905), AAKS, 14a:10775; see also Tirpitz to Foreign Office (July 11, 1905), AAKS, 14a:12147.

126. It was postponed indefinitely; see Foreign Office to Tirpitz (Aug. 21, 1905), AAKS, 15:14765. Note how the army continued to want it, in Foreign Office memorandum (Oct. 14, 1905), AAKS, 16a:18557. There is no evidence the survey was ever carried out.

127. Mumm to Foreign Office (Oct. 17, 1905), AAKS, 16a:18341. Vagts, II, 1251, mentions the rumor of an aggressive German intent which led to the halting of these naval surveys.

128. Mumm to Bülow (Aug. 14, 1905), AAKS, 15:17094.

129. Mumm to Foreign Office (Sept. 4, 1905), AAKS, 16a:18844.

130. Telegram of von Semmern (Truppel's deputy) to Mumm (Aug. 21, 1905), quoted in Mumm to Foreign Office (Sept. 4, 1905), AAKS, 16a:18844.

131. *Ibid.*

132. Betz to Mumm (Mar. 24, 1906), DGSE, 5:1532/06.

133. Bülow to kaiser (Oct. 18, 1905), AAKS, 16a:18171.

134. Text in MacMurray, I, 118.

135. *WCSL*, 195:15 (Dec. 27, 1905).

136. See *ibid.* for the quotation; see also Tirpitz to Foreign Office (Jan. 25, 1906), AAKS, 16b:2055.

137. Von Semmern, quoted in Tirpitz to Foreign Office (Jan. 25, 1906), AAKS, 16b:2055.

138. Yang's memorials in *WCSL*, 195:13ff (Dec. 27, 1905) and 196:17bff (April 26, 1906).

139. *WCSL*, 196:18b (April 26, 1906).

140. Von Semmern, quoted in Tirpitz to Foreign Office (Jan. 25, 1906), AAKS, 16b:2055.

141. *WCSL*, 195:15b (Dec. 27, 1905).

142. Report on police (Mar. 24, 1906), enclosed in DGSE, 5:1532/06.

143. Semiannual report of governor (Feb. 11, 1904), MK, 5.7:84ff.

144. Naval Ministry to Senden-Bibran (Feb. 28, 1905), MK, 5.7:102ff; semiannual report of governor (July 31, 1906), MK, 5.7:131ff.

145. Mumm to Bülow (June 3, 1905), AAKS, 15:14104.

146. Mohr, p. 442; Wilson Leon Godshall, *Tsingtao under Three Flags* (Shanghai, 1929), p. 172.

147. Mumm to Bülow (Feb. 2, 1904), AADE, 12:3423.

148. See sections on "Communications" in *Denk.* from 1901 onwards.

149. *Denk.*, 1901, p. 2889.

150. Mumm to Bülow (Feb. 2, 1904), and its enclosures, AADE, 12:3423.

151. Hildebrandt to Goltz (Dec. 20, 1902), DGSE, 2:48/03; *NCH*, July 9, 1902, pp. 67–68.

152. Lieder to Cordes (Nov. 14, 1904), enclosed in DGSE, 4:5980/04.

153. Yuan Shih-k'ai to Wai-wu-pu (1903), in *Pei-yang kung-tu lei-tsuan*, comp. Kan Hou-tz'u (originally published 1907; reprinted Taipei, 1965), 13:2b–3. This continued also; see, for example, *ibid.*

154. *NCH*, Aug. 6, 1902, p. 268; *Denk.*, 1906, p. 29; *HFT*, vol. IV, pt. 3, doc. 1882 (May 17, 1904); *NCH*, April 15, 1904, p. 758. For more details on Chinese postal development see the second section of chap. vi.

155. Ohlmer's report is appended in full to dispatch of Chou Fu (June 1, 1903), *HFT*, vol. IV, pt. 3, doc. 1829.

156. *HFT*, vol. IV, pt. 3, doc. 1882 (May 17, 1904) and doc. 1908 (Sept. 16, 1904). The regulations are appended to doc. 1908, and the quotation is from the covering memorandum on the regulations.

157. Ohlmer's report appended to *HFT*, vol. IV, pt. 3, doc. 1829, speaks of

a set of regulations in eight articles covering the relationship between the post and railroads; however, Ohlmer implies that some railroads were not covered by these regulations and that others were evading them.

158. Lieder to Cordes (Nov. 14, 1904), enclosed in DGSE, 4:5980/04.

159. Goltz report (June 12, 1904), enclosed in AADE, 13:12667.

160. Von Semmern to Mumm (Mar. 25, 1905), DGSN, 1:1787/05.

161. Mumm to Bülow (Aug. 14, 1902), AAKS, 15:17084, enclosure 1.

162. Texts in MacMurray, I, 594–595.

163. *Denk.*, 1907, p. 40.

164. *HFT*, vol. IV, pt. 3, doc. 2098 (June 3, 1907); chronology is at the end of this *HFT* volume, p. 21 (1906, first month).

165. On some of these, in addition to *HFT*, vol. IV, pt. 3, doc. 2098 (June 3, 1907), see Chang Hsin-ch'eng, *Chung-kuo hsien-tai chiao-t'ung shih* (Shanghai, 1931), pp. 462–463.

166. Texts and accompanying documents are in *Ch'ing-mo tui-wai-chiao-she t'iao-yueh-chi*, comp. Wang I et al. (1914; reprinted Taipei, 1963), vol. II (Kuang-hsü period), pp. 932–937.

167. Report appended to *KWT*, II, doc. 592 (May 12, 1902).

168. Lange to Bülow (Sept. 21, 1902), AAKS, 10:17414; Chou Fu, *Complete Works, tsou-kao*, 2:28b (July 9, 1904); Shen Tsu-hsien and Wu K'ai-sheng, *Jung-an ti-tzu-chi*, 2:26.

169. Letter of Hildebrandt quoted in a decree of the Shantung Yang-wu-tsung-chü (August 1902), DGSE, 2:3329/02; Lange to Mumm (Sept. 5, 1902), DGSE, 2:3667/02.

170. Lange to Mumm (Sept. 5, 1902), DGSE, 2:3667/02.

171. Goltz to Bülow (Sept. 18, 1902), DGSE, 2:3667/02.

172. Newsclipping from China *Times* (June 27, 1902), enclosed in DGSE, 2:2242/02; annual report of SEG, 1902, enclosed in DGSE, 3:2902/03.

173. Decree of Shantung Yang-wu-tsung-chü (August 1902), DGSE 2:3329/02.

174. Lange to Bülow (Sept. 21, 1902), AAKS, 10:17414.

175. Lange to Mumm (Sept. 5, 1902), DGSE, 2:3667/02.

176. Goltz to Bülow (Sept. 18, 1902), DGSE, 2:3667/02; annual report of SEG, 1902, enclosed in DGSE, 3:2902/03. The shares were not carried on the Shanghai stock exchange after they were initially offered (see *NCH*).

177. Chou Fu to Chang Chih-tung and Sheng Hsuan-huai (Dec. 12, 1902), Chang Chih-tung, *Works*, 185:12b.

178. Lange to Bülow (Oct. 8, 1902), enclosed in DGSE, 2:4044/02.

179. Quotation is in letter to Chang (Dec. 12, 1902), Chang Chih-tung, *Works*, 185:12b; see also Lange to Bülow (Sept. 21, 1902), AAKS, 10:17414.

180. Truppel to Tirpitz on visit of Chou Fu (Jan. 4, 1903), enclosed in AAKS, 10:4679.

181. *Ibid.*; Lange to Bülow (Sept. 21, 1902), AAKS, 10:17414.

182. Chinese Legation to SEG (Dec. 29, 1902), enclosed in DGSE, 3:1139/03.

183. *Ibid.*

184. SEG to Chinese Legation (Jan. 23, 1903), enclosed in DGSE, 3:1139/03.

185. Chinese Legation to SEG (Dec. 29, 1902), enclosed in DGSE, 3:1139/03; *KWT*, II, doc. 602 (Jan. 20, 1903).

186. SEG to Chinese Legation (Jan. 23, 1903), enclosed in DGSE, 3:1139/03.

187. For the story given here see Mumm to Bülow (May 27, 1904), and its enclosures, AADE, 13:11992; SEG to Foreign Office (July 28, 1904), enclosed in DGSE, 3:2311/04; Betz to Mumm (Feb. 5, 1905), DGSE, 4:831/05; Hu T'ing-kan memorial (Mar. 17, 1905), *WCSL*, 212:7b (this memorial is out of order in *WCSL* and has the obviously erroneous date of KH 34, 2, 12; KH 31, 2, 12 reads perfectly); Yang Shih-hsiang memorial (April 27, 1905), *WCSL*, 188:26ff.

188. Betz to Mumm (March 27, 1905), enclosed in AADE, 14:9260. Yuan Shih-k'ai was also involved; see Yang Shih-hsiang memorial (May 16, 1907), *STTL*, p. 151.

189. See, for example, Mumm to Foreign Office (Aug. 30, 1905), and its enclosure, AAKS, 16a:18843.

190. Yang memorial (May 16, 1907), *STTL*, p. 151.

191. *Ibid.*

192. Text of agreements in MacMurray, II, 1904ff.

193. See third section of chap. vi for discussion of mining development.

194. *NCH*, Aug. 28, 1901, p. 410.

195. Hung Yung-chou petition (May 12, 1902), *HFT*, II, doc. 592, and its appended document 8 (Hung to provincial treasurer, sometime in 1901) are the sources of the basic story and the quotations.

196. SBG to Foreign Office (Aug. 30, 1902), enclosed in DGSB, 1:4236/02.

197. Sheng Hsuan-huai, *Collected Papers*, 58:25 (Oct. 16, 1902).

198. Lange to Goltz (Feb. 21, 1903), DGSB, 1:649/03; SBG to Mumm (Nov. 18, 1904), and its enclosures, DGSB, 1:5971/04.

199. Lange to Goltz (Feb. 21, 1903), DGSB, 1:649/03; Lange to Chou Fu (Feb. 22, 1903), enclosed in DGSB, 1:692/03.

200. Lange quoting SBG letter, in Lange to Goltz (Feb. 21, 1903), DGSB, 1:649/03.

201. Quotation is from Lange to Chou Fu (June 16, 1903), enclosed in DGSB, 1:4971/04.

202. Chou Fu to Lange (April 18, 1903), enclosed in DGSB, 1:5971/04.

203. *Ibid.*

204. SBG to Foreign Office (July 5, 1904), enclosed in DGSB, 1:4724/04.

205. See, for example, exchange of messages of June and July 1904, between SBG and Betz (Oct. 16, 1904), enclosed in DGSB, 1:5462/04.

206. Foreign Office to Mumm (Aug. 5, 1904), DGSB, 1:4724/04.

207. Mumm to Betz (Sept. 24, 1904), and its enclosure, DGSB, 1:4724/04.

208. SBG to Mumm (Nov. 18, 1904), DGSB, 1:5971/04.

209. *Ibid.*

210. Mumm to SBG (Dec. 13, 1904), DGSB, 1:5971/04.

211. Mumm's letter has been printed in *KWT*, II, doc. 614 (Dec. 16, 1904).

212. Mumm to Bülow (Dec. 17, 1904), DGSB, 1:5971/04.

213. *KWT*, II, doc. 616 (Dec. 23, 1904).

214. *KWT*, II, doc. 617 (Jan. 1, 1905).

215. *KWT*, II, doc. 618 (Jan. 8, 1905).

216. The provincial treasurer and the heads of the Bureaus of Foreign Affairs, Commerce, and Railways and Mines to Betz (January 1905), enclosed in DGSB, 2:628/05.

217. Quotation is from Betz to Mumm (Jan. 26, 1905), DGSB, 2:628/05.

218. For example, Mumm to Bülow (April 13, 1905), AAKS, 14:8774; Foreign Office memorandum (April 17, 1905), AAKS, 14:6549.

219. Ambassador in U.S. to Foreign Office (April 22, 1905), AAKS, 14:6825.

220. Foreign Office to Ambassador in U.S. (April 27, 1905), AAKS, 14:6825.

221. Note company's rationalizations in SBG to Mumm (Feb. 13, 1905), DGSB, 2:938/05, and the response, Mumm to SBG (March 11, 1905), DGSB, 2:938/05.

222. Goltz to Bülow (Aug. 16, 1906), AABK, 1:26227; SBG (Tsingtao) to SBG (Berlin) (May 10, 1906), enclosed in DGSB, 2:4113/04.

223. *Denk.*, 1906, p. 24.

224. See third section of next chapter.

225. Luxburg to Goltz (May 26, 1906), enclosed in AAKS, 17:13503.

226. SBG (Tsingtao) to SBG (Berlin) (April 27, 1906, and May 10, 1906), both enclosed in DGSB, 2:4113/06.

227. *Ibid.; KWT*, II, doc. 633 (May 21, 1906).

228. SBG (Tsingtao) to SBG (Berlin) (May 10, 1906), enclosed in DGSB, 2:4113/06; Consul Merklinghaus to Mumm (July 10, 1906), DGSB, 2:3239/06.

229. SBG (Tsingtao) to SBG (Berlin) (May 10, 1906), enclosed in DGSB, 2:4113/06.

230. *Ibid.; KWT*, II, doc. 633 (May 21, 1906).

231. SBG to Bülow (June 23, 1906), enclosed in DGSB, 2:4113/06.

232. SBG (Tsingtao) to Betz (July 12, 1906), enclosed in DGSB, 2:3238/06.

233. Quotation is from Goltz to Bülow (Aug. 20, 1906), DGSB, 2:3669/06; see also Mumm to Bülow (July 27, 1906), DGSB, 2:3239/06.

234. Merklinghaus to Mumm (July 10, 1906), enclosed in DGSB, 2:3239/06.

235. SBG to Bülow (Oct. 31, 1906), enclosed in DGSB, 2:888/07.

236. Merklinghaus to Goltz (Aug. 14, 1906), DGSB, 2:3669/06.

237. Merklinghaus to Mumm (July 10, 1906), DGSB, 2:3239/06.

238. Merklinghaus to Mumm (Oct. 29, 1906), DGSB, 2:4743/06.

239. On Chinese production and its economic effect on the success of the SBG, see third section of the next chapter.

240. Text in MacMurray, I, 261ff; see also Li En-han, p. 179.

241. Lenz letter, quoted in report of Yuan Shih-k'ai (June 16, 1901), *KWT*, II, doc. 526. The renewed German campaign for the five zones began in April; see Yuan report (April 11, 1901), *WCSL*, 146:6, and Wai-wu-pu report (April 22, 1901), *KWT*, II, doc. 522.

242. Yuan report (June 16, 1901), *KWT*, II, doc. 526.

243. Report of Acting Governor Hu T'ing-kan (Nov. 26, 1901), *KWT*, II. doc. 551. For a good example of the German approach see Goltz letter (Nov. 15, 1901), *KWT*, II, doc. 547.

244. *KWT*, II, doc. 567 (Jan. 19, 1902).

245. Yuan report (Nov. 12, 1901), *KWT*, II, doc. 545.

246. For example, many of the government records on mining had been burned during the rebellion and had to be reconstructed with the aid of provincial authorities.

247. Wai-wu-pu to Mumm (Jan. 21, 1902), *KWT*, II, doc. 573.

248. Report of Chang and summary of the regulations (Feb. 2, 1902), *KWT*, II, doc. 579.

249. *Ibid.*

250. Mumm to Wai-wu-pu (Feb. 13, 1902), *KWT*, II, doc. 580; Wai-wu-pu to Mumm (Feb. 17, 1902), *KWT*, II, doc. 583; Chang Jen-chün report (Mar. 1, 1902), *KWT*, doc. 586.

251. *KWT*, VIII, chronology at end of volume, pp. 11-12 (Jan. 10-Mar. 17, 1902), and the same period in Kuo T'ing-i, II, 1156-1160; for relation to German demands see also Wai-wu-pu to Mumm (Feb. 27, 1902), *KWT*, II, doc. 585.

252. Chang report (Mar. 1, 1902), *KWT*, II, doc. 586.

253. Richthofen to chancellor (Mar. 1, 1902), AAKS, 9:3448.

254. This and the paragraph on the 1902-1905 period are based on *KWT*, II, docs. 595-601, 605, 608-610, 612-613, 615, 619.

255. Company letter transmitted by German legation (Nov. 22, 1905), *KWT*, II, doc. 620.

256. *Ibid.*

257. Yang Shih-hsiang report (Mar. 5, 1906), *KWT*, II, doc. 624. The Germans were aware of this pressure: see *ibid.*

258. *KWT*, II, doc. 622 (Nov. 29, 1905).

259. *KWT*, II, doc. 624 (Mar. 5, 1906); see also Yang's memorial (Sept. 12, 1907), *STTL*, pp. 153ff.

260. Yang report (May 1, 1906), *KWT*, II, doc. 629.

261. Report of visit is in *KWT*, II, doc. 626 (Mar. 20, 1906).

262. Text of the agreement is appended to *KWT*, doc. 629 (May 1, 1906).

263. *KWT*, II, doc. 629 (May 1, 1906).

264. Shang-pu to Wai-wu-pu (May 9, 1906), *KWT*, II, doc. 631; Wai-wu-pu to Rex (Aug. 1, 1907), *KWT*, II, doc. 638.

265. Li En-han, p. 176.

266. See *ibid.*, pp. 176-179, for the information in this and the next text paragraph.

267. Sun E-tu (Zen), pp. 129ff, gives the history of the negotiations.

268. For a typical German presentation of the problems which faced Germany in confirming the concessions, see Tirpitz to Foreign Office (May 19, 1906), AADE, 15:9219.

269. Text in MacMurray, I, 684ff.

270. Great Britain, Foreign Office, "Confidential Print," *China, Annual Report,* 1907, F.O. 405/178, p. 23.

271. Quoted in Sun E-tu (Zen), p. 135.

272. Meribeth Cameron, *The Reform Movement in China, 1898-1912* (originally published 1931; reprinted New York, 1963), p. 187.

273. Yuan Shih-k'ai, *Selected Memorials,* 10:8 (Nov. 4, 1901).

274. Goltz to Bülow (Mar. 3, 1903), AAKS, 10:5184.

275. *Ibid.*

276. For example, see Lange to Bülow (July 22, 1903), AAKS, 11:13908; Goltz report on trip (June 12, 1904), enclosed in AADE, 13:12667.

277. Goltz to Bülow (Mar. 3, 1903), AAKS, 10:5184; Mumm to Foreign Office (June 27, 1903), AAKS, 11:12583.

278. Mumm to Foreign Office (June 27, 1903), AAKS, 11:12583.

279. Mumm to Bülow (Nov. 25, 1903), AAKS, 11:18865.

280. Seckendorff to Truppel (Aug. 22, 1904), enclosed in AAKS, 13:19731.

281. Truppel to Seckendorff (Sept. 7, 1904), enclosed in AAKS, 13:19731.

282. Betz to Bülow (May 26, 1906), AAKS, 16b:11873.

283. *NCH*, April 27, 1906, p. 180.

284. Shen Tsu-hsien and Wu K'ai-sheng, *Jung-an ti-tzu-chi*, 2:26, says Yuan bought the equipment for the mint in Tsinan from Japan. There is no evidence of his ever "buying German."

285. For evidence see *NCH*, Aug. 7, 1903, p. 284; Mumm to Bülow (Nov. 25, 1903), AAKS, 11:18865; Goltz report on trip (June 12, 1904), enclosed in AADE, 13:12267.

286. For evidence see Betz to Mumm (Aug. 5, 1905), enclosed in AAKS, 16a:18087; Goltz to Bülow (Aug. 29, 1906), AAKS, 17:17185.

287. For an example see Truppel to Tirpitz (Dec. 30, 1902) and its enclosures, all enclosed in AAKS, 10:3222.

288. Hart report (April 27, 1905), *WCSL*, 188:13bff; S. Wright, p. 705.

289. *AKV*, p. 206. *AKV* provided much of the material used in writing this section; however, Schrameier very much de-emphasizes the disinclination of the navy to establish a new tariff system.

290. *AKV*, p. 217.

291. Exchange quoted in S. Wright, p. 727.

292. *Ibid.*, pp. 700–701, 760–761.

293. *AKV*, p. 199.

294. *AKV*, p. 203.

295. Quoted at length in *AKV*, pp. 206–209.

296. *AKV*, pp. 213ff.

297. Schrameier implies that the navy was amenable to a change by 1900 (*AKV*, p. 203); however, this does not fit the other evidence. See the next text paragraphs, and also Truppel to Tirpitz (Jan. 4, 1903), enclosed in AAKS, 10:4679; *NCH*, July 16, 1902, p. 122, and Nov. 3, 1905, p. 252.

298. *AKV*, p. 217.

299. Quoted in *AKV*, pp. 211ff.

300. Transcript of discussion between Chou Fu and Truppel (April 28–29, 1904), enclosed in AAKS, 12:11296.

301. Text in MacMurray, I, 191; negotiations described in *AKV*, p. 199, and *Denk.*, 1904, p. 19.

302. *AKV*, p. 244.

303. Mumm to Bülow (Aug. 14, 1905), AAKS, 15:17084, enclosure 1.

304. *AKV*, pp. 218–220.

305. Text in MacMurray, I, 192ff; discussion in *AKV*, pp. 232ff.

306. *AKV*, p. 239; text in MacMurray, I, pp. 199–200.

307. *WCSL*, 188:16bff (April 27, 1905).

308. IMC, *Returns*, 1906, p. 76.

309. Wai-wu-pu report and enclosures (Sept. 29, 1907), *WCSL*, 205:15bff.

310. IMC, *Decennial*, 1902–1911, p. 237.

311. *AKV*, p. 243.

VI. The Germans and Development in Shantung

1. Mohr, pp. 442–445.
2. For this and other 1913 figures see Tahara, pp. 133ff.
3. *Denk.*, 1907, p. 45, and 1908, pp. 36–37.
4. The debate on the court is one of the most common topics covered in AAKS from late 1901 to 1907. For some typical documents laying out the positions of the two sides see: *Denk.*, 1901, p. 2891; Knappe to Foreign Office (Nov. 18, 1901), AAKS, 8:16303; Richthofen to Bülow (Aug. 6, 1902), AAKS, 10:10284.
5. *Denk.*, 1902, p. 21; see also sections on "Administration" in later *Denk.*
6. For example, Schrameier, *Kiautschou, Entwicklung und Bedeutung*, p. 62.
7. *AKV*, p. 110; *Denk.*, 1901, p. 2885.
8. For material on land purchases given here see the sections on "Land" in the successive *Denk.* after 1900, as well as *AKV*, section on "Landpolitik," pt. III. For figures given see, in particular, *Denk.*, 1901 and 1906; *AKV*, pp. 61–62; Mohr, pp. 452–453.
9. See sections on "Forestry" in successive *Denk.*
10. *NCH*, Feb. 23, 1906, p. 43.
11. William Blane, "Tsingtau," *Transactions of the Japan Society, London*, 13:10 (1915).
12. *AKV*, p. 152.
13. The information on the land tax in the rural zone comes, except as otherwise noted, from *Denk.*, 1904, pp. 6ff, and *AKV*, pp. 90–102.
14. For text of two sets of regulations involved, see Mohr, pp. 242–243, 282–283.
15. On Hart's plan see S. Wright, p. 794, in addition to *Denk.*, 1904, and *AKV*.
16. Except as otherwise noted, the information on health comes from the sections on "Health" in the successive *Denk.* The figure on rates given here is from the semiannual report of the governor (Aug. 3, 1902), MK, 5.7:54ff.
17. Semiannual report of the governor (Aug. 12, 1907), MK, 5.7:155ff.
18. On urban development see sections on "Land" in the successive *Denk.*, as well as Weicker, pp. 48ff, and *AKV*, pp. 27ff.
19. IMC, *Returns*, 1906, p. 79.
20. Tahara, p. 511.
21. Jefferson Jones, *The Fall of Tsingtau* (Boston and New York, 1915), pp. 162–163.
22. Mohr, p. 452.
23. Townsend, p. 240.
24. Mohr, p. 452.
25. Tahara, p. 203.
26. *AKV*, p. 152.
27. Tahara, p. 203.
28. *Stenographische Berichte über die Verhandlungen des Reichstages*, 202:4382ff (Feb. 27, 1905).
29. *Ibid.*, pp. 4834–4835 (speech of Gröber).
30. Information on Dernburg comes from Rubinstein, "Bernhard Dernburg."
31. *Stenographische Berichte*, 231:4174ff (Mar. 21, 1908).

32. The material on the port facilities is drawn from the sections on "Building Activities" in the successive *Denk.*, as well as IMC, *Returns*, 1907, pp. 123–124, and IMC, *Decennial*, 1902–1911, pp. 245–246.

33. *Denk.*, 1906, p. 10.

34. Blane, "Tsingtau," pp. 10 ("Prussian aggression") and 6 (harbor). For another typically glowing account of the harbor facilities and other related developments at Tsingtao see Great Britain, Foreign Office, "Confidential Print," *Further Correspondence respecting the Affairs of China*, July–September 1905, F.O. 405/156, doc. 103, p. 105; see also Tahara, pp. 321ff.

35. On roads see the sections on "Building Activities" in the successive *Denk.*; Great Britain, Foreign Office, "Confidential Print," *Further Correspondence respecting the Affairs of China*, July–September 1905, F.O. 405/156, doc. 103, p. 105; IMC, *Decennial*, 1902–1911, p. 259.

36. For information and statistics on the mail and telegraph in the leasehold, see sections on "Communications" in the successive *Denk.*

37. For the material on the railroad, in addition to the specific citations see sections on "Communications" in the successive *Denk.*, and Tahara, pt. V, chap. 1.

38. For example, *NCH*, Jan. 8, 1902, p. 21.

39. Weicker, p. 158.

40. For a convenient chart of stations and their distances along the route, see Tahara, pp. 437ff.

41. For confirmation of this, see, for example, Luxburg to Goltz (May 26, 1906), enclosed in AAKS, 17:13503.

42. Weicker, p. 159.

43. Mohr, p. 454.

44. *NCH*, Sept. 22, 1905, p. 660.

45. *NCH*, Nov. 13, 1901, p. 920.

46. The figures are collected most conveniently in Tahara, pp. 453–454. Other sources, such as Mohr or the *Denk.*, give slightly different figures because they use slightly different time periods.

47. Mohr, p. 455.

48. Figures for 1905 are in *Denk.*, 1906, p. 7; later ones in IMC, *Decennial*, 1902–1911, p. 253.

49. This has been calculated by using figures provided in Mohr, p. 456, and Tahara, pp. 453–454, which give the necessary information for a rough approximation, i.e., the yearly gross income and costs of the company, as well as its extraordinary expenditures.

50. Hou Chi-ming, pp. 112ff.

51. In addition to the materials on the railroad being used throughout, on the development of these roads see also *NCH*, April 16, 1903, p. 729, and Aug. 14, 1903, p. 346; Lange to Bülow (July 22, 1903), AAKS, 11:13908; Hildebrandt to Goltz (May 26, 1906), DGSE, 5:2558/06.

52. *NCH*, Oct. 8, 1902, p. 744.

53. The material on the Chinese postal developments comes from IMC, *Decennial*, 1892–1901, pp. 120–121, and 1902–1911, pp. 245–247.

54. The high estimation of the Germans for the Chinese post at this time can be seen, for example, in *Denk.*, 1906, p. 29.

55. On the canal see *NCH,* June 19, 1901, p. 1174, and Dec. 16, 1904, p. 1345; Great Britain, "Confidential Print," *Further Correspondence respecting the Affairs of China,* July–September 1905, F.O. 405/156, doc. 103, p. 100; Great Britain, Foreign Office, "Blue Book," China No. 1, 1907, p. 12, in *House of Commons Sessional Papers,* 1907, vol. XCIX.

56. On the wharf see *Denk.,* 1907, p. 18; IMC, *Returns,* 1905, 1907, and 1909 (introductory survey in Kiaochow section); Tahara, pp. 329–330; Weicker, p. 63.

57. IMC, *Returns,* 1905, p. 80.

58. The story of the navy's efforts to make the shipyard private and the quotations come from the report of Friedrich Krupp (Sept. 20, 1907), MK, 5. 7:149ff, and Krupp von Bohlen und Habach to kaiser (Sept. 23, 1907), MK, 5. 7:147–148.

59. On the electric works see *Denk.,* 1901, p. 2888, and 1904, pp. 12–13.

60. Except as otherwise noted, the information on mining comes from the section on "Industry," subsections on mining, in the successive *Denk.;* Tahara, pp. 376–386; IMC, *Decennial,* 1902–1911, pp. 249–250.

61. IMC, *Returns,* 1912, p. 231.

62. *Denk.,* 1905, p. 16.

63. IMC, *Returns,* 1906, p. 79.

64. *NCH,* Oct. 26, 1906, p. 232.

65. Betz to Bülow (Oct. 19, 1905), DGSB, 2:5942/05.

66. *Ibid.*

67. IMC, *Returns,* 1908, p. 133.

68. A convenient chart of coal production figures is to be found in Tahara, pp. 380–381.

69. The figures on distribution in 1911 come from IMC, *Returns,* 1911, p. 223; similar figures with somewhat different categories and time periods in Tahara, p. 382, yield the same conclusions.

70. The material on DCSIG comes from the sections on "Industry" in the successive *Denk.* from 1902 onwards; Tahara, pp. 367–368; IMC, *Returns,* 1905, p. 81; Weicker, pp. 139ff.

71. IMC, *Returns,* 1905, p. 81.

72. Except as otherwise noted, the material on these smaller industries comes from the sections on "Industry" in the successive *Denk.;* Tahara, pp. 364–368; IMC, *Decennial,* 1902–1911, pp. 249–252.

73. *NCH,* Feb. 8, 1907, p. 290.

74. *NCH,* Mar. 2, 1906, p. 496, mentions 7% dividend for the first year. In 1913 it was 8%, according to Tahara.

75. IMC, *Decennial,* 1902–1911, p. 249.

76. On the I-hsien mines see Li En-han, pp. 122, 285–286, 294; IMC, *Decennial,* 1902–1911, p. 250.

77. *NCH,* Dec. 30, 1904, p. 1464.

78. IMC, *Decennial,* 1892–1901, pp. 94–96; on the growth of production see next section.

79. IMC, *Decennial,* 1902–1911, p. 250. The general lack of financial success of the German enterprises in Shantung lends some support to the suggestion made by Frank King that China's overall difficulties with economic development were not primarily the result of ideological, administrative, or sociological

factors peculiar to China, but rather of more conventional economic problems associated with beginning modern enterprises in any underdeveloped country; see Frank King, *Money and Monetary Policy in China, 1845–1895* (Cambridge, Mass., 1965), pp. 231ff.

King suggests that this position would be supported by evidence that foreign businesses in China, despite their presumably modern management, independence, and sources of capital, had as little success as Chinese firms. This seems to have been the case with the German companies. The main causes of their failures were such common problems as finding markets able to afford the products of modern industry, recruiting a modern labor force, and competing with efficient traditional enterprises which were better fitted to local conditions. Such problems must have also affected Chinese companies and so played a significant role in their own lack of success.

80. IMC, *Decennial*, 1902–1911, p. 251.

81. IMC, *Returns*, 1907, p. 4.

82. *Ibid.*, p. 127.

83. The rise in value of imports at Tsingtao up to 1907 was paralleled by a similar decline in value at Chefoo; see successive IMC *Returns*. The impact on Chefoo's imports was also remarked upon by observers; see, for example, Great Britain, "Confidential Print," *Further Correspondence respecting the Affairs of China*, July–September 1905, F.O. 405/156, doc. 103, pp. 98–99, 105.

84. All the figures on the value of goods imported and exported come from Mohr, pp. 461ff. IMC, *Returns*, 1907, has the items by weight.

85. IMC, *Decennial*, 1892–1901, p. 96.

86. *Ibid.*, pp. 94–95.

87. These figures are based on Ohlmer's estimates of 1905, in Ohlmer to Bülow (May 3, 1905), AAKS, 14:8302. There is no indication that the situation had changed by 1907; see, for example, *Denk.*, 1906, p. 7.

88. IMC, *Returns*, 1907, pp. 7–8, gives totals of direct trade with each country. The German percentage of imports is about 3.8%. Most German goods were shipped direct by 1907, but to compensate for the indirect imports I have estimated the total percentage at a little over 4%.

89. IMC, *Returns*, 1910, p. 198.

90. *Denk.*, 1906, p. 13.

91. *Stenographische Berichte*, 231:4175 (Mar. 21, 1908).

92. IMC, *Decennial*, 1902–1911, p. 238.

93. IMC, *Returns*, pp. 36–37.

94. IMC, *Returns*, 1913, pp. 420–421, has these figures. The statements on Chefoo are again based on the figures for that port in the successive *Returns*.

95. This figure is an estimate based on the following figures available in IMC, *Returns*: Total German direct imports to Tsingtao were 2,887,000 tls. Gross foreign imports were 26,467,353 tls. Of the German total, 732,000 tls. were railroad materials. The German percentage of commercial goods was, thus, about 8%. The figures for direct trade can be used because almost all German imports to Kiaochow were direct by 1913 (Mohr, pp. 468–469, shows that in 1910 this was almost the case; by 1913 the percentage of direct goods had certainly risen rather than dropped).

96. The figure—something over 5%—is arrived at in the same way as the

figure for 1907 (n. 88), using 1913 data available in IMC, *Returns*, pp. 44–49, and making less compensation for indirect imports. The rough similarity between this figure and that for imports into Tsingtao would, in the historical context, tend to confirm both, for they are based on different statistics.

97. Except as otherwise noted, the information on the development of commercial, shipping, and financial institutions and on the junk traffic may be found in the sections on "Commerce" in the successive *Denk.*

98. Schrameier, *Kiautschou, Entwicklung und Bedeutung*, p. 51.

99. IMC, *Decennial*, 1902–1911, p. 238.

100. *Denk.*, 1901, p. 2884.

101. *Denk.*, 1907, p. 26.

102. *Ibid.*, p. 12.

103. Great Britain, "Confidential Print," *Further Correspondence respecting the Affairs of China*, July–September 1905, F.O. 405/156, doc. 103, p. 105.

104. Kobe consul to Foreign Office (June 5, 1903), AAKS, 10:10965.

105. *Ibid.*

106. Mumm to Bülow (Nov. 11, 1903), AAKS, 11:18037. Truppel denied encouraging the Japanese, though he does appear to have done so.

107. Foreign Office to Tirpitz (Mar. 16, 1904), AAKS, 12:18037.

108. IMC, *Returns*, 1907, p. 125.

109. *Ibid.*, p. 19.

110. IMC, *Returns*, 1908, p. 129, and 1909, p. 133.

111. IMC, *Decennial*, 1902–1911, p. 238.

112. *Ibid.*, p. 242.

113. IMC, *Returns*, 1913, p. 417.

114. See junk figures in successive IMC, *Returns*, statistical sections of Kiaochow reports.

115. IMC, *Returns*, 1907, p. 121.

116. IMC, *Returns*, 1908, p. 130; IMC, *Decennial*, 1902–1911, p. 245.

117. IMC, *Returns*, 1905, p. 80.

118. See inland steam figures in successive IMC, *Returns*, statistical sections of Kiaochow reports.

119. S. Wright, pp. 760–761.

120. Tahara, p. 335.

121. Great Britain, "Confidential Print," *Further Correspondence respecting the Affairs of China*, July–September 1905, F.O. 405/156, doc. 61, p. 48.

122. Tahara, p. 335; IMC, *Decennial*, 1902–1911, p. 244; IMC, *Returns*, 1913, p. 404; Schrameier, *Kiautschou, Entwicklung und Bedeutung*, p. 56.

123. For these changes elsewhere see King, chap. 4.

124. IMC, *Decennial*, 1892–1901, pp. 98–99.

125. My material on the development of currency at Kiaochow comes from *Denk.*, 1906, pp. 15–16, and 1907, pp. 29–31.

126. IMC, *Decennial*, 1902–1911, p. 244. See *ibid.* for a good summary of the monetary history of Kiaochow.

127. For an excellent description of this process see Hildebrandt to Goltz (May 26, 1906), DGSE, 5:2558/06.

128. See, for example, Great Britain, "Confidential Print," *Further Corres-*

pondence respecting the Affairs of China, July–September 1905, F.O. 405/156, doc. 103, p. 99; IMC, *Decennial, 1902–1911,* p. 248.

129. *Denk.,* 1907, pp. 37–38; IMC, *Returns,* 1904, p. 134; "Confidential Print," F.O. 405/156, doc. 103, p. 98.

130. For a detailed description of this activity see later successive *Denk.,* sections on "Forestry, Agriculture, and Animal Husbandry." The success of such efforts was frequently mentioned by others, as, for example, in the IMC, *Returns.*

131. William Skinner, "Marketing and Social Structure in Rural China," pt. II, *The Journal of Asian Studies,* 24.2: 217–219 (February 1965).

132. IMC, *Returns,* 1911, p. 242.

133. *Ibid.,* p. 253.

134. The material in this section, except as otherwise noted, comes from the sections on "Education" in the successive *Denk.*

135. Weicker, p. 123.

136. *Denk.,* 1901, p. 24.

137. Schrameier, *Kiautschou, Entwicklung und Bedeutung,* p. 56.

138. IMC, *Decennial, 1902–1911,* pp. 254–256.

139. On the curriculum of this and other schools, in addition to *Denk.* see Mohr, pp. 446ff.

140. Mohr, p. 449.

141. Quotation is from Schrameier, *Kiautschou, Entwicklung und Bedeutung,* p. 49.

142. *Denk.,* 1907, p. 16.

143. Schrameier, *Kiautschou, Entwicklung und Bedeutung,* p. 56.

144. This information is in a remarkable survey of traditional education which forms App. 1 to *Denk.,* 1906.

145. On the formation of this university and its relation to the railway, see Charles Corbett, *Shantung Christian University (Cheeloo)* (New York, 1955), pp. 60ff; John Heeren, *On the Shantung Front* (New York, 1940), pp. 137–138.

146. Heeren, pp. 107–108.

147. Couling, p. 20.

148. *Ibid.,* pp. 20–21.

149. IMC, *Decennial, 1902–1911,* p. 254.

150. The fall of Kiaochow is described in many works. My account is drawn from Russell H. Fifield, *Woodrow Wilson and the Far East* (originally published 1952; reprinted, Hamden, Conn., 1965), chap. 1; Schrameier, *Kiautschou, Entwicklung und Bedeutung,* pp. 92–96; Westel W. Willoughby, *Foreign Rights and Interests in China* (originally published 1927; reprinted Taipei, 1966), I, chap. 9; and from Jones, *The Fall of Tsingtau.*

151. Quoted in Schrameier, *Kiautschou, Entwicklung und Bedeutung,* p. 93.

152. Jones, p. 92.

153. On this point see Willoughby, I, chap. 9, and Fifield, chap. 1. Hsieh K'ai-hsün, *Chiao-chou-wan,* and T'an T'ien-k'ai, *Shan-tung wen-t'i,* not only provide information which reveals Japan's increased power but also indicate it by the comparatively hostile tone with which they describe the Japanese presence in the province.

VII. Conclusions

1. The terms for "sovereignty" included in the statistics are *chu-ch'üan* and *tzu-chu-chih-ch'üan;* the count is a complete one and not selective. The *WCSL* edition used is the Taipei reprint, and the statistics presented use "page" to refer to the Western-style pages of this edition. The word *kuo-ch'üan* was also counted; it was, however, used very rarely in all periods, though with a frequency which results in a curve having the same shape as that for the total of the other two terms.

2. Most importantly, Mary C. Wright, *China in Revolution: The First Phase, 1900–1913* (New Haven, 1968); see especially the introduction. This excellent book, which appeared as my study was being completed, is the most important work, to date, to show the more positive and hence revisionist approach to the late Ch'ing, the perspective this study shares. Another recent work which shows Ch'ing success in the important field of recovery of mining rights is Li En-han. An early work that now looks remarkably astute is Cameron.

3. Great Britain, Foreign Office, "Confidential Print," *Far Eastern Department,* 1908, "Kiaochau," F.O. 405/187, p. 2.

4. This facet of nationalism is clearly seen in a man like Yen Fu, as portrayed by Schwartz.

5. This theme is evident, for example, in M. Wright.

6. The issues surrounding this question are summarized in Hou Chi-ming's introduction, and in Jack M. Potter, *Capitalism and the Chinese Peasant* (Berkeley, 1968), chap. 8.

7. Potter is another case study which brings forth evidence to support Hou Chi-ming on both these points.

8. IMC, *Returns,* 1931, I, 78.

Bibliography of Materials Cited

This work has not exhausted the materials available for the study of the German sphere of influence, nor has it examined the topic from every possible angle. The most significant sources for further study are the archives of the Reichsmarineamt dealing with Kiaochow and its administration, which are located in the Militaerarchiv of the Bundesarchiv in Koblenz. The archives of various missionary groups, both German and foreign, might also be of interest. There are no significant Chinese materials that are available which have not been examined for this study; however, the Tsungli Yamen archives deposited at the Academia Sinica, Taipei, do contain a small file on Kiaochow which I did not see until the manuscript was at the press. Almost all the documents come from late 1897 and early 1898 and deal with the diplomatic interplay between Germany and China over the cession of Chiao-chou Bay; they add virtually nothing to what can be learned from other sources. Through the use of the additional foreign archives mentioned above, the German administration of Kiaochow could be examined in greater detail, and more could be learned about the internal history of the leasehold. Another interesting project would be to discover more about the relationship between the Germans and the Chinese "man in the street," both in the leasehold and in the interior.

AABK. *See* German Archives deposited in the Deutsches Zentralarchiv.

AADE. *See* German Archives filmed by Florida State University.

AAKS. *See* German Archives filmed by Florida State University.

AKV. *See* Schrameier, Wilhelm, *Aus Kiautschous Verwaltung*.

Armstrong, Alexander. *Shantung*. Shanghai, 1891.

Bee, Benjamin Ming-chu. "The Leasing of Kiaochow, A Study in Diplomacy and Imperialism," unpub. diss. Harvard University, 1935.

Behme, Friedrich, and M. Krieger. *Guide to Tsingtau and its Surroundings*. 2d ed. Wolfenbüttel: H. Wessel, 1905.

Blane, William. "Tsingtau," *Transactions of the Japan Society, London*, 13:2–17 (1915).

The Boxer Rising. Originally published Shanghai: *The Shanghai Mercury*, 1901; reprinted New York, 1967.

Brunnert, H. S., and V. V. Hagelstrom. *Present Day Political Organization of China*, trans. A. Beltchenko and E. Moran. Originally published 1912; reprinted Taipei, n.d.

Cameron, Meribeth. *The Reform Movement in China, 1898–1912*. Originally published Stanford: Stanford University Press, 1931; reprinted New York: Octagon Books, 1963.

Chang Chih-tung 張之洞. *Chang-wen-hsiang-kung ch'üan-chi* 張文襄公全集 (The complete works of Chang Chih-tung). 228 chüan. 1937 ed.; reprinted Taipei, 1963.

Chang Hao. "The Anti-Foreign Role of Wo-jen, 1804–1871," *Papers on China*, 14:1–29 (1960). Harvard University, East Asian Research Center.

Chang Hsin-ch'eng 張心澂. *Chung-kuo hsien-tai chiao-t'ung shih* 中國現代交通史 (History of communications in contemporary China). Shanghai, 1931.

Ch'en, Jerome. *Yuan Shih-k'ai, 1859–1916*. London: Allen & Unwin, 1961.

China, Imperial Maritime Customs. *Decennial Reports on Trade, Navigation, Industries....* 1892–1901, 1902–1911.

——— *Returns of Trade and Trade Reports*. Annual vols.

Ch'ing-mo tui-wai-chiao-she t'iao-yueh-chi 清末對外交涉條約輯 (Collected treaties of the late Ch'ing), comp. Wang I 汪毅 et al. Originally published 1914; reprinted Taipei, 1963.

Chou Fu 周馥. *Chou-ch'üeh-shen-kung ch'üan-chi* 周愨慎公全集 (The complete works of Chou Fu). Originally published 1922; reprinted Taipei, 1966.

Cohen, Paul A. "Wang T'ao and Incipient Chinese Nationalism," *The Journal of Asian Studies*, 26.4:559–574 (August 1967).

Corbett, Charles. *Shantung Christian University (Cheeloo)*. New York: United Board for Christian Colleges in China, 1955.

Couling, Samuel. *The Encyclopaedia Sinica*. Originally published 1917; reprinted Taipei, 1964.

Deimling, "Die Kolonie Kiautschou," *Abteilung Berlin-Charlottenburg der Deutschen Kolonial-Gesellschaft Verhandlungen, 1900/01*, vol. II.

Denk. See Germany, Reichsmarineamt, *Denkschrift betreffend die Entwicklung des Kiautschou-Gebiets*.

DGSB. *See* German Archives deposited in the Deutsches Zentralarchiv.

DGSE. *See* German Archives deposited in the Deutsches Zentralarchiv.

DGSN. *See* German Archives deposited in the Deutsches Zentralarchiv.

Djang Feng-djen (Chang Feng-chen). *The Diplomatic Relations between China and Germany since 1898*. Shanghai, 1936.

Eastman, Lloyd. "Ch'ing-i and Chinese Policy Formation during the Nineteenth Century," *The Journal of Asian Studies*, 24.4:595–611 (August 1965).

Fairbank, John K. *Trade and Diplomacy on the China Coast: The Opening of the Treaty Ports, 1842–1854*. 2 vols. Cambridge, Mass.: Harvard University Press, 1953.

Fang Chaoying. Review of *Wu-hsü pien-fa*, in *The Journal of Asian Studies*, 17.1:99–105 (November 1957).

Fifield, Russell H. *Woodrow Wilson and the Far East*. Originally published New York: Crowell, 1952; reprinted Hamden, Conn.: Archon Books, 1965.

Franzius, Georg. *Kiautschou: Deutschlands Erwerbung in Ostasien*. Berlin, 1898.

German Archives
    Deposited in the Deutsches Zentralarchiv (Potsdam)
        AABK—Archives of the German Foreign Office, Dep. II, Archival file 09.01, no. 5025, "Bergwerkskonzessionen in China." 1 vol.
        DGSB—Archives of the German Legation in China, Archival file 09.02, nos.

1294–1297, "Schantung-Bergbau-Gesellschaft." 4 vols.

DGSE—Archives of the German Legation in China, Archival file 09.02, nos. 1308–1316, "Schantung-Eisenbahn." 8 vols.

DGSN—Archives of the German Legation in China, Archival file 09.02, no. 1062, "Handelsniederlassungen in Schantung." 1 vol.

Filmed by Cambridge University and the University of Michigan

MK—Archives of the German Imperial Naval Cabinet, Admiralty Reference XXII.c, "Kiautschou." 7 vols. Cambridge-Michigan reels 5–7.

Filmed by Florida State University

AADE—Archives of the German Foreign Office, Dept. I, China 4, no. 1 *secr.*, "Deutsche Eisenbahn-Unternehmungen in China." 29 vols. FSU reels 66–71.

AAKS—Archives of the German Foreign Office, Dept. I, China 22, "Kiautschou und die deutschen Interessen in Schantung." 32 vols. FSU reels 84–88.

Germany, Reichsmarineamt. *Denkschrift betreffend die Entwicklung des Kiautschou-Gebiets* (*Denk.*). Berlin, 1899–1910.

Citations here refer to the appendix volumes which form part of *Stenographische Berichte über die Verhandlungen des Reichstages*:

Denk., 1898 (to Oct., 1898), vol. 172, doc. 79, pp. 560–576.

Denk., 1899 (Oct. 1898-Oct. 1899), vol. 175, doc. 516, pp. 2830–2852.

Denk., 1900 (Oct. 1899-Oct. 1900), vol. 189, doc. 115, pp. 716–742.

Denk., 1901 (Oct. 1900-Oct. 1901), vol. 193, doc. 436, pp. 2883–2906.

Denk., 1902 (Oct. 1901-Oct. 1902), vol. 196, doc. 832, bound following p. 5592.

Denk., 1903 (Oct. 1902-Oct. 1903), vol. 206, doc. 187, bound following p. 850.

Denk., 1904 (Oct. 1903-Oct. 1904), vol. 212, doc. 561, bound following p. 3562.

Denk., 1905 (Oct. 1904-Oct. 1905), vol. 222, doc. 174, bound following p. 2704.

Denk., 1906 (Oct. 1905-Oct. 1906), vol. 241, doc. 268, bound following p. 1768.

Denk., 1907 (Oct. 1906-Oct. 1907), vol. 245, doc. 585, bound following p. 3604.

Denk., 1908 (Oct. 1907-Oct. 1908), vol. 253, doc. 1131, bound following p. 7256.

Denk., 1909 (Oct. 1908-Oct. 1909), vol. 272, doc. 195, bound following p. 1352.

Germany, Reichsmarineamt. *Das deutsche Kiautschou-Gebiet und seine Bevölkerung, Kartenkrokis und statistische Tabellen.* Berlin, 1899.

Germany, Reichsmarineamt. *Marineverordnungsblatt.*

Germany, *Stenographische Berichte über die Verhandlungen des Reichstages.*

Godshall, Wilson Leon. *Tsingtao under Three Flags.* Shanghai, 1929.

GP: Die grosse Politik der europäischen Kabinette, 1871–1914, ed. Johannes Lepsius et al. 40 vols. Berlin: Deutsche Verlagsgesellschaft für Politik und Geschichte, 1922–1927.

Great Britain, Foreign Office. "Blue Books," in *House of Commons Sessional Papers.*

Great Britain, Foreign Office. "Confidential Prints," filmed by the Public Record Office.

Heeren, John. *On the Shantung Front.* New York: Board of Foreign Missions of the Presbyterian Church in the United States of America, 1940.

HFT: Hai-fang-tang 海防檔 (Archives on naval defense), ed. Wang Yü-chün 王聿均 et al. Academia Sinica, Institute of Modern History, Compilations of Source Materials on Modern Chinese History, no. 1. 5 vols. Taipei, 1957.

The Holstein Papers, ed. Norman Rich and M. H. Fisher. 4 vols. Cambridge, Eng.: University Press, 1955–1963.

Hou Chi-ming. *Foreign Investment and Economic Development in China, 1840–1937.* Cambridge, Mass.: Harvard University Press, 1965.

Hsieh K'ai-hsün 謝開勳. *Erh-shih-erh nien lai chih Chiao-chou-wan* 二十二年來之膠州灣 (Chiao-chou Bay during the last twenty-two years). Shanghai, 1920.

Hsü, Immanuel C. Y. *China's Entrance into the Family of Nations.* Cambridge, Mass.: Harvard University Press, 1960.

Hubatsch, Walther. *Die Ära Tirpitz.* Göttingen: Musterschmidt Verlag, 1955.

Hummel, Arthur W., ed. *Eminent Chinese of the Ch'ing Period, 1644–1912.* 2 vols. Washington, D.C.: U.S. Government Printing Office, 1943–1944.

I-ho-t'uan tang-an shih-liao 義和團檔案史料 (Archival materials on the Boxer Rebellion), comp. National Bureau of Archives, Office of Ming and Ch'ing Archives. 2 vols. Peking, 1959.

IMC, *Decennial. See* China, Imperial Maritime Customs, *Decennial Reports on Trade, Navigation, Industries.*

IMC, *Returns. See* China, Imperial Maritime Customs, *Returns of Trade and Trade Reports.*

Irmer, Julius. *Die Erwerbung von Kiautschou, 1894–1898.* Cologne, 1930.

Jerussalimski, A. S. "Das Eindringen der deutschen Monopole in China an der Wende vom 19. zum 20. Jahrhundert," *Zeitschrift für Geschichtswissenschaft*, 8.8: 1832–1861 (1960).

Jones, Jefferson. *The Fall of Tsingtau.* Boston and New York: Houghton Mifflin, 1915.

Kehr, Eckart. *Schlachtflottenbau und Parteipolitik, 1894–1901.* Berlin: E. Ebering, 1930.

Kent, Percy. *Railway Enterprise in China.* London: E. Arnold, 1907.

Kiaochow and Weihaiwei. Handbook prepared under the direction of the Historical Section of the Foreign Office, no. 71. London, 1920.

King, Frank. *Money and Monetary Policy in China, 1845–1895.* Cambridge, Mass.: Harvard University Press, 1965.

Kuang-hsü-ch'ao tung-hua-lu 光緒朝東華録 (Records of the Kuang-hsü reign). 5 vols. Peking, 1958; 1st ed., in different format, 1909.

Kuo T'ing-i 郭廷以. *Chin-tai Chung-kuo shih-shih jih-chih* 近代中國史事日誌 (Chronology of modern Chinese history). 2 vols. Taipei, 1963.

KWT: K'uang-wu-tang 礦務檔 (Archives on mining), ed. Wang Hsi 王璽 and Li En-han 李恩涵. Academia Sinica, Institute of Modern History, Compilations of Source Materials on Modern Chinese History, no. 3. 8 vols. Taipei, 1960.

Langer, William L. *The Diplomacy of Imperialism, 1890–1902*, 2d ed. New York: Knopf, 1951.

Latourette, Kenneth S. *A History of Christian Missions in China.* Originally published 1929; reprinted Taipei, 1966.

Lee Kuo-chi. *Die Chinesische Politik zum Einspruch von Shimonoseki und gegen die Erwerbung der Kiautschou-Bucht.* Münster: Fahle, 1966.

Li En-han 李恩涵. *Wan-Ch'ing ti shou-hui k'uang-ch'üan yun-tung* 晚清的收回礦權運動 (The late Ch'ing movement for the recovery of mining rights). Academia Sinica, Institute of Modern History, Studies in Modern History, no. 8. Taipei, 1963.

MacMurray, John V. A., comp. and ed. *Treaties and Agreements with and concerning China, 1894–1919.* 2 vols. New York: Oxford University Press, 1921.

Mi-hsien chih 密縣志 (Gazetteer of Mi-hsien, Honan), comp. Wang Chung 汪忠 and Lü Lin-chung 呂林鐘. 20 chüan. 1924.

MK. *See* German Archives filmed by Cambridge University and the University of Michigan.

Mohr, F. W. *Handbuch für das Schutzgebiet Kiautschou*. Tsingtao, 1911.

Morse, Hosea Bellou. *The International Relations of the Chinese Empire*. 3 vols. Originally published 1918; reprinted Taipei, n.d.

NCH: North China Herald and Supreme Court and Consular Gazette (Shanghai).

Norem, Ralph A. *Kiaochow Leased Territory*. Berkeley: University of California Press, 1936.

Ostasiatischer Verein Hamburg-Bremen, zum 60 jaehrigen Bestehen. Issued by the Verein. Hamburg: Kuhn Verlag, 1960.

Pei-yang kung-tu lei-tsuan 北洋公牘類纂 (A classified collection of public documents of the Commissioner for Northern Ports), comp. Kan Hou-tz'u 甘厚慈. 25 chüan. Originally published 1907; reprinted Taipei, 1965.

Potter, Jack M. *Capitalism and the Chinese Peasant*. Berkeley: University of California Press, 1968.

Purcell, Victor. *The Boxer Uprising*. Cambridge, Eng.: University Press, 1963.

Rawlinson, John L. *China's Struggle for Naval Development*. Cambridge, Mass.: Harvard University Press, 1967.

Rich, Norman. *Friedrich von Holstein*. 2 vols. Cambridge, Eng.: University Press, 1965.

Richthofen, Ferdinand von. *China, Ergebnisse eigener Reisen*. 5 vols. Berlin: D. Reimer, 1877–1912.

Rockhill, W. W. *Treaties and Conventions with or concerning China and Korea, 1894–1904*. Washington: Government Printing Office, 1904.

Rubinstein, J. "Bernhard Dernburg: Colonial Reform and German Politics, 1906–1910," unpub. seminar paper Harvard University, 1963. (Cited with author's permission.)

Schiffrin, Harold. "Sun Yat-sen's Early Land Policy," *The Journal of Asian Studies*, 16.4:549–564 (August 1957).

Schrameier, Wilhelm. *Aus Kiautschous Verwaltung (AKV)*. Jena: G. Fischer, 1914.

———— *Kiautschou, seine Entwicklung und Bedeutung*. Berlin: K. Curtius, 1915.

Schrecker, John. "The Pao-kuo Hui, A Reform Society of 1898," *Papers on China*, 14: 50–69 (1960). Harvard University, East Asian Research Center.

Schwartz, Benjamin. *In Search of Wealth and Power: Yen Fu and the West*. Cambridge, Mass.: Harvard University Press, 1964.

Shan-tung t'ung-chih 山東通志 (Gazetteer of Shantung), comp. Yang Shih-hsiang 楊士驤 and Sun Pao-t'ien 孫葆田. 200 chüan. 1915.

Shen Tsu-hsien 沈祖憲 and Wu K'ai-sheng 吳闓生. *Jung-an ti-tzu-chi* 容菴弟子記 (Biography of Yuan Shih-k'ai). Originally published 1913; reprinted Taipei, 1962.

Sheng Hsuan-huai 盛宣懷. *Yü-chai ts'un-kao* 愚齋存稿 (Collected papers of Sheng Hsuan-huai). 100 chüan. Originally published 1939; reprinted Taipei, 1963.

Skinner, William. "Marketing and Social Structure in Rural China," pt. II, *The Journal of Asian Studies*, 24.2:195–228 (February 1965).

SL. See Ta-Ch'ing li-ch'ao shih-lu.

Spector, Stanley. *Li Hung-chang and the Huai Army*. Seattle: University of Washington Press, 1964.

Steinberg, Jonathan. *Yesterday's Deterrent: Tirpitz and the Birth of the German Battle Fleet*. New York: Macmillan, 1965.

Stoecker, Helmuth. *Deutschland und China im 19. Jahrhundert*. Berlin: Rütten & Loening, 1958.

STTL: Shan-tung chin-tai-shih tzu-liao 山東近代史資料, vol. III (Source materials on the modern history of Shantung), comp. Shantung Historical Association. Tsinan, 1961; reprinted Tokyo, 1965.

Sun E-tu (Zen). *Chinese Railways and British Interests, 1898–1911.* New York: Columbia University, King's Crown Press, 1954.

Ta-Ch'ing li-ch'ao shih-lu 大清歷朝實錄 (Veritable records of successive reigns of the Ch'ing dynasty). Tokyo, 1937–1938; reprinted Taipei, 1964.

Tahara Tennan 田原天南. *Kōshū-wan* 膠州灣 (Chiao-chou Bay). Dairen, 1914.

T'an T'ien-k'ai 譚天凱. *Shan-tung wen-t'i shih-mo* 山東問題始末 (Complete history of the Shantung Question). Shanghai, 1935.

Tirpitz, Alfred von. *My Memoirs.* 2 vols. New York: Dodd, Mead & Co., 1919.

Townsend, Mary E. *The Rise and Fall of Germany's Colonial Empire, 1884–1918.* Originally published New York: Macmillan, 1930; reprinted New York, 1966.

Vagts, Alfred. *Deutschland und die Vereinigten Staaten in der Weltpolitik.* 2 vols. New York: Macmillan, 1935.

Wang Shu-huai 王樹槐. *Wai-jen yü wu-hsü pien-fa* 外人與戊戌變法 (Foreigners and the reform movement of 1898). Academia Sinica, Institute of Modern History, Studies in Modern History, no. 12. Taipei, 1965.

WCSL: Ch'ing-chi wai-chiao shih-liao 清季外交史料 (Historical materials concerning foreign relations in the late Ch'ing period, 1875–1911), comp. Wang Yen-wei 王彥威 and Wang Liang 王亮. 219 chüan. Peiping, 1932–1935; reprinted Taipei, 1963.

Weicker, Hans. *Kiautschou: Das deutsche Schutzgebiet in Ostasien.* Berlin: A. Schall, 1908.

Willoughby, Westel W. *Foreign Rights and Interests in China.* 2 vols. Originally published 1927; reprinted Taipei, 1966.

Wright, Mary C. *China in Revolution: The First Phase, 1900–1913.* New Haven: Yale University Press, 1968.

Wright, Stanley. *Hart and the Chinese Customs.* Belfast: Queen's University, 1950.

Wu-hsü pien-fa 戊戌變法 (The reform movement of 1898), ed. Chien Po-tsan 翦伯贊 et al. Modern Chinese Historical Series, no. 8. 4 vols. Shanghai, 1953.

Wu-hsü pien-fa tang-an shih-liao 戊戌變法檔案史料 (Archival materials on the reform movement of 1898), comp. National Bureau of Archives, Office of Ming and Ch'ing Archives. Peking, 1958.

Yuan Shih-k'ai 袁世凱. *Yang-shou-yuan tsou-i chi-yao* 養壽園奏議輯要 (Selected memorials of Yuan Shih-k'ai), comp. Shen Tsu-hsien 沈祖憲. 44 chüan. 1937 ed.; reprinted Taipei, 1966.

Glossary

Cha-lien-tao 炸連島
Chang Chih-tung 張之洞
Chang-ch'iu 章邱
Chang I 張翼
Chang Jen-chün 張人駿
Chang Ju-mei 張汝梅
Chang Kao-yuan 章高元
Chang-tien 章店
Chang Yao 張曜
Chang Yin-huan 張蔭桓
Chang Yü-chu 張玉珠
Ch'en Pao-chen 陳寶箴
Chi-mo 卽墨
Chi-ning 濟寧
Ch'iang-hsueh Hui 強學會
Chiao-chou (Bay) 膠州灣 (膠澳)
Chiao-she-chü 交涉局
chih-hsien 知縣
chih-li-chou 直隷州
Chih-shan tsung-tu 直山總督
Chin-ling 金嶺
Ching-hsin 敬信
ch'ing-i 清議
Ch'ing-tao (Tsingtao) 青島
Chou Fu 周馥
Chou-ts'un 周村
Chu-ch'eng 諸城
chu-ch'üan 主權
Chu I-hsin 朱一新
Chü-yeh 巨野
Fang-tzu 坊子
Hai-chou 海州

Han-chia-ts'un 韓家村
Hei-hui 黑會
Hsia 夏
Hsia Hsin-yu 夏辛酉
Hsiao-ch'ing-ho 小清河
Hsü Chi-yü 徐繼畬
Hsü Chien-yin 徐建寅
Hsü Ching-ch'eng 許景澄
Hsü Hui-feng 許會灃
Hu T'ing-kan 胡廷幹
Hua-te chung-hsing mei-k'uang kung-
   ssu 華德中興煤礦公司
Hung-shan 䰄山
Hung Yung-chou 洪用舟
I-chou-fu 沂州府
I-hsien 嶧縣
I River 沂河
I-shui 沂水
Jih-chao 日照
Jung Lu 榮禄
K'ang Yu-wei 康有爲
Kao-mi 高密
K'uang-cheng-tiao-ch'a-chü 礦政調查局
K'uang-wu t'ieh-lu tsung-chü 礦務鐵路總局
Kung-ch'e shang-shu 公車上書
kuo-ch'üan 國權
Lai-chou-fu 萊州府
Lai-wu-hsien 萊蕪縣
Lan-shan-hsien 蘭山縣
Lao-shan 嶗山
Li Chin-pang 李金榜
li-ch'üan 利權

315

Li Hung-chang 李鴻章
Li Ping-heng 李秉衡
Li-ts'un 李村
Liang Ch'i-ch'ao 梁啟超
Ling-shan-wei 靈山衛
Liu K'un-i 劉坤一
Liu-t'uan 柳疃
Lo-k'ou 濼口
Lü Hai-huan 呂海寰
Mao-shan 茅山
Nieh Shih-ch'eng 聶士成
Nü-ku-k'ou 女姑口
Pai-lien-ts'un 白蓮村
pao-kuo 保國
Pao-kuo Hui 保國會
Pei-yang-ta-ch'en 北洋大臣
Po-sha River 白沙河
Po-shan 博山
P'u-fa chan-chi 普法戰紀
Sha-ho 沙河
Sha-tzu-k'ou 沙子口
Shang-pu 商部
Sheng Hsuan-huai 盛宣懷
Shih-chiu-so 石臼所
Ssu-fang 四方
Sun Wen 孫文
Ta-pao-tao 大寶島 (大豹島)
T'a-pu-t'ou 塔埠頭
T'ai-hsi-chen 臺西鎮
T'ang Shao-i 唐紹儀

Te-chou 德州
Te-kuo i-yuan chang-ch'eng 德國議院章程
Teng-chou-fu 登州府
Ting-chia-ching 丁家井
Ts'ang-k'ou 滄口
Ts'ao-chou-fu 曹州府
Tsinan 濟南
Tung Fu-hsiang 董福祥
t'ung-shang-k'ou-an 通商口岸
tzu-chu-chih-ch'üan 自主之權
Tzu-ch'uan 淄川
tzu-k'ai-shang-pu 自開商埠
Wai-wu-pu 外務部
Wang Chih-ch'un 王之春
Wang T'ao 王韜
Wang Wen-shao 王文詔
Wei-hsien 濰縣
Wei Yuan 魏源
Weng T'ung-ho 翁同龢
Yang-chia-ts'un 楊家村
Yang-chiao-kou 羊角溝
Yang Shih-hsiang 楊士驤
Yang-wu-tsung-chü 洋務總局
Yen-chou 兗州
Yin-ch'ang 廕昌
Yin-tao 陰島
Yuan Shih-k'ai 袁世凱
Yung Wing 容閎
Yü-hsien 毓賢

316

Index

Harvard East Asian Series